Campaign 2010

THE MAKING OF THE PRIME MINISTER

Campaign 2010

THE MAKING OF THE PRIME MINISTER

Nicholas Jones

biteback

First published in Great Britain in 2010 by
Biteback Publishing Ltd
Heal House
375 Kennington Lane
London
SE11 5QY

Nicholas Jones has asserted his right under the Copyright, Designs and Patents
Act 1988 to be identified as the author of this work.

ISBN 978-1-84954-030-8

10 9 8 7 6 5 4 3 2 1

A CIP catalogue record for this book is available from the British Library.

Set in Bembo
Printed and bound in Great Britain by
CPI Cox & Wyman, Reading, RG1 8EX

CONTENTS

1
CAMERON IN DOWNING STREET

On 11 May 2010 David Cameron walked calmly through the door of 10 Downing Street after five days of political theatre which almost brought the administration of the country to a standstill and which then opened up a new chapter in the post-war government of Britain. The disappointment of managing to overpower his opponents but of still falling twenty seats short of winning the 2010 general election led to an end game that Cameron was able to play in a way which few in his party ever envisaged and which caught the news media on the hop. At one point the editors of several national newspapers, slavish in their support of the Conservative cause, were left standing on their heads, having to execute spectacular about-turns as Cameron cemented a coalition government with the Liberal Democrats which Labour mistakenly thought might have been theirs for the taking. For once the journalists who reported the affairs of Westminster and Whitehall were left in the dark, mere bystanders to a display of political brinkmanship which paid no heed to the whims of media proprietors, the deadlines of press, television and radio or the online chatter of a digital age.

Forging an audacious partnership with the Liberal Democrat leader, Nick Clegg, while Gordon Brown remained firmly in place in Downing Street as the incumbent Prime Minister, was a task fraught with difficulty and at one point seemed about to collapse. But Cameron did not waver from his 'big, open and comprehensive offer' to share power in the national interest and by the evening of the Tuesday – after polling day the previous Thursday – the Queen had invited him to form the next government and Clegg was the new deputy Prime Minister. Brown's resignation as party leader on the Monday, and then the following day his final farewell and departure from Downing Street, ushered in the first coalition government since Winston Churchill's cross-party administration during the Second World War. At the age of forty-three, Cameron was the youngest Prime Minister since Lord Liverpool in 1812 and the first former junior employee of the Conservative Party to make it all the way to the highest office in the land. Few political insiders of his generation could match his knowledge and experience and, together with colleagues whom he had known for twenty years, he was able to seize an historic opportunity to break the mould of two-party politics.

From the moment he started work for the party at the age of twenty-two, joining the Conservative Research Department in the autumn of 1988, Cameron had an opportunity to witness at first hand the make-or-break moments in the careers of the top politicians of his day; he could learn from their experience and prepare for the moment when he might be in a position to execute the riskiest moves on the political chess board. Cameron was no stranger to the drama of the unexpected, the occasions when party leaders try to hold their nerve as events slip out of their control. His first memorable experience was the ousting of Margaret Thatcher in 1990 and then the searing cliffhanger of the 1992 general election when all seemed lost for her successor, John Major. Within months of Major's re-election after a Conservative victory against the odds, he was the freshly appointed young adviser seen on television accompanying the Chancellor of the Exchequer, Norman Lamont, who emerged from the Treasury into a battery of camera lights to announce Britain's humiliating withdrawal from the European Exchange Rate Mechanism. In his final, traumatic years in office Major was subjected to a level of media hostility the like of which few Conservative Prime Ministers have had to endure, and the events leading up to his defeat in

1997 left a legacy of distrust in the minds of voters which Cameron was still encountering on the doorsteps thirteen years later.

Striking a balance between being able to take advantage of the news media while not becoming its slave was a feat which defied many of the politicians for whom Cameron had either worked or had the opportunity to observe. Tony Blair, and his infamous strategists Peter Mandelson and Alastair Campbell, never tired of justifying their obsession with media manipulation on the grounds that New Labour was the first party to have to govern under the duress of 24/7 news reporting. Cameron, the 'heir to Blair', was a child of that environment, but without their hang-ups. He was able to tackle political adversity without constantly worrying about the next day's headlines or fearing what the media might do. An inner confidence in his own ability to communicate, his willingness to take risks and a determination to play it long gave him the staying power which he needed during the four and a half years that it would take him to reach Downing Street.

Cameron's ability to shake off harsh setbacks, pick up the pieces and then play a master stroke was a skill which might have been mocked by his political opponents but they were the very characteristics which appealed to a dedicated group of former workmates who earned their spurs in the politics of the early 1990s and who shared his ambition to take their party from opposition to government. Cameron was blessed with a degree of good fortune which most up-and-coming politicians can only dream of. He was in the right place at the right time when his party was minded to contemplate jumping a generation after years of faltering leadership and three general election defeats. His path to the top was not without its mishaps and he was still trailing the front runner, David Davis, until the 2005 party conference, when he captivated Conservative activists with an off-the-cuff speech which transformed his chances. Cameron's fate as party leader, like that of his immediate predecessors, might have been sealed as early as the autumn of 2007 if Gordon Brown, not long installed as Prime Minister, had acted decisively and opted for a snap general election which many in the Labour movement were predicting he could have won. Instead of seizing the moment to secure his own personal mandate as Prime Minister, he dithered and eventually chose the certainty of completing Labour's term in office.

Cameron began the long run-up to the 2010 general election well ahead in the opinion polls, averaging a 40 per cent share of the predicted vote, more than enough to secure the 117 extra seats which he needed to return the Conservatives to power. But the party's fortunes took a turn for the worse after the shadow Chancellor, George Osborne, used his speech at the 2009 annual conference to warn of the biggest cuts in public spending for thirty years. 'We are all in this together' was his much-repeated refrain and it added weight to the news media's interpretation that the Conservatives' determination to reduce the record budget deficit was bound to lead to an 'age of austerity'. By contrast Gordon Brown's message was that only the re-election of a Labour government could secure the recovery and avoid the threat of a double-dip recession, an argument which began to resonate with voters, especially in areas of the country where employment was heavily dependent on the public sector.

A shaky start to a planned policy-driven agenda for the first three months of the year, and a narrowing in the opinion polls, fuelled speculation that Labour could still win the most seats in what might well become a hung parliament. Once the election was called for Thursday 6 May the Conservatives still seemed fairly certain that the four-week campaign and their well-resourced push in the marginal constituencies would deliver the seats they required to win. Their calculations were based on the confident assumption that Cameron's open and engaging demeanour would easily carry the day during the three televised debates between the party leaders which were to be held in the three weeks leading up to polling day. But believing that Cameron was more than a match for the dour and uninspiring on-camera presence of Brown overlooked the unique nature of their confrontation; instead of Cameron going head to head with Brown in the style of a US presidential debate, there was going to be a three-way discussion and equal time for Nick Clegg.

Broadcasters had been trying without success for almost fifty years to persuade the leaders to agree to pre-election debates and the historic breakthrough achieved by BBC, ITV and Sky News for three ninety-minute debates was being hailed as a potential game changer. Previous attempts failed because one or other of the two main parties had always pulled out at the last minute, not wishing to concede an advantage to their opponent. For the first time a Prime Minister and a leader of the opposition kept saying 'yes' simultaneously and they both agreed without an apparent hesitation to a three-way bout with the Liberal Democrats. Cameron pledged his support from early on in his 2005 leadership campaign. Brown was only the third incumbent to actively seek a debate; the option had also appealed to James Callaghan and John Major, two other Prime Ministers who believed they were staring defeat in the face and who were prepared to risk all in a televised confrontation in the hope of improving their chances.

Clegg's performance in the first debate was the turning point in the election, the moment the contest became a genuine three-horse race which would change the direction of post-war British politics. He was a natural on television up against a slick but nervous Cameron and a grumpy Prime Minister; he played to perfection his role as the fresh-faced challenger offering the electorate the chance to break free from the 'two tired old parties'. Cameron and Brown had been coached extensively by American advisers who had experience of presidential debates but neither the Prime Minister nor the leader of the opposition appeared to have a clue as to how to respond to an upstart who kept reminding viewers that only the Liberal Democrats offered a real alternative to voting Labour or Conservative.

Within the space of a week opinion polls were indicating a boost of ten to twelve points in the Liberal Democrats' projected share of the vote, the biggest increase ever recorded during an election campaign. Cameron fought back with renewed vigour and instant opinion surveys suggested he won the two later debates. Nonetheless, the Conservatives' election game plan of concentrating their attack on the unpopularity of the Prime

Minister had been knocked for six; tactics had to be changed on the hoof while staff at party headquarters went through one of the mid-election wobbles which had nearly derailed previous Tory campaigns. Two of the weekend opinion polls held in the wake of the first leaders' debate put the Liberal Democrats ahead of both the Conservatives and Labour in terms of popular support, for the first time in 104 years, but that surge fell away once Cameron began campaigning against Clegg's proposal for an amnesty for illegal immigrants and his support for British entry to the euro. What did not dissipate, however, was the notion that perhaps the country needed a change from the 'two old parties' and might benefit from a hung parliament – or 'balanced parliament', the term favoured by the Nationalists in Scotland and Wales and other smaller parties.

Cameron entered the final week of the campaign ahead in opinion surveys but psephologists were divided as to whether the Conservatives would succeed in winning enough seats for an overall majority. An anti-politics protest had shown no sign of abating and the apparent determination of a large swathe of the electorate to vote for 'change' had produced the most unpredictable election for years. An exit poll of 18,000 voters conducted at 130 polling stations on behalf of BBC, ITV and Sky News strongly suggested that the country was heading for a hung parliament. Cameron's fightback after the disaster of the first debate, and a well-resourced push in marginal constituencies funded with the help of the party's deputy chairman Lord Ashcroft, had failed to deliver the victory which had seemed assured for so long. A shortfall of nineteen was indicated if the exit poll was correct in projecting 307 seats for the Conservatives, 255 for Labour and 59 for the Liberal Democrats. The first hundred results suggested a swing to the Conservatives of 7 per cent but despite gains across the country the party was failing to take some of its key target seats. Nonetheless, Cameron felt confident enough in his acceptance speech in his Witney constituency to declare that the Labour government had 'lost its mandate to govern our country'. The initial results indicated that the country wanted change – 'strong, stable, decisive and good government' – and he promised he would be guided by the national interest. Cameron headed back to London after an election day that had been as confusing as the campaign had been frustrating; as late as their 4 a.m. final editions the morning newspapers said there was still no clarity as to the final outcome.

If voters appeared to be turning their backs on the dominance and certainties of the traditional two-party system, they had certainly not been entirely won over by what had become known as Cleggmania. The Liberal Democrats' tally of fifty-seven seats was five down on the 2005 general election and as he left his count in Sheffield, Clegg acknowledged that his party 'simply didn't achieve what we hoped'. But despite his disappointment he was rapidly emerging as the likely 'kingmaker', the party leader holding the balance of power, able either to support a Conservative-led minority administration or to back a pact with Brown to keep Labour in power. Overnight results confirmed the accuracy of the exit poll: the final projections gave the Conservatives 306 seats on a 36.1 per cent share of the vote, Labour 258 seats on 29.1 per cent and the Liberal Democrats 57 seats on 23 per cent.

On his arrival in London later that morning Clegg was the first to declare his hand and he told waiting journalists that he would stick to the policy which he laid out the previous November, that if there was no absolute majority, then the party with the most votes and the most seats would have the first right to seek to govern. 'That is why I think it is now for the Conservative Party to prove it is capable of seeking to govern in the national interest.' Under guidelines strengthened by the cabinet secretary, Sir Gus O'Donnell, the incumbent Prime Minister retained the right to try to form a government, as happened after the inconclusive result of the 1974 election when Edward Heath attempted but failed to reach an agreement with the Liberal Party leader Jeremy Thorpe. There had been speculation for weeks that Labour might have a chance to remain in government with the support of the Liberal Democrats and when Brown emerged on the steps of 10 Downing Street to acknowledge the voters' verdict, he had no wish to queer his pitch with the party leader who held the balance of power:

I understand and completely respect the position of Mr Clegg in stating that he wishes first to make contact with the leader of the Conservative Party . . . Should the discussions between Mr Cameron and Mr Clegg come to nothing, then I would, of course, be prepared to discuss with Mr Clegg the areas where there may be some measure of agreement between our two parties.

Cameron was facing the biggest challenge of his career. Could he devise – and then deliver – a strategy which took account of his failure to win a commanding majority, which avoided the perils of running a minority administration (Harold Wilson's choice in 1974), and which still enabled the Conservatives to take power and run a stable government? His team were full of praise for the sure-footed way he recovered from the disastrous outcome to the first televised debate; he was about to face the ultimate test of his ability to think on his feet, of his flair for turning adversity to advantage. Insiders subsequently gave their accounts of tense discussions in the 'war room' at Conservative headquarters as the key triumvirate of Cameron, his chief strategist, Steve Hilton, and the shadow Chancellor, George Osborne, agreed their tactics. Close aides were quoted as saying that Cameron remained pragmatic and unflappable, determined to outline a strategy which would catch his opponents off guard and present an option which the public might never have thought a Tory leader had the imagination to propose.

By mid-afternoon, secure in the knowledge that his party was on course to take at least ninety-seven seats from both Labour and the Liberal Democrats, he was ready to abandon the sloganising of the election campaign and embark on the hard bargaining which would be needed to pull off a daring political gamble. His short speech displayed a steely determination to build on a result which had delivered more Conservative gains than in any election for eighty years but which still fell short of an overall majority. He thanked Clegg for offering to have talks with the Conservatives; he was ready to see if the two parties could agree to more than a simple 'confidence and supply' agreement to keep a minority government in power:

It may be possible to have stronger, more stable, more collaborative government than that . . . So I want to make a big, open, comprehensive offer to the Liberal Democrats. I want us to work together in tackling our country's big and urgent problems, the debt crisis, our deep social problems and our broken political system.

While there were policy differences between the two parties on issues such as the European Union and defence, he said they agreed on tax reform and were both opposed to the government's identity card scheme. But Cameron did not offer a referendum on changing the voting system, a pledge which was included in Labour's manifesto and was a key demand of the Liberal Democrats. Instead the Conservatives were prepared to establish an 'all-party committee of inquiry on political and electoral reform'. Having spent the latter half of the campaign resolutely defending Britain's first-past-the-post system for parliamentary elections, Cameron could hardly have gone any further. An hour earlier, in his statement, the Prime Minister had pointedly strengthened the government's hand, signalling to the Liberal Democrats that Labour would offer them far more than the Conservatives. Brown gave a commitment to 'immediate legislation' to begin to restore public trust in politics: 'A fairer voting system is central. I believe you, the British people, should be able to decide in a referendum what the system should be.'

Cameron's offer to the Liberal Democrats to join a Tory-led coalition opened the door to the brutal reality of a hung parliament. During the four days of intense bargaining which ensued, there were almost constant negotiations between the three parties, usually involving their separate teams of negotiators but sometimes necessitating private conversations, leader to leader, either on the telephone or in person. On occasion it appeared that both Cameron and Brown were on the brink of clinching an early agreement with Clegg, only to have their hopes dashed, before eventually the historic deal was struck and a Conservative–Liberal Democrat coalition government emerged from the inconclusive outcome to the 2010 election. Together the two parties held 363 seats, enough to deliver a comfortable seventy-plus majority and the long-term stability which a minority government would lack.

After a campaign like no other, with the first-ever televised leaders' debates generating an all-embracing focus on the three personalities rather than their policies, some sections of the news media found it hard to make sense of the five-day hiatus and the confusion surrounding the negotiations for a possible coalition. For newspapers which had been ultra-loyal supporters of Cameron there was incredulity that Brown was still Prime Minister the day after losing ninety-one seats and when Labour's share of the vote fell to 29 per cent, the lowest since Michael Foot's disastrous defeat in 1983. 'Squatter holed up in No. 10' was the *Sun*'s take on Brown's explanation that he had a constitutional duty to try to resolve the current political deadlock for the 'good of the country'. *Sun*-speak put it differently: 'A man aged fifty-nine was squatting in a luxury home near the Houses of Parliament . . . denying entry to its rightful tenant.' The *Daily Express* was similarly outraged: 'Just how dare deluded Brown cling to power.' Richard Littlejohn, the *Daily Mail*'s columnist, claimed he had warned all along that Brown would 'simply barricade the door to No. 10' while he tried to stitch up a 'grubby deal' with the Liberal Democrats. 'If pretty boy Cleggy props up a shameless Brown, he'll never be forgiven.' Even the *Financial Times* seemed to share the sentiment of the tabloids: 'The show's over, Gordon, kindly leave the stage.' But the show was not over; the first act was only a curtain raiser for the political thriller that was about to unfold.

Brown's invitation to meet Clegg, a manoeuvre which neatly pre-empted Cameron's 'big, open and comprehensive offer', was no mere pleasantry. Once it became clear on Friday morning that the Conservatives were falling short of an overall majority the Prime Minister was joined in Downing Street by three of Tony Blair's former strategists, Alastair Campbell, Lord Mandelson, the Business Secretary, and Lord Adonis, the Transport Secretary. Their task was to help prepare and then promote Labour's negotiating strategy should Cameron fail to strike a deal. Ministers were soon appearing on post-election radio and television programmes arguing the case for a repeat of the Lib–Lab pact of the 1970s. Peter Hain, the Welsh Secretary, urged the Liberal Democrats to accept the Prime Minister's 'once-in-a-lifetime opportunity' to join with Labour and usher in reform of the voting system; Ben Bradshaw, the Culture Secretary, argued that by working together Labour and the Liberal Democrats could offer the country a 'progressive alliance' which had the backing of fifteen million voters as against ten million for the Conservatives; and in an attempt to win over critics in the parliamentary party, Mandelson hinted that Brown might be ready to stand down as soon as he had steered the country through the recession and delivered electoral reform.

After being filmed together on Saturday morning laying wreaths at the Cenotaph to mark the sixty-fifth anniversary of VE Day, the three leaders waited impatiently for news from the discussions being conducted on their behalf. Cameron told veterans attending the celebrations that he thought the Conservatives were 'close' to a power-sharing agreement. Clegg met Liberal Democrat MPs to sound them out on Cameron's offer and was greeted by shouts of 'fair votes now' from a demonstration organised by 1,000 supporters of electoral reform.

Brown's continued tenure of No. 10 was still irritating the Tory press, which deployed one of its favourite weapons, an immediate opinion poll with politically loaded questions. Instant online surveys completed within minutes of the end of each of the three leaders' debates had given newspapers an opportunity to drive the agenda forward and polls for two Sunday papers did the Prime Minister no favours. 'Voters tell Brown to quit as Cameron races to secure deal' said a banner headline on the front page of the *Sunday Times* over a YouGov poll which indicated that 62 per cent of those questioned wanted Brown to resign immediately. A BPIX survey for the *Mail on Sunday* suggested a higher figure of 68 per cent. There were divided opinions over Cameron's offer to work with the Liberal Democrats: 50 per cent were against a pact; 58 per cent wanted Cameron to govern on his own.

Conservative and Liberal Democrat negotiators spent Sunday locked in talks at the Cabinet Office. Clegg told journalists that he met Cameron the previous evening and took a call from the Prime Minister. 'Everyone is trying to be constructive for the good of the country.' Cameron sent an e-mail to Conservative supporters explaining why the negotiations would 'inevitably involve compromise'. Michael Gove, the shadow schools secretary, added to the sense of give and take by telling *The Andrew Marr Show* that in a 'spirit of co-operation' he was quite prepared to let a Liberal Democrat have his job in a future Conservative government. The prospect of Liberal Democrats joining a Cameron cabinet was floated by the former Conservative Prime Minister John Major within hours of Cameron's initial offer of talks. 'If that's the price to ensure we have economic stability, then that's the way I think we should go.'

Despite the belligerence of the Tory press and requests from three Labour MPs that he should stand down as leader, Brown returned to Downing Street after spending Saturday night at his constituency home seemingly as determined as before to try to reach an agreement with the Liberal Democrats. To underline his resolve to remain in government, he sent an e-mail to party supporters praising them for withstanding the 'roar of a hostile media and a very well-funded opposition'. Brown said it truly was 'the word of mouth' election campaign and 'hundreds of thousands of activists' answered his call by attempting to convince an unprecedented number of undecided voters to stay loyal to Labour. 'On polling day you excelled yourselves again and the excellent results in so many of our most marginal seats are testament to that.' As a result of their efforts to stem the Conservatives' advance, no single party could form a majority government. Their fightback meant Labour entered a 'political landscape not considered possible a few short weeks ago' and that gave him the chance to do everything in his power to 'secure the recovery . . . to fight for a future fair for all'.

Brown's carefully crafted rallying cry to the party faithful was a prelude to another day of gripping political theatre. Monday began inauspiciously with the confirmation that there had been more one-to-one meetings and conversations between the leaders; fresh negotiations were planned between the Conservatives and Liberal Democrats; and journalists and broadcasters feared they probably faced more confusion and fresh intrigue. There had been intense speculation overnight suggesting the Prime Minister would step aside as party leader if that was the price of a pact, a prospect being talked up with greater vigour by Mandelson the likelier it seemed that a deal might be slipping away from Cameron due to the Conservatives' inability to match Labour's offer of a referendum on electoral reform.

By mid-afternoon there was still no clarity. Cameron's deputy, William Hague, said further progress had been made. A meeting of Liberal Democrat MPs broke up with the party saying it wanted to seek fresh clarification from the Conservatives on 'certain points' while still listening to representations from Labour. Then, with hardly any warning, the apparent impasse was broken; instead of Cameron heading to Downing Street as had been widely predicted, Brown unveiled a last-ditch attempt to forge a power-sharing deal. Suddenly all bets were off and the blessing of the Liberal Democrats was up for grabs. As the implications reverberated around Westminster, the Conservatives' negotiating team hurried to up their game.

Brown announced his audacious attempt to keep Labour in power from the steps of No. 10: 'Mr Clegg has just informed me that, while he intends to continue his dialogue that he has begun with the Conservatives, he now wishes also to take forward formal discussions with the Labour Party. I believe it is sensible and it is in the national interest to respond.' What gave the new bidding war so much potency was the second half of the Prime Minister's statement: Brown intended to step down as Labour leader, thus removing the chief road block to a Lib–Lab coalition. In the closing stages of the election campaign Clegg had said repeatedly that he would not countenance doing a deal which allowed Brown to remain in Downing Street if Labour were no longer the largest party. From the start of their discussions with their Labour contacts, the Liberal Democrats' negotiators made no secret of their insistence that the Prime Minister would have to stand aside if there was to be any chance of making progress. Brown made no mention of this ultimatum in his statement but for the first time he publicly acknowledged that he had lost the authority to govern. 'No leader was able to win the full support of the country. As leader of my party I must accept that as a judgement on me.' A leadership election would be held and a new leader would be in place in time for the autumn party conference. But in the meantime, in response to Clegg's request for talks, the Prime Minister intended to ask the cabinet to approve a formal process for negotiations. 'There is a progressive majority in Britain and I believe it could be in the interests of the whole country to form a progressive coalition government.' Therefore if the national interest could best be served by a coalition between the Liberal Democrats and Labour in order to ensure a deficit reduction plan to support economic growth and a 'stable, strong and principled government', then he would discharge that duty. 'Only such a progressive government could meet the demand for political and electoral change which the British people made.'

Clegg was walking a political tightrope by starting parallel negotiations with Brown while continuing what he insisted were 'very constructive' talks with Cameron. His justification was that his party had not 'reached a comprehensive partnership agreement for a full parliament' with the Conservatives; therefore opening up negotiations with Labour on the same basis was the 'responsible thing to do'. Clegg praised the Prime Minister for having taken a 'difficult personal decision in the national interest'; by agreeing to step down, Brown could help ensure 'a smooth transition to the stable government that everyone deserves'.

A fresh counter-proposal made almost immediately by Cameron's negotiating team raised the stakes still further. William Hague said the Conservatives were prepared to make a 'final offer'. They would match Labour and agree to hold a referendum on electoral reform; the British electorate would be asked whether they wanted to change the voting system from first-past-the-post to alternative vote. Also on the table was a promise of a fixed-term parliament and an undertaking to give the Liberal Democrats several seats in the cabinet.

The first hint to the Tory high command that all was not well, and that their offer would have to be improved, had been the request for 'clarification' followed by a call from Clegg in which he insisted on a full coalition government rather than an agreement to offer support on a bill-by-bill basis. Conservative MPs were briefed that evening at the House of Commons and they thumped their desks in approval after being told by Cameron that the country's economic stability might be jeopardised unless they went the extra mile and offered a generous coalition deal. Despite the brave show of support there were real fears that the premiership might be slipping from Cameron's grasp and mounting anger that Labour and the Liberal Democrats had been secretly negotiating an agreement that might allow the Prime Minister to cling to power until the summer at least. Tory elder statesmen reacted furiously to Brown's attempt to deny Cameron the ultimate prize. Lord Hurd said it was a 'shabby, shameful and unfair' attempt to prevent the largest party taking power; Lord Heseltine accused him of engaging in 'party politics at its most sordid'.

If the hierarchy was reluctant to cut to the chase there were no such inhibitions on the part of Cameron's attack dogs in the Tory press; they were in no doubt that Clegg was the villain of the piece. 'Clegg's Lib Dems are a bunch of two-faced shysters,' thundered the headline over the thoughts of the *Sun*'s associate editor, Trevor Kavanagh. He believed the only consolation for Cameron in this blatant act of betrayal by 'double crossing, two-faced shysters who would sell their mothers for political gain' was that it might ultimately prove to be a lucky escape for the Conservatives because any deal that had been stitched up would be 'doomed from birth'. Across at the *Daily Mail*, Peter Oborne fired another broadside at Clegg's 'immaturity and treachery': his secret negotiations with Brown behind Cameron's back were 'cheap and dishonest behaviour'. The front page of the *Daily Express* denounced 'This shabby stitch-up'; Britain was facing the prospect of being ruled by a 'sordid coalition of losers'.

In their rush to denounce Clegg the Tory tabloids made the

assumption that the Labour government was capable of striking a deal; they also failed to take sufficient account of Brown's beleaguered position and the groundswell of criticism within the party against his attempt to construct a shaky coalition. Unlike the proposed Con–Lib agreement, a Lib–Lab pact would still lack an overall majority and be dependent on the support of the Scottish Nationalists, Plaid Cymru, the Democratic Unionists and MPs from the other smaller parties. Creating a rainbow alliance was untenable in the opinion of the former Home Secretary, David Blunkett. It would be dependent not just on the 'vagaries of a Liberal Democrat party prepared to get into bed with whoever is offering the most' but on Nationalists who could 'pull the plug on a coalition of the defeated at any time'. John Reid, another former Home Secretary, was convinced that a Lib–Lab coalition would result in 'mutually assured destruction' for both parties. Jack Straw, the Justice Secretary, shared their fears and thought Labour's only option was to accept the result of the election and go into opposition. Another unspoken concern was that if Brown managed to remain in office, negotiate a coalition and then hand over to a new leader, the country would not be prepared to accept a second unelected Labour Prime Minister.

The stark reality of Labour's plight was not lost on the parliamentary party, where the focus of attention had rapidly switched to the leadership election triggered by Brown's decision to step down. Likely contenders included the Foreign Secretary and the Climate Change Secretary, David and Ed Miliband respectively, the Schools Secretary, Ed Balls, and the Health Secretary, Andy Burnham. Their backers were more interested in rounding up support among newly elected Labour MPs than in trying to talk up the Prime Minister's chances of securing a Lib–Lab coalition.

Another tell-tale sign was the paucity of ministers and MPs prepared to do Brown's bidding. Of the inner circle who had been advising the Prime Minister over the weekend, only Lord Mandelson and Alastair Campbell appeared to be manning the Downing Street barricades. Brown's two remaining cheerleaders were busily patrolling Westminster on a propaganda offensive, talking up the prospects for a deal to stop the Conservatives taking power. Mandelson hailed the possibility of a 'progressive coalition' as the 'most dramatic development in post-war British politics'. Campbell took on all comers in his defence of the Prime Minister and was more than happy to go the distance in an on-air shouting match with Adam Boulton, political editor of Sky News. When asked whether the 'national interest' would be served by Brown 'limping on' in Downing Street for another four years, Campbell replied that obviously Boulton was 'upset David Cameron is not Prime Minister'. Boulton retaliated: 'I'm not upset . . . Don't keep casting aspersions on what I think . . . I'm fed up with you telling me what I think.' Within an instant they were head to head, interrupting each other, jabbing their fingers. Boulton demanded to know why there had been no meeting of either the cabinet or parliamentary party to approve Brown's strategy. When Campbell insisted that those meetings were taking place, Boulton jumped in: 'In other words, it's you, totally unelected, have plotted this . . . You are the one who has cooked this up with Peter Mandelson.' Campbell, no stranger to the art of provoking television interviewers, instantly assumed an air of injured innocence. 'Oh my God, unbelievable. Adam, calm down, calm down'. A much-viewed bust-up starring one of the original architects of New Labour came to symbolise the desperate, pathetic last-minute manoeuvring which tarnished Gordon Brown's final days in Downing Street. The evident disarray in Labour's ranks, and the bluster of the farewell appearances of Mandelson and Campbell, were in stark contrast to the disciplined, tightly run operations mounted by the Conservatives and Liberal Democrats.

Having had his hopes upended so spectacularly on Monday, Cameron appeared resolute as he left home on Tuesday for a fourth day of hard bargaining and political drama at Westminster: 'It's now, I believe, decision time, decision time for the Liberal Democrats and I hope they will make the right decision to give this country the strong, stable government that it badly needs and badly needs quickly.' Clegg's negotiators were about to have their first meeting with a team which Brown had hurriedly assembled but the noises off that morning from Labour MPs were hardly encouraging. David Blunkett's language was getting more colourful by the hour. He accused the Liberal Democrats of acting like 'every harlot in history' by offering their support to the highest bidder. Diane Abbott denounced a Lib–Lab pact on the grounds that it would destroy the Labour Party. Andy Burnham added his voice to those saying the party could not 'get away from the fact that Labour didn't win'. Hearing some of their potential partners describe their proposed link-up as a 'coalition of losers' was not an inspiring start and on their return from the talks the Liberal Democrats' team were clearly disappointed. There had been no movement by Labour on key demands such as dropping identity cards or abandoning a third runway at Heathrow airport and the negotiators' conclusion was that the dogged determination of several senior leading Liberal Democrats to try to keep Labour in the game was being met by a surprising degree of uninterest.

A parallel meeting between Cameron and Clegg with Sir Gus O'Donnell near at hand appeared to have been far more constructive and was a positive precursor to the resumption of negotiations at the Cabinet Office that afternoon between the Conservatives and the Liberal Democrats. William Hague was armed with an improved offer and by late afternoon, despite Labour's claim that their talks were still going positively, a breakthrough seemed imminent. Vince Cable, the Liberal Democrats' Treasury spokesman, confirmed that a deal was 'very, very close to being done'; Cameron returned to give staff at party headquarters the clearest signal that the Conservatives were about to emerge victorious; his MPs were put on standby for a meeting that evening.

Just after 7 p.m. a lectern was placed outside the No. 10 front door; the stage had been set for the final scene. Sarah Brown stood beside her husband as he announced that he intended to tender his resignation to the Queen and advise her to invite the leader of the opposition to form a government. He wished the next Prime Minister well. Only those who had held the office could understand the full weight of its responsibilities. 'I loved the job not for its prestige, its titles and its ceremony – which I do not love at all. No, I loved the job for its potential to make this country I love fairer, more tolerant, more green, more democratic, more prosperous and more just – truly a greater Britain.'

His voice cracked with emotion as he paid tribute to the armed forces; he would 'never forget all those who have died in honour and whose families today live in grief'. In thanking his staff, he said they had been friends as well as brilliant servants.

Above all, I want to thank Sarah for her unwavering support as well as for her love, and for her own service to our country. I thank my sons John and Fraser for the love and joy they bring to our lives. And as I leave the second most important job I could ever hold, I cherish even more the first – as a husband and father. Thank you and goodbye.

His dignified, heartfelt statement was a moment for reflection, blotting out the opportunism and prevarication of the previous four days. Brown turned to his wife as their sons were ushered out through the No. 10 front door and together, all four holding hands, they walked towards the car that was to take him to Buckingham Palace. As his thirteen years in Downing Street, holding the two highest offices of state, drew to a close, the civil service were preparing for the reality of a political realignment which the New Labour pioneers would not have thought possible. Westminster and Whitehall were to get their first taste of coalition government for sixty-five years. Two leaders who had been so contemptuous of each other during a hard-fought election campaign were to be yoked together as Prime Minister and deputy Prime Minister, leading an administration which promised to put political differences aside in the national interest.

While the ex-Prime Minister and his wife were having their audience with the Queen, the two teams of negotiators concluded their talks at the Cabinet Office and immediately headed off to report back to Cameron and Clegg. Less than an hour after Brown's resignation, Cameron and his wife Samantha arrived at the Palace. Within half an hour of being asked by the Queen to form a new government, becoming the twelfth Prime Minister of her reign, he finally reached Downing Street. His prolonged tussle with Brown had kept Westminster on a knife edge, as did Harold Wilson's ousting of Edward Heath following the inconclusive result of the February 1974 general election, but instead of a minority government the hung parliament of 2010 broke the mould of two-party politics. Even before he took office Cameron was ready to endorse a new era in politics and he gave up the long-standing right of a Prime Minister to choose when to go to the country. A fixed-term parliament of a full five years was one of the shared commitments of Britain's first post-war coalition government. Barring a defeat, it meant the date of the next election would be on Thursday 7 May 2015, a constitutional change that promised the politicians of Westminster an unprecedented degree of certainty in place of the traditional vagaries of the British political calendar.

Cameron's opening words on the steps of No. 10 were a tribute to Brown's 'long record of dedicated public service' coupled with praise for the outgoing government. Britain was 'more open at home and more compassionate abroad' and that was something the whole country should be grateful for. There was no sense of triumphalism and he gave a frank assessment of the troubled state of the economy. He said the country had to come to terms with a hung parliament and pressing issues such as a huge deficit, deep social problems and a political system in need of reform. 'For those reasons I aim to form a proper and full coalition between the Conservatives and Liberal Democrats . . . to provide this country with the strong, the stable, the good and decent government that I think we need so badly.' Party differences would be put aside so that he and Nick Clegg could work hard for the common good and for the national interest. 'I came into politics because I love this country. I think its best days still lie ahead and I believe deeply in public service.' Cameron would want to make sure that his government always looked after the elderly, the frail and the poorest. 'We must take everyone through with us on some of the difficult decisions we have ahead . . . This is going to be hard and difficult work. A coalition will throw up all sorts of challenges. But I believe together we can provide that strong and stable government.'

On entering No. 10 with his wife Cameron was greeted by Gus

O'Donnell and within a matter of minutes he took a call from Barack Obama offering his congratulations and another from Chancellor Merkel of Germany. George Osborne was confirmed as Chancellor of the Exchequer, William Hague named the Foreign Secretary; and then the new Prime Minister had to attend to the unfinished business of the evening. Such was Brown's determination to make a swift exit once he realised that Labour's coalition talks were floundering that he pre-empted a final agreement between Cameron and Clegg. They were still waiting to hear the outcome of their negotiations and had no opportunity to secure the endorsement of their respective parliamentary parties. But once Liberal Democrat MPs were briefed and Cameron was given a tumultuous reception by Conservative MPs, Clegg was confirmed by the Queen as deputy Prime Minister.

Throughout the day there had been hard bargaining on both sides. On the key issue of the economy, the Liberal Democrats dropped their opposition to the Conservatives' election commitment to start making immediate cuts of £6 billion in public spending; they also agreed to a significant acceleration in plans to reduce the structural deficit over five years. In order to move towards honouring the Liberal Democrats' goal of a £10,000 personal tax allowance, the Conservatives agreed to increase capital gains tax and to accept the previous government's decision to introduce higher national insurance contributions for employees, a proposal which had been attacked as 'Labour's jobs tax' during the election campaign. Another concession was the postponing of the Tory plan to increase the threshold for inheritance tax to £1 million. Both parties agreed not to join the euro or transfer more powers to the European Union; the Liberal Democrats accepted a cap on the number of immigrants from outside the European Union; and they opted to disagree over the Conservatives' commitment to Britain's Trident nuclear missile system and the nuclear power programme. In addition to fixed-term parliaments and a commitment to hold a referendum on the alternative vote electoral system, the coalition partners signed up to a 'wholly or fully elected' House of Lords.

Clegg's final task, not completed until after midnight, was gaining the overwhelming endorsement of his federal executive. Earlier his parliamentary party gave unanimous support to an agreement which guaranteed the fifty-seven Liberal Democrat MPs a total of five cabinet posts and fifteen other ministerial jobs across Whitehall. After a momentous twenty-four hours and having achieved far more influence for Liberal Democrats than his contemporary predecessors might ever have imagined, Clegg acknowledged there 'may be many questions, many doubts' in both his party and the public about the new governing coalition:

> *I hope this is the start of the new politics I have always believed in – diverse, plural, where politicians of different persuasions come together, overcome their differences in order to deliver good government for the sake of the whole country . . . But I want to reassure you that I wouldn't have entered into this arrangement unless I was genuinely convinced that it offers a unique opportunity to deliver the kind of changes you and I believe in. So I hope you'll keep faith with us, I hope you will let us prove to you that we can serve you and this country with humility, with fairness at the heart of everything we do, and with total dedication to the interests and livelihoods of everyone in Great Britain.*

As the Liberal Democrats' negotiators celebrated the realisation that their party had the chance to honour hard-fought commitments there was little sympathy for the Labour ministers who had persuaded Gordon Brown to sacrifice his job in a desperate attempt to secure a 'progressive' alliance, only to find that he was then being deserted by his own MPs. Labour's negotiating team was accused of being more attracted to the challenges of opposition than in creating a coalition. Lord Adonis, the cabinet minister who had argued most forcibly in support of Lib–Lab agreement, accused Clegg of being 'dead set' on a coalition with the Tories. 'They should have been straight about this fact rather than playing silly games.'

Having accused Clegg of treachery and betrayal in gruesome headlines the previous day, the Tory tabloids adopted their other favourite tactic next morning and did their best to sideline his contribution in their adulatory coverage of the new Prime Minister's arrival in Downing Street. David Cameron seemed to know intuitively what the photographers would be looking for as he stood outside the No. 10 front door with his wife. 'Dave New World' was the *Sun*'s headline over a front page picture of the new Prime Minister giving the pregnant Samantha 'a loving pat on her baby bump' as he arrived from the Palace 'at the dawn of a new era of Conservative rule'. Well down an editorial on page ten the paper said that Clegg 'finally did the right thing – but only after tarnishing his reputation. The "rainbow coalition" was nonsense. Clegg should recognise he is the junior partner in government.' The *Daily Mail* chose the same picture of Cameron, 'his hand resting gently on his pregnant wife's bump', under the headline 'Baby, we made it'. Possible disaffection in the ranks of the Liberal Democrats was identified as the greatest threat to Cameron's 'historic power-sharing deal' and it prompted another *Daily Mail* headline, 'Can Clegg keep a lid on rebellion?' Underneath was a photograph of Clegg sitting in his car the previous day 'carelessly brandishing' a memo which revealed in his 'spidery handwriting' the six steps that would need to be achieved in a coalition agreement. 'Under "roles" appears the telling word: "Me". Is this the "new politics" of which he speaks so piously? Truly, Mr Clegg is the Madame Fifi of British politics, fluttering his eyelashes at one suitor before sneaking off in secret to play footsie with another.'

Rarely had there been five days in British politics when all sections of the news media had been so impotent in influencing events, reduced to mere onlookers of a political tug of war which was reshaping the way the country was about to be governed. There was no opportunity or advantage to be gained in giving off-the-record advance briefings about the momentous steps which Cameron intended to take, nor were there any attempts, given the great uncertainty and the need for secrecy, to try to spin the coverage one way or another. The tabloids' savaging of Clegg on the morning of the final day of negotiations was an illustration of the degree to which journalists were in the dark about the true state of play.

During the four and a half years that it took Cameron to lead the Conservatives into power there was often speculation about whether he would ever stand up to his party in quite the same way as Tony Blair did when he abandoned Clause IV in Labour's constitution and dropped its historic commitment to public ownership. Blair's speech to the 1994 annual conference was a much-manipulated moment in the moves being taken to cement his grip on New Labour; it became an essential reference point in the media's narrative of his rise to power. Daniel Finkelstein, chief leader writer for *The Times* and a former director of the Conservative Research Department – where the new Prime Minister started work – believed Cameron had finally achieved his 'Clause IV' moment. His 'generous offer' to Clegg, inviting the Liberal Democrats to join a coalition on such broad terms, was 'far more audacious' than Blair's initiative. Proposing a partnership agreement which the Liberal Democrats were not expecting was 'an extraordinary political coup'; it meant the traditional anti-Conservative majority represented by Labour and the Liberal Democrats was 'no longer an anti-Conservative majority'.

Establishing a coalition government gave Cameron and his party an unparalleled opportunity to rise above partisan party politics and rewrite contemporary political history. His initiative dominated the rolling news stories for well over a week, and rightly so. The twists and turns of the story spoke for themselves and left few opportunities for the kind of behind-the-scenes manipulation which he always promised he would avoid if he became Prime Minister. Without knowing what lay in store, he used an interview on the final Sunday of the election campaign to reiterate his undertaking that any administration he led would turn its back on the spin of the Blair and Brown governments. He told *The Andrew Marr Show* that he aspired to a style of government of 'quiet effectiveness' and he would 'put aside the tools of the short-term politics, of the 24-hour news agenda'. He would not be sitting in his office with the '24-hour news blaring out, shouting out the headlines'. Labour's obsession with seeking to exploit the news media had been incredibly damaging: 'I think we've run government in the last thirteen years as a sort of branch of the entertainment industry. It's been sort of 24-hour news and sort of 24-hour government.'

In the final stages of the election campaign the fawning of the Tory press in their coverage of Cameron was matched only by the brutality of their treatment of Gordon Brown and their savage character assassination of Clegg. Polling evidence suggested that sustained attacks on the Liberal Democrats for backing the euro and proposing an amnesty for illegal immigrants was partly responsible for the reduction in the initial surge in the party's support, although it did not appear to have had the same effect on the aspiration of many voters for a hung parliament. Media analysts disagreed on the impact of press reporting on voting intentions but political strategists considered that the cumulative effect of the treatment their parties received did influence their electoral prospects.

The *Sun*'s sycophantic reporting was rewarded on his second day in office with an exclusive 'first interview' with the new Prime Minister. Cameron 'thanked *Sun* readers who backed his bid to oust Gordon Brown'. In a list of staff changes at No. 10, Cameron announced that Andy Coulson, his chief media strategist at party headquarters, had been appointed the new director of communications in Downing Street. Coulson, a former editor of the *News of the World*, played a key role in the campaign, providing an invaluable link with the national press. All four of Rupert Murdoch's national newspapers – *The Times*, the *Sunday Times*, the *Sun* and the *News of the World* – urged their readers to vote Conservative in 2010, a complete about-turn from the 2005 general election, when they each recommended the re-election of Tony Blair. A week into the new government Gary Gibbon, political editor of *Channel 4 News*, reported that Murdoch was one of Cameron's first visitors, seen going 'up the back stairs into No. 10'. Gibbon remarked that Murdoch had never been a huge fan of the Liberal Democrats so may have been seeking reassurance. 'In one of his television interviews in the campaign, Adam Boulton of Sky News asked whether David Cameron would resist the power of Murdoch if he gets into No. 10. He said "Of course", if my memory serves. Watch this space.'

Gibbon's tease reflected the reality of modern-day politics in an incessant news environment. Cameron's promise to eschew the manipulative techniques of Blair and Brown had the ring of poacher turning gamekeeper. When he graduated from the Conservative Research Department after the 1992 general election and became an aide to Norman Lamont and then Michael Howard, he had his first taste of the secretive basis on which information is traded between ministers and journalists. Cameron's job description was 'special adviser' and he showed every sign of enjoying his new-found freedom to give political correspondents off-the-record briefings. For a few years at least he operated as party political spin doctor and introduced himself to the black arts of a hidden world in Westminster and Whitehall. By dint of perseverance and shrewd political judgement he built a coalition government out of the inconclusive result to the 2010 general election and in doing so he became the first special adviser to rise through the ranks to reach the highest office of state.

2
EARLY YEARS

Still in his early twenties, fresh from Eton and Oxford, David Cameron served a political apprenticeship with the Conservative Party which gave him direct personal experience of the highs and lows that followed the upheaval of Margaret Thatcher's ousting from Downing Street in November 1990. His steep learning curve would help instil the drive which took him to the top of his party. In the 1992 general election campaign, when John Major won against the odds, the young Cameron was in the team which briefed the Prime Minister before his daily news conferences. Six months later, having been promoted to the role of special adviser to the Chancellor of the Exchequer, he was standing in the Treasury courtyard when the then Chancellor, Norman Lamont, had to announce that due to the devaluation of the pound, Britain had been forced to withdraw from the European Exchange Rate Mechanism. Cameron had been on the inside track at the two events which marked the rise and fall of Major's recently re-elected administration, a reality check on the harsh misfortunes of political life. Within the space of a few years he had become steeped in politics and already seemed to have acquired the approachable personality of a future public relations professional. Beneath the smooth exterior there were also the emerging signs of an astute political operator whose early grounding would be put to good use once he had the chance to lead his party.

Political history is littered with lessons for the politicians of the future;

a mark of leadership is the ability to learn from the past. Cameron, who read politics, philosophy and economics at Brasenose College, Oxford, joined the Conservative research department in September 1988 after gaining a first-class honours degree. To have started work for a political party at the impressionable age of twenty-two, and then to have had such an illuminating range of insights so early in his career, gave him an invaluable head start, a political induction which few of his contemporaries would be able to match. He had observed at first hand the unrelenting pressures faced by a Prime Minister whose authority was under attack; he had seen how the conduct of a general election campaign could confound the direst predictions of the opinion pollsters; and then, within months of becoming a ministerial aide, he found himself in the Chancellor's private office in the midst of the financial crisis which shattered the Conservatives' reputation for sound economic management and resulted in personal disaster for Lamont. Cameron's introduction to the inner workings of both the party machine and the administration of Whitehall was a curtain raiser for the dramatic shifts which were about to unfold and reshape the political landscape: the slow, debilitating collapse of the Major government; the catastrophic rout of the Conservative Party in the 1997 general election; the rise of New Labour, culminating in Tony Blair's landslide victory; and then, in their wake, almost a decade of introspection and infighting over the future direction and leadership of the Tory Party. As he rose through the ranks, becoming first an MP and then a shadow minister, Cameron had ample opportunity to compare and contrast the successes and failures of the Blair and Brown governments with what he had witnessed in the final years of the Thatcher and Major premierships. In the four and a half years he spent as party leader reorganising and rebranding the Conservatives in readiness for the 2010 general election, he demonstrated that he had not wasted his long apprenticeship and that he was more than capable of putting the lessons of the past to good use.

Former contemporaries at Conservative Central Office recall how the newly appointed Cameron revelled in political argument. He was self-assured, keen to display his command of statistics and clearly determined to succeed in politics. The ambitious Cameron had talents which would help him come to terms with the age of media-driven politics and the unrelenting pressures of the 24/7 news agenda: he had a flair, when discussing politics, to treat it as a conversation, an all-important accomplishment when he had to start speaking to an audience or answer questions in a one-to-one with a constituent or an interviewer. From his earliest days as a party researcher he seemed determined to get to grips with the love–hate relationship between politicians and journalists. Whatever he might have thought privately about political correspondents and commentators, he was eager to make their acquaintance, quick to learn how they could be exploited to promote his career. His undoubted skill in dealing with reporters, photographers and television crews was evident from the moment he began campaigning for the Tory leadership. So too was his supreme confidence in front of a camera, a priceless gift for an ambitious politician. In fact, his presentation was so slick that it immediately became a source of comment and criticism among friend and foe alike. What was so striking about his on-screen behaviour was his easy-going nature and friendly repartee when being bombarded with reporters' questions; it all seemed so effortless. Cameron's advantage over his political rivals and opponents was that he had cut his political teeth in the daily dogfights between journalists and politicians. He knew from his first years in politics what it was like to get entangled in a media feeding frenzy or trapped by a reporters' stakeout; he understood why it was so important not to appear flustered or become aggressive. Cameron had built up an intimate knowledge of the tricks of the trade on both sides of the fence: he had served an apprenticeship as a political attack dog and trainee spin doctor and in addition he had acquired an equally strong grasp of the media mindset, only too well aware of how low journalists were prepared to stoop in pursuit of an exclusive story. Yet once elected leader, Cameron was able to project the on-air persona of the man in the street, a hint almost of naivety, as though he was an innocent abroad when it came to the dark arts of media manipulation.

My first chance to assess Cameron's potential as a political operator was in the 1992 election campaign when, like other reporters, I became aware of the antics of what was variously dubbed the 'brat pack' or 'Patten's pups', a young and motley crew recruited by the Conservative chairman, Chris Patten, and in whom the Prime Minister was foolishly said to have rested his fate. Under the guiding hand of Peter Mandelson, the Labour Party had widened its appeal, having shown far greater flair than the Conservatives in exploiting television and radio. In an attempt to make up lost ground, the former *That's Life* producer Shaun Woodward had been hired to give Major's campaign a televisual makeover. Woodward's appointment as director of communications was considered to be quite a coup and his association with Esther Rantzen, star presenter of *That's Life*, gave the Tory campaign some much-needed sparkle. Nonetheless, Conservative Central Office was gripped by uncertainty, denuded of many of the older, experienced hands who had guided Margaret Thatcher to three general election victories. In their place the party had recruited a much younger team, some fresh faced and not long out of university, who were enthusiastically taking orders from a light entertainment producer who freely admitted to journalists that he was modelling himself on Mandelson, much feared by Tory strategists because of his success in repackaging the Labour Party and in promoting Neil Kinnock.

Journalists could hardly believe their good fortune when Woodward's team began acting out the kind of stunts which would have earned their place in the running order alongside Rantzen's singing dogs and comic characters. In the second week of the campaign reporters and television crews were told to assemble outside Central Office for what we were promised would be a good picture story. Maurice Saatchi, who was supervising the party's advertising campaign, insisted we would witness a 'strong visual message'. Laid out on the pavement was a large wooden model of a factory. Written on the chimneys were the words 'investment', 'jobs' and 'recovery'. No sooner were the television cameras in place than a steamroller trundled into Smith Square. Its livery was funereal and the only splash of colour amid all the black paint was a superimposed red L (for Labour), matching the L-plate used by learner drivers. 'Patten's pups', who were lined up on the pavement, whooped with delight as the steamroller proceeded to smash the wooden model to smithereens, stopping only a few feet short of the front door of Central Office. Sean Holden, the Conservatives' head of broadcasting and a former political reporter with TV-am, told me the story would have great impact on both television and radio. 'We are trying to talk to the C2s and this will get the message across to them that their jobs are at risk if Labour get elected.' Equally enthusiastic was Steve Hilton, who was co-ordinating campaign policy with Saatchi and Saatchi. He claimed it was a 'very effective piece of media campaigning' because it was symbolic of what Britain would be like under Labour. As they were speaking a large shroud was being thrown hurriedly over what remained of the factory. Whereas Holden and Hilton seemed convinced the stunt had been effective, other young researchers and strategists thought differently. Having seen that photographers were lining up shots to include the smashed words 'investment', 'jobs' and 'recovery', they obviously feared that newspaper pictures of a shattered factory might give the wrong impression.

The 'brat pack's' exuberance was a gift for political columnists and diary writers and, as if almost on cue, David Cameron seemed to emerge as their leader and spokesman, gathering increasingly flattering mentions as the campaign progressed. Initially Major was mocked by David Seymour, writing in the now-defunct newspaper *Today*, for having put his faith in the 'clammy hands of Patten's puppies'. Seymour could not believe that the Prime Minister was relying on a team that was 'wet behind the ears'. How at the age of twenty-five could 'David Cameron, an old Etonian' have the experience to head the political section at Central Office? How could Hilton – 'yes, only twenty-two' – be 'campaign co-ordinator' when he 'had only just left public school' at the time of the previous general election? 'Sleep, little babies' was the headline next day on the lead item in the *Times* diary, which revealed that Cameron and Hilton were up at 4.45 each morning in order to prepare press briefings for Patten and

Major. Billeted round the corner from Smith Square in Gayfere Street, in a house owned by the then Conservative candidate Alan Duncan, they worked an eighteen-hour day. After giving Patten a rundown of what had appeared in the press they briefed Major at 7.30 a.m. and, after a full day's work, monitored television and radio coverage each evening until Patten returned from campaigning in his Bath constituency. Ann Leslie, the *Daily Mail*'s celebrated feature writer, described her encounter with the 'Tory teenies': they were 'a bunch of eager, muddled young beavers' who had never fought an election.

'Patten's pups' literally had to flee the scene in panic when a misguided news conference descended into chaos. This happened on the third day of what journalists dubbed the 'war of Jennifer's ear', the row about the leaking of the name of a young girl with excruciating earache who was featured in a Labour Party election broadcast. My last sight of the 'brat pack' was watching them beat a hasty retreat up the stairs of Central Office looking as if they were the culprits in the kind of consumer scam exposed by *That's Life*. In a bid to reassure voters that the government's health reforms were working, sympathetic hospital consultants and doctors had been lined up on the platform and at the end of their presentation the Secretary of State for Health, William Waldegrave, was ambushed by journalists demanding to know why the Conservatives had leaked Jennifer Bennett's name. Once Waldegrave admitted that Central Office had 'helped' Jennifer's consultant make contact with the *Daily Express* there was pandemonium; reporters rushed forward to ask questions. In the hue and cry which followed an ashen-faced Sean Holden was pushed against a Tory poster; Shaun Woodward tried unsuccessfully to stop television crews who were filming him without his permission; and Cameron, who was standing with Patten's special adviser, Patrick Rock, ended up being pinned against a wall. When I asked a question, Rock shouted back at me: 'We didn't give out the name. Ask the editor of the *Independent*.' Cameron gave his own account of what happened in a comment column for Guardian Unlimited shortly after being elected an MP. He described himself as a veteran of the 'war of Jennifer's ear' and the unseemly row which erupted after the Conservatives tried to wind up their press conference: 'I vividly remember being pinned to the wall and screamed at by Alastair Campbell, then political editor of the *Daily Mirror* . . . I'm still waiting for my campaign medal from John Major.' 'Dirty Little Trick' was the headline next morning on Campbell's front-page splash for the *Mirror*, which said the 'sickening truth' was that it was the Conservatives who had thrust 'little Jennifer Bennett into the glaring spotlight of the general election battle'.

I could not remember a Tory news conference ending so chaotically and Cameron had been wise to keep his head down and let Rock do all the talking before they all hurried out of camera range. Even so, Cameron's presence had been noticed by the press pack and he was definitely making a point of cultivating the younger and newer reporters, hoping no doubt to build up a nucleus of critical friends in the media. Much of the legwork for the diary columns of national newspapers is done by trainees, often graduates starting out on a career in journalism, and they are an obvious target for a political activist trying to make his name. In the third week of the campaign a diary paragraph in *The Times* described Cameron as 'one of the brightest young people in the party'. Not surprisingly, when reporting the celebrations at Central Office after Major had returned victoriously to Downing Street with a personal mandate and an overall majority of twenty-one seats, *The Times* turned among others to Cameron, whose quotes were considered far more newsworthy than Woodward's. 'Chris Patten's babes came of age yesterday' was the opening line in Andrew Pierce's report describing the smiles on the faces of the youthful campaigners as 'they opened yet another bottle of champagne'. Having been blamed initially for a lacklustre campaign, they had come close to cracking under the strain and, as Pierce observed, their eighteen-hour days had taken their toll: 'Bags under their eyes. Pallid skin. They used to catnap at their desks during any lull in proceedings.' Cameron had not only volunteered the kind of colourful lines which *The Times* needed but had also delivered the quote which topped the story: 'The brat pack hits back . . . Whatever people say about us, we got the campaign right.'

In seizing the opportunity to capture the headlines and vindicate their role, Cameron gave an early demonstration of his flair for amusing self-deprecation, an invaluable skill for an up-and-coming politician: 'Not being battle-hardened veterans, we had to take the flak on the chin. But after the first two weeks we just got our heads down and decided to listen to what we were being told by our workers on the ground rather than the opinion pollsters, and especially newspaper reporters.' On polling day his fellow 'Patten's pup' Steve Hilton, who was too young to have voted in the 1987 general election, rang Cameron to say: 'I have done it. I have finally voted. They can't write that about me any more.' Once the results starting coming in they were unable to hide their excitement and Cameron led Hilton and the rest of his crew across Smith Square to chant and jeer outside Transport House, head office of the Transport and General Workers' Union and former headquarters of the Labour Party.

Having emerged as de facto cheerleader and spokesman for the 'brat pack', Cameron was savouring his first taste of political success, which in his case was all the sweeter because of a personal setback immediately prior to the election. He had spent the previous year seconded to the team which helped to brief John Major in preparation for the then twice-weekly sessions of Prime Minister's Questions. Much of his time was spent reading the text of speeches and interviews given by Labour politicians as he hunted for embarrassing quotes or slip-ups which could be used when attacking the opposition. Cameron told Guardian Unlimited that being 'plucked' from Central Office and 'sent to No. 10' had taught him how to respond to the daily news agenda. By scanning the papers he was able to work out the likely questions and then he had to try to 'think of killer facts and snappy one-liners'. His skill in identifying punchy responses which Major could use to undermine Neil Kinnock had not gone unnoticed. In June 1991, the Atticus diary column in the *Sunday Times* credited Cameron with finding the 'timely anti-Labour ammunition' which explained why the Prime Minister's performances in the House of Commons had become 'sharper of late, unlike his platform set-pieces'. Major had left Kinnock 'squirming' on the opposition front bench after he brandished a 'dreadful piece of doublespeak' from Labour's then employment spokesman, Tony Blair, about the impact which a minimum wage would have on unemployment. The following week, Gordon Greig, political editor of the *Daily Mail* – and then the doyen of the Westminster lobby – complimented Major on the 'brisker, more business-like atmosphere' in the Downing Street kitchen cabinet which had been evident since the arrival of 'a razor-sharp script man, David Cameron, from the Tory Central Office political desk'. On the strength of his contribution to the Prime Minister's pre-election fightback Cameron had been tipped by the *Times* diary for promotion to Downing Street. Major's political adviser Judith Chaplin was leaving to become the Conservatives' general election candidate in Newbury. Cameron was described as the 'man to watch', a sentiment shared by the *Mail on Sunday*'s Black Dog column, which claimed he was one of two 'extremely ambitious politicos' mounting formidable campaigns to get her job. In the event Chaplin's post was filled by Jonathan Hill; Cameron continued in his role as head of the Central Office political section. Preparing daily briefs for the Prime Minister and party chairman for the duration of the 1992 campaign proved quite an ordeal but, as he told *The Times* years later, he learned there was all to play for in a general election. 'Major was the only person who thought we were going to win. A pretty hairy job but it turned out he was right.'

Cameron's aptitude for briefing ministers and his ability to conjure up jokes and insults with which to taunt Labour's front bench was put to immediate use. During the heat of the campaign his advice had been widely sought ahead of news conferences and speeches. His popularity came as no surprise to Alistair Cooke, then the deputy director of the Conservatives' research department, who interviewed Cameron in 1988 when he first applied to join the staff. 'There were all these panicking ministers who wanted briefing every five minutes and Cameron calmed them all down. He was the perfect hand holder.' Norman Lamont, who had seen Cameron in action, briefing Major in the build-up to the election, was highly impressed and as soon as he returned to the

Treasury after their unexpected victory, the Chancellor immediately offered him a job. Lamont reflected on the strengths of his young adviser in an interview for the *Independent* shortly before Cameron was declared party leader: 'Cameron was very quick, very alert and I thought "I want him". He was a political rather than an economic adviser, so he would help with speeches; he would be in on briefings for parliamentary questions; he would be present at some of the tax meetings to do with the Budget, and might give it a political angle.' Another characteristic which the former Chancellor highlighted was that Cameron could be good company and was 'very likeable', an observation which would subsequently prove to underline Cooke's conclusion that Cameron was the 'perfect hand holder' for a panicking minister.

Lamont was in desperate need of a makeover. His lacklustre delivery at the despatch box was proving no match for his erudite Labour shadow, John Smith. When the Chancellor delivered 'a rattling good speech' in May 1992, which for once was said to have 'discomforted' Smith, the *Sunday Times* gave Cameron another plug. Atticus said the 'young Tory whizz-kid', brought in to spice up Major's Question Time performances, had 'hit the ground running' at the Treasury. Cameron's promotion was said by the *Independent* to be 'an ideal stepping stone' towards becoming a prospective parliamentary candidate, and the year he was about to spend with the Chancellor would transform the young researcher and speech writer into a hardened media handler whose privileged background of Eton and Oxford appeared to prove no handicap when he had to cope with the excesses of the tabloid press and the seedier side of journalism.

Lamont faced a gathering economic storm that summer: sterling was under pressure and British membership of the Exchange Rate Mechanism was being tested to the limit. Age and a lack of City know-how did count against Cameron and at the end of August 1992 there was a snide reference in the *Times* diary to a hole in Lamont's kitchen cabinet: while it did include a leading aide from the Conservatives' election-winning 'brat pack', it lacked an adviser with 'hands-on market experience'. Three weeks later, on 17 September, Lamont floundered in the maelstrom of

Black Wednesday. In a desperate attempt to stem the collapse of the pound the Chancellor raised interest rates twice in a day by a total of 5 percentage points but the slide continued and Britain was forced to leave the ERM at a cost to the taxpayer of anything from £4 billion to £5 billion. Television news footage of Lamont's announcement shows Cameron at the edge of shot, standing to one side of the Chancellor. Thirteen years later, in his first speech on the economy as party leader, Cameron spoke ruefully of the day the Conservatives lost their reputation for economic competence. He told *The Times*: 'If you cut me down the middle, you would find "Exchange Rate Mechanism" written on me like a stick of rock.'

With his back firmly against the Treasury wall and his credibility in tatters, Lamont was forced to defend himself in the face of sustained calls for his resignation, a dire change of fortune which required his young attack dog to learn new tricks. Even further disasters were afoot and the beleaguered Chancellor would need all the support he could muster, not least from his talented wordsmith, who was about to get his first taste of a media feeding frenzy. Having endured what economic pundits calculated was the most costly mistake ever made in a single day by any Chancellor, the hapless Lamont was about to entertain the nation by revealing that he was apparently equally incompetent in managing his own financial affairs. Details of his credit card account were leaked to the *Sun*, which alleged that Lamont was £470 overdrawn and had been sent five warning letters for not making his monthly payments. The last purchase was £17.47 spent at a Thresher off-licence near Paddington, which a shop assistant claimed was for a bottle of Bricout Brut champagne and a packet of Raffles extra-long cigarettes. 'What Were You Up To Norm?' was the question posed in capital letters on the front page of the *Daily Star*. Its story line about the Chancellor's 'mystery shopping trip in a seedy part of London' was carefully balanced with a stout denial from the Treasury, which insisted the Chancellor was in Whitehall when the purchase was supposed to have been made. A Treasury statement about the Chancellor's movements that afternoon and evening was quoted verbatim and it said his schedule included 'meetings at the Treasury with his special adviser David Cameron'. A similar name check in the *Daily Express* also cited Cameron's presence in support of Lamont's rebuttal. By drawing attention to his meetings with his special adviser in the time line of that day, the Chancellor strengthened his version of events and the Treasury's statement was accepted immediately by Thresher's management, which apologised for the embarrassment caused by inaccurate statements by its staff; Lamont's bill showed that he had in fact purchased two bottles of claret and a bottle of Margaux at another branch the previous day.

Sensing the Chancellor's vulnerability, Labour's increasingly effective publicity machine had identified him as the most promising target in their campaign to destabilise John Major's administration. Three days after the leak about his overdrawn credit card, Lamont was accused of a cover-up by the then shadow Chancellor, Gordon Brown, when the *Sunday Times* disclosed that the Treasury had secretly paid his legal costs the previous year during the saga of 'Miss Whiplash'. On moving into 11 Downing Street, Lamont rented out his home in Kensington, only for the *News of the World* to reveal that the tenant in the basement was a sex therapist. Fearing that the story presented a threat to his authority as Chancellor, Lamont sought the advice of the leading libel lawyer Peter Carter-Ruck and the Treasury paid £4,700 towards the bill, a payment which officials subsequently insisted was wholly justified.

Nevertheless the Chancellor had become a marked man and for Cameron, who spent much of the time briefing newspapers like the *Sun*, it was a chilling baptism into the cruel world of crisis PR, not something he had sought or perhaps expected, but an insight into the dark side of politics and a formative sequence of events for any young and ambitious party activist. During his first six months as a special adviser – and still only twenty-six – he had acquired an awareness which other political aides might have had to wait a lifetime to experience. He had been in the Chancellor's private office during an unprecedented financial crash and then had to observe an unfolding personal tragedy as a minister's reputation got repeatedly trashed in a tabloid frenzy. In the event

Cameron's walk-on role in 'Threshergate' and the resurrection of the 'Miss Whiplash' story were merely curtain raisers for the dramas which were to follow and in which he would play a more prominent part. Within a matter of months Lamont would become the first Conservative Chancellor in thirty years to be sacked and his political adviser would find himself caught in the cross-fire of the savage battle between his embittered former boss and the then Tory chairman, Sir Norman Fowler. Cameron was about to be tested as never before: he had to show loyalty to his beleaguered ex-boss but at the same time avoid doing anything to damage the Major government or the Conservative Party.

Increasingly at odds with the Prime Minister, the Chancellor had become isolated from many of his cabinet colleagues. He cut a lonely figure around Westminster and was in desperate need of Cameron's company and moral support. Instead of being left behind at the Treasury, the Chancellor's young adviser would be wined and dined in the company of the cream of the House of Commons press corps. Cameron had already become a valuable source of quotes and tip-offs and now he was about to make his mark not just among diary writers and tabloid journalists but also with senior lobby correspondents and political editors; he was about to earn his spurs as a Treasury 'insider' and 'cabinet source', a trader in sensitive, off-the-record information.

The week before the cabinet reshuffle of May 1993 Lamont delivered the wind-up speech on the third reading of the Maastricht Bill and after a 'glass or two of champagne' in the whips' office, Cameron was invited to join the Chancellor and two correspondents for 'a light supper of scrambled eggs, smoked salmon and mineral water' at Shepherd's restaurant in Marsham Street. By then Lamont's fate had probably been sealed and the two journalists, from the *Independent on Sunday*, noted that he seemed to fear the worst, appearing 'tired and subdued'. In their account of the 'Chancellor's ignominious end', Donald Macintyre and Stephen Castle admitted to being bowled over by the political acumen of their young guest. They were particularly impressed by the way Cameron subsequently handled his relations with lobby correspondents during Lamont's sacking, probably the most acrimonious departure since Margaret Thatcher's spectacular disagreements with Michael Heseltine and Geoffrey Howe.

Initially, in the face of continuing speculation about a cabinet reshuffle, Cameron's role was to insist that it was 'business as usual' in the Treasury; Lamont was said to be busy preparing a second Budget to be delivered the following November. Macintyre and Castle could not fault the conduct of the Chancellor's aide: 'Cameron, politically mature beyond his years, fought a doughty campaign for his boss but one that was free of hype or dishonesty. He tirelessly told MPs and journalists up to the last minute that Lamont was hard at work on his planned unified Budget and determined to give it.' Lamont's sacking meant Cameron was out of a job, and praise from the *Independent on Sunday* for having given journalists even-handed guidance was an accolade which would add gravitas to the CV of any unattached political adviser. But Cameron, who was anxious to preserve the confidence of the journalists he had been briefing, had first to steer his way through the post-reshuffle repercussions. The story had moved on and so had the speculation: journalists wanted to know precisely when and how Lamont would exact his revenge on Major. I was about to experience at first hand the moment when Cameron's guidance failed to reflect reality. Spin doctors have to put the best possible gloss on what they know but the cardinal rule is not to get caught supplying inaccurate information.

Cabinet reshuffles have become far more civilised affairs in recent years. Outgoing ministers are usually informed by telephone and spared the embarrassment of being trapped on camera as they are forced to walk up to the No. 10 front door simply to receive their marching orders from the Prime Minister. By today's standards Lamont's sacking was brutal. When he called in to see Major he was able to slip through a connecting door from No. 11 to No. 10 without emerging into Downing Street but his movements during the rest of the day would be followed by the media every step of the way. When offered the alternative but rather lowlier cabinet post of Secretary of State for the Environment, the

Chancellor refused to accept the demotion, turned on his heels after a 'flaming row' with Major, stepped 'expressionless' from No. 11 and was driven smartly away, only to return unexpectedly half an hour later telling reporters he had 'never felt better'. During an agonising wait for the official reshuffle announcement, Cameron once again became the Chancellor's companion and his presence was duly noted in newspaper timetables of the Downing Street drama: '11.06 a.m.: Lamont, who has been back at Downing Street for an hour, leaves again in his Jaguar accompanied by his adviser David Cameron. He smiles but says nothing [*Daily Express*].' Reporters were in hot pursuit and the pair were spotted next having lunch at Toto, a small Italian restaurant in Knightsbridge. Cameron had got drawn into a stakeout where journalists would make a note of Lamont's every move: 'Lunching alone with his adviser, the deposed Chancellor nevertheless managed two glasses of champagne' (Press Association); 'After his £34-a-head lunch of pasta and fruit salad there was no official car to whisk him away' (*Today*); 'Shorn of his ministerial limousine, Lamont had to flag down a taxi' (*Daily Mirror*).

Any slip-up by a high-profile politician whose behaviour is being closely monitored in a restaurant or similar venue can easily be magnified out of all proportion. Given Lamont's seething sense of injustice he would have been at even greater risk without the additional safeguard of Cameron's eyes and ears. Lamont had chosen wisely: his adviser was not only likeable and good company, but was also the 'perfect hand holder' and must have offered great reassurance with his presence, even if it might not have been much fun at the time. Cameron was getting dragged ever deeper into the task of helping to pick up the pieces as Lamont's career veered off into an uncontrolled tail spin. As the denouement approached he would discover to his own cost how a wounded minister seeking revenge can compromise the position of friends and colleagues. Lamont's petulance would take some beating and Cameron's only consolation was that he was unlikely to be fazed in his future career by any similarly acrimonious reshuffle.

On arriving at the Treasury immediately after being sacked, Lamont informed Cameron that he would not be following the traditional courtesy of exchanging a resignation letter with the Prime Minister. Instead he issued a personal statement insisting that the success of the policies he had put in place at the Treasury would 'become increasingly clear with the passage of time'. Lamont's snub to Major was highlighted by the *Sunday Times* in its background report on the reshuffle: 'Cameron was instructed to issue an unprecedented statement of self-justification to the Press Association, omitting any reference to Major or any mention of his continuing support for his government. According to Treasury insiders, the first No. 10 heard about it was when the news agency put it out at 4.03 p.m.' Asking the Press Association rather than the Downing Street press office to release the statement was quite a coup for the news agency, which reproduced the *Sunday Times* report about Cameron's role in a series of full-page promotional advertisements in *UK Press Gazette*. Flagging up the identity of Lamont's spokesman in a weekly magazine for the news media meant that any journalist inquiring about the ex-Chancellor's intentions would be in no doubt that Cameron was the right person to contact.

Lamont's statement to the Press Association included the tantalising line that he did not 'intend to make any further comment for several weeks', which only served to fuel the speculation that he would indeed exact revenge at some point. Two weeks elapsed, then he seized the opportunity to cause maximum embarrassment for the Prime Minister by opting to make a personal statement immediately before an Opposition Day debate criticising the government's handling of the economy. Cameron, still without the firm promise of a new job, had been asked repeatedly by lobby correspondents what Lamont intended to do. No doubt thinking about his own future and anxious to avoid harming his chances of getting placed with another cabinet minister, Cameron consistently played down any suggestion that Lamont was seeking retribution; he told correspondents that he had been in touch with Lamont that weekend and was confident the former Chancellor had no intention of retaliating.

While Cameron was doing his best to serve the interests of the Prime Minister and the Conservative Party by trying to damp down speculation, it was a mistake to have paraded himself as a point of contact for the ex-Chancellor and it might perhaps have been a wiser course of action to have told journalists he was no longer in a position to help with their inquiries. Although I did not speak to Cameron myself, I knew his guidance to the lobby was not only out of date but was also misleading. David Hart, a friend of Lamont's and a former adviser to Margaret Thatcher, had told me on the night of the reshuffle that the former Chancellor blamed Sir Norman Fowler for having urged Major to dismiss him. 'Lamont is boiling over with rage. He purposely did not write a letter of loyalty because he wants room for manoeuvre. He will not say anything for the next few days but he will cause a lot of trouble. He thinks the offer of environment is an insult and he told Major so.'

When news of Lamont's intention to make a personal statement finally emerged it caught Westminster by surprise. The first official notification was at noon, when the House of Commons annunciators listed the day's business. With only a few minutes to spare before the start of *The World at One*, I managed to contact Hart and he confirmed that Lamont's speech would be a 'bombshell'; it was definitely intended to discomfort the Prime Minister. 'Lamont has kept quiet about it on purpose. He feared that Major and the whips would try to screw it up if they got wind of what he was planning.' When asked on air what Lamont might say, I went hard in predicting that 'a very aggrieved ex-Chancellor' would launch a calculated attempt to embarrass Major; it promised to be a 'riveting' speech about his sense of having been betrayed by the Prime Minister and made a scapegoat. My broadcast was immediately challenged on its accuracy by the press office at Conservative Central Office, which accused me of 'going over the top'. While waiting in the press gallery for the statement I was also cross-questioned by the *Daily Mirror*'s political editor, John Williams, who said Cameron had personally assured him that Lamont had no intention of speaking out of turn.

Hart's guidance was spot on: Lamont launched a damning indictment of the Prime Minister, accusing him of being obsessed with his image to the point that his government 'gives the impression of being in office but not in power'. Political journalists drew immediate comparisons with Geoffrey Howe's statement in the autumn of 1990 which precipitated the fall of Margaret Thatcher. Lamont's friend Woodrow Wyatt, the *News of the World* columnist, was credited with having written much of the speech, which perhaps explained why Cameron was out of the loop. 'Mr Whiplash' was the bold headline on the *Daily Mail*'s front page next morning above a report that suggested Lamont had meted out the sort of punishment which a sex therapist would have been proud of. No doubt Cameron was mightily relieved that for once his speech-writing skills had not been called upon. Although some lobby correspondents might have felt they had been misled by his briefings, he had demonstrated some neat political footwork in smartly detaching himself from the ex-Chancellor and in repositioning himself firmly behind the Prime Minister and the party.

Lamont's final few weeks at the Treasury would have tested Cameron's loyalty to the limit, because he was being asked to spin the line that it was 'business as usual' when it was becoming all too obvious that the Chancellor would be a casualty in the looming reshuffle. The last straw for the Prime Minister and the party hierarchy was the Conservatives' humiliating defeat in the Newbury by-election after a disastrous campaign blighted by Lamont's infamous line '*Je ne regrette rien*'. Shortly before he was sacked, in a belated attempt to apologise, the Chancellor used a speech at the Scottish Conservatives' annual conference to try to make amends. On this occasion the speech writer was not Cameron but Hart, who was doing his best to stiffen the Chancellor's resolve to ride out the reshuffle speculation, not least because he believed that Lamont's continued presence at the Treasury would safeguard the position of the then chief secretary, Michael Portillo, who was committed to the task of trying to curb public spending. Hart wanted Lamont's speech in Edinburgh to show that the Chancellor could take it on the chin. 'I got Lamont to say: "I regret the hardship that getting inflation down has caused. But I do not regret taking the tough but necessary decisions to get inflation under control." I thought it was time he made the point that he regretted the effects of what had happened.'

Given all the manoeuvrings behind the scenes, Cameron could not be faulted on the way he managed to extricate himself from the bitter post-reshuffle recriminations. After the scandal and intrigue surrounding Lamont's downfall, he was about to secure the patronage of a cabinet minister who was renowned for being meticulous in his efforts to micro-manage his media personality. Staying on at the Treasury was not an option because the new Chancellor, Kenneth Clarke, had already chosen two special advisers to work in his private office. As any aspiring politician knows only too well, a lucky break can make all the difference and accepting the offer to become an adviser to the newly appointed Home Secretary, Michael Howard, was by far the most fortunate move Cameron could possibly have made. He was about to establish a relationship which would further strengthen the foundations of his rise to the top of the Conservative Party. Howard's friendship and support would prove to be invaluable after the Conservatives' defeat in the 2005 general election when the baton of leadership would be handed on to the next generation.

The new Home Secretary's principal special adviser was Patrick Rock, with whom Cameron had worked during the general election campaign; he was largely responsible for assisting Howard in his contacts with the news media. Cameron's task, in addition to supporting the other Home Office ministers, was to help with speech writing and policy research, again another highly propitious opportunity. Howard had not expected to get the home affairs brief and he realised immediately that he faced an uphill task in trying to re-establish the Conservatives' reputation as the party of law and order. Tony Blair, then shadow Home Secretary, had stolen a march on the Tories with his promise in January 1993 that a future Labour government would be 'tough on crime and tough on the causes of crime'. Howard was determined to find a way to retaliate and he believed his first party conference speech as Home Secretary in October

1993 was the ideal occasion on which to launch what he hoped would be seen as a radical crackdown on crime. In the weeks leading up to his appearance before the annual gathering of Conservative representatives at Blackpool he gave Cameron a masterclass in preparing and then implementing a strategy designed to capture the news agenda. With the help of his advisers he drew up a total of twenty-seven new measures which he told the conference amounted to the 'most comprehensive programme of action against crime that has ever been announced by any Home Secretary'. Headline writers on the tabloids gave the speech an ecstatic welcome: 'The law goes to war' (*Sun*); 'Back to real Tory values' (*Daily Express*); 'Steps back to sanity' (*Daily Star*).

When I was handed a copy of the speech at the party press office I saw straightaway that it was not the usual conference rhetoric. Stapled to the back were five additional pages headed 'notes for editors' giving precise information about how each new provision would be implemented. Although it was obviously a Conservative news release and was printed on party paper, the document exuded a sense of authority and was clearly designed to give the impression that these were official government announcements. Conference speeches are often short of detail, especially on controversial subjects like law and order, and Howard knew that if journalists were to be convinced, there would have to be some real substance to back up his proposals. As I listened to Howard and checked off his announcements against the text, the vast range of his proposals was striking: 'I'm going to introduce tougher powers to allow the police to stop and search cars for weapons and explosives . . . We will sweep away many of the complex legal restraints on DNA . . . This may mean that more people will go to prison. I do not flinch from that . . . Let us be clear. Prison works . . . We shall build six new prisons.'

During the pre-conference build-up there had been no mention of Howard's plan to deliver what the London *Evening Standard* dubbed 'Britain's biggest ever crime-busting package'. The conference agenda did contain more resolutions on law and order than any other subject and journalists were anticipating that Howard would have to face the delegates' wrath. However, by taking the news media by surprise, he succeeded in dominating much of that day's radio and television coverage and provided front-page leads next morning for most of the national newspapers. Cameron's supporting role in ensuring that the Home Secretary grabbed the conference headlines gave him an insight into Howard's Machiavellian talent for managing his coverage in the news media. Of all John Major's ministers, he was the one with the clearest grasp of the agenda-setting ability of the press and the likely response of broadcasters. But he was also the minister that radio and television producers feared most. A particularly menacing attribute was his deadly accuracy when making complaints, as I had learned to my cost. During the build-up to the 1992 general election I was reprimanded by my editors when Howard, who was then Secretary of State for Employment, complained directly to the BBC's director general, John Birt, about the accuracy of my reporting for Radio 4. Birt's letter of apology, regretting my failure to have been 'very cautious of reporting detailed and substantial allegations', was leaked to the *Daily Express* with the inevitable headline 'BBC says sorry'.

When reporting Howard's speech at Blackpool my suspicions were aroused by the quasi-official nature of the Conservatives' news release. Its presentation suggested there might have been a degree of political collusion within the Home Office. In fact the opposite was the case: several senior officials told me subsequently they had been caught off guard by the scope of the twenty-seven steps which the Home Secretary said he intended to take to protect 'people's freedom to walk safely on their streets and to sleep safely in their homes'. Howard had purposely drawn up his package with the help of his advisers rather than civil servants; Rock and Cameron had both prepared numerous policy papers examining various proposals. In challenging the traditional thinking of both the Home Office and the criminal justice system, Howard had delighted the 'hanging and flogging' brigade at conference but his ideas attracted widespread criticism, not least because it was increasingly apparent that most of the initiatives had emerged from the

Home Secretary's private office rather than his departmental officials, who had not been shown an advance copy of the completed text with its five pages of detailed proposals. After both the BBC and the *Guardian* reported that Home Office civil servants had privately complained that their department was being turned into 'a PR machine' for the Home Secretary, the input of his two ministerial aides was called into question. Sir Clive Whitmore, permanent under-secretary at the Home Office, wrote to the *Guardian* defending the Home Secretary: Howard did debate policy issues 'fully with officials' but it was for the Home Secretary and 'his ministerial colleagues' to reach decisions. Nonetheless, the point had been made: special advisers had played their part in what Whitmore stated had been a 'vigorous and healthy' process of policy formulation.

Howard's conference pledges had to be translated into firm proposals ready for the Queen's Speech the following month. Columnists began to speculate on what new ideas Rock and Cameron might be asked to conjure up. Melanie Phillips, writing in the *Observer*, accused Howard and his aides of coming up with 'one loopy idea after another' in an attempt to build his profile as 'leader of the demagogue tendency'. 'The Weasel', diarist for the *Independent*'s magazine, dreamed he had been at a private brainstorming session for Howard's 'speech writers and spin doctors' where they had suggested impaling offenders ready for stoning, only to be told by 'a wet blanket from Central Office' that this would be rejected on grounds of cruelty. Cameron's input into the Blackpool speech was derided by Mark Lawson in the *Independent on Sunday*'s review. Though 'crudely written' it was 'a formidable technical achievement' because it could be 'spoken, or more nearly shouted, on a single note of indignation' and enabled Howard to explain why the criminal justice system would now be weighted in 'favour of pippill rather than crimnills'. After hearing the Home Secretary outline his law-and-order programme in the debate on the Queen's Speech, the hapless Rock and Campbell were firmly in Alastair Campbell's sights in his comment column in *Today*: 'It must have been tossed together by a couple of special advisers over lunch. It was dreadful, deplorabull, terribill and once again Labour's Tony "tough on Howard, tough on the causes of Howard" won the day.'

Campbell and the other columnists were proved correct in their deduction that Howard had given free rein to his young advisers to think the unthinkable on law and order. Seven years later the newly elected Conservative MP for Witney let slip, perhaps inadvertently, that some of the policy proposals he put forward as Howard's special adviser might have been considered off the wall. In an online diary for Guardian Unlimited in June 2001, Cameron described listening to his first Queen's Speech as a new MP and his disappointment that Labour had failed to honour their pledge to reform licensing hours, an objective he supported in the early 1990s. 'I wrote endless papers about scrapping our ludicrous laws. The permanent secretary, who was also tiring of my missives about stiff minimum sentences for burglars, summoned me to his office and said: "Cameron, as far as I can see you want half the population in prison and the other half in the pub." Fair point.'

During the year he spent at the Home Office, Cameron could not have failed to notice that although Howard was on good terms with certain newspaper editors and radio and television executives, his relations with leading broadcasters and producers were often abrasive and not helped by his predilection for complaining. Whereas Norman Lamont had found it impossible to come to terms with the intense scrutiny of the media and only exacerbated his troubled relations with journalists, Howard was always ready to defend himself and if necessary mount a counter-attack. Peter Mandelson had the same, steely approach. Reporters and production staff soon came to realise that the Home Secretary, like Mandelson, thought nothing of going over their heads direct to the management in order to demand an apology. Once politicians acquire a reputation for being not just difficult but perhaps even vindictive towards broadcasters and their technicians, it can be hard to shift. Viewers and listeners sense the tension during interviews and it is not long before cartoonists and satirists pick up the on-air nuances, often with deadly effect. Howard certainly marked Cameron's card when it came to the ABC of complaining and once a politician has understood how to retaliate, it can become addictive.

Family breakdown and the punishment of young offenders were two of the issues in which Cameron had taken a great interest at the Home Office and his input was reflected in Howard's speech to a fringe meeting at the 1993 party conference. His address was entitled 'Picking up the pieces' and the Home Secretary dealt at length with the rapid increase in the number of single mothers, their reliance on social security benefits and the lack of peer pressure on their offspring, often resulting in 'rebellious boys thinking they can get away with anything' because of the trend away from the 'deterrent effect of punishment'. Reference to various studies at home and abroad indicated his aides had carried out extensive research and the examples he quoted included evidence from a trial in New Jersey where single mothers had their benefits capped for second and subsequent children.

In a report for *News at Ten*, ITN's political correspondent Mark Webster highlighted the Home Secretary's undertaking that he would study the New Jersey experience to see if it contained any lessons for Britain. Howard was annoyed by the broadcast; he considered Webster had gone too far in suggesting that the Conservatives wanted to bear down on single mothers. ITN's political editor, Michael Brunson, told me he had to pick up the pieces: 'Howard's adviser Patrick Rock complained straight to ITN in London. It would have been better if Howard had dealt with me directly. Mandelson is more of an operator in that respect, at least he has learned that I can communicate quickly with the rest of the ITN team and sort things out.' Webster's report was amply vindicated next morning: 'Crackdown on lone mothers' was the front-page splash in the *Daily Mail*; 'End of welfare mothers,' said the *Daily Express*; and the *Guardian* reported that Howard had become the 'first senior cabinet minister to court publicly' the idea of a benefit crackdown.

While the nitty-gritty of these complaints might seem an irrelevance to the outside world, I knew from my contacts inside the Home Office information department that they were viewed entirely differently within the Home Secretary's private office. His determination not to be tripped up on air was all-consuming and when helping to brief Howard on the issues involved, Cameron would have tried to cover every possible eventuality. If Howard was about to be interviewed live, his aides would demand to be told the names of any other guests as it might influence his decision as to whether to take part in the programme; he would always insist on having the last word on the subject; and would ask for the chance to listen to any contributions pre-recorded in advance, so as to reduce the chances of being caught off guard.

My own previous conviction for having been found guilty by John Birt of offending Howard thwarted my one and only opportunity to have lunch with the Home Secretary. I had been hoping it might give me the chance to renew my fleeting acquaintance with Rock and Cameron. Two BBC colleagues had booked a table at Simply Nico and when they both had to cancel unexpectedly my name was put forward as a substitute. First thing next morning Howard's private office rang to say that he was now 'too busy' to attend. Before I even had time to ring Simply Nico, the restaurant telephoned to say Howard had pulled out.

Cameron's career was approaching a turning point. In spring 1994 he told Howard that he intended to look for a job outside politics as he felt he needed to widen his experience if he was to secure a place on the candidates' list and stand for Parliament. The six years he spent at Westminster had been a roller coaster ride, taking him from the research department at Conservative Central Office straight to Downing Street to help brief the Prime Minister, and then on to two of the great departments of state, the Treasury and the Home Office.

During his two years as a special adviser he could not have served two more contrasting politicians of the Major government. The Chancellor and the Home Secretary were travelling in opposite directions: Lamont was sacked and his ministerial career ended in humiliation; the highly ambitious Howard would go on to have a central role in rebuilding his party and would later lead the Conservatives into the 2005 general election. Both had given Cameron an exceptional opportunity to see if the ideas and beliefs of a young political researcher could be translated into firm policy proposals. Helping to write speeches and prepare media briefs had required Cameron to get to grips with the twists and turns of economic management and then the ever-expanding home affairs remit. But more importantly, because they were at different stages in their political careers, Lamont and Howard had divergent experiences at the hands of the news. In their own individual way, they each gave their young aide a front-row seat for observing how politicians have to cope with a non-stop barrage of headlines. In his year at the Treasury, Cameron saw how even desperate crisis PR could not keep pace with the accident-prone Lamont and the calamities which dogged his final months as Chancellor. At the Home Office, Howard was firmly on the way up; he was commanding the news agenda by challenging the criminal justice system, and he had yet to face the kinds of crisis in the prisons and law enforcement which have tended to destabilise most recent Home Secretaries.

The two cabinet heavyweights were also opposites in the way they treated journalists and tried to withstand media vilification. Lamont was often aloof, unable to come to terms with the cut and thrust of the daily dogfight at Westminster, seemingly in despair at ever getting a good press or a fair hearing, whereas Howard's obsession with scoring points and trying to put journalists and broadcasters in their place bordered on the kind of control freakery which New Labour's spin doctors finally realised, too late in the day, was almost always counter-productive.

The year Cameron spent with Howard was cited a decade later as having been 'useful training for an apprentice politician' because it had been a 'good vantage point to observe political failure'. When commenting on the line-up in the Conservatives' 2005 leadership election, the *Independent*'s columnist Bruce Anderson reminded his readers that Howard was the most right-wing Home Secretary for many years, determined to counter the institutional pessimism of the Home Office that nothing could be done to prevent the rise in crime. He ought to have been the hero of the popular press and the public's darling. His lack of popularity was an instructive lesson for Cameron because if a party leader was to stand any chance of succeeding, it was 'helpful to work out why others had failed'.

Cameron joined the corporate affairs department of Carlton Television in September 1994, first as personal assistant to the chairman, Michael Green, and then, within a few months, becoming director of corporate communications, or 'head of corporate affairs' as he liked to be known. Again, perhaps without realising what lay in store, he had made another fortuitous move. The seven years he spent at Carlton would give him an exceptional insight into the hidden world of the collusive relationships which tend to flourish when the commercial interests of media proprietors are at stake and when the government of the day or an opposition party are seeking to gain favourable treatment from journalists and broadcasters. The television moguls of the 1990s, like the press barons of old, were ever mindful of their potential role in influencing public opinion and they tended to be as promiscuous as newspaper editors when extending political favours and patronage. Cameron would see for himself what went on behind the scenes when owners and proprietors were being courted assiduously by politicians and sometimes being handsomely rewarded with the honours which have been bestowed by successive Prime Ministers.

Cameron had joined an industry which at the time was enjoying rapid expansion but which was also highly regulated. If television and radio companies were to prosper, they had to establish and maintain an effective relationship across Whitehall, and the insights gained at Carlton would stand Cameron in good stead once he had the chance to shape Conservative policy for the digital age and begin the hard slog of trying to win the respect and support of the all-important media proprietors.

3
THE BIG SPEECH

Many are the times a long-awaited and much-rehearsed speech to a party conference has failed to deliver. When he walked on to the platform at the Blackpool Winter Gardens in October 2005 and spoke without notes for twenty minutes, David Cameron transformed his chances of winning the race for the leadership of the Conservative Party. In the event, a single conference speech did succeed in changing the political weather. What added to the theatre of the occasion was the element of surprise; few of the pundits had seen it coming. Perhaps even more surprising was that in reacting to the speech many seasoned commentators did not appear to take full account of the way party representatives were responding to what was after all Cameron's first-ever speech to a party conference and the first such high-profile address of recent years to have been delivered without the aid of a teleprompter. In their instant analysis most political journalists failed to spot the turning point that it would become in the leadership election. Cameron's debut on the conference platform was about to earn its place in the contemporary folklore of his party, the moment when the Conservatives could at last look ahead with some confidence to returning to government. After having been written off for much of the leadership campaign as an eager but inexperienced also-ran, he had risked all, taken on the party's heavyweights and delivered the performance of a lifetime.

Defining moments are all-important in the careers of aspiring politicians. The most celebrated event in the early progression of Tony Blair was what became known as his 'Clause IV' speech at Labour's 1994 annual conference. Blair's audacity in taking on the left of his party was promoted subsequently as an occasion of high drama, just as the political theatre surrounding Cameron's off-the-cuff performance improved greatly with retelling. In both cases it was the post-speech spin which helped to cement them as ground-breaking episodes. Unlike Blair, whose stand against the trade unions won immediate praise, Cameron had to wait for five days before his debut finally attracted the almost unanimous approval of the news media. In some respects Blair's speech was a sleight of hand because it contained no direct mention of his plan to remove Clause IV from the party's constitution and abandon Labour's commitment to 'common ownership'. Instead he spoke of the need for 'a clear up-to-date statement' about the party's objectives and it was only after the speech, once journalists were briefed that Blair was absolutely determined to rewrite Clause IV, that its true significance was realised. Eleven years later Cameron at least had the personal satisfaction of knowing that his address had captivated the conference but in contrast to the reception for Blair's speech it took far longer to convince journalists that this was the event which would have the greatest influence on the outcome of the Conservatives' leadership election.

The tortuous path which he had to negotiate during the summer and autumn of 2005 was a test of stamina in the face of hostile fire, a dress rehearsal for the endurance that would be required four years later for the long haul to a general election. During the opening rounds of the contest, when Tory big hitters such as David Davis and Kenneth Clarke were making all the running, Cameron and his aides had struggled to attract the attention of the news media but they held their nerve, tried to build up support and waited for the right moment to grab the spotlight and reach out to activists, over the heads of the parliamentary party. Cameron's X-factor, which he was about to deploy with unexpected panache, was an ability to memorise a speech and then, however daunting the prospect, address a crowded conference hall and hold the attention of the audience. His informality was engaging, but exceptional presentation would not have been enough on its own to outsmart his opponents. Organisation was just as important and his campaign team demonstrated an ability to choreograph a big event and seize the moment, a flair for tactical timing which would become a hallmark of Cameron's leadership during the protracted lead-up to polling day in 2010.

Faced by the widespread predictions that the leadership contest was likely to develop into a straight fight between Davis and Clarke, the Cameron campaign had little alternative but to hold firm and do their best to talk up his chances. His age and a relatively brief career in the House of Commons counted against him but conversely his pitch for modernising the party was said to have strengthened his appeal among newer and younger MPs, who were being courted assiduously. A prolonged contest was working to his advantage and he held off as long as possible before publicly declaring his hand. Cameron's inner circle of advisers included the shadow Chancellor, George Osborne, and other former colleagues from his days at Conservative Central Office. Like him they were seasoned party professionals, well versed in the structures and procedures that link the constituencies to the staff at headquarters, and their combined knowhow as insiders meant Cameron was able to draw on the encouragement of some up-and-coming political strategists at a time when most columnists and commentators persisted in writing off his chances.

A summer of uncertainty started the day after the Conservatives' defeat in the general election of May 2005, when Michael Howard announced that he would step down once rules were agreed for a new leadership contest. He favoured the election of his successor being restricted to the 197 Conservative MPs at Westminster rather than being opened up again to a vote by the party membership. Conservative MPs had been stripped of the final say after the party's defeat in 2001, when Iain Duncan Smith was elected on the strength of a mass vote in the constituencies only for the parliamentary party to launch a putsch against him two years later and elect Howard in his place. Once they heard of the intention to deny party members a say in electing a new leader, many constituency workers and grassroots campaigners voiced their opposition and a seemingly interminable debate over the conduct of the contest was not finally resolved until late September, only a matter of days before the start of the annual conference. To the surprise and disappointment of the party hierarchy the constitutional college failed to ratify Howard's proposal; MPs backed the change but only 58 per cent of party representatives agreed, less than the necessary two-thirds majority. A decision to keep to the existing system and embark on another vote by the rank and file required a rethink all round. Instead of a swiftly conducted contest restricted to the parliamentary party there would have to be an initial series of MPs' ballots to choose two candidates whose names would then go forward to a postal ballot of the party's 300,000 members, a process that would not be completed until early December. Seven months would have to elapse between the Conservatives' third election defeat and the installation of a new leader.

By announcing that he intended to stand down, without having first ensured there were settled rules in place for the selection of a new leader, Howard had effectively fired the starting gun for a race that lacked a finishing line. Potential contenders were unsure about their tactics: should they concentrate their campaign in Westminster or appeal directly to party members in the constituencies? Initially it was open season, with all and sundry letting their names go forward. Within a week of Howard's announcement that he would stand down, twelve potential candidates were identified by the *Daily Telegraph*: David Davis, John Redwood and Liam Fox were contenders for the right; David Cameron, George Osborne, Sir Malcolm Rifkind and David Willetts were seen as the most likely to appeal to the solid centre ground of the party; and Kenneth Clarke, Andrew Lansley, Damian Green, Tim Yeo and Alan Duncan were named as candidates thought to be favoured by the left.

Osborne was the first to stand aside and he immediately became the de facto organiser and spokesman for Cameron's campaign team, or the 'Notting Hill set', as the young modernisers had come to be known.

Osborne and Cameron had been friends since their paths crossed as political aides under John Major's government, a friendship that had deepened when they were elected MPs in the 2001 general election. They had homes in Notting Hill and they often cycled together, through Kensington Gardens and Hyde Park, on their way to the House of Commons. Both were regarded as potential high flyers and when the success of their partnership began attracting wider attention, Michael Portillo wondered if they could be the Tories' answer to Tony Blair and Gordon Brown. Portillo had failed to reach the final ballot when he made his own bid for the leadership in 2001 and two years later, when Howard replaced Duncan Smith, he looked ahead in a column in the *Observer* to the days when a future generation of Conservatives might have a chance of regaining power. Although Portillo stressed that these 'two bright young things, unsullied by having held office in a previous administration', were not ready to stand for the leadership, his suggestion that they might have the appeal of a Blair–Brown ticket helped to reinforce their image as the two most promising young pretenders of the 2001 intake.

They both won rapid promotion once Howard was appointed leader. Osborne became shadow Treasury chief secretary and Cameron joined the shadow cabinet in September 2004 as head of policy. Within a matter of weeks Cameron's next appointment made the *Daily Telegraph*'s front-page splash: 'Howard gives protégé major election role'. Party insiders were quoted as saying that Howard's decision to give Cameron the job of co-ordinating Conservative policies for the 2005 general election was part of his 'master plan' to groom him as a future party leader. Their favoured status continued after the Conservatives' third successive defeat. Once Howard had made it clear that he intended to remain leader while a debate took place about the process of electing his successor, he reshuffled his frontbench team. Osborne was promoted to shadow Chancellor and Cameron appointed shadow Education Secretary. Again the inside talk was that Howard had acted strategically. Whereas Osborne would have his work cut out trying to challenge Brown and his team of Treasury ministers, Cameron would not be as hard pressed when shadowing Ruth Kelly, the Secretary of State for Education, and unlike other potential challengers, Cameron would have both the time and the greater freedom to float new policies and promote his bid for the leadership.

Being identified as Howard's protégé gave Cameron every incentive to refresh the easy-going political repartee which he had adopted since his earliest days at Conservative Central Office and which he tended to use whenever he was caught off guard or forced to respond to awkward questions. 'Well, at least we talk to each other' was his riposte if asked by journalists how he and Osborne reacted to being hailed the 'Blair and Brown' of their generation. He ridiculed suggestions that he might stand for the leadership should Howard be defeated in the 2005 general election: 'It's absurd. I mean, it can be quite flattering to read these things about yourself. But it is for the birds.' Barbed comments about having been to Eton and Oxford were more troubling. When asked initially whether his privileged education might hamper his political career, he revealed his inner doubts: 'I don't know. You can try to be logical about it and say the upside is a terrific education. The downside is the label that gets attached and mentioned in every article.' Later he took shelter behind an array of self-deprecating one-liners which could be delivered with a smile: 'Yes, I know I have this terrible CV . . . Conservatives judge people on their merits, not where you come from but where you are going to, so that should apply to Old Etonians as well as everybody else.' Once he and Osborne began to be pilloried for being 'Notting Hill Tories', Cameron often hit back with a question of his own: 'Is it going to stick, this dreadful label?' Sniping about their privileged backgrounds and inherited family wealth was again harder to deflect and once Osborne ruled himself out as a potential leader, Cameron's campaign team became a ready-made target for the Labour Party's spin doctors. They were instantly dubbed 'Toffs on Tour' by Downing Street aides, a line of abuse which, although predictable, was also persuasive, likely to stick and much more difficult to shake off.

To begin with the odds seemed stacked firmly in favour of the shadow

Home Secretary, David Davis, who at the age of fifty-six had years of political experience behind him and still had every hope of pulling off the top job. He claimed to have the backing of twice as many MPs as either Clarke or Cameron. A head start at Westminster was strengthened by claims that Davis was also in front in the constituencies, one reason why it was said Howard had argued that the vote should be restricted to the parliamentary party, in the hope that a 'stop Davis' candidate might emerge. A YouGov opinion poll conducted in June among the party's rank and file put support for Davis at 54 per cent, with 30 per cent for Cameron, 24 per cent for Fox and 19 per cent for Clarke. Such was the strength of his lead both at Westminster and in the country that some pundits appeared to think Davis would be a shoo-in. William Rees-Mogg, writing in *The Times*, concluded that no other candidate had a body of support equal to Davis's. Cameron and the other challengers were 'rolling stones' who had gathered no 'moss' and in his opinion the party should adopt the same 'short cut' which had been used to elect Howard. The *Evening Standard*'s Anne McElvoy concurred: Davis was 'looking unbeatable' unless Clarke decided to stand, which she thought would be the 'only contest worth having'; potential candidates such as Cameron looked 'lame or unready'.

From the start the one columnist to champion Cameron was Alice Thomson, assistant editor of the *Daily Telegraph*, who revealed that after Michael Howard announced his resignation the Notting Hill Tories met at an Italian restaurant, Zucca, to plan their tactics. She judged that Cameron and Osborne were at the 'tougher' end of the leadership spectrum, 'aspirational but also pragmatic'. Cameron told her that voters needed to be inspired but they also wanted the Conservatives to 'fess up when we haven't got the answers'. A fortnight later Thomson gave her take on why Cameron and his team had been so encouraged by Howard's prediction that the election contest could become a marathon and might last until Christmas: the Notting Hill set needed 'as much time as possible to grow some stubble and look serious'.

As the summer progressed Cameron's campaign was still failing to generate any real momentum. A Populus opinion poll published by *The Times* at the end of July drew attention to the candidates' fluctuating fortunes. Among Conservative voters, experience seemed to count for most: if it was a straight choice, Davis would trounce Cameron by 53 to 14 per cent but Clarke would narrowly defeat Davis by 29 to 26 per cent. An online Populus poll assessing voter recognition of the seven leading candidates produced an equally dispiriting result: Cameron had the lowest score, having been recognised by a mere 6 per cent of the sample, well behind Clarke (50 per cent) and Davis (27 per cent).

Among commentators the emerging consensus was that the young modernisers would have to wait their turn. Some suggested Cameron should consider stepping aside. Michael Portillo, although among the first to have written up the prospects of Cameron and Osborne, was no longer so sure. He doubted whether Cameron had the experience to cope with shadowing Blair and then possibly Brown. He concluded his comment column in the *Sunday Times* by admitting that if he was still an MP, he would consider voting for Davis, who was evidently a 'shrewd political operator', and he would advise Cameron to withdraw. Other columnists lined up with similar advice: John Rentoul (*Independent on Sunday*) said it was too late for Cameron to change the tempo and catch up with the favourite; Steve Richards (*Independent*) thought Cameron was 'intelligent, charming and capable of engaging beyond the Conservative Party' but was too young and inexperienced for the second-toughest job in politics; and, while agreeing he was an 'exceptionally plausible' candidate, Simon Heffer (*Daily Mail*) derided Cameron for not having 'a clue how to connect with the mass of voters that the Tories need to haul on board'.

What many journalists had under-estimated was the tenacity of the Notting Hill set and the interest which Cameron was beginning to generate for his promise to deliver 'compassionate Conservatism'. In mid-June he used an article for the *Mail on Sunday* to argue that the party should refocus on 'helping the most vulnerable'. His pitch was well timed, not least because the former party chairman Theresa May had entered the fray, prompting fresh headlines about her claim at the 2002 annual conference that people regarded the Conservatives as the 'nasty party'. In signalling her intention to join the leadership race, May told *The Politics Show* that although the party was no longer judged so harshly, Conservatives were too often characterised as 'negative, self-interested and out of touch'. In attempting to define 'Conservative compassion', Cameron drew heavily on his experience as the father of a two-year-old disabled boy. Ivan Cameron suffered from severe epilepsy and cerebral palsy and the daily struggle faced by the parents of disabled children became a recurring theme in Cameron's speeches, interviews and articles. When he was questioned by *The Times* for a profile published immediately after his promotion to the shadow cabinet in September 2004, he readily agreed that to be appointed minister for the disabled would give him great personal satisfaction. Cameron had a no-nonsense reply when asked how he answered those Conservatives who believed he should not talk publicly about his disabled son or appear to use him for political advantage: 'Ivan is part of who I am. He is a very special child. We adore him in ways that you will never love anybody else, because you feel so protective.'

Given his previous experience as a political adviser at Westminster and the seven years he spent in corporate communications, Cameron was obviously more streetwise than most MPs when it came to dealing with journalists and he seemed to know almost intuitively where he and his wife Samantha intended to establish the boundaries regarding access to their private life. He had seen for himself how debilitating it could become when politicians failed to achieve a comfortable balance between the demands of the news media and the need to protect their families from intrusive publicity. Perhaps the greatest dilemma for any MP with a young family is deciding whether to allow the children to be photographed and filmed. Should they become part and parcel of a politician's public persona?

Photographs of wives, husbands and children do often appear in election literature but for many politicians that is as far as they are prepared to go. They fear that once they have ticked the box for family publicity there may be no way back. Two spectacularly misjudged photo-opportunities involving politicians' children in the early 1990s were seared into the collective memory of Conservative MPs. At the height of the concern about eating beef, due to the scare over 'mad cow disease', the agriculture minister, John Gummer, was photographed feeding his four-year-old daughter Cordelia with what the newspapers dubbed a 'BSE-burger'. Two years later, in a desperate attempt to deflect attention from his affair with the actress Antonia de Sancha, the National Heritage Secretary, David Mellor, compounded media outrage about the hypocrisy of Conservative ministers regarding family values when he arranged for his wife, two young sons and his parents-in-law to join him looking over a garden gate for the benefit of newspaper photographers.

Having seen how dangerous it could be to misjudge media access, Tony and Cherie Blair were determined to protect their children from intrusive publicity when they moved into 10 Downing Street in 1997. In the hope of satisfying media demands for at least a degree of access they did pose for a limited number of family photo-opportunities outside No. 10 and again either before or after general elections. However, because of the large number of photographers and camera crews working in and around Downing Street, the task of trying to shield children on their way into and out of No.10 was a perpetual problem and the Blairs complained frequently about unnecessary intrusion into their family life, especially if their offspring became embroiled in embarrassing incidents. Sometimes pictures were taken inadvertently, prompting fresh complaints, even if they were not published or broadcast. The suspicion took hold that the Blairs were quite prepared to parade their children for the cameras if it suited their political purposes but otherwise demanded total privacy, a balance which became increasingly hard to justify.

Therefore when Cameron invited a photographer into his home for his profile in *The Times* and agreed to be photographed in various poses with Samantha, Ivan and their nine-month-old daughter Nancy, he had clearly taken a calculated decision. His openness was refreshing.

Whereas he might have attracted criticism on the grounds that given his privileged upbringing he was only too keen to portray himself as a typical family man, the counterpoint was that any publicity that he was able to command as an MP could then be used to help to drive up the level of care for disabled children from less advantaged backgrounds. Whatever his private calculations, Cameron was always frank and engaging in front of the camera and eager to discuss the problems which parents faced.

Shortly after he began raising disability issues in speeches in the House of Commons, the London *Evening Standard* reported that Cameron and his wife had joined other parents from west London in campaigning to prevent the closure of the Cheyne Day Centre, an intensive therapeutic unit for severely disabled children. His support for threatened special needs schools became something of a crusade once the leadership campaign gave him a wider platform on which to promote future Conservative thinking on education. He wrote in the *Independent* about the 'wonderful revelation' it had been when he and Samantha had found a school that could cope with what were judged to be Ivan's 'profound and multiple learning difficulties'. His argument that parents should have a choice between special and mainstream schools challenged the accepted thinking that a sprinkling of special needs children in every classroom encouraged inclusion, a policy of integration which had resulted in the loss of around 100 special schools under Labour. By speaking out so forcefully in support of state-run day centres for disabled children, Cameron widened his appeal beyond the ghetto of political reporting. 'At last, a fanciable Tory' was the headline over India Knight's column in the *Sunday Times* praising his 'impressive' campaign on behalf of children like Ivan. 'This man isn't an alien . . . He looks, you know, nice . . . The things he says are humane and intelligent and make sense.'

Ivan's frequent admission to hospital deepened his parents' experience of the National Health Service; in one six-month period he was in for sixteen overnight stays. Cameron told correspondents that turning up for work at the House of Commons after spending a night in hospital with his son put politics into perspective. When interviewed by the *Guardian* at the Conservatives' 2004 party conference, the paper's columnist Jackie Ashley concluded that Cameron had probably spent 'more time in NHS hospitals than anyone else in politics' and she made much of the fact that he 'raves about the quality of care'.

The more journalists began to appreciate the full extent of his involvement in caring for Ivan, the greater seemed to be the attention which Cameron commanded when he pledged to put the family at the heart of Conservative policies. In a speech to Policy Exchange, a think tank favoured by the Notting Hill set, he proposed that tax breaks and benefits should be used to support marriage. Most newspapers interpreted Cameron's personal manifesto as an uncompromising attempt to champion Tory modernisation and by mid-August he was able to demonstrate that his support was holding firm at Westminster. A survey of Conservative MPs conducted by the *Daily Telegraph* showed that while David Davis was still well in front with sixty-two confirmed backers, Cameron had collected twenty-three declarations of support, one more than Kenneth Clarke, which the paper said showed after three months of 'thinly veiled campaigning' there was still all to play for.

Perhaps of even greater encouragement was the evidence that Alice Thomson was no longer a lone voice among the commentariat. Political pundits who had previously failed to express an opinion, or who had been dismissive of Cameron's chances, were beginning to warm to his campaign. By the end of August the *Independent*'s long-established columnist Bruce Anderson confirmed that he had been won over by the Notting Hill Tories. Initially Anderson considered Cameron no more than a 'possible' candidate; in mid-August his weekly column favoured Sir Malcolm Rifkind due to his 'distinguished record of high office'. But a week later Anderson acknowledged that Cameron was 'a principal contender' and that his campaign team had been right to avoid 'dramatic gestures' when the Davis camp claimed the leadership was already in the bag. 'Cameron was unmoved, insisting that the man who was leading the marathon after the first quarter of a mile rarely won the race.' Anderson endorsed Cameron the following week, declaring that, as Margaret

Thatcher would have said, 'there is no alternative'. Cameron was the only candidate who could restore two words which had vanished from the Tory vocabulary: 'hope and future'.

Anderson's endorsement was a much-needed fillip for Cameron's campaign team because late August delivered an unexpected twist in the contest. 'Enter the Big Beast' was the *Daily Mail*'s front-page headline over an exclusive interview in which Kenneth Clarke declared that he was convinced he could beat both the front runner and the young pretender and be a 'better leader' than both of them. At sixty-five, the former Chancellor was making his third bid for the party leadership. He had lost out in previous contests to William Hague and Iain Duncan Smith. Clarke believed he had a 'much better footing' to lead the party because he had opposed from the outset the Iraq War, which both Davis and Cameron had backed, and he relished the chance of taking on Gordon Brown's economic record, which he would regard as a 'home fixture'. *Daily Mail* readers were told it was up to Clarke to convince them that he had the 'hunger, energy and ideas' to deserve the leadership. The worry about choosing Davis was that he would 'engender further hatred and factionalism in this already riven party'. Cameron had produced some 'polished if tantalisingly insubstantial speeches on big policy issues' but it was hard to shake off the feeling that at thirty-eight he was too young and inexperienced and 'too obsessed with aping Tony Blair rather than furthering conservative principles'. By showing his hand almost a month before the party's constitutional college had decided the form of the leadership election, whereupon nominations would be invited, Clarke had upstaged his rivals and the *Daily Mail*'s political editor, Benedict Brogan, proved correct in his prediction that the former Chancellor's entry into the race would 'electrify a moribund contest that has so far failed to catch the public imagination'.

Cameron had been put on the spot and next day he interrupted his family holiday in Devon to insist he was best placed to help the Conservatives reconnect with younger voters, a step which he believed was 'a precondition for our future electoral success'. In a speech at a local party function, Cameron had no need to mention the disparity in their ages, because it was reflected in much of the press reaction. There were several pointed quotes from Cameron's supporters suggesting that Clarke was too old to lead the party as he would be seventy by the next election. Nevertheless Clarke had succeeded against the odds in mounting by far the strongest challenge to Davis and to the evident disappointment of the Notting Hill set, Cameron was again being dismissed in much of the resulting media commentary as an also-ran, alongside Liam Fox, Sir Malcolm Rifkind and David Willetts.

Such was the initial momentum behind Clarke's advance that Cameron came under intense pressure to stand aside so as not to split the moderate vote. When endorsing Clarke as 'incomparably the most popular and experienced' candidate, the former Conservative deputy Prime Minister Lord Heseltine raised the possibility of a 'dream ticket'. He suggested that an 'obviously young' Cameron might welcome a period 'very close to the top' and gain the experience of working with 'a professional bruiser, which Ken is'. Clarke himself dismissed the idea as a fanciful notion and he used his *Daily Mail* interview to renew his appeal to Cameron's supporters by reassuring Eurosceptics in the party that they could rely on his volte-face on Europe. The previous week Clarke had renounced his passionate support for British membership of the euro. The launch of the single currency had been a 'technical success' but he said it had failed to increase efficiency or stimulate policy reforms. Now he was ready to go further: if he led a Conservative government he would not seek to take Britain into the euro and he was almost certain such a step would not happen during his political career. Cameron responded by using a column in the *Daily Telegraph* to take a swipe at Clarke's pro-European sympathies and to renew his pitch to the right of the party. He urged Conservatives to do more to challenge the culture of the European Union by fighting to end its 'damaging social role' and to press for the return of employment and social regulation to UK control.

However hard Cameron tried to retaliate, he could not dent the perception that the contest had become a two-horse race between

Davis and Clarke, a scenario which was given further weight by the constitutional college's ruling that the membership rather than the parliamentary party would make the final decision. A ballot restricted to MPs would have put Clarke at a disadvantage but there were indications that his popularity in the party at large had increased since he began to distance himself from some of his earlier pro-European views. 'Clarke boost as grassroots Tories keep vote' was the *Daily Telegraph*'s take on the story. A YouGov poll identified Clarke as the favourite: 33 per cent of the party faithful regarded him as the best person to succeed Howard compared with 27 per cent for Davis. Bill Deedes, the paper's celebrated columnist, gave Clarke his endorsement, arguing that age was immaterial and that the former Chancellor had the experience to be a strong leader of the opposition. Chris Patten suggested in the *Guardian* that Clarke would be the leader most able to drag the party back to 'a more sensible and comprehensible European posture'.

As underdog, Cameron had no alternative but to hold tight: if he could reach the last two, the longer the contest lasted, the greater his chances of promoting his agenda for change and of persuading the party to jump a generation. He did attract a few more endorsements but once most pundits began to assume it was becoming a straight fight between Davis and Clarke, Cameron's press coverage remained dire by comparison, even in newspapers sympathetic to the Conservative cause. Favourable mentions for his brand of 'compassionate Conservatism' were few and far between and some of his initiatives were being greeted with outright derision. 'Heaven help us all' was the concluding line of a *Daily Mail* editorial ridiculing his suggestion that governments worldwide should 'keep an open mind' about legalising drugs in order to tackle the global crisis in narcotics. 'Wannabe Tory leader who wants to go soft on drugs' was the inevitable headline, followed a few days later by a similar drubbing in the *Daily Express*, which accused a 'grasping' Cameron of resorting to ageism in his bid to defeat Clarke. In reinforcing his argument that younger generations cared just as much about quality-of-life concerns as economic stability and prosperity, Cameron had assured his audience in

Devon that he was convinced this was 'how young people feel because this is how I feel'. Patrick O'Flynn, *Daily Express* political editor, saw an open goal: 'young Master Cameron' could afford to take economic stability and prosperity for granted because his was guaranteed by dint of enormous inherited wealth. 'But the notion that a Notting Hill silver spoon merchant is in touch with ordinary young people saddled with huge student debts and struggling to get a foot on the property ladder is laughable.'

To have spent five months promoting himself as a future leader and to find that jibes about being a toff were still surfacing in the Tory press was hardly the encouragement which Cameron needed as he prepared for the official launch of his leadership bid. Although Clarke had pre-empted the process, Cameron and Davis had both held back, waiting for the constitutional college to give its verdict on the conduct of the election. Opening up the vote to the constituencies gave Cameron another two months to promote his 'change to win' manifesto but bearing in mind the party's ageing membership, he realised his inexperience might count against him. The challenge to his campaign team was to devise a strategy to persuade the rank and file to opt for his vision of the future rather than rely on established heavyweights. If Cameron was to reinforce the message that it was a mistake to look to senior figures from the past, he had to find positive ways to accentuate the age difference between himself and his rivals and demonstrate that he could rally the younger and newer party members.

In the event there could hardly have been a greater contrast between the two leadership launches: Davis staged a worthy, no-frills affair but Cameron broke free from the usual, staid political backdrop. Journalists were greeted with funky music and a video; the room had been decorated with trendy drapes in white and pale blue; strawberry smoothies and chocolate brownies were on offer; and Osborne was on hand to introduce 'Dave'. Cameron spoke without notes for twenty minutes promising that only he could 'drag the party' into the modern day. He answered head on the charge that he was too young and inexperienced: 'If you have got the right ideas in your head and the right passion in your heart, and if you know what this party needs to do to change, then you should go for it.' An hour earlier Davis had been decidedly low key, careful not to jeopardise his commanding lead in the parliamentary party. He too called for radical modernisation, urging the Conservatives to offer 'real change, not just a change of management'.

After endless skirmishing the two Davids had finally squared up to each other, reinvigorating the contest. Among political correspondents the general consensus was that Davis remained the clear front runner with the support of fifty-five MPs, well ahead of the sixteen declarations for Cameron. While the figures looked bleak there were some encouraging signs: Cameron had impressed the sketch writers for having spoken 'impressively without notes', with his 'polished' launch and with his 'slick presentation'. His theme, that the Tory Party had to 'think, look, feel and sound like a completely different organisation', had obviously struck a chord. He promised to get more women into Parliament and encourage candidates from the ethnic minorities. Several columnists highlighted the generational and cultural gap between the Davis and Cameron camps, the very point which the Notting Hill media strategists had been trying to make and which to their relief was being reinforced in press commentary: 'There were few women [at the Davis launch]. One man wore a turban. The rest were white blokes in dark suits' (Quentin Letts, *Daily Mail*); 'There were lots of beautiful Sloaney gals at Cameron's do, yummy mummies with babies in designer gear . . . The Davis launch was . . . attended by a rather less attractive bunch of men in pin-stripe suits' (*Sun*); 'Davis's huge gang of obscure MPs turned out to support him' (Andrew Gimson, *Daily Telegraph*).

Securing at least a modicum of respect from leading commentators is essential when fighting a potentially divisive event like a leadership election. Much of the news coverage tends to revolve around the personality of the candidates rather than their policies. Rival campaign teams search out favourable reportage and are constantly on the lookout for sympathetic columnists. If a journalist's support can be relied upon, his or her name will be passed on to television and radio producers who might want to arrange discussion programmes and who will be under pressure to offer viewers and listeners a balanced debate. Cameron's campaign had taken time to gain momentum and the more seriously he was being taken by the pundits, the greater the chance of him influencing the direction of mainstream news coverage. A run off between Davis and Clarke was still judged to be the most likely scenario, a perception which the *Independent*'s Bruce Anderson did his best to dispel in his account of the launch. Having become an unexpected Cameron convert the previous month, Anderson acknowledged that initially many in the party thought a bid for the leadership was premature at the age of thirty-eight. But those doubts had been silenced by 'force of personality'; Cameron was 'a real-world Tory' determined to 'force his party to make the changes necessary to achieve power'. Like other commentators, Anderson had been struck by Cameron's ability to speak without notes and deliver a 'formidable speech'.

From his earliest days at Conservative Central Office Cameron had enjoyed presenting and developing a political argument, a talent which served him well when briefing John Major during the 1992 general election campaign and later during his two years as a special adviser to Norman Lamont and Michael Howard. The private office of a world-weary minister can be an unforgiving arena for an eager young researcher but Cameron's perseverance paid off and his mastery of the techniques for talking through a policy paper marked him out when he left Westminster and became head of corporate affairs at Carlton Communications in September 1994. Michael Green, the group chairman, was engaged in a series of mergers and acquisitions requiring a constant round of strategy presentations in the UK, Europe and the USA. 'Sometimes we'd get absolutely exhausted, the finance director and me, and we'd say: "David, for Christ's sake can you do this one?" And he did. And he did it better than us sometimes.'

Cameron's ability to take command of a brief and then speak off the cuff with confidence in front of an audience, while keeping to a carefully constructed line of argument, gave him a distinct edge once he tried to get selected as a parliamentary candidate. His first unsuccessful attempt, within a few months of joining Carlton, was at Ashford in Kent, where he attended a drinks party given by the local Conservative association. He was selected for Stafford but failed to win the seat in the 1997 general election, such was the extent of the Labour landslide. This was followed by two further unsuccessful attempts at selection: first for Kensington & Chelsea and then, six months later, for Wealden. His selection meeting for the Witney constituency, where he was elected MP in 2001, was a memorable event for Lord Chadlington, president of the West Oxfordshire constituency association. 'Cameron was the only candidate out of twenty who delivered his speech off by heart standing in front of the lectern,' he said. Having observed him subsequently over the years, Chadlington found that Cameron remained 'very self-analytical' about his presentation, always anxious to learn from his mistakes.

Given the praise Cameron attracted from hard-bitten sketch writers for the flair he had shown when speaking without notes at the launch of his bid for the leadership, his aides knew that if he could deliver a similar tour de force at the annual conference in Blackpool the following week, it would give his campaign the boost it so desperately needed. Cameron was one of five declared candidates, who would each get the chance to speak. Conservative MPs remained a prime target because they would be balloting first at Westminster but the last-minute decision to widen the franchise for the final ballot meant the party at large had assumed a critical role and the Winter Gardens were about to become the setting for a glorified talent contest.

The party representatives relished their sense of empowerment, eager to see how the contestants performed on the conference catwalk. Two opinion polls published on the first morning underlined the range of opinion and the significance of their reaction. A panel of floating voters canvassed for an ICM poll in the *Guardian* suggested that the candidate best placed to take on a Labour government led by Gordon Brown was Cameron. Among potential Conservative voters, 50 per cent supported him, well ahead of both Davis (43 per cent) and Clarke (41 per cent). But when party members were asked for a *Daily Telegraph*/YouGov poll who they thought should succeed Michael Howard, there was a dead heat between Davis and Clarke, who each secured 30 per cent. Cameron was way behind on 16 per cent, followed by Liam Fox (13 per cent) and Sir Malcolm Rifkind (4 per cent).

Spreading the five speeches over the first three days of the conference heightened the tension between the rival camps. Journalists revelled in the opportunity to treat the conference as a prolonged beauty parade. Matthew Parris entered into the spirit of the occasion by suggesting in *The Times* that Cameron's X-factor was an appealing, 'indefinable quality' which meant voters would like the 'look and sound of him'. The headline writers for the tabloids had even greater fun with the warm-up acts. In justifying his claim to be the only true moderniser in the contest, Cameron implied that Davis was a fake: 'I would say buy Coca-Cola. If you like Coke, get the real thing.' Davis was swift to retaliate: 'I'm Mr Heineken. I want a Tory Party that reaches the parts of Britain it never reached before.'

Such are the pressures imposed by live television coverage that keynote speeches from a conference platform have to be well rehearsed. In recent years they have almost always been presented with the help of a teleprompter so as to limit the chance of stumbles or mistakes. To deliver a speech of up to twenty minutes or more without either a written text or any other form of back-up is a high-wire act which most party managers would consider far too risky for such an important debut. In Cameron's case any slip-up could prove fatal to his leadership bid: if he lost his thread or his voice dried up, he knew he would get slaughtered by the media and screw up his one and only chance to impress the wider membership.

Rifkind opened the proceedings and effectively stole Cameron's thunder; he abandoned the lectern and spoke without notes or teleprompter when presenting his appeal for a revival of Conservatism that was 'generous, sensible and moderate rather than ideological'. But the press pack was in an unforgiving mood: *The Times* claimed he slipped up twice in his delivery, 'losing his thread and stammering for a moment'. Next day there was no going back for Cameron. Having spoken from memory at his launch he could hardly fall back on a text, especially as he had been upstaged by Rifkind. In contrast to the former Foreign Secretary, who was an experienced House of Commons debater, Cameron was a novice, so untested as a public speaker that he had never led for the party in a big debate in Parliament or even spoken before at the annual conference. Press commentary that morning fuelled the unease of his campaign team: even the *Daily Telegraph*'s Alice Thomson, the first columnist to fly the Notting Hill flag, acknowledged that there was 'only one obvious contender for the crown' – Davis. Cameron was mocked or written off by other pundits: 'He'd be toast faced with either Blair or Brown' (Polly Toynbee, *Guardian*); 'When he talked about the poor his eyebrows created the shallow V of toff earnestness, often seen when Royalty visited bombed-out Cockneys during the war' (David Aaronovitch, *The Times*). Aides waiting anxiously for him to speak, desperate to counter the negative coverage, handed out photocopies of the ICM poll suggesting Cameron was the most likely to persuade wavering voters.

Undaunted by the prospect of a make-or-break appearance, he strolled on to the platform and launched into what the media had been briefed would be another impromptu speech. When practising to an empty hall the previous evening, Cameron had been overheard promising that he could build and lead 'a new generation' of Conservatives. His freestyle delivery reinforced his optimistic pitch and he told delegates they should 'feel good about being a Conservative again'. After three consecutive election defeats he was convinced that what Brown feared most was a Conservative Party which had the courage to change, a stance which required changing their 'culture and identity and making it right for today'. He wanted a Britain that was self-confident, outward-looking and engaged both ethically and enthusiastically with the wider world.

Cameron paced around the stage, varying his pitch. During an emotional passage which drew on his experience caring for Ivan, he promised to assist the parents of disabled children, especially when they faced heartbreak over the closure of special schools. A government he led would improve childcare and support marriage through the tax system. His finale built on the renewal he had promised and the prospect of a return to power: 'Let's dream a new generation of Conservative dreams.' Cameron's ambition and enthusiasm were infectious; if he could not offer experience, he could offer hope and he succeeded in capturing the mood of the conference. Samantha, expecting their third child and paying her first visit to an annual conference, joined him on the platform for a three-minute standing ovation which he milked for all it was worth; at one point he even patted the bump on his wife's tummy. Cameron's tactic of presenting himself as a fresh face for the future with an unashamedly modernising message had paid off but the young pretender was still at the mercy of events; Clarke was next to speak.

For a self-proclaimed 'big beast' there was nothing for it but to talk up his own achievements when the Conservatives were last in power. Clarke had not addressed the annual conference since 1996, when he was Chancellor of the Exchequer in John Major's government, and the genuine warmth with which he was welcomed was a tribute to his popularity and the party's respect for his record of economic competence. He took delight in reminding his audience that he cut 2p off the basic rate of income tax, the kind of reduction he would aim for again once he became Prime Minister. If the Conservatives were to have any chance of winning the next election, they had to choose 'an even bigger beast' than either Tony Blair or Gordon Brown. Clarke won a two-minute standing ovation, which was only brought to a halt when he walked off the platform.

Next day's newspapers were eagerly awaited: would there be any sign of them moving in Cameron's favour? His aides had been working feverishly behind the scenes, trying to convince journalists that the media's focus on the rivalry between Clarke and Davis was misplaced; the party at large was ready to jump a generation. Despite the best efforts of the Notting Hill set, the threat to Davis posed by the enthusiastic reception for Clarke's speech dominated much of the conference coverage in *The Times*, the *Independent* and the *Guardian*; their reports of Cameron's debut were inside the paper, well down the page. The *Sun*, however, was an exception. Instead of concentrating on the fortunes of the 'big beasts', it had detected a change of direction within the party. 'Cam On You Blues' was the bold headline over a double-page spread which declared that 'young gun Cameron' had become the 'darling of the Tory beauty contest'. Trevor Kavanagh, the paper's political editor, praised Cameron's 'prodigious performance', a fifteen-minute address delivered off by heart and without a single mistake. The *Sun*'s leader comment verged on the ecstatic: a 'rare mood of optimism' swept the conference once Cameron had brought the Tories to their feet by offering an 'inspirational, uplifting' vision of the future. An equally enthusiastic leader in the *Daily Telegraph* concluded that Cameron had proved he was 'more than a smooth operator'. He had shown sureness and confidence that was greatly to his credit when he spoke without notes to 'the largest and certainly the most important audience of his life'.

Impressing the country's largest-selling tabloid and the Conservatives' house journal was no mean achievement; their opinions mattered and could not be ignored by commentators and broadcasters. Cameron's daring presentation was cited in justification for their acclaim. Other papers described his off-the-cuff speech as engaging and impressive but the heads of their correspondents had not been turned to anything like the same degree, a failing which the Cameron camp would seek to rectify. If his barnstorming debut had won over the *Sun*, and if Kavanagh thought political speeches would 'never be the same' again after such an 'audacious effort', the Notting Hill spinners had more than enough favourable material to work with. Identifying and then backing potential winners is regarded by the *Sun* as its forte; this was an invaluable endorsement so early in Cameron's career and another illustration of the promiscuous exercise of political patronage which has helped to underpin the success of the Murdoch press. For the first time there was a chance to build some real momentum behind Cameron's campaign and influence the direction of the news agenda. All too often it is the constant retelling of political events that helps to get them remembered as mould-breaking moments. Cameron's Blackpool speech certainly had lift-off; it could be presented, and would come to be regarded, as an event that changed the political weather and transformed his chances of becoming party leader.

Two well-acclaimed speeches had opened up the contest once again. Davis, as front runner, was in the unenviable position of having to embark on his presentation against a backdrop that was far less encouraging than at the start of the week, when most commentators had predicted that the blessing of the conference was his for the taking. Not only did he face a twin assault from Cameron and Clarke but some well-meaning supporters had failed to foresee a looming public relations car crash. Ill-thought-through photo-opportunities are not to be recommended in the goldfish-bowl atmosphere of the annual conference. When several well-proportioned women were seen on parade in the Winter Gardens wearing 'It's DD for me' T-shirts and two posed with him for press photographs, the crass sexist overtones did not go unnoticed and the subsequent embarrassment in the Davis camp reflected the challenge his aides faced in trying to appeal to the young, modernising wing of the party.

Nonetheless, bolstered by the declared backing of sixty-six MPs, Davis presented himself as the only candidate who could unite all sections of the party and get the Conservatives to 'walk tall again'. Changes were needed but he rebuked the activists – and by implication Cameron and his supporters – for effectively paralysing the party with their prolonged debate on modernisation. 'We don't need a collective nervous breakdown. So let's stop apologising and get on with the job.' Tough measures on law and order constituted the main thrust of his policy platform. A future Conservative government would recruit more police, build more prisons, deport terror suspects and shake up Labour's 'utterly ridiculous' laws on 24-hour drinking. Media expectations had been dimmed in advance because journalists were told that Davis was not a good set-piece speaker but that was hardly sufficient warning for the lukewarm response and somewhat perfunctory standing ovation he received. His lacklustre performance drew immediate comparison with the final presentation and the assured delivery of Liam Fox, who succeeded in outflanking the front runner from the right. Like the shadow Home Secretary, Fox mocked the modernisers for not being proud of the way the last Conservative government had changed Britain: 'You don't set an agenda for the future by trashing the past.' Fox reinforced his Eurosceptic credentials by promising that he would seek to lead a Europe that was decentralised, outward-looking and competitive. As a first step he would end the Conservatives' relationship with the pro-integration European People's Party (EPP) in the European Parliament. If they were to be true to their belief that they would never accept that 'Britain's destiny lies in a United States of Europe', then the party could not be seen to be 'saying one thing at home and another in Brussels'. Fox had broken new ground by proposing this withdrawal, a pledge which highlighted the Eurosceptics' distrust of the pro-Europeans among their group of MEPs and an initiative which could not be ignored by a future leader.

At last broadcasters, columnists and sketch writers had an opportunity to assess all five contenders and the news media's consensus was that after a mediocre performance, support for Davis was ebbing away fast. His supporters did little to hide their dismay at his failure to seize the moment and their pained reaction fed the story line that there was all to play for. Cameron's speech the previous day continued to attract positive comments and there were some signs that the narrative started by the *Sun* and the *Daily Telegraph* was beginning to take hold. The *Independent* considered that his 'powerful performance turned him into a serious contender'; the *Guardian* quoted party representatives who thought Cameron had been the most inspiring; and the *Daily Mail* said the speeches of Clarke and Cameron were 'magical moments' when the party found a new sense of purpose. But with journalists still so uncertain about the final outcome, Cameron's aides were desperate to find a way to capitalise on the success of his conference debut.

Political correspondents do tend to hunt as a pack when working to deadline at pressurised events and they will follow each other once a clear story line has emerged. Help was at hand in the farewell address of the outgoing leader, Michael Howard, who all but declared his personal preference when he urged the party to understand young people's aspirations and start to demonstrate that it was ready to talk about the 'world as it is, not the world as it was'. Howard delivered a blunt message to his largely elderly audience whose average age was probably sixty to sixty-five. Party representatives had an obligation to look to the future, as happened in the 1979 general election, when Margaret Thatcher had succeeded in appealing to younger people. Her supporters wanted 'more opportunity and more power to better themselves and their families'. In what Howard hoped would be a repeat of the politics of the 1980s, he wanted to see a Tory leader able to relate to young people who had been shaped by 'the internet and the iPod, by cheap flights and mobile phones' and who had been fired up by impatience for action on climate change and desperate poverty in Africa.

Howard's plea that the party should skip a generation when choosing his successor became the tipping point which the Notting Hill Tories had worked so feverishly to engineer. A bandwagon was gathering pace and aides could finally point to a definite shift in opinion. Cameron overtook Davis as the bookies' favourite after William Hill slashed his odds from a 10-1 long shot at the start of the conference to 11-10 favourite at the end of it. Betting on politics might be regarded as a fringe activity but bookmakers eager for publicity are only too well aware that the latest odds are often seized upon by headline writers desperate to liven up their take on a long-running event such as a leadership election. Next morning the *Sun*'s top line was that the contest had already attracted bets worth £1 million, most of which were on Cameron. Political journalists were unanimous in interpreting Howard's farewell as a carefully coded recommendation in favour of his young protégé. Sketch writers and columnists acknowledged that a herd mentality was beginning to click in: 'People are scrambling to get on board the SS *Cameron* before it's too late' (Simon Hoggart, *Guardian*); 'Newspapers rush to endorse his candidacy' (Steve Richards, *Independent*).

Where Cameron and his aides had a distinct advantage over Davis, Clarke, Fox and Rifkind was that because of their age and outlook they had the greatest affinity with the journalists they were seeking to influence. Diarists, fashion writers and photographers regarded Samantha Cameron as a far more newsworthy proposition than the other wives and partners. She had carved out a career as a window dresser and designer and within months of reworking the interior of the Bond Street stationery and leather goods retailer Smythson she was appointed the company's creative director. The 'sleek black dress and fishnets' which she wore to her husband's launch won praise from the *Sun*; when David and Samantha strolled along Blackpool's North Pier, the caption to the photograph in *The Times* complimented her on the 'understated elegance of the Smythson handbag, demure skirt and perfect white T-shirt'; and the *Daily Telegraph* judged 'Sam, 34, who has a tattoo (of a little green dolphin) on her ankle' to be the 'most modern of the Tory wives'. Cameron knew from his days in public relations that flattering coverage on the inside pages was a vital component to a long-running media campaign. Readers, viewers and listeners who might be turned off by political news do often engage at a more personal level and although the impact of the softer side of journalism might seem marginal it requires careful planning, cannot be taken for granted and does have a cumulative effect.

Once the conference finished Cameron's aides had to get grips with their next challenge, working out how best to influence coverage in the weekend press. Sunday newspapers play a pivotal role during the party conference season; they not only look ahead but also give their all-important opinion on the conference that has just taken place. Offering background briefings to correspondents and columnists cannot be left to chance. Their assessment tends be more reflective than that of their colleagues in the daily press and because there is less hard news around, agenda-setting stories and comment columns are more likely to influence broadcasters and feed through to weekend television and radio coverage.

Howard's helping hand supplied the traction which the Cameron campaign sorely lacked and to the great relief of his team most of the Sunday newspapers followed suit, giving his debut their seal of approval. 'The force is with him' was the headline over a leading article in the *Sunday Times* which said he had a 'star quality' rare among politicians and deserved the 'ballistic blast-off' which the conference bestowed after his 'barnstorming performance'. Other editorials were just as flattering: the *Observer* said his 'daring speech made without notes' made him look the candidate of the future and the *Sunday Telegraph* considered he was the 'conference darling' for good reason because he 'grasped the changed mood of the activists and took the plunge, responding to their appetite for a fresh start with wit and confidence'. In sharp contrast to rave reviews for Cameron, the verdict on Davis was dire and the post-conference reportage was peppered with references to his 'stale', 'uninspiring', 'abysmal' speech. Sunday papers offer not only insight but also pride themselves on being able to generate fresh impetus to a developing story and Cameron was the beneficiary of their endeavour. A *Sunday Times* YouGov poll of grassroots support in the constituencies suggested that nearly half of the party's membership had changed sides as the conference progressed. Cameron had leapt into first place, increasing his tally from 16 per cent the previous week to a commanding 39 per cent share, well ahead of Clarke (26 per cent), Davis (14 per cent), Fox (13 per cent) and Rifkind (1 per cent). The timing of the survey, and its publication ten days before the first ballot by the parliamentary party, presented Conservative MPs with a stark choice: if they were going to declare for Cameron, there could be no better moment. A *Sunday Telegraph* exclusive claimed that Cameron had begun planning what he would do in his 'first 100 days' as party leader, another hint to potential backers that they had no time to lose.

By exploiting every opportunity to follow through Cameron's daring debut, the Notting Hill Tories had secured pole position in the struggle to command the news agenda during the two months that would have to elapse before the final vote. It had taken five days to secure the all-embracing recognition which his campaign team thought he deserved and as far as the news media was concerned there was now an established 'fact' to work on: Cameron's intrepid conference speech was the defining event, the moment that he leapt ahead of the party's big hitters and assumed the mantle of leader in waiting. Another 'fact' that was rapidly being woven into the narrative was that Davis's failure to deliver an effective speech had probably put paid to what had previously looked like an unstoppable bid for the leadership. Political and media analysts lent their weight to this thesis. In his column in *PR Week*, the former Labour Party spin doctor Charlie Whelan conceded that the Tories had done a service to the art of political communications. Delivering a speech without notes or an autocue had been a 'revelation'. Cameron's leadership campaign had been 'a faultless demonstration of great PR', in the view of Julian Henry, a director of Henry's House PR consultancy. In his column in *Media Guardian*, Henry described the Blackpool speech as 'a snappy and eloquent display' which set the tone with 'a master's precision'.

Even for a consummate public relations practitioner there are nightmare scenarios which can spiral out of control and Cameron's time at Oxford University had come back to haunt him. While he was busy promoting himself around the conference fringe, journalists had identified a weak spot in his academic CV: did he ever take drugs when he was a student? Broadcasters were ready to return to the question time and again and Cameron's knack of coming up with rather trite one-liners in the hope of defusing tricky situations would be tested to the limit. His opaque, light-hearted responses were interpreted by the news media as a 'yes' but refusing to be specific only encouraged the next interviewer to try again. Each new story line provided further ammunition for the *Daily Mail*, which had returned with a vengeance to its criticism of Cameron for having expressed a liberal approach towards tackling drug abuse. At issue was his work with the Home Affairs Select Committee, which in 2002 recommended the reclassification of cannabis and ecstasy, and then his subsequent support for the Labour government's decision to downgrade cannabis from a class B to a class C drug. Almost alone in his party he had stood out against the constant demands for a 'war on drugs' and argued for crack cocaine and heroin addicts to be weaned off their habit with prescription substitutes. Having been such an outspoken campaigner, Cameron was particularly vulnerable should the press start a witch hunt about his past and, after his own walk-on parts in the firestorms which engulfed Norman Lamont's final year as Chancellor of the Exchequer, the would-be party leader was about to experience for himself the debilitating consequences of becoming a high-profile victim in a media feeding frenzy.

Cameron had his back to the wall from the moment he was challenged at a fringe event by the *Observer*'s columnist Andrew Rawnsley. 'I'm human enough to have done all these things, but I'm too much of a politician to tell you what they were.' His pre-prepared line of defence was hardly likely to suffice and when pressed again he acknowledged he did have 'a normal university experience, let's put it that way', a reply interpreted by Rawnsley as an 'effective admission'. Aides briefed political journalists that Cameron was determined not to give a categorical answer either way but next day Daisy McAndrew of *ITV News* reminded him that if he was 'really so normal' he must have tried drugs at university, 'a spliff, if not something stronger'. He responded by giving the same easy-going but vague non-denial: 'I'm human enough to have done lots of things I shouldn't have done. But even after four years in Parliament, I'm too much of a politician to tell you what they all are.' When Andrew Marr tried again on *Sunday AM*, Cameron was ready to turn the tables on his inquisitors: 'Are we going to have some sort of McCarthyite hearings into every Member of Parliament?' His tactic was to try to draw a clear line between the indiscretions of his youth and public life: 'I did lots of things before I came into politics which I shouldn't have done. We all did.'

Being needled by interviewers about his time at Oxford and hailed as 'Cannabis Cameron' by several Labour MPs at the House of Commons was what he might have expected but the story line became more threatening when the focus switched to his possible use of class A drugs.

Firm denials had been obtained by the *Mail on Sunday* from the four other leadership contenders and some supporters of David Davis could not resist the opportunity to turn up the heat. Their chance came at a hustings organised by the right-wing 92 Group. Kenneth Clarke was the first candidate to speak and when asked by Mark Pritchard, MP for the Wrekin, whether he had ever used class A drugs, the cigar-smoking former Chancellor replied that if anybody was interested he had never 'taken cocaine'. But Clarke did jump to Cameron's rescue: he did not think questions about their private lives should be put to the candidates because they reduced the leadership election to a 'tabloid sideshow'. Pritchard refrained from posing the same question to the other contestants.

Cameron's patient, good-humoured responses flew in the face of the clamour in the news media for some straight talking but his refusal to confirm or deny what might or might not have happened when he was younger was a tactic which was beginning to work to his advantage. When he and Davis appeared together on *Question Time* he again fended off repeated calls to come clean by insisting they were both 'allowed to have had a private life before politics in which we make mistakes . . . We are all human and we err and stray.' The audience clapped and cheered, a response which mirrored the applause on the Blackpool fringe when he rebuffed the drugs question for a third time. Despite a show of public sympathy and some supportive comment columns and editorials in newspapers such as the *Daily Telegraph*, the *Guardian* and the *Independent*, there was no let-up on the part of the *Daily Mail*, which published a full-page editorial under the headline 'Drugs, David Cameron and a question that must be answered'. It claimed there were 'whispers abounding' that some in Cameron's inner circle were 'habitual drug users' and demanded that he be 'open and frank', a phrase which Davis repeated in a television interview. When asked on the Channel 4 programme *Morgan and Platell* whether someone who had taken class A drugs could lead the party, the shadow Home Secretary piled on the pressure: 'It's a breach of the law, so if it was recent, the answer would be no.'

Having had all week to trawl over the story Cameron's aides feared the worst as they waited to discover whether there would be fresh revelations in the Sunday newspapers. If there were going to be damaging personal disclosures the most dangerous moment was the weekend before the first ballot. There was heightened uncertainty when the London *Evening Standard* revealed that a close family member had been addicted to heroin. Cameron's response was that he was 'incredibly proud' of the way his relative had overcome a drugs problem after going through rehabilitation. In the event the newspapers contained no new horror stories but instead offered a wide range of advice, much of it supportive. Michael Portillo told the *Observer* he thought Cameron was right not to answer the question because once there was a fact on the record, the newspapers knew they could 'print anything – true or false'. In his column in the *News of the World*, William Hague suggested there would be gaps in the higher ranks of most professions if everyone who had ever taken drugs was denied a top post. Despite having commissioned an opinion poll which showed that 61 per cent of Conservative supporters did not think a leadership candidate who had tried hard drugs should be forced to stand down, the *Mail on Sunday*'s headline writers could not shake off their addiction to class A substances: 'Tories for Cameron – even if he has taken cocaine'. An editorial renewed the paper's demand for full disclosure: if Cameron remained silent, the party would have to hope that 'no skeletons come clattering out of the cupboard in mid-general election'.

His campaign team's confidence that he would emerge unscathed from the drugs furore was vindicated when Cameron finished a close second to Davis in the first round of voting. Sir Malcolm Rifkind had withdrawn in the hope of boosting Clarke's chances but the former Chancellor secured only thirty-eight votes and was eliminated. Davis (62), Cameron (56) and Fox (42) went through to another ballot the following day. With the tide of opinion at Westminster beginning to flow firmly in his direction Cameron topped the second ballot, ensuring his place in the wider constituency contest. Davis had lost support among MPs, finishing up with fifty-seven votes, but Cameron had motored ahead, polling ninety votes. Liam Fox (51 votes) was eliminated, leaving Cameron and Davis to fight it out head to head in a six-week campaign which would culminate in a postal ballot of party members. There had been some suggestion Cameron might be 'crowned' leader if Davis did badly and could be persuaded to stand aside, but such talk was scuppered by Cameron's failure to secure more than half the 198 votes in the parliamentary party. Nonetheless, backed up by the findings of a YouGov poll which showed he remained the runaway choice in the constituencies, the *Daily Telegraph* nailed its colours to the mast in a bold front-page headline: 'Cameron's bandwagon rolls on into the country'.

Except for a potentially dangerous ten-day hiatus generated by persistent questioning over possible drug taking, Cameron had been able to take advantage of what until then had been a somewhat leisurely five-month campaign and he had roamed freely over a diffuse agenda. But once two candidates had been selected to go before the membership, opinions began to polarise and there was a far sharper focus on policy differences. A harder edge to the contest put Cameron under the most pressure because of a clear divide between the young modernisers and the right-wing forces which had coalesced behind Davis. Thatcherites, Eurosceptics and Tory 'knights of the shires' were alarmed by Cameron's reformist programme and his talk of 'modern, compassionate Conservatism'. Lining up alongside party grandees to put the front runner under far greater scrutiny were assorted pundits in the news media and various attack dogs from the left of British politics. At their fourth attempt the Tories seemed close to electing a party leader who stood a real chance of rebranding the Conservatives and establishing the wherewithal to beat Labour. Cameron was about to be attacked from all sides and his vulnerability had been heightened by the tight schedule for the run-off. In addition to a packed agenda which included eleven regional hustings and numerous party gatherings, the two candidates were desperate to gain the maximum possible exposure on television and radio.

When attempting to hold politicians to account during an election or a leadership contest, broadcasters have a tactical advantage over their colleagues in the press. Most news and current affairs programmes are transmitted live and as Cameron had discovered when challenged about drugs, campaign minders can exercise little if any control over the questions which might be asked. The greatest risk during a newspaper interview, even when certain subjects have been ruled off limits in advance, is that an interviewee might get lulled or even tricked into being indiscreet or going off message. Once a politician appears in front of a camera or is live at a microphone, there is a constant danger of being ambushed. Party spin doctors know they are powerless to intervene and if backed into a corner, an interviewee can easily trip up. Cameron's slick presentation and friendly put-downs had helped him fend off awkward questions about his university life. But for the news media, the task of investigating possible drug taking remained unfinished business and the *Daily Mail* was lying in wait. Given his astute defensive footwork and the lack of fresh disclosures about his past, journalists realised that the likelihood of them advancing the story probably depended on the ingenuity and persistence of programme presenters.

Within a few hours of topping the parliamentary poll, Cameron appeared on *Channel 4 News* and inadvertently delivered the headline which the *Daily Mail* had been itching to write: 'Cocaine and me, by Cameron'. Instead of asking whether he had smoked cannabis at university, newscaster Alex Thomson turned to class A drugs, the question which had been left hanging in the air. In his first answer Cameron insisted that 'what is private in the past should remain private', but Thomson persisted and asked whether he would deny ever having 'snorted cocaine as an MP'.

CAMERON: *That's right, but please, I mean, I think we've dealt with this issue. . .*
THOMSON: *So that's a 'No'?*
CAMERON: *I've absolutely answered your question.*
THOMSON: *Say 'No'.*
CAMERON: *I've just said 'No'.*

Once the focus of the questioning began to probe his conduct during the four and a half years he had served at Westminster, there was no way out. Cameron's nerve had been tested and for the first time he had given a specific answer. His ability to ad lib while sticking to a carefully vetted line of argument had finally been found wanting and his reply would encourage other programme presenters to persevere, a slip-up which the *Daily Mail* suggested 'could revive speculation that he experimented with drugs' before he became an MP in 2001. Once rekindled there was no telling which direction the firestorm might take and the following morning, no doubt fearing a wider conflagration, Davis told *Today* that for the remainder of the contest he would not be answering 'any questions on drugs – policy or otherwise'. Nonetheless Cameron had, as journalists like to say, given the story fresh 'legs' and the hunt was on again among the tabloids to find a potential knockout blow. George Osborne was the *Mail on Sunday*'s target and it published an exclusive interview with a former 'vice girl' who alleged that Cameron's campaign manager had a 'youthful fascination with cocaine'. When her story first surfaced the previous weekend in the *News of the World* and the *Sunday Mirror*, Osborne dismissed it as a 'desperate smear' that dated back to 1993. He said the woman concerned did have a child with a friend of his who had since overcome a drug addiction but that was his only connection with her. A rather flattering in-house story was all that the *Mail on Sunday* could offer about the man himself: Caroline Graham, the paper's correspondent in Los Angeles, wrote about her first teenage crush on a 'fresh-faced, slightly chubby' David Cameron. Another non-story was offered by the *Sunday Telegraph* after its reporters tried without success to discover whether security vetting might have thrown up incriminating details about his time at university or early career. When hired as Norman Lamont's political adviser in 1992, Cameron was checked out by the Treasury to see if he suffered from any 'defects of character' which might expose him to blackmail. In a dead-bat response to a freedom of information request, the Treasury said personal information gathered during recruitment was never released. Undaunted by the lack of evidence, the paper tried to turn its story into an attack on the government. Under the headline 'Labour's "dirty tricks" over secret Cameron dossier', it claimed Treasury insiders had suggested there was 'sensitive security information' about the Tory front runner.

Press fascination with his past meant there was no escape from a continuing inquisition and when the two candidates went head to head on *Question Time* there was no point him trying to stonewall during an edgy confrontation about the reclassification of ecstasy. Cameron continued to favour downgrading: 'What people want is a realistic and sensible policy that gets to the bottom of the drugs problem.' He was equally robust during a Sky News debate and was applauded by a young studio audience when he repeatedly defied questioning by the columnist Amanda Platell, who ran William Hague's media department during the 2001 general election. Cameron's final set-to was a much-heralded but much-delayed showdown with *Newsnight*'s Jeremy Paxman. Hoping no doubt to minimise the risk of a vote-losing encounter, the interview had been postponed for as long as possible but it had given Paxman and his researchers ample time to lay a potential trap. Cameron was well and truly ambushed in the opening seconds:

> PAXMAN: *Do you know what a Pink Pussy is?*
> CAMERON: *I don't think I do.*
> PAXMAN: *Do you know what a Slippery Nipple is?*
> CAMERON: *That is a drink.*

Cameron managed to keep his cool in the few moments it took him to realise that Paxman was referring to two of the suggestive cocktails sold at city centre nightclubs run by the West End bar owners Urbium, a company of which he had been a non-executive director until his resignation the previous month. He disagreed with the suggestion that some of Urbium's venues had been linked to disorder and he maintained his support for the Labour government's decision to lengthen pub opening hours, a reform which he had argued in favour of since his spell at the Home Office as Michael Howard's political adviser. When it came to the ritual foray over drug taking, Paxman tried an all-embracing question. Was it correct that he did take drugs as a young man but had not done so since becoming an MP?

> CAMERON: *I have been very clear that I think you are entitled to a private past.*
> PAXMAN: *Is that analysis correct?*
> CAMERON: *Yes . . . yes, that is correct.*

As there appeared to be nothing new to say on the drugs front, Paxman needed to engineer an unexpected opening gambit in the hope of catching Cameron off guard and their clash over binge drinking delighted the *Sun*, which led its inside page next morning with a report on the 'Pink Pussy punch-up'. Tabloid headlines apart, the *Newsnight* interview earned its place alongside his noteless speech as another celebrated moment in the leadership campaign because Cameron managed to turn the tables and ambush Paxman. To the delight of the Tory faithful, old scores were settled and a BBC presenter put in his place. During an infamous interview in 1997 about the dismissal of a director general of the prison service, Paxman persisted in asking Howard the same question fourteen times, a duel which enthralled most *Newsnight* viewers but enraged the former Home Secretary and in the opinion of many senior Tories justified their frequent complaint that there was left-wing bias to the BBC's news reporting. Howard's protégé had prepared and memorised a pointed response should Paxman become aggressive. When he judged the moment had arrived, Cameron was ready:

> *This is the trouble with these interviews, Jeremy. You come in, sit someone down and treat them like they are some cross between a fake or a hypocrite. You give no time to anyone to answer any of your questions. It does your profession no favours at all and it's no good for political discourse.*

For good measure, Cameron interjected again after another interruption: 'Let's have a deal. Maybe I can get two sentences out, then you can interrupt.'

Media commentators applauded his feisty performance and afterwards Cameron made no secret of the fact that he had thought long and hard about how best to turn Paxman's inquisitorial style against him. Confronting television's big beasts in the final stages of a volatile finale to the leadership contest was a risk but one well worth taking, at least in the view of the London *Evening Standard*'s columnist John Lloyd, who praised Cameron's strategy because it 'lets viewers judge whether or not politicians can handle aggression'. Conservative websites reflected grass-roots satisfaction: 'DC monstered Paxo' said one appreciative text. Perhaps more importantly, by asking no more than a couple of matter-of-fact questions about possible drug taking, Paxman had effectively drawn a line under the frenzied reporting of the previous weeks. If *Newsnight*'s fearless interrogator considered there was no more mileage to be had, Cameron's aides could safely conclude that the story had run its course. He had not been caught out by the publication of incriminating evidence and had easily withstood all that the tabloid press could throw at him.

Winning sympathy and support from audiences during televised confrontations was a testament to his skill in responding in a credible way to difficult questions about his personal life. His critics tended to dismiss him as nothing more than a pale imitation of Tony Blair but few of them could deny that after a six-week grilling on drugs, the public at large seemed to think that his answers were definitely on the right side of sincerity.

Cameron's polished performances and engaging punchlines had begun to unnerve the government and ministers could see the threat that he might eventually pose to both Blair and his likely successor, Gordon Brown. Labour's media strategists considered one area of potential vulnerability was his seven-year career as corporate affairs director for Carlton Television, which could be exploited by political opponents to give weight to their charge that he was all spin and no substance, nothing more than a shallow public relations front man who lacked guiding principles and beliefs. Unless asked by journalists, Cameron rarely mentioned his own background in corporate communications but whenever the opportunity arose he was quick to explain why he believed that a deeply rooted culture of spin within the Blair administration had corrupted the process of government. Writing in the *Sunday Telegraph* about his promise to deliver a 'thoughtful, measured and moderate' regime, he berated the 'belligerent, partisan and macho style of politics' which had become the defining characteristic of the Blair era. 'You can see it in the swaggering culture of spin personified by Alastair Campbell and deployed against anyone who dares challenge New Labour's moral righteousness.'

Since his ignominious resignation midway through the 2003 Hutton inquiry into the death of the weapons inspector Dr David Kelly, Campbell had become a tireless defender of the communication techniques which he deployed on behalf of the Prime Minister during his nine years as Blair's press secretary. Ever the self-publicist Campbell rose to the bait and used his column in *The Times* to deliver a tit-for-tat demolition job. Exuding all the modesty he could muster, Campbell suggested that he rather than Blair had been Cameron's true role model:

> *Watching Cameron trying to soundbite his way through his television debate with David Davis, it was clear Cameron is not remotely in Blair's league. Far from being the new Blair, he may actually be the new Alastair Campbell. He knows how to craft a line and put it over. He has a feel for what tickles the media's fancy, what makes a story and how to get it up as a headline, what combination of action and demeanour keeps the photographers happy.*

But being a press officer was different to leading a political party and Campbell justified his conclusion that Cameron felt 'more comfortable with spin than substance' on the grounds that he had been a public relations man for a television company and 'you can't get much more spin-doctory than that'.

While Cameron did seem to have neutralised rumour-mongering about his days at university and the company he might have kept in later years, there was another skeleton in his cupboard which Campbell had tried to rattle and which some in the news media believed might be of interest to the Westminster village. However much Cameron sought to disparage Campbell's addiction to spin, his time at Carlton Television had coincided with the ascendancy of New Labour and ever-more sophisticated techniques for manipulating the news media. During his spell at Conservative Central Office and later as a ministerial aide Cameron had gained wide experience of potential pitfalls when briefing journalists. His final year as a political adviser had given him an insight into Michael Howard's dogged determination to secure favourable headlines and the Home Secretary's refusal to take prisoners if crossed by errant reporters. By the late 1990s aspiring political activists and trainee spin doctors were mesmerised both by Campbell's early success and by the awe which he inspired among journalists. He had indeed become a role model for many eager recruits in the public relations industry. Conscious no doubt of the possibility that Campbell and his ilk might succeed in prodding the memories of business and media correspondents, Cameron did his best to counteract suggestions that his PR regime at Carlton Television had been based on the teachings of the Howard–Campbell school of abrasive spin doctoring. He betrayed his anxiety when interviewed by the *Sun* for a flattering two-page exclusive under the headline 'The real David Cameron'. He conceded that journalists who dealt with him at Carlton during take-over talks might well have concluded he was 'not as nice as he looks'. So much was at stake during merger negotiations in the television industry that he had to be tough but he liked to believe that his 'fair share of media disasters' resulted either from him not knowing the answer or when he did, of not being able to give it. 'I had a reputation for being quite tight lipped. It is important not to lie to the press and sometimes I had to stonewall and be terse.'

If Cameron thought his apologetic 'prebuttal' might have helped in some way to assuage bruised egos he was sorely mistaken. Ian King, the

Sun's business editor, waited until the eve of the final ballot result before putting the boot in:

> *I was unfortunate enough to have dealings with Cameron when he was PR man for the world's worst television company. And a poisonous slippery individual he was, too. Back then, Cameron was far from the smoothie he pretends to be now. He was a smarmy bully who regularly threatened journalists who dared to write anything negative about Carlton . . . he loved humiliating people.*

Jeff Randall, editor at large of the *Daily Telegraph*, nursed an explicit grievance from his time as editor of the *Sunday Business*: he believed Cameron misled him about a potential merger involving Carlton. Randall's character reference was hardly what a leader in waiting wanted to hear: 'I wouldn't trust him with my daughter's pocket money.' Cameron's insistence in his *Sun* interview that he had not crossed the line and actually lied to reporters did not cut much ice with Randall: 'In my experience, Cameron never gave a straight answer when dissemblance was a plausible alternative, which probably makes him perfectly suitable for the role he now seeks: the next Tony Blair.'

I knew from my own experience and subsequent inquiries that one element of Cameron's defence rang true. He had some justification in arguing that he always tried to be 'polite and friendly' when briefing journalists. During the recriminations which followed Norman Lamont's sacking by John Major in the 1993 cabinet reshuffle, Cameron's mistake was that he probably tried too hard to engage with political journalists. He chose to deny speculation that Lamont was about to seek retribution against Major, which I happened to know was true. In my opinion he would have been far safer adopting the line that there was nothing he could say, and then stuck to it.

The low opinion of Cameron held by business and financial correspondents was not shared by some of the senior journalists employed in the newsrooms of the television franchises owned by the Carlton group.

Laurie Upshon, editor and later news controller of Central Television, which became a Carlton subsidiary, had dealings with Cameron both in his capacity as corporate affairs director and also as a Conservative candidate in Stafford and later Witney, two constituencies covered by Central.

> *His ambition was obvious, but he was always very affable. When we attended Conservative conferences as representatives of the Midlands franchise he didn't treat us as the country cousins, he was never condescending. I found him a smooth operator, always focused on what he did. After the birth of Ivan I got the feeling that he mellowed, he was less thrusting and more humane than previously.*

Campbell's taunt that Cameron knew what tickled the 'media's fancy' and how to keep the 'photographers happy' was a classic backhanded compliment from Blair's spinmeister. Press pictures and television footage of the Camerons en famille had become a regular feature of the extensive reportage surrounding the leadership election and a powerful political tool. He appeared with Samantha in numerous poses, relaxing at home, in the kitchen or out walking in the country, often with Ivan or Nancy, sometimes held in their arms or in push-chairs. Having adopted an open-door approach to the news media, photographers and television camera crews reciprocated and an ever-changing array of well-chosen images of a young family man presented David Davis and his supporters with a dilemma. His attitude towards the opposite sex had taken a knock since the 'It's DD for me' T-shirt episode and he faced renewed criticism for a condescending approach towards women after he lost out in what was dubbed the 'battle of Tory underpants'. Martha Kearney, presenter of *Woman's Hour,* caught the two candidates by surprise when she asked them to reveal their choice of underwear. Cameron said he preferred boxer shorts; Davis admitted he wore briefs, forgetting that Campbell's assertion that John Major tucked his shirt into his underpants resulted in the former Prime Minister being lampooned mercilessly in countless cartoons. When Kearney inquired whether they preferred blondes or brunettes, Davis blurted out 'blondes' while Cameron remained silent, another black mark given that Davis was then heard to mutter that his wife Doreen was a brunette. On being reminded that she had described her husband as 'a male chauvinist pig', Davis insisted his wife was only teasing but he incurred further feminine wrath when asked by Kearney to justify the sexist photo-shoot at Blackpool. 'These things happen, they go wrong and they go right. The idea came from a girl and some people were upset by that and I am sorry. But it was a sense-of-humour failure all round.' Davis fared no better when he and Cameron were questioned later that day at the annual conference of the Conservative Women's Organisation. Its president, Pamela Parker, was 'horrified' by the 'patronising' manner which Davis had adopted. When invited to vote on a show of hands, the result was said to have been five to one in Cameron's favour.

Although Samantha Cameron was photographed quite often at her husband's side, she steadfastly refused all interview requests and except for a few innocuous answers about herself and her children she had steered clear of the political fray. Doreen Davies was also at her husband's side in Blackpool on the day of her husband's conference speech and she too was photographed with him but otherwise she had remained at their constituency home in Haltemprice and Howden and had not been on the campaign trail. Her low profile had not gone unnoticed. Given that women accounted for over half the party's membership and that Davis seemed to have annoyed so many feminists, he had to move fast if he was to stand any chance of demonstrating that he was serious about taking positive steps towards advancing female equality. Anxious no doubt to help her husband reassure party members about the depth of his commitment to family values, Doreen Davis agreed to be interviewed by a *Daily Mail* reporter. Rebecca Hardy discovered that the shadow Home Secretary's wife was 'an extraordinarily nice woman, without a nasty bone in her body' but 'painfully shy'; did not like the media spotlight; and had never before given an interview to the press. 'Doreen is not frivolous. She is pragmatic. She married a man whose life was politics and she'll stick by him, come what may.' Their three children had left home, each having been through university; they had two grandchildren. In her husband's absence at Westminster, she ran the constituency office from their former farmhouse. It could be 'quite lonely' and when he was in London 'very often, days go by and we don't speak on the phone'. Hardy's account of the life of an MP's wife who had spent thirty years dedicated to her husband and children divided opinion among the *Daily Mail*'s columnists. Amanda Platell argued that Britain would 'fall apart if it were not for the quiet care of women like Doreen Davis'. Although she sympathised with a 'long-suffering' wife left 'sitting alone in her farmhouse in Yorkshire', Rosie Boycott considered the insight into the couple's private life told female voters in the leadership election 'more than any hustings ever could'. Boycott drew an immediate comparison with Samantha Cameron, who had worked hard to help turn round an ailing company, brought up a severely disabled son and found time to stand by her husband's side. 'She has been able to do all this only because her husband clearly treats her like an equal.'

In their own personal way, under the cruel glare of the media's spotlight, the two candidates had done what they could to reassure the party about the strength of their individual commitment to their families. An age gap of almost twenty years and differences in their lifestyles and approach to marriage had influenced the way the contest was reported. However much media intrusion into their private lives might be resented, David Cameron had shown that aspiring politicians had little alternative but to come to terms with ever-greater scrutiny and try to work out how to use it to their advantage. From the start of the campaign he had acknowledged that the public had a right to see how a potential party leader lived his life, at home as well as at Westminster. David and Doreen Davis, not having been affected perhaps to the same degree by influences such as reality television and the cult of celebrity, had different strengths and qualities to offer and, as the contest drew to a close, policies rather than personalities presented a sharper dividing line.

David Davis could be forgiven for appearing somewhat relaxed because he believed the endorsements he was attracting were far more likely to influence the Conservatives' core vote than the opinions of a few fussy feminists. Lord Tebbit pledged his support in a letter to *The Times* in which he launched a scathing attack on Cameron for having made the 'fundamental error' of trying to copy Tony Blair: 'It's no good aping New Labour and fighting on the ground which Labour voters are leaving in droves.' Against the run of findings in other opinion surveys, a Populus poll for *The Times* showed that Davis led Cameron by 50 to 37 per cent among Tory supporters, suggesting further confirmation of the popularity of his policy platform. Commitments which appeared to appeal to the rank and file included a plan for £38 billion of tax cuts, a double referendum on membership of the European Union to ensure the 'full-scale return of power from Brussels to Britain' and a promise to preserve the autonomy of local Conservative associations.

To the annoyance of the Davis camp, Cameron made a calculated pitch for the support of Eurosceptics by promising to adopt the hard-line approach first proposed by Liam Fox that the Conservatives should withdraw from the European People's Party, the main centre-right grouping in the EU. Cameron's pro-European supporters, including some leading Conservative MEPs, reacted furiously. They feared his aim of establishing a new right-wing group which was Eurosceptic, free market and pro-American would leave the Conservatives utterly marginalised in the European Parliament. Their analysis was shared by *The Times'* columnist Peter Riddell, who said Cameron's unexpected move was 'his first big mistake' as future party leader, a last-minute attempt to appease the hard-line right which threatened 'a serious split within the party and a rupture with European allies'. Whatever qualms Cameron might have held about the undertaking he had given, Fox's supporters were encouraged and the prominent Eurosceptic MP Bill Cash, together with nine of his parliamentary colleagues, wrote to the *Daily Telegraph* praising Cameron's 'sound judgement'. Their promises of support took his pledges past the half-way mark to reach 100, a key moment for the parliamentary party. As the contest drew to a close there was a further flurry of endorsements and the first opinion surveys began to indicate that party members were voting two to one in Cameron's favour. His high-profile backers constituted a roll call of the party's big names. Boris Johnson used an appearance on *Desert Island Discs* to reveal that he was preparing to give up his part-time editorship of the *Spectator* in the hope of serving in a Cameron shadow cabinet; for Fox it had been a 'close call', but he wanted the leadership to pass the 'next generation'; William Hague's endorsement prompted immediate speculation that he would return to the front bench as shadow Foreign Secretary; and Iain Duncan Smith urged the party to unite around Cameron and stop the 'poisonous' briefings which had undermined his own two-year stint as party leader.

Once the outcome seemed beyond doubt editorial opinion swung firmly behind Cameron. While much of the laudatory commentary was late in coming, the Tory-aligned press had finally been won over and the positive tone adopted in leader columns reflected the influence which the Notting Hill set had been able to exercise behind the scenes. Cameron had spent his career striving to engineer favourable publicity for political and business leaders, struggling to come to terms with the fickle nature of the British press, and he was about to be beguiled by seductive flattery of a kind he could only have dreamed of when he started work as a 22-year-old political researcher at party headquarters. Giving its verdict on a 'gladiatorial contest', the *Sun* praised the Conservatives for choosing a 'statesman-in-waiting' who looked good on television and had the 'rare gift as a Tory of making voters feel good about life'. A party which had 'seemed almost obsolescent' had rediscovered 'vigour and optimism' and the *Daily Telegraph* had no hesitation in declaring it would 'enthusiastically back' Cameron, 'a natural winner'. The *Daily Mail* agreed that a party which 'once seemed dead in the water' had been transformed. Cameron was capable of reaching people who would never usually dream of voting Conservative. 'He has star quality. In a matter of months he has shot from obscurity to become one of the most fascinating figures in politics.'

Davis conceded defeat on the eve of the result, giving the party machine a free hand to help choreograph Cameron's coronation. Genealogical research published that morning revealed that he was the most blue-blooded Tory heir apparent for four decades. Debrett's Peerage released a family tree which indicated that Cameron was related to the Queen through King William IV's illegitimate daughter. Analysis by Cracroft's Peerage showed that Samantha Cameron, the daughter of a baronet, was descended from Charles II and Nell Gwyn. Undaunted by the fuss over their aristocratic lineage, David Cameron set off by bicycle for the House of Commons from his home in Notting Hill. Wearing a red jacket, helmet and gloves he made his way through a throng of photographers and television crews; hovering above was a BBC helicopter. As the leader-to-be reached Westminster, he unstrapped his helmet for the final approach. Predictions of a two-to-one majority were confirmed at the official declaration: Cameron won by 134,446 votes to 64,398 on a 77.8 per cent turnout in a postal ballot.

After a leadership election which had lasted for 214 days the result was a foregone conclusion but the decisiveness of his victory was greeted with a new-found sense of euphoria and enthusiasm which Cameron interpreted as a mandate to change the way the Conservative Party looked, thought and behaved. He repeated a pledge given during the leadership campaign to end the 'scandalous under-representation' of women in the parliamentary party; he was fed up with the 'Punch and Judy politics of Westminster, the name calling, backbiting, point scoring, finger pointing'; and under his leadership, the party would establish what was right for the long term and not 'invent policies for newspaper headlines'. In a deliberate break with the Conservatives' Thatcherite past, Cameron distanced himself from one of the former Prime Minister's most controversial statements and he promised to develop policies for the good of the country and communities. 'There is such a thing as society, it's just not the same thing as the state.' He even made fun of his attempt to reinforce his green credentials: 'I tried to make a start this morning by biking to work. That was a carbon-neutral journey until the BBC sent a helicopter following me.'

His first parliamentary duty as newly elected leader of the opposition was to lead for the Conservatives at Prime Minister's Questions. Sketch writers were waiting with pens poised: would Cameron deliver on his promise to eschew 'Punch and Judy' politics? Help was at hand in that morning's *Guardian*, which reprinted Cameron's account for Guardian Unlimited of the day in May 2002 when, as a new MP, he put his first question to Tony Blair. His own experience as a party worker in the early 1990s, when he had to think of 'killer facts and snappy one-liners' for John Major, had convinced him that the perceived theatrical weakness of PMQs, the waving of order papers and cheering by MPs, was in fact its greatest strength. A leader of the opposition who was 'slow witted, corrupt or simply not up to the job' would not survive the adversarial combat of the House of Commons. Cameron could hardly have set the bar higher for himself. Three and a half years after writing about the day he waited with 'palms running with sweat, throat dry, chest pounding' to be called by the Speaker for his first brush with the Prime Minister, Cameron was about to square up to Blair, having been described that morning by the *Daily Telegraph* as the 'most inexperienced opposition leader for 80 years . . . an MP for less than five years who had made only a handful of frontbench speeches'.

A five-word punchline which Cameron could only have prepared earlier was all that it needed to delight Conservative MPs and rattle Blair. Their encounter opened with Cameron twisting the knife in a seemingly non-confrontational manner by offering to work with the government to get the 'good bits' of Labour's educational reforms approved by Parliament. He urged the Prime Minister to be as 'bold' as he wanted to be because that was when Blair always believed Labour were at their 'best'. When Blair tried to retaliate by asking whether the new Conservative leader still believed that schools should be free to set their own admission procedures, Cameron's skill in unsettling the Prime Minister was acknowledged by the sketch writers to have been a parliamentary tour de force: 'It's only our first exchange and already you are asking me the questions. This approach is stuck in the past and

I want to talk about the future. He was the future once.' The roar of approval from the opposition benches for Cameron's savage put-down was interpreted as confirmation of the spin that he was the true 'heir to Blair'. The strategy was not without risk because the accusation that Cameron was merely 'aping Blair' had dogged him throughout the leadership campaign. After the success of his speech in Blackpool, *The Times* revealed that at a conference dinner Cameron told guests 'I am the heir to Blair', a story he denied but one which gained credence after the host, the *Daily Telegraph*'s editor, Martin Newland, not only confirmed that the conversation had taken place but said he had advised him not to repeat the claim. Davis used Cameron's boast to advantage during a spirited comeback in a *Question Time* debate when he accused his opponent of imitating Blair's 'policy-lite' approach to politics. While insisting he was amused by the jibe that he had become a 'Tory Blair', Cameron used an article in the London *Evening Standard* to explain why he disagreed with those Conservatives who claimed they could see 'nothing good' in the Prime Minister. 'When it comes to domestic policies, it's pretty difficult for anyone sensible on the centre-right to avoid sounding like Blair, for the simple reason that he has adopted most of our language.'

Seven months after having been dismissed as a rank outsider, when the party's big beasts seemed to have every justification for convincing themselves that the leadership was theirs for the taking, Cameron had pulled off a stunning victory and then topped it off with an assured debut in the House of Commons. Nonetheless the long, gruelling campaign and frequent setbacks had served a purpose, strengthening his resolve and the dedication of his back-room team. Not only had the leadership passed to the next generation but so had control over the party machine and Cameron's aides were the first to admit that the ups and downs of the contest had shown they needed time, and plenty of it, to find their feet. If they were to have any chance of giving meaning to his promise to deliver 'modern, compassionate Conservatism', the last thing the party needed was an early general election. Uppermost in their minds was the nightmare scenario that a mid-term handover of power from Tony Blair to Gordon Brown could give Labour an opportunity to go to the country and a chance to pull off a fourth general election victory. Michael Howard had helped to engineer a protracted contest to choose his successor, giving Cameron and his allies every opportunity to learn from their mistakes. Labour were unlikely to be anywhere near so accommodating, or so it must have seemed to an inexperienced opposition front bench facing such a well-entrenched government machine.

4
THE NON-ELECTION OF 2007

On becoming leader of the opposition in December 2005 the challenge for David Cameron mirrored the task which a decade earlier faced the newly elected Labour leader, Tony Blair. Both struggled with the twin objectives of reforming their parties while trying at the same time to get a raft of fresh policies taken seriously by the news media and then by the wider electorate. Under Blair the process of modernisation spawned the creation of New Labour, which was launched at the party's 1994 annual conference with the slogan 'New Labour, New Britain'. Cameron held back from seeking a name change but he was equally ambitious in his plans for rebranding the Conservatives. Both leaders inherited parties which remained resistant to new thinking despite having suffered successive election defeats. Blair and his advisers realised full well that their key aims went hand in hand. They were convinced that changes to the structure and outlook of the party had a greater chance of being accepted the more Labour's new ideas were scrutinised and talked about. If the reforms could be presented as news stories in themselves, and if they were favourably received by political journalists, the backing of the media could be used as a justification for speeding up the process and if necessary helping to force through unpopular measures. A decision to rewrite Clause IV of the constitution and abandon an historic commitment to public ownership was sprung on the party without warning but it was greeted with wide acclaim in the press and hastened the party's rehabilitation. During the long run-up to Labour's historic victory in the 1997 general election, Blair often reflected on the limitations of opposition. His priority as party leader was to engage potential voters and convince them that Labour had changed but, having no power to decide or implement public policy, he had to come to terms with the harsh reality that his ability to influence the electorate depended almost entirely on what he said rather than on what he could do.

To begin with Cameron faced a near-identical challenge: lack of interest on the part of much of the news media and a membership hostile to reform. Four years later, riding high in the opinion polls, the Conservative Party's website paid an unintended compliment to the effectiveness of the approach which Blair adopted during his early struggles to get New Labour taken seriously. When there was still much uncertainty about the timing of the 2010 general election, Cameron's official online biography could not have been more explicit about his proudest political achievement to date: 'getting the Conservative Party listened to again'. Although they would perhaps have been reluctant to concede the claim that the Conservatives had become a force to be reckoned with, the priority which Cameron had given to the importance of making the Tories relevant once again was a tactic which would have won a grudging acknowledgement from Blair's three leading media strategists, his campaigns director Peter Mandelson, press secretary Alastair Campbell and pollster Philip Gould. In their individual way they each played a crucial part in shaping New Labour and they bequeathed Cameron and his aides an invaluable route map for the tortuous task of rebuilding a dysfunctional political party and reconnecting it with the electorate.

Because he was up against a hard-pressed John Major, who won the 1992 general election against the odds and who then doggedly stayed the course, hanging on until the bitter end so as to complete a full term as Prime Minister, Blair was fortunate in having three years in which to refashion and re-energise the Labour machine before having to face the electorate. The trials and tribulations of an increasingly fractious

Conservative Party provided an easy target and his team of advisers had ample time to devise and implement strategies designed to command the news agenda and promote the policies of New Labour. They were so successful in taking advantage of the instability generated by rebellious Conservative Eurosceptics and in exploiting the backlash which engulfed Major after the failure of his 'back to basics' initiative that the near certainty of winning the 1997 election was turned into an unprecedented Labour landslide. Campbell and his team succeeded in hanging the word 'sleaze' around Major's neck with devastating consequences for the Conservatives' reputation for probity, a slur which the former Prime Minister blamed on the fabrication and deceit of Labour's burgeoning band of spin doctors.

In the event Cameron finished up having much more time than Blair to rebrand and reorganise his party but he had no way of knowing that would be the case when he set off on what turned out to be a 4½-year trek to polling day. Indeed in the early months of his leadership he had every justification for fearing he might become the fall guy in a snap general election. Blair's declaration ahead of the 2005 election that he intended to serve a full term but step down before the Labour Party went to the country to seek a fourth mandate was unprecedented in an age of media-driven politics. His immediate predecessors dared not reveal their true intentions so far in advance for fear of being written off as a lame duck Prime Minister. By prematurely declaring his hand, Blair unsettled not only his own party but also the opposition. While he did all he could to quell persistent speculation about the likely timing of his departure, he faced growing pressure within his parliamentary party to agree to an early handover to the Chancellor of the Exchequer, Gordon Brown. Among political strategists there was a widespread belief that a newly installed Prime Minister would be sorely tempted to go to the country almost immediately in order to seek a fresh mandate for Labour, rather than hang on until 2009 or 2010.

Having worked so hard to choreograph a stunning victory in the leadership contest, Cameron's aides knew there was no time to lose if he was to stand any chance of mounting a credible fightback against a well-entrenched Labour government backed by a comfortable sixty-plus majority. A mid-term handover to Brown seemed increasingly likely because Blair's authority at Westminster and his personal ratings in the opinion polls had been in freefall for months. His unprecedented achievement in leading Labour to three general election victories seemed to count for nothing when set against the mounting evidence that he misled the country in 2003 about the extent of Saddam Hussein's weapons of mass destruction and was open to the accusation that he persuaded Britain to join the US-led invasion of Iraq on the basis of a 'lie'. His integrity was further undermined by constant allegations about the degree to which he had exploited his position as Prime Minister by offering business leaders peerages in return for donations to the Labour Party in what became known as the 'cash for honours' scandal.

An untested Conservative leader, barely recognised by much of the electorate, found he was up against another moving target: instead of the blemish of Blair there might soon be a Brown bounce and a rush to the polls. Offsetting Cameron's political inexperience were the strengths which emerged so forcefully during the leadership contest and which his aides wanted to put to immediate use. He was an assured performer in front of the camera, able to shine against the big beasts of politics and the media, and, more to the point, he was a fresh face, desperate to attract attention and raise public awareness for himself and his party. Journalists and programme producers sensed that Cameron was prepared to come out to play and had something akin to the instant appeal of a new arrival in a reality television programme. Like a surprise guest in *I'm a Celebrity. . . Get Me Out of Here*, he seemed to be gagging to be part of the action, quite prepared to volunteer for the next bush tucker trial.

For a revamped publicity team at Conservative campaign headquarters it was a case of all systems go: at last the party had a leader who was in tune with popular culture, impatient for the news media's embrace and only too happy to be filmed and photographed in family settings, either at home or out and about with his wife and children. After having put so much effort into winning over doubtful members of the Tory Party, Cameron was able at last to concentrate his fire on the government. The ease with which he was starting to command editorial space and air time unnerved the Labour machine and the scale of the threat which they thought he might pose at a forthcoming general election was one of the few issues where there was a measure of agreement between the warring Blair and Brown factions. David Hill, one of Labour's most experienced media strategists, had succeeded Campbell as No. 10's director of communications and in theory he had the unenviable responsibility of having to co-ordinate the response of the seventy or so special advisers whose task it was to brief journalists on behalf of ministers and their departments. Downing Street's pro-Blair team of political aides was regularly in conflict with its rival at the Treasury under the command of Brown's media chief, Damian McBride. Such was the hostility between the two camps that they rarely worked in unison but with Cameron it would be different; here was a ready-made target and the Labour spin machine was yearning to exploit stories about his privileged background and wealthy friends. Despite their addiction to factional infighting and the damage which this was inflicting on Blair's premiership, Labour's network of special advisers remained a force to be reckoned with and, when not turning in on themselves, they could still exert considerable influence over the story lines appearing in key media outlets. Confidential documents, exclusive information and private briefings were all on offer to favoured journalists and once they got wind of what the Tory leader and his party were up to, government insiders knew they would have no difficulty farming out tip-offs and anonymous quotes to their trusted clientele. In ticking the box for publicity, and in offering himself up to the media, Cameron had taken a calculated risk. Ex-ministers and former party colleagues who had fallen out with either Blair or Brown complained bitterly about having been the victims of anonymous briefings; Cameron was about to experience for the first time the full force of the black arts of Labour's infamous attack dogs. Thanks to the ingenuity of journalists and Labour's rapid counter-spin, the attention-seeking escapades of the new Tory leader were about to result in some telling images which in some cases would develop a life of their own, prove difficult to erase and provide useful ammunition for his opponents.

Politicians rarely hit on a memorable photo-opportunity which can be repeated time and again and yet remain plausible with the public, but Cameron's trick of cycling to the House of Commons on mornings such as the day of Prime Minister's Questions certainly ticked all the relevant boxes as far as the news media was concerned. Photographers and television crews could be sure of a fresh supply of pictures and footage ready to feed into news bulletins and next day's newspapers. There was also the added bonus of a visual image which connected with many younger voters and was in tune with their concerns about the environment and their desire for a healthy lifestyle. Cameron did his best to publicise his green credentials during the leadership campaign; he promised he would take climate change out of party politics by establishing an independent authority to ensure future governments kept to year-by-year reductions in carbon emissions. One of his first initiatives after choosing his shadow cabinet was the appointment of a policy group on the quality of life under the co-chairmanship of the environmentalist Zac Goldsmith, editor of the *Ecologist*, and John Gummer, the former Conservative agriculture minister. Full-page advertisements promoting the party's agenda for change declared that the Conservatives would 'stand up to big business' to secure reductions in carbon emissions so as to halt the rise in global temperatures. Cameron promised to reduce his and his family's carbon footprint: he planned to install solar panels and a small wind turbine on the roof of his London home.

Within days of Cameron taking office opinion surveys began to reflect a sizeable Conservative bounce. The first poll of polls suggested that an eight-point Labour lead had been reversed and transformed into a two-point advantage for the Tories. Unlike previous Tory leaders, Cameron scored well on green issues and potential voters thought he would do more for the environment than either Blair or Brown. If he was to continue setting the pace on climate change the Conservatives needed to conjure up a succession of memorable, headline-grabbing initiatives, a task which was being given the highest priority by Cameron's chief strategist, Steve Hilton. Since their days together in the research department of Conservative Central Office, when they cut their political teeth as two of 'Patten's puppies' in the 1992 general election, they had been close friends and Hilton became a constant source of inspiration during the leadership contest. 'Change to win' was the slogan he devised for Cameron's campaign manifesto; he helped to prepare the no-notes speech for the official launch; and his was the guiding hand behind much of the tactical repositioning which in a matter of months propelled Cameron from rank outsider to party leader.

Rebranding the party was the next step on the long route march to polling day and the challenge was irresistible for a marketing guru who shunned personal publicity but who had played a key role in devising controversial advertisements for the Conservatives in the two general elections fought by John Major. Hilton subsequently built a name for himself and his agency, Good Business, by advising leading consumer brands on ethical practices and socially responsible behaviour. Guidance was given on how brands could benefit from social programmes 'without being – and looking – superficial', precisely the kind of strategy which would be needed to promote Cameron's green agenda.

My first contact with Hilton was in 1992 when, at the age of twenty-two, he was appointed a campaign co-ordinator and was responsible for liaising with the party's advertising agency, Saatchi & Saatchi. Major's government had been unsettled by opinion polls suggesting victory for Neil Kinnock, or at least a hung parliament, but early on in the campaign, the shadow Chancellor, John Smith, made the tactical mistake of presenting an alternative tax and benefits package which the Conservatives attacked immediately on the grounds that it represented 'Labour's tax bombshell'. Dramatic posters rammed home the message on 7,000 billboard sites. Hilton also helped to co-ordinate the Conservatives' election broadcasts, which were usually shown to journalists a few hours before transmission. After one preview late in the campaign I could see Hilton was excited, itching to brief the assembled correspondents before they left. On being given the go-ahead, he told us that when the latest broadcast was transmitted that evening it would include a superimposed flashing message giving the telephone number of Labour's London headquarters. 'We are telling voters who are fed up with the way Neil Kinnock is knocking Britain to ring up Labour's headquarters if they wish to protest. There is something they can do.' Despite protests from Labour about possible incitement, broadcasting organisations were powerless to stop its transmission because they said there was nothing unlawful in publicising the party's telephone number. Maurice Saatchi was so impressed with Hilton's flair for political campaigning that he recruited him for the agency, saying: 'No one reminds me as much of me when young as Steve.'

Four years later, in the lead-up to the 1997 election, Hilton took the credit for having been the inspiration behind the infamous advertisement featuring a photograph of Tony Blair with a big grin on his face and red, demon-like eyes over the slogan 'New Labour, New Danger'. Peter Mandelson, backed by the Bishop of Oxford, the Right Reverend Richard Harries, censured the Conservatives for daring to portray Blair as the devil but the demon-eyes image acquired cult status and was named advertisement of the year by the magazine *Campaign*. Another Hilton-inspired image produced by Saatchi's new agency, M&C Saatchi, was an advertisement which featured a puny Blair sitting on the knee of the German Chancellor, Helmut Kohl.

In contrast to 1992, when he was an active member of the 'brat pack' and upfront with journalists, Hilton kept his distance from political correspondents during the controversies of the 1997 campaign, fearing he might be the target of another well-executed Labour sting. Two months before polling day a Labour activist handed the *Observer* the transcript of an interview in which he admitted that Major was the Conservatives' greatest weakness. Hilton said he fully expected Labour to 'go for Major in a big way, portraying him as a wimp'. The interview was with a sixth-form student and according to her account he spoke frankly about the behaviour of political propagandists and the tricks of their trade. Private polls were often quoted by the Conservatives but he said they were a myth: minimal polling was actually done and the party often lied about the results. Hilton insisted he had no recollection of what in fact was a three-year-old private conversation but Labour's spin machine, determined to get even with the author of 'New Labour, New Danger', went into overdrive, pushing the line that a leading Tory strategist had branded Major 'a wimp'.

Having been so badly bruised in the past, Hilton did his utmost to remain in the shadows once he was back on the party's payroll giving Cameron advice on media strategies. Publicists and spin doctors always go to extraordinary lengths to keep out of camera range during contrived photo-opportunities and Hilton was doubly careful, especially when promoting Cameron's green crusade and choreographing what became an iconic image of the new Tory leader riding a dog sleigh over a retreating Arctic glacier. His visit to the remote Norwegian island of Svalbard in April 2006 was designed to highlight the impact of global warming, a visual reminder of the Conservatives' promise to introduce a 'green revolution', a key plank in their campaign for that year's local elections. Photographs and television footage of Cameron driving his pack of huskies secured extensive coverage across the media and praise for the leader's image-maker included what the *Guardian* claimed was a text to Hilton from an ally at party headquarters which read: 'Simply brilliant – that was worth a thousand speeches.' But several newspapers which only weeks earlier had been singing Cameron's praises were less than impressed. 'The Ice Man cometh' was the *Daily Mail*'s headline over a two-page spread which mocked his attempt to prove his green credentials by travelling 2,000 miles by car and private jet, 'burning 30,000 gallons of fuel', for a fifteen-mile journey by sleigh.

While some commentators lampooned Cameron for engaging in photo-opportunities far removed from the reality of the council elections coming up the following month, his aides were delighted with the publicity he achieved for his Arctic adventure and were convinced that it gave added force to an election broadcast which promoted the eco-friendly initiatives of Conservative-controlled local authorities. Labour's first response to the success of Hilton's marketing ploys was an election broadcast which depicted a computer-generated 'Dave the chameleon', a sleazy swivel-eyed reptile sipping champagne and eating flies in a stretched limousine before spewing out policies at a lectern under the caption 'I am the heir to Blair'. In one scene, in which Labour took a swipe at Cameron's Eton education, the chameleon wore a boater; in another the creature remained true blue despite attempting to appear green. The script leant heavily on what the newly elected Tory leader was said to have learned during his career in public relations: 'Dave the Chameleon changed into every colour of the rainbow as he told everyone just what he thought they wanted to hear.' Portraying him as a beguiling blue reptile riding a bicycle seemed to work to his advantage rather than against him and more than a third of those questioned for a *Mail on Sunday* opinion poll said they thought the chameleon was 'likeable', despite apparently being fork tongued. At least one seasoned Labour Party campaigner agreed that the broadcast backfired: the industry minister Margaret Hodge admitted that voters in her Barking constituency found the concept of a reptile which 'flip-flops' politically far too complicated to understand.

For Labour to have felt the need to mount a pointed attack on Cameron's personality within five months of him becoming leader was seen by his advisers as vindication of the tactics they were adopting. In an interview for the magazine *Credit Today*, George Osborne was surprisingly honest about the time and thought which went into generating photo-opportunities. 'Just creating the positive image of David Cameron as a relaxed family chap who enjoys cycling has taken months of effort.' Lord Bell, who as Tim Bell made his name advising Margaret Thatcher, told *PR Week* he was sure Cameron's ability to present himself as 'a celebrity' was a 'positively intoxicating' experience for most Conservatives. 'He is a bright and attractive face with a glitzy past and a glitzy present. This is why he was able to dress up in his cycling kit without the derision William Hague got for wearing a baseball cap.' Nonetheless, as the *Sun* noted,

Cameron refused to wear any kind of headgear while being photographed in the Arctic, despite having to endure temperatures of minus 20 degrees, so determined was he to make sure he did not look 'daft in a hat'. Tory pundits who took the greatest comfort from Cameron's success in giving 'surprising speeches at surprising events' were some of those who suffered most at the hands of New Labour's spin doctors. Daniel Finkelstein, the Conservatives' director of research in the 1997 election, urged the party to do even more to champion populist issues. 'Talking about the environment and posing with huskies was not an embarrassing PR stunt, it was a master stroke.' Michael Portillo thought the image of Cameron as 'a green Adonis (dressed in blue) on his dog-drawn sledge' was as emblematic as Thatcher appearing as 'a goddess of war mounted on a battle tank'. Until he went 'wheelless' on the Norwegian ice, the pictures of him arriving at Parliament on his bicycle had been the most successful piece of political propaganda for years. 'One snapshot of his two-wheeler on our front pages suggested that he is young, unpompous, unaffected by success, keen to keep fit, concerned about the planet and a Tory leader like no other. Six messages from one photo is good going.' A slightly discordant voice was that of Zac Goldsmith, who told the *Daily Mail* that 'chasing votes on the green ticket' was opportunism when the only answer might be to tax over-consumption of energy. 'Norway is a stunt, but it's a good stunt and there's no other way of interpreting it.'

Amid the self-congratulation of the Tory hierarchy one important detail had been overlooked: what happened to the leader's parliamentary papers on the mornings he cycled to the House of Commons? Hugo Rifkind's diary column in *The Times* noted this inconsistency and Cameron's press officer George Eustice was asked whether Cameron's box of documents went by 'official car when he pedals'. If that was the case, it would not be 'very carbon neutral'. Eustice promised Rifkind the problem would 'get sorted' but weeks later the *Daily Mirror* hit the bull's eye in its campaign to expose Cameron's hypocrisy. 'Con yer bike' was the headline over an exclusive sequence of pictures showing Cameron apparently flaunting his green credentials while he had 'a flunky following behind in a gas-guzzling motor carrying his shoes and briefcase'. *Mirror* photographers watched the 'born-again environmentalist' leap on his bicycle and pedal off only for his official car to arrive a few minutes later and the driver to be handed 'a briefcase, a shirt and a pair of highly polished shoes'. At last Cameron's political opponents had the ammunition they had longed to find, the evidence that he was guilty of gesture politics and that his slogan for the council elections, 'Vote blue, go green', was a fraud.

By puncturing the ballyhoo surrounding his regular cycle rides, the *Daily Mirror* made sure Cameron faced some difficult questions next time he was interviewed. On *The Politics Show*, he was forced to admit that his government car often had to follow behind with a 'huge box full of work . . . dozens of letters and papers'. Pressed further by John Humphrys on *Today*, he denied he misled anyone by sending his documents by car: 'I don't get on my bike to prove green credentials; I get on my bike as it is a lovely thing to do . . . for the exercise and a breath of fresh air.' But as with persistent questioning over possible drug taking, there was to be no escape: broadcasters would not be satisfied until Cameron showed at least a degree of contrition. Finally, on Radio 1's *Newsbeat*, he confessed to having made a mistake; his chauffeur had been banned from following him to work in future. 'That did happen once or twice and I've now made sure it will never happen again.' He continued to cycle to the House of Commons each Wednesday morning because it 'gets me going for Prime Minister's Question Time'.

Deconstructing the Conservatives' carefully arranged photo-opportunity delighted Kevin Maguire, the *Daily Mirror*'s associate editor and political columnist, who had been waiting for the chance to rubbish Cameron's green credentials. He said he purposely wrote 'ferocious leaders' about Cameron and made sure they were short and direct so they would be 'very quotable' for broadcasters. Although alone among the tabloids in expressing such outright hostility, its exclusive could not be ignored and once Cameron's crafty stage management had been exposed other newspapers piled in with negative stories. There were reports he had refused the cleanest option in the government's car pool in favour of a faster model while at the same time advising parents to abandon the school run and instead walk with their children.

Undaunted by the criticism, he used an article in the *Sunday Telegraph* to promise that a future Conservative government would encourage a new generation of greener cars and would cut vehicle emissions by more than a third. By generating so much coverage for his green agenda, Cameron stole a march on Gordon Brown, who, not to be outdone, used a speech to UN ambassadors in New York to argue that tackling environmental pollution could become a driver for economic growth. He announced plans for a 'global solution to a global problem' and later, in a BBC interview, challenged Cameron to spell out how the Conservatives intended to meet his pledge to replace the climate change levy. Treasury aides said the Chancellor was 'telling it straight to an American audience' while a 'policy-lite' Cameron cycled to work and took television crews to the Arctic; they agreed this was confirmation that Brown was determined to do battle with the new Tory leader without waiting for Tony Blair to step down.

While both Labour and the Liberal Democrats derided the 'Vote blue, go green' slogan, the May local elections delivered the best result for the Conservatives for more than a decade. Labour lost over 300 council seats and, after analysing the figures, the Electoral Reform Society predicted that if the Conservatives' 40 per cent share of the vote was repeated at a general election, Cameron would be on the 'verge of an overall majority' at Westminster. But progress in northern England was nothing like as strong as the party hoped for, another reminder of the lengths to which he believed the Conservatives would have to go if they were to reverse years of retreat in Britain's industrial heartlands. In a clear break with Thatcherism and the devastation left after her decade in power, Cameron was about to start a fresh page in his attempt to define 'modern, compassionate Conservatism'. In a series of speeches he set out to explain why 'there's more to life than money' and why a government he led would focus 'not just on GDP but on GWB [general wellbeing]'. As proved to be the case with his green crusade, Cameron was about to discover that he could not always rely on the sure touch of his strategists and speech writers. Another indelible image was about to be created to take its place alongside film of him driving a pack of huskies and photographs of a chauffeur carrying his shoes and briefcase; on this occasion the credit would go to the rapid response of Labour's spin machine.

Young parents were Cameron's first target as he argued the case for employers to offer more flexible work patterns so that families could enjoy a better work–life balance. Working mothers were a priority for help and he told the National Family and Parenting Institute that a policy review team was examining whether a future Conservative government could give tax breaks to all working parents who had to pay for childcare; any new tax relief for married couples would also apply to civil partners. 'Tories end war on single mums' was the *Sun*'s take on a pledge to 'break with the past' which the paper said would 'infuriate grassroots Tories' opposed to going soft on feckless young women. Cameron's intention was to challenge the assumption that family-friendly policies were Brown's sole preserve:

> *So for the Conservative Party today, it's not just a case of the war on lone parents being over . . . We want to promote stable relationships and to support married couples . . . and we need to think more about how society can help increase the wellbeing of lone-parent families.*

Speech by speech Cameron started to set out an agenda for a social affairs programme which was beginning to capture the attention of charities, pressure groups and opinion formers. 'The muesli offensive' was the headline for the *Observer*'s analysis of Cameron's courtship of the 'muesli-eating classes', who felt their causes were being neglected by Labour. Gaby Hinsliff, the paper's political editor, said the effort being made to woo such campaigners was reminiscent of Blair's 'prawn cocktail circuit', when New Labour wined and dined business leaders in the City of London ahead of the 1997 general election. Hinsliff trailed ahead to Cameron's next speech in July 2006, which she said would outline ideas for tackling gang culture, his attempt to match Blair's much-publicised but much-derided commitment to be 'tough on crime, and tough on the causes of crime'.

A more detailed preview the following Sunday claimed that Cameron was about to 'completely re-engineer the Conservatives' image on crime' by arguing that a long-term answer to the social influences which were driving children to offend was to 'show a lot more love'. He thought some of the youngsters who wore tops to hide their faces did so because of a 'sense of menace' in town centres and their own fear of becoming victims of crime. Hinsliff gave a direct quote from the speech Cameron intended to give next day to a conference organised by the Centre for Social Justice: 'Hoodies are more defensive than offensive. They're a way to stay invisible in the street. In a dangerous environment the best thing to do is keep your head down, blend in and don't stand out.'

Providing news agencies, newspapers and broadcasters with an advance copy of a text has long been standard practice but in their determination to influence the news agenda politicians increasingly run the risk of giving their opponents the chance to misrepresent a speech before it has even been delivered. Such is the demand for comment and reaction that political parties have been forced to establish sophisticated departments to monitor news output; they are programmed to offer instant rebuttal to stories which are damaging or inaccurate and they aim whenever possible to undermine the forthcoming announcements or initiatives of their rivals. The *Observer*'s headline that Sunday was based not on Cameron's own words but on Labour's spin about what he was expected to say the following day: 'Cameron softens crime image in "hug a hoodie" call'. Tucked away at the end of Hinsliff's story was a quote from the Home Office minister Vernon Coaker, giving Labour's withering response to what the Tory leader was due to announce: 'Cameron's empty idea seems to be "let's hug a hoodie", whatever they have done.' Next day Labour reworked the quote to get the same headline in the London

Evening Standard; this time it was in the name of the police minister, Tony McNulty, who ridiculed Cameron for sending out a 'vacuous hug-a-hoodie message to troublesome teenagers'. Labour's spin doctors had succeeded in persuading journalists to accept their interpretation of the speech. The meaning had been twisted to put the words 'hug a hoodie' into Cameron's mouth when his text drew a clear distinction between the tough sanctions required for offenders and the need to 'show a lot more love' to those youngsters who stayed within legal boundaries but who needed more support. By reinterpreting the line to imply that Cameron wanted society to hug the hoodies who terrorised housing estates and shopping centres, Labour fired up not only headline writers and cartoonists but also the disgruntled and often anonymous band of rent-a-quote Tory right-wingers who immediately accused Cameron of failing to recognise the reality of life on the streets. 'He's gone bonkers,' one unnamed MP told the *Evening Standard*. Cameron's aides insisted that his speech was a clear declaration that youngsters who broke the law should be punished but protests were too late. Whether he liked it or not, it was now an established 'fact' that he had gone soft on anti-social behaviour. Martin Newland, former editor of the *Daily Telegraph*, observed in his column in the *Guardian* that a thoughtful speech had been transformed by 'Labour's formidable spin' into 'hug a hoodie' headlines. Cameron was also forced to acknowledge that it was a soundbite which he would always be associated with: 'Those three words never passed my lips. It is incredibly annoying if you never utter them.'

After pursuing him for a matter of months Labour's attack dogs felt they were well on the way to establishing in the public's mind an enduring identikit image of the new Conservative leader as an inept Tory toff so pampered that a chauffeur carried his shoes and briefcase; so remote from the real world that he imagined driving a pack of huskies across a glacier was the answer to global warming; and so misguided to think that love rather than punishment would curb menacing young tearaways. These were precisely the taunts which would be used time and again in the speeches of Labour politicians and appear in the pages of the *Daily Mirror* as Blair and Brown attempted to come to terms with the Conservatives' steady advance in the opinion polls. But as soon as Cameron began to shift his focus onto social issues, however hard opponents tried to question his sincerity and ridicule his ideas, the press pictures and television footage told a different story. Cameron's role as a caring father was there for all to see; photographers and camera crews continued to be offered access at work, home and play. A great variety of shots of the couple out with their children, often pushing buggies, gave newspapers and magazines a chance to offer readers the kind of images which would take pride of place in any family photo album.

Such repeated visual confirmation of his support for and devotion to his wife and children was adding a powerful human dimension to the family-friendly political agenda which he had been outlining and which he hoped would produce better childcare and public support for working parents. Cameron had also made it harder for his opponents. His privileged background remained a liability but his personal life was becoming a no-go area for political attack dogs. After his second son, Arthur, was born in February 2006, he took paternity leave only for the Labour Party to remind journalists that he voted against new rights for fathers when they were first approved by the House of Commons. David Hill, Blair's director of communications, denied a report in the *Mail on Sunday* that Downing Street had been plotting a smear attack. 'It was perfectly reasonable to state that having opposed paternity leave when it was introduced in Parliament, Cameron then took it.' Cameron voted against the bill on a three-line whip within months of becoming an MP in 2001, the year before the birth of his first son, Ivan.

Cameron was more than a match for Labour's spin machine: on his first day back at work he joined an online forum to answer questions from mothers on the Mumsnet website; he entered a sponsored walk with two-month-old Arthur peeping out from a trendy baby sling ('A picture of hands-on fatherhood,' said the *Daily Mail*); and he spoke openly on *Desert Island Discs* about the anguish of learning of Ivan's diagnosis of cerebral palsy and severe epilepsy. He and Samantha took time to get over the shock, as though they had been bereaved: 'You are mourning the gap between your expectation and what has happened.' Cameron's care for Ivan, his frankness about coping with a disabled child and his obvious empathy with other parents of children with disabilities made him even more quotable on Father's Day. When interviewed by Gloria Hunniford for the BBC show *Heaven and Earth*, the Archbishop of Canterbury, Dr Rowan Williams, singled out Cameron and the England football captain David Beckham as two role models for modern fatherhood because they both took 'their fathering seriously'. In his own Father's Day article for the *Sunday Times*, Cameron said his family and children would always be more important to him than becoming Prime Minister. 'I passionately want to have the chance . . . but the fact is that whatever I do or don't achieve in politics, nothing matters as much as my family . . . on Father's Day we should remember the simple truth that a successful dad spends time with his children.'

Having had their fingers burned when challenging Cameron for taking paternity leave, Labour's media strategists were forced to look on with envy as he continued to generate tabloid stories which suggested he was more in tune with popular culture than either the Prime Minister or the Chancellor. An air of disbelief greeted Gordon Brown's revelation in an interview for *New Woman* that listening to the Arctic Monkeys on his iPod 'really wakes you up in the morning'. Yet the self-same columnists and commentators who reacted with incredulity on hearing of the Chancellor's choice of music were tickled pink when Cameron selected Benny Hill's 1971 chart topper, 'Ernie (the Fastest Milkman in the West)', as one of his eight favourites for *Desert Island Discs*. He told Sue Lawley that he learned the 600 words of the song as a five-year-old and the disc would be a reminder of his childhood. 'When you are asked to sing a song, this is, I'm afraid, the only song whose words I remember.' As he still performed it occasionally as a party piece, Lawley asked for a rendition but he ducked the chance and spoke the opening line instead.

His appearance on *Friday Night with Jonathan Ross* succeeded in generating even more column inches and some rave reviews for the way he kept his cool during what the *Mail on Sunday* declared was a 'lewd and grossly offensive' interview. When asked by Ross whether he ever had sexual fantasies about Lady Thatcher 'in stockings' when he was a teenager, Cameron tried to change the subject. But Ross persisted: 'But did you or did you not have a wank thinking "Margaret Thatcher"?' Initially he burst out laughing, along with the audience, but after a quick double take, simply replied 'No'. Ross was triumphant: 'See? I'm like Paxman.' Such was the furore that the BBC banned repeats and removed the question and answer from the video version on the BBC's website. Cameron took the row in his stride; his office said guests on the show knew what they were letting themselves in for. Jonathan Ross was credited with having asked the 'knockout question of the week' by the *Sun*'s television critic, Ally Ross, and the *Guardian*'s political columnist Michael White thought that by showing he could cope with the 'street-smart zeitgeist' of a non-deferential age, Cameron would probably reap a dividend among young voters.

Politicians are renowned for lacking a sure touch when trying to relate to the latest craze but again Cameron had no difficulty upstaging Blair in the build-up to England's first match in the 2006 football World Cup. On the morning of Prime Minister's Questions, Cameron set off from home with the flag of St George fluttering behind his bicycle, an instant and visible sign that he was ready to mix it with the numerous lorry drivers and white van men who were already flying the flag in support of their team. In a hurried response, Downing Street announced Blair had sent a handwritten letter of support to the team's manager, Sven-Göran Eriksson; No. 10 would also fly the England flag on match days.

Political honeymoons can be a mixed blessing but Cameron's frenetic first six months as party leader succeeded in transforming Tory fortunes. An opinion poll for the *Sun* put the Conservatives on 41 per cent, ten points ahead of Labour, their biggest lead since John Major won the 1992 general election. In his column in the *Guardian*, Max Hastings said his respect for Cameron was 'almost unbounded' because he took 'no heed of Conservative geriatrics' and told the old guard the unpalatable truth that the British people had changed immeasurably. 'If I sound somewhat star struck, so I am . . . I did not believe that a clutch of old Etonians would ever again prove acceptable to the British electorate as its rulers.' A subsequent probe by the *Guardian* revealed that fifteen of the 130 office holders on the Tory front benches in the Commons and the Lords were educated at Eton. Notwithstanding his reliance on the most prestigious of old-boy networks, a willing news media had given Cameron ample opportunity to be heard and he was an obvious choice for the *House Magazine*'s award for opposition politician of the year. Unlike his three immediate predecessors, he had forged what the columnist Peter Oborne described as an 'alliance' with the media class. Instead of resisting the media and seeking to speak beyond it to Tory voters, Cameron and his adviser Steve Hilton ('the most important man in Conservative politics') had recognised that the only way back to power was to follow New Labour's example: engage with journalists and make 'gigantic changes in style and substance'. Nonetheless, as he set off for a family summer holiday in Corfu, wiser heads in the Conservative hierarchy doubted whether the party had changed fundamentally. Some nagging questions were left hanging in the air. Were Labour's spinners right after all in depicting him as a chameleon? Was he presenting the Conservative Party in what he hoped was a more acceptable hue but one which was only skin deep? In Lord Bell's view Cameron's transformation into a Tory leader different from the public's normal expectation had been 'brilliantly done' but the party itself was exactly the same as it was before. He told the BBC4 documentary *The Worst Job in Politics – Leader of the Opposition* that the electorate's perceptions might have changed but in reality the party had not moved 'one inch'.

On his return from Corfu, Cameron planned to spend the rest of the summer preparing for the Conservatives' 2006 annual conference in Bournemouth, his first as party leader, a chance to reassure the party faithful about the wisdom of following a new and different path. He did not know it at the time but some of his efforts to accelerate the process of reform would end up having to take second place behind the fallout from a seismic convulsion within the Labour Party. After months of intrigue among ministers and MPs, the Blair–Brown divide was tearing the government apart and the tail end of the summer would see a decisive step towards a handover of power, heightening speculation that an inexperienced Cameron might be forced to lead the Conservatives into a general election far sooner than the party wanted. To begin with, in the apparent calm of mid-August, Cameron stuck closely to New Labour's handbook on seizing the initiative.

During a long summer recess, when ministers are not under anything like the same pressure to respond to the daily news agenda, opposition parties have a greater chance of influencing the media. A tactic for manipulating the Sunday newspapers, which was first deployed by Peter Mandelson and his deputy Colin Byrne in the run-up to the 1992 general election, was about to make a reappearance. Under Neil Kinnock, John Smith and then Blair, the priority in presentational terms was always the need to convince commerce and industry that a future Labour government would curb trade union power and adopt business-friendly policies. Exclusive stories about shifts in Labour policy were invariably offered first to the *Sunday Times*, which was seen as having the greatest influence in the City of London and the business community. For Cameron the target audience was different but the challenge similar: he was eager to convince liberal-minded and socially aware opinion formers that the Conservative Party which he led was ready to apologise for Margaret Thatcher's worst mistakes. After a short visit to South Africa and a private meeting with Nelson Mandela, he selected the *Observer*, one of the fiercest critics of Thatcher's refusal to support the African National Congress, to explain why his party 'got it so very wrong on apartheid'. Cameron's placing of his exclusive article was a carbon copy of Mandelson's technique: choose the newspaper which has traditionally been the most hostile. If the editorial staff is convinced that a significant shift has taken place, then the story will get top billing and will be more likely to influence the rest of the media. The *Observer*'s front-page splash – 'Tory leader dumps key Thatcher legacy' – provoked widespread comment and reaction. Lord Tebbit considered Cameron was 'too young to know what he was talking about' when he denounced Thatcher for having branded the ANC as 'terrorists' but veterans of the anti-apartheid movement welcomed the Tory leader's recognition that Mandela was one of the 'greatest men alive'.

Without exclusive articles and confidential briefings the Sundays would struggle to compete in a crowded market. To gain the greatest advantage, media strategists have to learn how to play off one newspaper against another. Whereas the *Observer* was an obvious choice for trailing speeches on family-friendly initiatives or soul searching about apartheid, Cameron's green agenda was of particular interest to the *Independent on Sunday*, which regularly campaigned for action on global warming. On the Sunday following his tribute to Mandela, Cameron used another exclusive article to outline Conservative plans for 'year on year targets' to cut Britain's greenhouse gas emissions. The *Independent on Sunday* praised Cameron for putting the environment at the top of his party's priorities; readers were reminded that it was his trip to the Arctic ahead of the local elections which helped him 'win, and win handsomely'. In his day, Mandelson's aim was to use positive coverage in newspapers which were not Labour's natural supporters as a way of encouraging change in the face of internal opposition, a tactic warmly endorsed at Conservative campaign headquarters.

After being criticised in an editorial for failing to show a 'sustained interest in foreign affairs' Cameron offered the *Guardian* an exclusive article promoting his four-day trip to India in early September; he wanted the visit to revitalise Britain's strategic interest in working with a huge potential trading partner and in sharing 'global leadership with both India and China'. Pictures of him in Mumbai sporting the traditional Hindu red dot on his forehead appeared in British newspapers alongside reports of turmoil at Westminster. Blair had been ambushed by Brown's supporters and the Prime Minister was left with no alternative but to agree to a timetable for a handover of power. A round robin letter signed by Tom Watson, a junior defence minister, and seven parliamentary private secretaries called on him to resign so as to enable the government 'urgently to renew its leadership'. In the face of mounting resignations from junior ranks, Blair had a three-hour meeting with Brown and a smiling Chancellor finally left Downing Street, looking, said the *Daily Mail*, 'like the cat that got the cream'. Next day Blair announced that Labour's annual conference in Manchester, only a fortnight away, would be his last as party leader; he refused to elaborate on the timing but indicated he would stand down before the start of the 2007 summer recess.

Opinion polls suggesting the Conservatives had recovered sufficiently to gain an overall majority undoubtedly stiffened the resolve of the Chancellor's colleagues and admirers; they were anxious to start a fightback under a new Prime Minister; and they were annoyed Blair intended to hang on until the following summer instead of departing ahead of the council elections in May. Polls barely budged in the first nine months after William Hague, Iain Duncan Smith and Michael Howard began their leadership and not surprisingly Cameron's rapid progress encouraged a mood of eager anticipation at Conservative campaign headquarters for what the *Daily Telegraph* was confident would be a proper contest between a 'relaxed and personable' Cameron and the 'grim Fifer', described even by his own side as 'psychologically flawed'. There was also an unspoken sense of relief among Cameron's aides: at least the Conservatives would not be thrown into an instant election knowing they had insufficient resources, no detailed policies and few selected candidates. Blair's ousting, although delayed, was nonetheless a signal to Cameron that he had no time to lose if he was to win approval at his first annual conference for the rebranding and repositioning of the party.

In an attempt to answer criticism that his leadership was light on policy, Cameron's mission statement for the future, entitled 'Built to Last', was rewritten and strengthened. When first published in February 2006 it was dismissed by the right of the party for failing to promise tax cuts and being light on specifics; the August version listed more than fifty proposals including his much-trailed ideas for a 'green growth' economy and family-friendly initiatives. In a fresh renunciation of the Thatcher years, he used a speech in Glasgow to apologise for a series of blunders north of the border: 'The imposition of the poll tax was the most egregious . . . to treat Scotland as a laboratory for experimentation in new methods of local government finance was clumsy and unjust.' The fifth anniversary of the 9/11 terrorist attack gave Cameron the chance to break another link with the past. While Lady Thatcher was being escorted by Vice-President Dick Cheney to an act of remembrance on the lawn of the White House, Cameron signalled an end to the Conservatives' flirtation with the neo-conservative policies of right-wing Republicans by declaring in London that he believed Britain should be 'solid but not slavish' in its friendship with the United States. His call for a 'rebalancing' of the relationship tapped into mounting public anger at Blair's uncritical support of President Bush's use of pre-emptive military action against Iraq.

Cameron's detachment from the Conservatives' Thatcherite legacy had to be handled sensitively, step by step, and he proceeded cautiously when introducing a new emblem, the ultimate symbol of a rebranded political party. Peter Mandelson took much of the credit for negotiating the delivery of a red rose at Labour's 1986 party conference after Neil Kinnock ditched further use of the red flag. The Conservatives' logo of a flaming torch of freedom, first introduced by Margaret Thatcher in 1977, went through several makeovers but had survived for nearly three decades and was a reminder of past glories for former party chairmen like Lord Tebbit. Cameron wanted to adopt a softer image in time for his first party conference; he regarded the torch as 'old fashioned and too strident'. A fuzzy picture of an oak tree emerged as a favourite once the design agency Perfect Day began consulting focus groups and the final choice was a squiggly drawn version standing beside the word 'Conservatives'. An oak was chosen because it represented 'solidity, tradition, friendliness towards the environment and Britishness', a concept mocked by Tebbit, who likened the smudgy green branches and blue trunk to a 'bunch of sprouting broccoli'.

Steve Hilton's efforts to promote a refashioned party faced an acid test in the constituencies, where Cameron was struggling to persuade members to accept an A-list of parliamentary candidates for consideration at selection meetings. Priority in winnable seats was being given to women and applicants from black and ethnic minorities in a desperate attempt to achieve a more balanced representation in the parliamentary party. Of the 198 Conservative MPs elected in 2005, only seventeen were women and two from ethnic minorities. Having interviewed Cameron for *Catalyst*, published by the Commission for Racial Equality, I knew he regarded it as a test of his leadership to gain the membership's approval for a priority list of candidates for target constituencies. When we met in the spring a panel at party headquarters had just begun choosing candidates for the A-list; half were to be women and 10 per cent black and minority ethnic. 'We need to look more like the country we are trying to represent . . . and that means Muslim and black communities.' In their ongoing effort to ensure they were more representative of Britain's multi-racial society, the party had established an ethnic diversity council, an Asian network and Chinese and Turkish Conservative associations.

The more Cameron extolled the benefits of a diverse Britain and the need for his party to celebrate the massive contribution made by immigrant communities, the more determined I became to hark back to the Conservatives' 2005 general election campaign and the part he played in preparing Michael Howard's manifesto. I could see his brow puckering but I pressed on: did he feel uncomfortable about a campaign which warned the country of the dangers of 'five more years of asylum chaos' and which used billboards to ask the electorate 'Are you thinking what we're thinking? It's not racist to impose limits on immigration'? Looking me straight in the eye, he replied without hesitation: 'I have not suddenly woken up to the benefits of a diverse Britain. I have always believed in the massive contribution which the immigrant communities have made but I also believe in fair and firm immigration control.'

Another pained expression greeted a follow-up question: had the Conservatives made a miscalculation in being alone among the three main parties in promising to 'put a limit on immigration'? After insisting that he was not being contradictory in standing up for 'fair and firm immigration control' while celebrating the benefits of diversity, Cameron said he had no wish to 'refight' the battle over the 2005 manifesto: 'You fight an election as a team, you win as a team, you lose as a team and then you have got to learn as a team. I don't want to get into how I feel now about what was said then.'

In the six months that had elapsed since our discussion the A-list had become one of the main talking points in the party. At campaign headquarters there was great enthusiasm for the rapidly expanding cast of high-flyers seeking to become Conservative MPs; out in the constituencies there was often resentment. Some associations openly accused the leadership of undermining their independence by seeking to exclude local candidates at selection meetings. When Cameron announced that the A-list had been expanded to 150 names he faced up to his critics and told associations he might have no alternative but to impose all-women shortlists. 'No one inside or outside the party should have the slightest doubt about how seriously I take this issue.'

What irked Gordon Brown's advisers as they prepared the ground for his first party conference as heir apparent was the success of the Conservatives' makeover and the plaudits Cameron was attracting for his efforts to fast-track high-profile women into Parliament. Early hopefuls included the novelist Louise Bagshawe, businesswoman Margot James, television presenter Esther McVey and former Conservative spin doctor Priti Patel. In a blatant repeat of the famous 1997 'Blair's Babes' photo-call with Labour's newly elected women MPs, Cameron posed with his candidates at Westminster, an event which the *Evening Standard* reported with the headline 'Dishy Dave and his Tory dolls'. Others added to the elite list included the *Coronation Street* star Adam Rickitt, the black entrepreneur Wilfred Emmanuel-Jones and the environmentalist Zac Goldsmith. When interviewed on *GMTV* ahead of his speech to Labour delegates in Manchester, Brown was irritated on being asked whether he intended to soften his image once Blair stood down. Stability and security mattered more and he was convinced voters could tell the difference between style and substance: 'I don't claim to be a celebrity. What I do is get on with the job.'

A carefully arranged pre-conference truce between the warring Blair and Brown factions fell apart almost as soon as the Chancellor had completed his keynote address. After declaring that he would 'relish' the chance to take on Cameron, Brown began the party's long goodbye to Blair with his own tribute: 'It has been a privilege for me to work with and for the most successful ever Labour leader and Prime Minister.' Cherie Blair watched the speech on a television monitor just outside the main hall and was overheard saying: 'Well, that's a lie.' Mrs Blair immediately denied having said anything of the sort but Carolin Lotter, a television producer with the American news agency Bloomberg, stuck to her story, which dominated coverage of the speech. 'Cherie rains on Gordon's parade' was the *Daily Mail*'s front-page headline next morning. In his farewell address Tony Blair tried to make light of the spat with a joke at his wife's expense: 'I don't have to worry about her running off with the bloke next door.' His parting shot was aimed over Brown's head to the party at large: 'You're the future now. Make the most of it.' Blair's masterful oratory was contrasted with what many commentators judged was a pedestrian address from Brown and the Prime Minister left Manchester having won the freedom to decide for himself the timing of a final handover.

In the lead-up to that summer's putsch Brown made strenuous efforts to soften his image as a dour Scotsman and convince the public that he was as cuddly, normal and human as Cameron. Giving his first-ever interview to a woman's magazine in May 2006, he offered a glimpse of his private life to Helen Johnston, editor of *New Woman*. She visited his Downing Street flat and found him amiable and relaxed. Brown dodged answering the 'boxers or briefs' question which Martha Kearney put to Cameron and Davis by insisting that he wore 'whatever comes to hand but they're all M&S'. He was a fan of *The X Factor* and his iPod selection included the Beatles, Coldplay and also the Arctic Monkeys (although he subsequently denied having chosen tracks from the Arctic Monkeys). A month later the *Mail on Sunday*'s political editor, Simon Walters, was invited to the Chancellor's flat only to find him in an armchair, 'hunched over the television, nervously watching' England's World Cup match against Trinidad & Tobago. Easily the most eye-catching illustration of a relaxed husband was a family portrait of himself, his wife Sarah and their two sons John and Fraser. Fraser was a month old and the photograph, which was taken by a family friend, Lesley Donald, was reproduced in the form of a card and sent to well-wishers, including Cameron, who was among those who had congratulated the couple on the birth of their second son. Unlike the Tory leader, Brown had gone to great lengths to keep his children out of the public eye and except for a shot of the couple holding Fraser shortly after his birth, this was the first photograph of the enlarged family. Previously aides had advised the media that he would never pose with his children for a photo-shoot; the Chancellor was even heard to mock the Blairs for using family photographs on their Christmas cards.

'Project Gordon' held the key to the transformation: Cameron was being challenged head on in the public relations stakes by the Chancellor's wife, herself an experienced media strategist. She had become the linchpin of a concerted attempt to widen the Chancellor's appeal among women and to ensure he appeared more natural to Middle England. Before their marriage Sarah Macaulay was in partnership with Julia Hobsbawm and their public relations agency, Hobsbawm Macaulay, worked for several causes close to Labour. Under her guidance the Chancellor had smartened up his appearance, swapped crumpled red ties for pastel colours and usually remembered to smile for the cameras. Not to be outdone by the images of Cameron's domestic prowess, he invited Kay Burley of Sky News to follow him around as he discussed his household chores. Brown spoke movingly about the loss in January 2002 of their first baby, Jennifer Jane, who died from complications ten days after birth. Close to tears, he recalled the moment she died in their arms: 'You never come to terms with it . . . you always know there's something missing.'

For all Labour's criticism of Cameron's knack of coming up with slick photo-opportunities, the Conservatives were often much more innovative, able to call on the far greater expertise of their natural allies in the advertising and public relations industries. On the eve of the party conference the *Guardian* was allowed advance access to WebCameron, a website for video blogs by Cameron and guest bloggers. His first webcam showed him washing up in the kitchen while the family ate breakfast. 'Watch out BBC, ITV, Channel 4, we're the new competition.' Cameron wanted to offer 'behind-the-scenes access' so that people had 'a direct link' and could see that politicians were not 'a race apart'. There were glimpses of Samantha, a cradle containing baby Arthur and the sound of constant interruptions from Nancy as her father attempted to present some of the key messages for the conference. He said more work needed to be done on his speech but 'right now, I'm going to wash up the porridge'. Online traffic to WebCameron increased dramatically after two of the Labour MPs who played a central role in the plot to oust Blair hit back on YouTube. Tom Watson posted a homage called 'Watsocam' which showed him doing the washing up while demanding at the same time that Cameron should reveal the identity of secret donors to the Conservative Party. A posting by another of Brown's ardent supporters, the Birmingham MP Siôn Simon, proved so controversial he was forced to remove it from YouTube and issue an apology. 'Yo. My name's Dave, yeah? Thing is, I'm just like you' was the opening line of an Ali G-style spoof. Simon delivered his one-minute parody wearing a baseball cap and T-shirt: 'Want to sleep with my wife? That's cool . . . I got my two kids . . . You like them? Take one . . . My name is Dave. And I'm just like you.' Initially Simon insisted his video was meant to be funny but he beat a hasty retreat after being rebuked by the leader of the Commons, Jack Straw, who called on Labour MPs to avoid personal attacks. Having dented Sarah Brown's efforts to present her husband as a pleasant and relaxed family man in contrast to his reputation at Westminster as a grim political bruiser, the two scheming Brownites back-pedalled on their plan to match Cameron blog by blog and expose him as a 'cardboard-cut-out Tory toff'.

By beginning the countdown to his departure but without giving a date Blair handed Cameron a useful stick with which to beat critics in his party. Journalists thrive on uncertainty, and mounting speculation about what Gordon Brown and his acolytes might do once they had command of Downing Street fuelled comment about the future direction of Conservative policy, especially in the key area of taxation. Cameron's August mission statement disappointed the Tory right because of his refusal to commit himself to the party's traditional tax-cutting agenda; growing friction over future economic policy was singled out by the news media as the most likely issue to provoke confrontation at the annual conference in Bournemouth. Blair's first year as party leader supplied a useful template for political correspondents: if the 'heir to Blair' was to prove he could exercise real authority, he needed a 'Clause IV' moment. A possible dogfight over taxation fitted the bill for the pundits and in turn provided Cameron with an opportunity to insist he was not going to make rash promises which Brown could exploit. 'I'm not going to be pushed around' was his response on *Sunday AM* when Andrew Marr asked him whether he would agree to right-wing demands. 'I'm not going to flash up unfunded tax cuts . . . If people want the old policies back they can't have them . . . We fought elections on upfront tax cuts and lost.'

His conference speech was equally blunt. There were no pain-free solutions and he wanted to offer substance rather than the spin of 'some pie-in-the-sky' tax cuts. Whereas Blair explained his priority in three words, 'education, education, education', Cameron used three letters: 'NHS'. For the first time since its foundation in 1948, the task of maintaining and improving the National Health Service became the Conservatives' overriding commitment to the electorate, a pledge which Cameron reinforced by quoting the experience of his own family in relying on the NHS 'all the time, day after day, night after night'.

Traditionalists were warned there was 'no going back': unless the Conservatives were 'on the side of the next generation' they had no chance of regaining power. The strength of his rejection of homophobia and his backing for gay marriage caught the conference by surprise but nonetheless was greeted with applause. He said a future Conservative government would support civil partnerships because what mattered was commitment, 'whether you're a man and a woman, a woman and a woman or a man and another man'. Labour's efforts to put more money into childcare would be encouraged and as there was also a 'social responsibility' to tackling climate change, if Blair included a bill in his final Queen's Speech to put a price on carbon use, the Conservatives would back it.

While Blairites marvelled at the speed with which Cameron was able to colonise the centre ground of politics without the backlash the pundits had predicted, Brownites were alarmed by the transformation which was taking place and also angered by Blair's failure to give the Chancellor his unequivocal endorsement. Prime Minister's Questions were an opportunity for Cameron to twist the knife. 'Do you back the Chancellor as your successor? Yes or no. I mean, I do; do you?' Blair dodged the question and kept Brown waiting until the Queen's Speech debate the following month before finally giving his blessing. He predicted the next election would be between a flyweight and a heavyweight and, however much Cameron danced around the ring, at 'some point he'll come within the reach of a big clunking fist' and become the fifth Tory leader to be carried out, with 'a fourth-term Labour government still standing'.

Yet more accolades and favourable newspaper reviews greeted the completion of Cameron's first twelve months as leader. He was named the 2006 politician of the year by the Political Studies Association and communicator of the year by *PR Week*, whose editor, Danny Rogers, made a light-hearted reference in Cameron's absence to the debate about 'style over substance'. I detected a sense of collective pride at the awards dinner that the industry was able to honour one of its own although I did hear a few boos from some guests none too pleased that a politician rather than a PR practitioner had scooped the top award. *PR Week* praised the launch of WebCameron for offering 'a new era of transparency' after Blair's 'age of spin' which it thought might help cut through the 'media circus in favour of direct dialogue with the public'. Plaudits from the PR industry only served to draw attention to doubts within the party: PR stunts might have helped make it fashionable once again to be a Conservative but that was no substitute for a clear vision on future policy. Cameron marked the anniversary by promising that in 2007 voters would get a clearer idea of what life would be like under his premiership. 'You're going to hear real grit in terms of how we're going to change this country for the better.' He used a New Year article in the *Daily Telegraph* to reassure his critics that the foundation stones for his alternative government would be built on the enduring ideas which first encouraged him to join the Conservative Party and work for Margaret Thatcher: 'freedom under the law, personal responsibility, sound money, strong defence and national sovereignty'.

Before he could make much progress in delivering a harder edge to the party's policy agenda he was derailed by fresh and embarrassing reminders of life at Eton and Oxford. The *Mail on Sunday* was finally able to deliver a hitherto elusive front-page headline: 'Cameron did smoke cannabis'. A new biography revealed that in 1982, at the age of fifteen, he was involved in Eton's 'worst-ever drugs scandal' when seven boys were expelled, two told to leave at the end of the summer term, and another nine, including Cameron, fined and 'gated' but allowed stay on at school and take their O-levels. His limited response to the story followed the pattern of previous statements: 'I did things when I was young that I shouldn't have done and that I regret. But politicians are entitled to a past that remains private.' Labour's attack dogs were soon off the leash: a 'senior source' was quoted in the *Sunday Times* as saying the incident could not be dismissed as a 'schoolboy prank' because it pointed to 'the same casual, dilettante "anything goes" attitude to drug abuse' that still persisted in Cameron's inner circle. But yet again Labour's spinners had over-reached themselves because ministers and MPs held back from criticism, having no wish to see escapades from their own school days splashed over tabloid front pages. An unexpected ally was the Home Secretary, John Reid, who offered his support for party leaders with a past: politics would not be well served by 'plastic politicians produced off some colourless and characterless conveyor belt'.

Although his reported confession to the headmaster, Eric Anderson, about having smoked the odd spliff at Eton did not provoke the anticipated furore, the same could not be said about one of the photographs reproduced in *Cameron: The Rise of the New Conservative*. In their research for the book, the authors, Francis Elliott and James Hanning, tracked down a 1987 photograph of the Bullingdon Club, an exclusive Oxford University dining society. Standing at the back wearing a wing collar and double-breasted tailcoat was Cameron; seated on a step in the front row was a similarly attired Boris Johnson. Having bought the serialisation rights, the *Mail on Sunday* needed to teach its caption writer no lessons in exploiting Cameron's embarrassment. Readers were reminded that when seeking to become Prime Minister, he liked to be photographed in 'an open-necked shirt discussing the environment or African debt', but when a 21-year-old student at Brasenose College he 'styled himself on the starched Edwardian look made famous by *Brideshead Revisited* and revelled in his cloistered world of champagne-quaffing privilege'.

Elliott and Hanning had unearthed an unforgettable image which encapsulated Cameron's rarefied upbringing and pointed to a lifestyle remote from the average voter. The photograph was widely reproduced before being withdrawn from circulation by the university photographers Gillman and Soame. Newspaper columnists pontificated at length on the activities of the Bullingdon Club, 'a byword for drunkenness and vandalism', and explored the family backgrounds of the ten wealthy students who posed for the picture. Labour's media strategists were convinced the previously unseen image of Cameron in a tailcoat would have a lasting impact and a spokesman was quoted in the *Independent on Sunday* suggesting the party would use the 'now iconic photograph' in a future election poster to show that Cameron and Johnson, resplendent in their wing collars, were 'out of touch with modern Britain'. Political cartoonists were even more relieved than Labour's spin doctors: Cameron was instantly recognisable as a Tory toff in top hat and tails, a caricature to rival Martin Rowson's regular depiction in the *Guardian* of a plump, purple-pantalooned popinjay.

Unwelcome publicity about the antics of the Bullingdon Club was only one of the factors contributing to the effective sidelining of Cameron's policy-driven agenda during the late winter and early spring of 2007. Politicians and journalists were becoming increasingly preoccupied by all manner of permutations for the likely fallout from the looming departure of Blair and his deputy, John Prescott. An eventual handover to Brown was always regarded as a foregone conclusion but the ramifications were unpredictable: would Labour hold a leadership election? Would Brown seek a fresh mandate? Were the opinion polls correct in suggesting that instead of a Brown bounce there might instead be a boost for Cameron? Initially a united front was needed as Labour prepared for the council elections in May. Blair and Brown hit the campaign trail for one last time as Prime Minister and Chancellor but their joint ticket lacked the potency of the 2005 general election and the Conservatives took the spoils, gaining 900 seats on a 40 per cent share of the vote.

Cameron's control over the destiny of his party seemed unshakeable: he was breaking free from Thatcherite dogma, updating Tory values and putting in place a strategy in case Brown decided to go to the country. He was convinced the coming election would be dominated by quality-of-life issues. 'The great challenge for the 1970s and 1980s was economic revival. The great challenge in this decade and the next is social revival.' Labour continued to ridicule his argument that there was 'more to life than money'; that general well-being mattered as much as gross domestic product. In a parting shot at the inherited wealth of Cameron and George Osborne, Blair dismissed their 'sunshine' agenda by reminding them that it was easier to say 'happiness is more important than money if money is not a problem'.

Within days of Labour's drubbing in the council elections Blair responded to the pent-up anger of Brown's supporters by finally honouring his promise to give a date for his departure: he would step down at the end of June, giving the party seven weeks to elect a new leader and deputy. His announcement marked the start of a tumultuous summer at Westminster. A sea wall had been breached on a high tide of economic growth and an unstoppable flood of unprecedented events was about to sweep away the widely shared political expectations for the post-Blair era. Cameron's uninterrupted advance would be checked and then thrown into reverse as Labour's opinion poll ratings recovered. His well-honed pitch as an affable, regular guy would also prove no match for the gravitas of Brown once the former Chancellor was able to play to his strengths during a summer of unexpected crises. Before the year was out a financial tsunami would begin to threaten and then start to demolish the very foundations of the policies which Cameron had campaigned for during his bid for the leadership and which he then persuaded the party to adopt. Ultimately much of his original election strategy would be turned on its head as the certainties which he had relied upon began to crumble and politicians were forced to apply their minds to saving money rather than spending it.

Labour's upward trajectory in the opinion polls during the summer of 2007 was kick-started by the Conservatives' worst internal dissent since Cameron took power. A partial retreat was required before he was able to patch up his differences with MPs angered by the apparent ditching of the party's long-standing faith in the superiority of grammar schools. Although he had already reiterated the established line that the party was no longer committed to opening new grammars, there was alarm in local authorities which retained selective education after the shadow Education Secretary, David Willetts, declared that 'academic selection entrenches advantage, it does not spread it'. Tory MPs from the shires, already concerned by Cameron's support for city academies, feared that existing selective schools might be threatened. When the shadow Europe minister Graham Brady persisted in publishing data which showed that 'selection raises standards for everyone' he was reprimanded by the chief whip but he resigned rather than face the prospect of being sacked in Cameron's first shadow cabinet reshuffle. Unrest among Tory MPs and continuing campaigning by grassroots activists in favour of the 11-plus provoked news reports suggesting that Cameron would relish the chance to take on right-wing rebels in another 'Clause IV' confrontation. In his opinion they were being 'delusional' in thinking a future Conservative government would build more grammars when for far too long nostalgia about the benefits of the 11-plus had been 'a chain around our necks'. Nonetheless he was forced to accept that new grammar schools might have to be built in areas which retained selection. In a BBC interview, he acknowledged events had not been 'as smooth' as he would have liked but he was sure that when the 'smoke clears' the party would understand why he was not prepared to 'flinch or stop making' the changes needed to keep the Conservatives on the centre ground.

Presenting a united front was a priority for Cameron the closer it got to the special conference to announce the result of Labour's leadership elections. Brown's only challenger, the MP John McDonnell, failed to attract sufficient nominations for a contest; Harriet Harman beat Alan Johnson by the narrowest of margins to become the new deputy. Blair brandished his P45 at his final session of Prime Minister's Questions and bowed out with the words: 'I wish everyone, friend or foe, well, and that is that. The end.' He was given an unprecedented two-minute standing ovation which Conservative MPs were urged to join after Cameron praised him for his 'huge efforts in terms of public service'. Blair's handover of power was the moment Cameron had been waiting for, a chance to galvanise the party behind his leadership in preparation for what he feared would be an inevitable Brown bounce.

Aides recognised that the bruising dispute over grammar schools was a reminder that the support of the parliamentary party could not always be taken for granted but they had not expected that on the eve of assuming office the new Prime Minister would be able to welcome the defection to Labour of Quentin Davies, a pro-Europe Tory MP of twenty years' standing. Davies had found himself increasingly in agreement with

Labour's policies; Brown was a leader with a 'towering record' whose 'clear vision' for the future was one he shared and wished to follow. By contrast he thought the Conservatives had ceased 'collectively to believe in anything'; Cameron had replaced a sense of mission with a public relations agenda which demonstrated his 'superficiality, unreliability and an apparent lack of any clear convictions'. Another backbencher was equally disenchanted: Ann Winterton told the *Parliamentary Monitor* that grassroots supporters were 'baffled' by the row over whether the party's traditional support for grammar schools had been abandoned. Willetts paid a heavy price for the confusion and in a summer reshuffle he was moved from education to become shadow spokesman on universities.

Cameron's misfortunes were multiplying: high-profile campaigns during July in two critical by-elections ended disastrously for the Conservatives, provoking a fresh round of recriminations. In the hope of snatching victory, he visited Ealing Southall five times and was unstinting in support of the Sikh candidate Tony Lit, who had been hand picked for the constituency and who in a controversial move was listed on the ballot paper as representing 'David Cameron's Conservative Party'. Labour held the seat with ease, finishing well ahead of the Liberal Democrats; the Conservatives remained stuck in third place. In Sedgefield, although they were never likely to take Blair's former constituency, the Conservatives fell from second to third place, rounding off a dismal performance. Having failed to achieve the breakthrough in the by-elections which he so desperately needed, Cameron faced a mini-rebellion and some dreadful headlines. 'Could Cameron turn out to be the Tories' Kinnock?' was the question posed by Andrew Rawnsley in the *Observer*. Melissa Kite led the *Sunday Telegraph*'s coverage with the ominous claim that 'up to half a dozen' Conservative MPs had lodged formal requests for a vote of no confidence in Cameron's leadership. Undaunted by the criticism, he donned a pair of wellington boots to visit homes in his constituency threatened by summer floods. He told Sky News there would be 'no retreat to the comfort zone' of failed policies which would take the Conservatives away from the centre ground of

British politics. That evening, despite evident unease within the party, he flew to Rwanda to join a dozen Conservative volunteers who were helping to repair and refurbish an orphanage, the kind of initiative which he believed Britain had a 'moral imperative' to support. Cameron was in a no-win situation: pulling out of a long-planned aid project would have led to questions about the depth of his commitment towards assisting developing countries but he left behind an impatient party, a country inundated with floodwaters after unprecedented summer rainfall, and a new Prime Minister motoring ahead in the opinion polls.

Another round of unforgiving headlines reflected the shift which had taken place in the media's narrative. Cameron's hitherto easy ride was due in part to the role which he had been assigned in helping to fuel the Blair–Brown feud but that was yesterday's news. Instead of continuing to give him the benefit of the doubt, which suited the previous story line, journalists were falling over themselves to indulge Brown and extend him a political honeymoon. Conservative campaign headquarters were caught on the hop by the sudden switch from being praised to being pilloried. 'Sham Cam' was the *News of the World*'s send-off for the Rwanda trip. His 'hug-an-orphan stunt' was said to take some beating even for a party leader so addicted to photo-opportunities; was it time he was renamed 'Camera On?' There could hardly have been a greater contrast between the criticism heaped on Cameron's head for his 'In and Out of Africa' flying visit and the blitz of favourable headlines which greeted his announcement within weeks of becoming leader that Bob Geldof, champion of the Make Poverty History campaign, had been appointed a consultant to the Conservatives' policy group on global poverty. If it had not been for the summer floods, the headline writers and columnists might not have hit the target with such ease: 'So where's the Rt Hon. member for washed-out Witney?' asked the *Daily Mail*'s front page. Trevor Kavanagh was so disheartened he predicted in the *Sun* that Brown could 'win big' at the next election because after eighteen months of Cameron's 'promising leadership, the party is once more dead in the water'.

The Conservatives' calculation that the country might turn against an unelected Prime Minister who had seized power as a result of a Labour coup was proving to be a non-starter. Within days of the handover Brown was able to project himself in a way no one had quite predicted. A series of national emergencies, which began with two daring attempted terrorist attacks, in central London and at Glasgow airport, gave him the opportunity to assume a commanding position. When unexpected events speak for themselves, and an authoritative Prime Minister has seized control of the news agenda, there is no need for a spin doctor. Brown's own innate understanding of how to influence news reporting, and his agility in meeting the media's deadlines, allowed him to discard the political baggage of the past and begin reinventing himself in the eyes of the public. Having contributed so much to the clamour for a change of Prime Minister, journalists were almost duty bound to give him every encouragement.

Brown the 'action man' co-ordinating help for the flood victims of Gloucestershire was the theme of a report by the BBC's political editor, Nick Robinson, who was billed as having been given 'exclusive access to the Prime Minister'. The *Sun* was awarded the same preferential treatment, gaining the 'first newspaper interview' with Britain's new 'workaholic' premier. Within four hours of his arrival in Dorset, Downing Street told journalists that he would abandon his family's summer holiday next morning and return to London to deal with an outbreak of foot and mouth disease at a farm in Surrey. Every day there was news of the Prime Minister chairing another session of the government's emergency committee. Brown was on camera yet again after the murder in mid-August of the eleven-year-old Liverpool schoolboy Rhys Jones, said to have been Merseyside's youngest-ever victim of gun crime. Whoever was responsible would be tracked down and punished for 'a heinous crime that shocked the whole country'. However adverse the circumstances the Prime Minister took them in his stride and his sombre, matter-of-fact appearances on television, and his serious turn of phrase, complemented his hands-on approach.

Ever the political street fighter, Brown still had time for some point scoring; he knew precisely how to upstage his opponents and get true Thatcherites grinding their teeth in resentment at Cameron's smug line about having successfully detoxified the Tory brand. In mid-September, in a pre-conference display of mischief, he posed at the front door of 10 Downing Street with Lady Thatcher, who was about to be ushered in for tea with the family. She had written a letter of congratulation to the new Prime Minister and he responded by inviting her to meet Sarah and their two boys, John and Fraser, who reportedly played with toy cars which she had bought for them in Hamleys. A return to her old haunt, the first such visit for seven years, was a moment to be savoured at the age of eighty-one. Wearing a striking cerise dress rather than her usual blue, she displayed no inhibitions about standing next to a Labour premier who as a shadow minister had regularly sought to hound the Conservatives and damage her government. Journalists were reminded that shortly after becoming Tory leader Cameron turned down a chance to be photographed with her.

Labour's recovery in the opinion polls began immediately Blair handed over power. After his first week in office a poll of polls for the *Independent* indicated that a Brown bounce had wiped out the solid lead which the Conservatives had enjoyed for the previous fifteen months. An uninterrupted surge in support constituted what the *Guardian* said was 'a dream start' and by mid-August the *Sunday Times* was reporting that a YouGov poll had recorded a ten-point Labour lead, the highest since November 2002, well before the start of the Iraq War. Runaway speculation that Brown would seize the moment and seek a fresh mandate was encouraged by Downing Street briefings. In their off-the-record guidance to journalists, three of Brown's closest cabinet colleagues, Ed Balls, Douglas Alexander and Ed Miliband, did little to hide their enthusiasm and delight at the prospect of a snap election and a possible fourth election victory. But the spin was running well ahead of the Prime Minister and he was on the point of becoming a victim of his own success that summer in having turned a series of calamitous events to Labour's advantage. Public opinion was about to prove as fickle as the weather. Storm warnings of turbulence in the financial markets were upgraded to hurricane level after an emergency Bank of England loan to keep Northern Rock afloat failed to reassure panicking customers, who queued up in their thousands to empty their savings accounts. Calm was only restored after a series of unprecedented measures: Northern Rock's deposits were guaranteed by the government; the Treasury agreed to act as a guarantor for other lenders in difficulty; and, in a surprise U-turn, the Bank of England offered to pump £10 billion of emergency funding into the money markets.

Initially public anger at the scale of the crisis led to volatility in the opinion polls, reflecting also the squeeze on family finances after five interest rate rises within a year and higher energy costs and food prices. Nonetheless Brown was able to argue that his decisive action had worked: 'It is because of the strength of our economy that we have been able to take these measures.' Labour's lead in the polls stabilised and then recovered as a result of positive coverage following his first appearance as Prime Minister at the party's annual conference in Bournemouth. In what some commentators considered was one of Brown's least partisan speeches, he did all he could to court middle England by declaring he would 'stand up for British values' so as to create a Britain where there was 'no longer any ceiling on where your talents and hard work can take you'. He developed his theme of promoting 'Britishness' by giving an unexpected pledge that his government would be 'drawing on the talents of all to create British jobs for British workers'. He was a 'conviction politician' and his 'moral compass' would hold firm to the words of his father, a minister of the church, who had preached that 'we must be givers as well as takers'. Brown promised that mothers would get more paid maternity leave and children free education between the ages of three and eighteen, plus college grants for poorer youngsters. 'So this is my pledge to the British people: I will not let you down.' Next morning, Peter Mandelson, visiting the conference in his role as European Union trade commissioner, told *Today* that the Prime Minister had positioned the government firmly in the centre ground, in his 'own style, but under the New Labour handbook'. The fissure over the leadership was behind them: 'Brown has taken the Blair big tent and thrown it wide open.' Among delegates there was a buzz of speculation about a possible snap election, an option on which Brown refused to be drawn. During a round of interviews he stuck steadfastly to the line that he was intent only on 'getting on with the job . . . my focus is entirely on the issues which affect the country'.

Lord Kinnock raised one of the few Labour voices ruling out an autumn poll: 'Brown's instinct is not to go for a snap election . . . there is not going to be an election in 2007.' His confident prediction on *Today* did little to reassure Conservatives arriving for their annual conference in Blackpool. Their sense that an election was imminent was reinforced by dire results in weekend opinion polls. Labour led by ten points according to Populus in *The Times*. In his commentary for a YouGov survey for the *Daily Telegraph*, Professor Anthony King said voters regarded Cameron as 'well meaning but ineffectual and politically inept . . . as glib and insubstantial as Tony Blair'. Journalists were keen to stir up a sense of crisis: Cameron's authority was on the line and that meant he would have to deliver another make-or-break speech. 'Mission impossible' was the *Sun*'s assessment of the daunting task he faced in trying to turn around his 'ailing party' in time to head off a Labour 'rout' if Brown decided to opt for a November election. Initially all eyes were on George Osborne, the shadow Chancellor, as the party waited to hear evidence of the new policies which the leadership had promised in support of their 'summer heat on Brown' campaign. Osborne's initial response to the run on Northern Rock failed to impress business commentators, who said that he and Cameron looked lightweight and inexperienced against Brown and the Chancellor, Alistair Darling. Financial journalists on the *Guardian* told me Osborne's office was caught off guard and was next to 'useless' during the first couple of days of the crisis when television footage of British people queuing for their money went round the world.

However, when it came to economic policy, Osborne had kept his word and an exclusive report in mid-August by the BBC's economics editor, Evan Davis, gave a hint of the first tax cuts of Cameron's leadership. Abolition of inheritance tax and a lower stamp duty for house buyers were two of the options which Davis claimed were being given the highest priority. Although only 6 per cent of estates were affected, the shadow Chancellor was said to be sure he was on to an election winner, as inheritance tax was the 'most hated among voters because it was disproportionately worrying for families whose main asset was their home'. On the eve of the party conference, Nick Robinson revealed that Osborne intended to promise that a future Conservative government would increase the threshold for inheritance tax and recoup the lost income through a new charge to be levied on non-domiciled residents. Osborne trailed his own announcements on *Today* next morning: by increasing the threshold to £1 million, 98 per cent of family homes would be taken out of inheritance tax altogether; people who registered for non-domiciled status would pay an annual levy of £25,000 on their untaxed offshore income; and by raising the threshold to £250,000, nine out of ten first-time home buyers would be taken out of stamp duty. Osborne's dramatic embrace of the party's traditional tax-cutting agenda electrified the conference. 'Not for nothing was he cheered to the creaking rafters of the Winter Gardens,' said the London *Evening Standard*'s city editor, Chris Blackhurst.

Cameron relished the advanced billing for his own 'speech of a lifetime': he spoke without a script for sixty-seven minutes, his off-the-cuff delivery designed to recapture the passion of the address which he gave on the same stage in 2005 and which helped clinch the leadership. Flourishing four sheets of handwritten notes, which listed his bullet points and key phrases, he did his best to put party representatives at their ease. 'I haven't got an autocue and I haven't got a script . . . so it might be a bit messy, but it will be me.' By memorising his speech he hoped to demonstrate spontaneity and sincerity, a technique which *The Times* said Cameron had seen used with great effect by the former shadow health secretary Ann Widdecombe when she won over activists at the

1998 conference by 'delivering her speech striding around the stage'. Cameron's vow to promote marriage and help wives who gave up work to raise their children attracted the biggest cheer. 'The family is the best welfare system of all.' After widespread acclaim for Osborne's audacious pledge on inheritance tax and stamp duty, Cameron had no hesitation in taunting the Prime Minister: 'So, Mr Brown, what's it going to be? Why don't you go ahead and call that election?' For next morning's newspapers the unanswered question was whether the Conservatives would bounce back in the opinion polls. The *Daily Telegraph* was sure Cameron had 'done enough' to deter Brown from calling a snap election; the *Sun*'s verdict was that Brown was likely to 'think twice' about going to the country because winning a snap election seemed 'mission very possible' for the Tories.

Brown did his best to keep the Conservatives off the front pages during the first two days of their conference. He made a surprise visit to Iraq, where he gave a pledge that 1,000 British troops would be home by Christmas, pre-empting a statement which he had promised to the House of Commons and opening himself up to the accusation that he was playing politics with the armed forces. Although irritated by what they considered was a blatant attempt to upstage the speeches of Osborne and Cameron, Tory strategists were convinced their announcement on inheritance tax would probably succeed in torpedoing Labour's talk of an early election. Brown had three days in which to make up his mind and the countdown was played out step by step through the news media. Opinion polls, press comment and television news programmes assumed pivotal roles in a drama which exposed the Prime Minister as a ditherer, a charge which his opponents would ruthlessly exploit.

Within twenty-four hours of Cameron's speech closing the Conservative conference on Wednesday afternoon, a YouGov opinion poll for *Channel 4 News* indicated that Labour's lead had been cut from eleven points to four, enough to get the government re-elected but with a much reduced majority. Unnamed ministers were quoted by the programme's political correspondent Cathy Newman as saying a four-point margin looked 'very scary, too risky'. But the *Guardian*'s columnist Jackie Ashley put a counter-view: Labour were 'so geared up' for an election, Brown could not ignore the momentum and would find it difficult to wait. She told *Today* that Labour were still likely to win by a margin of thirty to forty seats, which was 'not a bad working majority', and if Brown left it a year the Conservatives would be able to step up their campaigning in the marginal constituencies.

Two more polls on Friday morning confirmed the trend: a Populus poll in *The Times* suggested the Conservatives had narrowed Labour's lead to three points and an ICM poll for the *Guardian* put them neck and neck on 38 per cent. Brown had boxed himself in because a decision had to be taken that Sunday if an election was to go ahead on either 1 or 8 November, which Labour strategists thought were the last possible dates before the onset of winter. To keep up the pressure Cameron asked the Prime Minister to authorise civil servants to start pre-election meetings with members of the shadow cabinet so they could discuss issues like inheritance tax and prepare for the introduction of new policies by a new government. Osborne tried a different tack: either Brown called an election which the Conservatives have got 'a good chance of winning – or he bottles it'. By Friday evening there was no going back: editors and political correspondents on Sunday newspapers were told that early on Saturday afternoon Brown would pre-record an interview with Andrew Marr for transmission next morning on the BBC; transcripts would be issued after the recording.

Once Brown's aides confirmed to journalists that the Prime Minister had abandoned the idea of a November election the news spread like wildfire. During a gap in a rugby commentary, Nick Robinson told listeners to Radio 5 Live that the election was off; word soon reached Conservative campaign headquarters and the Tory blogosphere buzzed with jibes about 'bottler Brown'. In a clip from Marr's interview broadcast later that afternoon on the *PM* programme, the Prime Minister insisted Labour would have won an election 'today, next week or the week after' but he wanted to be judged on his long-term competence.

'I want a chance to show the country that we have a vision for the future of this country . . . I want a mandate to show the vision of the country that I have is being implemented in practice.' By giving an exclusive interview to Marr rather than hold a news conference open to all journalists or offer a pooled interview available to all news outlets, the Prime Minister had fallen into the trap of trying to divide and rule the media, a costly mistake when a politician's reputation is at stake. Brown's hole-in-the-corner approach angered broadcasters such as ITN and Sky News; rival television crews assembled in Downing Street just in case the Prime Minister appeared at the No. 10 front door; and more critically the pre-recording of his interview gave Cameron ample opportunity to record his reaction in good time for the early evening news bulletins. In response to questions from Sky News, he accused Brown of 'trying to spin himself into an election' and then in an act of 'great weakness and indecision' head for the exit. 'This is not a vision for change but a strategy to cling to office.' Brown's miscalculation in allowing Cameron the chance to launch a point-by-point demolition even before the BBC had broadcast Marr's interview was compounded by the fact that by timing the announcement for Saturday afternoon he gave the Sunday newspapers ample time to prepare in-depth coverage and put the boot in. 'Brown bottles it' was the *Mail on Sunday*'s all-too-predictable front-page headline. The *News of the World* claimed the election was scrapped after its political editor, Ian Kirby, informed the Prime Minister that an ICM opinion poll in key marginal constituencies suggested that forty-nine Labour MPs would lose their seats. An election U-turn was a gift for the *Sun*'s headline writers: 'He's in the brown stuff'.

By leaving his decision until the last possible moment Brown turned his eventual retreat into a public relations disaster. Instead of having the foresight to rein in the ministers and aides who were busily talking up Labour's prospects in the weeks leading up to the party conference, he reinforced the spin by taunting the Conservatives, ignoring the danger that the speculation might go too far, that he was needlessly limiting his own room for manoeuvre, and that by letting expectations rip, he would make it all the harder for Labour MPs, party officials and activists should he ultimately rule out an early election. 'Loose talk' among Brown's aides was largely to blame in the view of Matthew Taylor, formerly Tony Blair's head of policy in Downing Street. In his interview for *The Andrew Marr Show*, Brown stressed that he did take account of what he had been told by those in the party who wanted a November election but in the end he felt the priority for the public was that he 'got on with the job'. An insight into the cost to the party of the Prime Minister's indecision emerged in 2010. Peter Watt, Labour's former general secretary, revealed in his book *Inside Out* that the party ran up a bill of £1.2 million preparing for the election that never was. Because of the Prime Minister's refusal to end the pretence that he might still go to the country, Watt had to wait until the final announcement before he could release a fleet of cars which had been kept idling in Westminster that Saturday morning just in case ministers had to be taken round the country on campaign visits.

Brown's ignominious retreat was a prize scalp for the Conservatives, not least for George Osborne, whose pledge to raise the threshold for inheritance tax triggered the all-important boost in Tory support, a surge which opinion polls continued to reflect. When asked on *PM* whether his announcement was simply a ploy to derail Labour, the shadow Chancellor denied that he was forced to make a premature announcement simply because the Conservatives feared a possible election. 'I would have introduced inheritance tax at the conference. Hand on heart; I would have done it anyway.' Nonetheless Osborne was desperate to restore Tory morale and do what he could to ease a crisis of confidence in the leadership. By playing one of the potential aces in the Conservatives' pack of electoral goodies, the shadow Chancellor trumped Brown but his gamble highlighted the underlying weakness of their position. Cameron was close to completing two years in office and the events of the summer had demonstrated all too clearly his shaky hold on the party. The row over grammar schools was an illustration of his uneasy relationship with shire Tories; slow progress was being made in persuading constituency associations to select women and candidates from ethnic minorities; and the volatility in the opinion polls was a constant reminder that their own on–off revival was in large part due to voters' dissatisfaction with Labour rather than clamour for a Conservative government.

Cameron's second year in office had also revealed his vulnerability when trying to cope with the fickleness of the news media. Policy initiatives and carefully crafted photo-opportunities were just as likely to be ridiculed as treated positively. Politicians expect a love/hate relationship with journalists but Conservative campaign headquarters lacked the forward thinking which had benefited Blair after he was elected Labour leader. Through the combined efforts of Peter Mandelson and Alastair Campbell, Blair was able to rely on a media regime which helped to orchestrate favourable coverage in sympathetic news outlets and, more importantly, which ensured at least a degree of advance warning of the publication of hostile stories.

When explaining why he pulled back from a snap election, Brown was clearly anxious not to close off the option of going to the country in 2009, but in similar circumstances Jim Callaghan and John Major both hung on to complete a full parliamentary term and their record in office suggested that in all likelihood the Prime Minister would wait until 2010. Brown had given Cameron the precious gift of time, at least a year and most probably up to two and a half, in which to get to grips with the many fault lines which the summer had exposed. One priority was to take another leaf from the New Labour handbook and work out how to get greater leverage over the way the policies of a rebranded Conservative Party were being presented to the public while at the same time securing at least a degree of protection from the worst excesses of the news media.

5
MURDOCH SWITCHES

When steeling himself and his party for the long march to a general election which Gordon Brown seemed most likely to hold in the spring of 2010, David Cameron needed above all to establish a more stable relationship with the news media. The Prime Minister's extended honeymoon grappling with a summer of emergencies had done wonders for Labour's morale at the party's 2007 annual conference. Confusion over Conservative policy towards grammar schools, together with a series of similar presentational mishaps, had triggered the first serious questioning of Cameron's competence as leader, which only began to subside after Brown abandoned talk of an autumn election. Tory strategists were alarmed by the fragility of Cameron's lead in the opinion polls and the speed with which hitherto friendly political commentators had turned against him. A worrying degree of uncertainty as to how journalists might respond sapped the confidence of staff at Conservative campaign headquarters and hampered their future planning. They lacked contacts in the wider media fraternity and had little expertise in understanding how to exploit populist campaigns in the tabloid press or how to avoid getting ensnared in damaging story lines. A network of sympathisers with eyes and ears in the right places can provide a political party with at least a degree of advance warning of potentially hostile coverage.

Cameron's aides and advisers were well plugged into new media: the Tory blogosphere was thriving, dwarfing the offerings of Labour activists. But despite the steady rise in the internet's influence on political discourse, established news outlets remained the dominant force in setting the agenda. Much of the traffic to blogs, Twitter and social networking sites was a response to the stories in the daily papers or the latest twists and turns broadcast on radio and television. On occasion the online world of citizen journalism called the shots but more often than not it was the banner headlines of the press rather than the web which retained the clout to transform internet chatter into mainstream news. Bloggers and the twitterati liked to deride the importance of old media but newspapers and not websites had the money to buy up exclusive stories or commission opinion polls and it was their executives who were about to be subjected to a calculated charm offensive by Cameron and his closest aides.

Tony Blair's landslide victory in the 1997 general election became a certainty once he succeeded in turning the media juggernaut in his favour. Three previous Tory leaders failed abysmally in their attempts to win a sympathetic hearing but Cameron was different. His entire career had been spent at the interface of politics and the media and the challenge for an avid student of the New Labour phenomenon was to see if he could get the media supertanker to change course once again. Blair had bequeathed him a set of charts but was Cameron prepared to make the compromises which might be required in return for the kind of patronage which could help sway the electorate?

New Labour's initial strength was undoubtedly due in large part to a critical realignment in the editorial sympathies and commercial interests of the communications industry. With the help and guidance of media-savvy aides and advisers, Blair succeeded in the mid-1990s in decoupling the Conservatives from many of their natural allies in newspapers, broadcasting, advertising and public relations. His achievement was all the more remarkable given the inherent weakness of being in opposition and the ongoing ability of the government of the day to command the news agenda. Once in office, New Labour's increasing rapport with journalists and editors was reinforced with a business-friendly approach towards the needs of media proprietors. Labour's long-standing commitments towards attempting to increase media diversity by tackling abuses within the sector were quietly dropped; Blair was ready to turn a blind eye to continuing complaints about the predatory pricing of newspapers and the dangers of increased cross-media ownership between press and television. Instead of seeking to interfere and curb the freedom of the owners, New Labour was laissez-faire: the newspaper industry was left unhindered to police its own editorial standards and behaviour through a system of self-regulation administered by the Press Complaints Commission. Public service broadcasting enjoyed similar freedom and the expansionist plans of the BBC's director general, John Birt, were backed with healthy increases in the licence fee. Having found New Labour a friend rather than a foe, the communications industry was only too happy to reciprocate.

What Blair's media strategists wanted more than anything was a better understanding of, and if possible direct access to, the inside track of the decision-making processes of the news industry's major players. Advance warning of likely story lines in evening news bulletins or the next day's newspapers is invaluable when planning how to promote a political party. Unless they can predict how the media are likely to react, campaign managers are at the mercy of the 24-hour news cycle, unable to plan events and policy launches to their leader's best advantage. While few journalists would admit to willingly relinquishing an element of surprise by alerting a political party to the potential top line of a story, the reality is different. I certainly experienced a fundamental shift in attitudes during my thirty-year career as a BBC correspondent. In the 1970s, well before the advent of rolling news, when there were far fewer bulletins and programmes, a political speech or event would be reported when it happened; reaction would be covered in subsequent reports; responses would rarely if ever be sought in advance. With the rapid expansion in radio and television output during the 1980s, and the growth in the number of news bulletins and current affairs programmes, Labour strategists saw a chance to develop a mutually beneficial two-way trade. Editors and producers needed more exclusive interviews, faster access to information and operational guidance on what was being planned; in return a political party could demand an advance briefing on the direction and content of future coverage.

Peter Mandelson was the first political tactician to apply systematic pressure on broadcasters. When responding to competing bids from radio and television programmes, he had the authority to determine which Labour politician would be offered for interview. His pivotal role under Neil Kinnock and later Tony Blair strengthened the party's hand when BBC journalists were asked before transmission to reveal the way events were likely to be reported. Mandelson's writ was exercised over the years with even greater rigour by Alastair Campbell, Charlie Whelan, David Hill and a succession of key personnel in New Labour's increasingly sophisticated media operation. At the peak of their influence the party's spin doctors had unprecedented access: they would be able to extract information about the day's running order, the angle to be taken in reporting speeches and events, and even the names of the correspondents being assigned to the top stories of the day. While day-to-day detail was always important, advance notice of hostile stories was what mattered most of all. Rapid rebuttal was a key weapon in the armoury of the New Labour spin machine and the aim was always to try to neutralise damaging revelations, ideally even before a story had been broadcast. Critical newspaper reports would be rubbished; the relevance and accuracy of facts and quotations would be questioned; and the work of troublesome correspondents would be deemed 'unreliable', a label which New Labour's media czars had no hesitation applying to some of my 'unhelpful' reporting.

Given the flexible political affiliations of the national press, once Blair had won the sympathy of the leading proprietors the editorial line tended to follow suit. No newly elected government can expect anything other than a brief honeymoon. Laudatory coverage during the first few months in office inevitably becomes more critical but Blair, like Margaret Thatcher before him, continued to enjoy a benign relationship which lasted far longer than that afforded to Jim Callaghan, John Major or Gordon Brown. Powerful new administrations need to be nurtured and at critical moments the greatest favour which a newspaper can extend is to play down or perhaps even ignore damaging stories. When embarrassing revelations are in the offing, and there is the possibility of getting favours in return, friendly journalists will often alert their political contacts to what is afoot and perhaps even breach news embargoes in order to give party officials and ministerial advisers much-needed time to limit or even forestall negative publicity. If established news outlets do not rate certain stories, their lack of interest can then be used by spin doctors to browbeat broadcasters who are warned they are in danger of being duped into running a 'non-story', a common refrain once Mandelson and his acolytes managed to breach the BBC's editorial defences in their attempts to persuade producers to drop damaging items.

Cameron had first-hand experience of the devastating consequences for Major's government of New Labour's superiority in manipulating journalists. Although he said repeatedly he deprecated the ruthlessness of Campbell's regime in Downing Street, he knew that in a media-saturated age he had no alternative but to follow Blair's template for wooing key players in the communications industry. Campbell's network of insiders was impressive but he and Mandelson had nothing like the hold over the national press which had been exercised on Thatcher's behalf by advisers such as Bernard Ingham, Gordon Reece and Tim Bell. The days of their legendary influence over what then constituted Fleet Street were but a distant memory for Cameron and his colleagues and if they were to stand any chance of establishing and then maintaining a substantial lead in the opinion polls, the Conservative Party needed an enhanced level of protection from the media firestorms which proved so debilitating in the summer of 2007. After suffering the indignity of having the line 'hug a hoodie' written into his speech and then hung round his neck by Labour's spin machine, Cameron realised that if he was to enjoy anything like the support and loyalty which so many journalists initially offered Blair, then he had to immerse himself in the murky world of media manipulation. Only by cultivating proprietors, editors, commentators and correspondents did he stand any chance of establishing an all-important early warning system.

In the run-up to the 1997 general election, Mandelson and Campbell helped to design and install what to all intents and purposes was a media firewall around Blair, a line of defences which they hoped would detect and repel news stories which might threaten him. New Labour's well-oiled relationship required constant care and attention. In return for the favourable treatment which Blair was receiving there had to be a payback. Rather like the protection money collected by the mafia, politicians have a price to pay; media barons expect a sympathetic hearing and hopefully preferential treatment if their interests are at stake. Blair's persistence in wooing Rupert Murdoch has been well chronicled over the years. Nonetheless, bearing in mind the political promiscuity of the proprietors, Labour's ability to retain the support of Murdoch's British newspapers during three general election campaigns was a remarkable feat and a reflection of the close personal interest which Blair maintained in the fortunes of media companies. Researchers had to wait until October 2008, long after his departure from Downing Street, before obtaining two rare insights into the true extent of the day-to-day co-operation between a British Prime Minister and an American media tycoon. As a result of an application under the Freedom of Information Act, the Cabinet Office finally released a note of a discussion held in Downing Street in January 1998 when Murdoch met Blair in the presence of three advisers, Campbell, Jonathan Powell and James Purnell. Murdoch complained that a long-running European Commission investigation was delaying a new interactive digital satellite service which had already been cleared by the UK's regulators and in which Sky Television had invested £800 million. Blair said he was 'instinctively sympathetic' to what Murdoch was aiming to achieve and the government believed it was 'important that the UK remained at the cutting edge' in the kind of media products which Sky was developing. After the meeting officials were instructed to look into the situation 'ASAP' and give advice on tactics to get round the 'stumbling block' in the EU. The second disclosure related to a telephone call in July 2002, eight months before Britain joined the American-led invasion of Iraq. Murdoch gave Blair a rundown on his attempt to launch a Sky-like channel in Italy and then reassured the Prime Minister that there would be no wavering by the *Sun* in its backing for American and British action to deal with Saddam Hussein's weapons of mass destruction. The last sentence of the note revealed that Murdoch had given Blair an explicit pledge: 'He praised the Prime Minister for his position on Iraq and said that his newspapers would strongly support the government on Iraq and foreign policy.' Documentary evidence of the Prime Minister's conversations with Murdoch confirmed what most political observers believed was the case: Blair, like Thatcher, knew that at critical moments he could rely on the loyalty of the *Sun*, the country's largest-selling daily newspaper.

Cameron was no stranger to the discreet hard bargaining which can take place between ministers and business leaders. He attended such meetings during his time as a special adviser in John Major's government and then sat on the other side of the table when he became head of corporate affairs for Carlton Television and accompanied the chairman, Michael Green, during negotiations affecting the broadcasting sector. Carlton was in competition with Sky and as an industry insider he would have watched with fascination and perhaps a degree of trepidation once rumours began to circulate early in 1997 that Murdoch had given up on the Major administration and was about to switch his allegiance from the Conservatives to Labour. By rejecting the possibility that a future government which he led might try to curb the power of media conglomerates, Blair convinced Murdoch that New Labour posed no threat. Cameron would have observed and taken on board the shift which had taken place under Blair: a political party which seeks an accommodation with media companies has to make sure that it has a policy agenda which appeals to the industry. Although Blair's repositioning would almost certainly have had implications for the future activities of Carlton Television, Cameron was more concerned by the prospect of an imminent switch in the editorial stance of Murdoch's newspapers because his own political future was on the line. Having been adopted the previous year as the parliamentary candidate for the new constituency of Stafford, he was preparing to fight his first general election.

Six weeks before polling day a newspaper front-page headline became a news item in itself: 'The *Sun* backs Blair – give change a chance'. Murdoch's backing was the breakthrough which Alastair Campbell had worked tirelessly to achieve and the endorsement of Blair was an historic moment in Labour's troubled relationship with the tabloid press. Campbell believed the *Sun*'s vilification of Neil Kinnock contributed to Labour's defeat in the 1992 general election; he was convinced that unless its right-wing opinions could be neutralised and hopefully turned to the party's advantage, Blair remained vulnerable to hostile coverage. Sales of Murdoch's four titles – *The Times*, the *Sunday Times*, the *Sun* and the *News of the World* – commanded 42 per cent of the national newspaper market, a far larger share than any competitor and a weight of editorial opinion which no political party could afford to ignore.

After he became party leader, when thinking through possible Tory tactics to woo Murdoch, Cameron and his contemporaries would have had their own vivid memories of the alarm and despondency within the Conservative Party once the *Sun* started idolising Blair in the way that it had previously glorified Thatcher. A glance at newspaper front pages on polling day in 1997 would not have been an encouraging experience for candidate Cameron as he prepared to face the voters of Stafford. A colour photograph of Blair filled the *Sun*'s front page; superimposed was a star-studded 'lucky finger' from the National Lottery advertisements which pointed to the headline 'It must be you'. Murdoch's loyalty to Blair, a constant source of strength during the Iraq War, remained undiminished during the first two terms of his premiership. In the 2005 general election all four Murdoch titles urged their readers to stick with the Labour government. 'Put in your X for Britain . . . and Blair' was the *News of the World*'s banner headline on the Sunday before polling day. The

Sun, mindful that Blair was likely to be succeeded by Gordon Brown, put both their pictures on the front page. 'Come on you reds' was the polling day message, with the Prime Minister and Chancellor of the Exchequer pictured wearing red football shirts numbered respectively 10 and 11, providing a visual reminder of the link to Downing Street. Their double billing on the *Sun*'s front page was a tribute to the care which the Chancellor had taken to maintain the closest possible relationship with Murdoch and the editors of his British newspapers. Brown's media team at the Treasury ran a rival network of briefings to that operated by Downing Street; the Chancellor prided himself on the degree of access which he had personally established with key players in the media industry; and if and when Blair departed, he remained convinced he would be able to retain the support of the Murdoch press.

Labour's re-election in 2005 with a commanding majority of sixty-six seats was a bittersweet victory: Blair won an historic third term but his achievement was time limited. If he was to stand any chance of fulfilling his pre-election promise to serve a full term he needed to heal the internal split over the future leadership of his party. But Brown's supporters had no intention of settling their differences with the Blairites and the infighting became more acute after Cameron's decisive victory in the Conservatives' leadership election. Blair was emerging as the fall guy in a narrative which took hold in the news media: a divided government was being led by a lame duck Prime Minister and either Labour MPs agreed on a new leader or they would end up being defeated by a resurgent Conservative Party. Plotting to hasten his departure intensified once allegations started to emerge in March 2006 that several businessmen had been made life peers in return for donations to the Labour Party. Blame for the 'cash for peerages' scandal was laid at the door of the Prime Minister because he had made the nominations. Blair was questioned as a witness by the Metropolitan Police and it was not until a month after he left Downing Street that the Crown Prosecution Service finally announced there were insufficient grounds for any of the individuals to be charged. As the investigation dragged on month after month, Blair's authority ebbed away and the tenor of his treatment in the tabloid press turned from contempt to almost a sense of loathing. The respect which Blair enjoyed in the pages of the *Sun* at the height of New Labour's influence was rarely if ever extended to his entire cabinet; readers were continually being reminded of the dangerous influence which the trade unions exercised over Labour's affairs. Whenever the paper's editors and correspondents were asked for their opinion on radio and television programmes they did little to hide their contempt for left-wing politics; they were keen to make the point that their support for Blair did not mean the paper had abandoned its Thatcherite beliefs in small government and a state which taxed less. Having suffered three election defeats and tried three different leaders, Cameron's barnstorming performance at the 2005 conference was the moment the *Sun*'s political team had been waiting for, a sign that the Conservative Party might at last have found a successor to Thatcher. Their immediate acclamation of Cameron's off-the-cuff speech, well ahead of many other correspondents and commentators, helped to build an unstoppable momentum behind his leadership campaign. Such was the *Sun*'s growing disenchantment with Labour that within a matter of months Cameron would find that he was pushing at an open door once he was in a position to generate the story lines which fitted the paper's agenda.

Much fun has always been made of the infamous front-page headline 'It's the *Sun* wot won it', which was published after Neil Kinnock's defeat in 1992. The suggestion that a tabloid newspaper had swung the result of a general election was always considered far-fetched and the claim became a source of embarrassment for the editor, Kelvin MacKenzie, but Kinnock was never in any doubt that the constant campaign against him in right-wing newspapers like the *Sun* was one of the main reasons for the Conservatives' narrow victory. It was because Peter Mandelson and Alastair Campbell were so convinced that a continuous diet of slanted stories had scuppered Labour's chances that they put so much effort into trying to neutralise and then win the backing of the Murdoch press. By the time Cameron was elected the tide was well and truly on the turn and the flow of anti-Labour stories was again gathering pace. Brown was waiting impatiently for his chance to put a stop to the sense of drift in the government's relationship with the news media; his aides were sure that once they had control over Downing Street's communications department they would be able to regain command of the news agenda. Cameron's task was threefold if he was to succeed in weakening the links between Murdoch and Blair and subsequently Brown: he needed to persuade the *Sun* to turn up the heat against Labour and print more items favourable to the Conservatives, and he needed to find a way of enlisting a coterie of friendly journalists who might help protect his back against the full impact of hostile story lines. For decades the *Daily Mirror* has provided comparable editorial support for successive Labour leaders. A damaging story which grabs the headlines in the *Daily Mail* or *Daily Express* might well be relegated to a few paragraphs in the *Mirror*, perhaps tucked away on an inside page or even ignored altogether. A similar prize was within Cameron's grasp once the Conservatives started to address the concerns of the *Sun*'s readers and the party began to develop a policy agenda which was more appealing to the commercial interests of the media proprietors than anything which Blair or Brown could offer.

Max Clifford, the celebrated publicist, has spent most of his career devising similar strategies to protect celebrities. He makes no secret of his ability to persuade newspapers to drop stories damaging to one or other of his clients in return for an equally sensational disclosure about someone else. Guidance on how to keep information out of the news media does not come cheaply and Clifford has claimed his agency has consistently earned more money from advising public figures on how to avoid unsavoury publicity than from the 20 per cent commission it receives from brokering the sale of exclusive accounts of celebrity misdemeanours or extra-marital affairs. Clifford's trick of playing off one newspaper against another in return for exclusive access or interviews is standard issue in a spin doctor's toolbox. Party leaders try to avoid getting involved in unseemly double dealing but they know that sometimes their aides have no alternative but to engage in similar sharp practices. Whereas Cameron was anxious to steer clear of Clifford's trade in sensational stories, he was well placed to take advantage of another preoccupation of tabloid newspapers. They see themselves as defenders of the public interest and are keen to promote their role campaigning against what they believe to be injustice or unfairness. If Cameron could tailor Conservative policies to chime with the latest editorial objectives of the popular press, there was every chance he could gain valuable publicity.

Both the Prime Minister and the Chancellor were being targeted by the *Sun* for failing to provide sufficient support for the armed forces; Blair was being criticised for committing troops without adequate back-up and Brown was under attack for withholding the funds which the Ministry of Defence needed to purchase the right kit and equipment. Under Murdoch's ownership the *Sun* has never wavered in its support for 'our boys', from the Falklands War in 1982 through to the conflicts in Iraq and Afghanistan, and as the litany of grievances lengthened, Cameron was presented with an open goal. Day after day the *Sun* – 'proud to be the Forces' paper' – mounted campaigns on behalf of the troops. Press reaction to the escalating casualties and the distress of their relatives was contributing to a change in public attitudes. Service personnel were encouraged by the *Sun* to wear their uniforms with pride when returning from tours of duty and the paper heaped praise on the people of the market town of Wootton Bassett once they started the habit in April 2007 of assembling along the route of the funeral corteges carrying bodies repatriated to RAF Lyneham. A constant round of investigations into shortages of items such as boots and body armour and stories which exposed squalid conditions in the married quarters of the families waiting at home piled on the pressure.

Cameron's first visit to Afghanistan as party leader took place in July 2006 and he was mentioned in a throwaway line in a report on how ministers had finally acted on 'a *Sun* campaign' to ensure British soldiers had bomb-proof patrol vehicles. There was a snide reference to Cameron having worn a flak jacket whereas Blair never donned 'a protective jacket on war zone trips'. Three months later at the Tory Party conference,

Cameron got his act together and he managed to steal a march on the government. 'Tories to axe our boys' tax' was the headline on a *Sun* exclusive about Cameron's intention to offer 'a tax holiday for our brave troops'. In a signed article, he said the Conservatives were putting together a 'forces' manifesto' and the party would consider whether to suspend income tax while service personnel were on operations in Iraq and Afghanistan. Next day the *Sun* claimed that after 'a flurry of calls' between Blair and Brown, the Treasury signalled it would match the Conservatives' offer. But the following month he was targeted by the *Sun* for having instructed Conservative MPs to vote with Labour rebels in favour of an immediate inquiry into the Iraq War. 'Tory turncoats' were accused of playing politics by offering a massive boost to terrorist enemies just when 'our boys' were engaged in intense fighting with the Taliban. By a process of trial and error Cameron began to understand the paper's mindset and in January 2007 he was back in favour after repeating his conference pledge of a 'forces' manifesto' which would address the neglect of service accommodation. Thanks to his initiatives the *Sun* and the Conservatives were back in business but Murdoch's newspapers were hedging their bets; Brown was still an unknown quantity as a future Prime Minister; there was no immediate prospect of an election; and Cameron would have to be far more convincing in defending Conservative beliefs if he was to stand any chance, come the next election, of securing the *Sun*'s endorsement.

After spending most of the Thatcher decade as an industrial correspondent reporting her government's success in defeating strikes such as the 1984–5 dispute with the National Union of Mineworkers, I was never in any doubt that the *Sun* prided itself on being regarded as 'one of us', her ultimate term of approval. From my many subsequent discussions with journalists and editorial executives who joined the exodus to Murdoch's union-busting printing plant at Wapping in east London in January 1986, I felt they always regarded their editorial support as being on loan to Blair and that should a true heir to Margaret Thatcher emerge, their affinity to the Conservative cause could easily be rekindled. Their strident opposition to the mass picketing of the pit strike, which was reinforced when they were besieged themselves by sacked print workers during the Wapping dispute, strengthened the conviction of editorial staff on the *Sun* and the *News of the World* that in the competitive arena of tabloid journalism they were the only true champions of the forces of law and order. A testament to that close relationship is the *Sun*'s continuing support for those either serving on the front line or helping to protect the public. Sponsored events include the *Sun*'s 'Millies' awards for the 'bravest of the brave' in the military and the annual police bravery awards organised by the Police Federation. Both have become star-studded occasions which attract leading members of the royal family, celebrities and politicians and which generate extensive coverage in both print and on television.

Designing policies to fit the story lines of newspapers which spoke up for the Tories' traditional allies in the police and armed forces was always going to be relatively straightforward, a far easier proposition than the task of trying to gain and maintain Rupert Murdoch's personal approval. The commercial interests of his UK companies BSkyB and News International and the views of their respective chief executives, Murdoch's son James and Les Hinton, would always have to be taken into account when exercising political patronage. No media conglomerate operating in the much-regulated world of communications was likely to be in any rush to jeopardise its ongoing relations with the government of the day, especially if Blair's successor looked like being equally amenable towards the proprietors and their needs. But the new Tory leader had social as well as political strengths which worked in his favour when embarking on a charm offensive and which allowed him to take advantage of the petty rivalries of the Blairites and Brownites and their reluctance to socialise together.

Most of Cameron's closest advisers, their wives and partners, were well known within the media elite, either in their own right or through business and family connections, and the Notting Hill set became increasingly well represented at industry gatherings. David and Samantha were high up on the 'must invite' list – indeed, *Tatler* put them at the top of the magazine's 2006 'hot 100' list of party animals and their presence ensured even greater publicity for fashionable social events. In May they were the guests of the *Sun*'s editor, Rebekah Wade, and her husband, the *EastEnders* actor Ross Kemp, at a lavish pre-World Cup party held at the Hertfordshire mansion of the footballer David Beckham and his wife Victoria. Such was the demand for tickets for the hottest social event of the sporting calendar that the *Daily Mail* took delight in pointing out that 'gatecrasher Cameron' was so desperate to attend, once he found out that Blair had declined, that he 'wangled an invite' from Wade. Diary writers and columnists competed with each other in describing how 'call me Dave' and his wife rubbed shoulders with the world of 'showbusiness and bling' at 'Beckingham Palace'. But the subtext of the coverage was unmistakable: no previous Conservative leader would ever have been considered remotely cool enough to have mingled with the England football squad and A-list celebrities in the company of Wade.

Being seen socialising with the *Sun* prompted questions about Murdoch's opinion of his editor's guest and the future political loyalties of his newspapers, speculation which he seemed only too keen to promote. Within weeks of Cameron's election he told the BBC he thought the new Tory leader was 'very bright' but seemed to be 'all about image'; people needed to know much more about his vision for the country. Five months later, in an interview for the *Australian*, he hinted that his British newspapers might well abandon Labour and return to the Conservatives. If and when Blair stood down, he believed there should be a stand-off lasting at least twelve to eighteen months before a general election so that voters could see how Brown fared as Prime Minister and then had a chance to compare that with what Cameron had to offer. Murdoch has always insisted he does not dictate the editorial line taken by his newspapers but there was no mistaking the strength of his wait-and-see edict, a message which he repeated in an interview for American television in July 2006. He was quite open about the influence which the *Sun* was exercising over the Blair government: 'Right now we are giving them a bad time . . . We fought him pretty hard on Europe. We said "Stay away from there". He's come round.' Murdoch was withering in his assessment of Blair's tactics: the Prime Minister became a 'lame duck' the day he announced he would not fight a fourth general election. 'You can feel within his own party the left rising up and challenging him.' He liked Brown 'very much, on a personal level' but still did not think 'much' of Cameron. 'He's totally inexperienced. I do not know what substance is there or what he really believes in.' Murdoch's remarks became even more pointed in an interview for the *New Yorker* when he complained about the tiresome nature of the rivalry between Blair and Brown. 'Whenever I'm in town they say: "Can't you come over for a cup of tea?" It's sometimes very inconvenient . . . And you have to be careful to have a cup of tea with them both, or they are very suspicious that you are lining up with the other one.' Again he could not resist flattering himself as a potential puppet master: 'The sooner we can see a face-off between Gordon and Cameron, the sooner we can see the future.' The choice which his newspapers made would depend 'entirely on Gordon's performance and on the state of Britain'.

Murdoch's grandstanding on the future direction of British politics was brought to a sudden halt by a serious setback to the expansion of BSkyB and a looming crisis at News International. Investigations were ordered by the media regulator Ofcom and the Office of Fair Trading when BSkyB purchased a 17.9 per cent stake in ITV in November 2006 in what the markets considered was a surprise move to frustrate a merger with NTL. Sir Richard Branson's Virgin group, NTL's leading shareholder, claimed the £940 million share purchase was an attempt to stifle competition and 'secure creeping control of the British media'. BSkyB's audacious move triggered the first investigation under Labour's regime for regulating broadcasting; there were immediate calls for the government to intervene to protect the public interest; and renewed demands for BSkyB to be stripped of its monopoly of live broadcasting rights for Premier League football matches. Cameron must have had a sense of déjà vu on seeing Rupert and James Murdoch being thwarted by the constraints of a heavily regulated television industry, a scenario which he had experience of during his time as head of corporate affairs for Carlton Television. In his day the challenge for the ITV network, of which Carlton was part, was to establish a digital rival to the satellite services of Sky Television. OnDigital, an ill-fated joint venture by Carlton and Granada, was seen off by Sky Digital and collapsed despite an investment of £1.2 billion. But BSkyB was not the only part of the Murdoch empire facing months of uncertainty during the latter half of 2006. News International's management were on edge following the arrest in August of the *News of the World*'s royal editor, Clive Goodman, and a private investigator, Glenn Mulcaire, who were charged with tapping the mobile telephones of aides to members of the royal family.

Murdoch's misfortunes were to have a silver lining for the Conservatives: not only did Cameron see an opportunity to develop new and what he hoped would be more appealing policies for the broadcasting industry, but his party was about to become an unexpected beneficiary of the fallout from the police investigation into the *News of the World*'s activities. After pleading guilty to being part of a conspiracy which used criminal methods to access mobile phone voicemails, Goodman was jailed for four months and Mulcaire for six months. Immediately the sentences were passed in January 2007, the paper announced that the editor, Andy Coulson, had resigned. He said he deeply regretted the interception of personal voicemail messages, which was 'entirely wrong', and as it occurred on his watch, he accepted his position had become untenable. If the *News of the World* held people to account, then its 'own house' had to be in order. 'As the editor of the newspaper, I take ultimate responsibility for the conduct of my reporters.' His swift departure had to be seen as part of a calculated exercise in damage limitation by News International. If Coulson was no longer editor and had become a private citizen, he could not be questioned or held to account by the Press Complaints Commission, a move which the management hoped might limit the scope of any future inquiries into illegal phone tapping by its journalists. News International's tactics could not be faulted: Coulson was deemed to be 'no longer answerable to the PCC' and an inquiry found no evidence that the editor was aware of Goodman's illegal activities.

Coulson's comeback caught the Westminster village on the hop. His appointment as the Conservatives' director of communications, four months after his resignation from the *News of the World*, was a genuine surprise and one which caused consternation among Labour's media strategists. In his interviews the previous summer Rupert Murdoch had left the door firmly ajar to the prospect of his newspapers switching to the Conservatives. What Cameron lacked was a media technician with the clout and experience who could help shape and manage an agenda which would appeal to the popular press and hopefully win the support of the proprietor of Britain's two most widely read tabloids.

Coulson's CV was tailor made for the task which Cameron had in mind and although political correspondents drew an immediate parallel with Tony Blair's appointment of Alastair Campbell in 1994, the two journalists were polar opposites in several crucial respects. Campbell was beginning to promote himself as a personality in his own right long before he became Blair's press secretary. As political editor for the *Daily Mirror* and then the *Today* newspaper, he was in regular demand on television and radio as an opinionated commentator and, despite being a committed Labour Party propagandist, he sometimes stood in as a programme presenter. His Achilles heel during his stint as the Prime Minister's director of communications was an inability to control his addiction to self-publicity; he could not stop himself becoming the story. His highly publicised fight to the finish with the BBC reporter Andrew Gilligan, which culminated in his ignominious departure from Downing Street after giving evidence to the Hutton inquiry into the death of the weapons inspector Dr David Kelly, was a salutary lesson in what can happen when a spin doctor presses the self-destruct button.

Coulson by comparison appeared to have no wish to become a personality and he shunned the celebrity status which proved so alluring to friends and colleagues like Rebekah Wade and also the *Daily Mirror*'s editor, Piers Morgan, with whom he had worked as a reporter on the *Sun*'s showbusiness column, Bizarre. Rather than take personal advantage of numerous award-winning scoops during his three years editing the *News of the World*, he asked Stuart Kuttner, the managing editor, to speak on the paper's behalf on radio and television. Coulson rarely gave interviews and his few responses were limited to matter-of-fact comments about his role as editor. His run of notable exclusives included revelations about the private lives and secret affairs of David Beckham, the England football coach Sven-Göran Eriksson and the Home Secretary, David Blunkett. When accepting awards, including 'newspaper of the year' in 2005, Coulson never shied away from the criticism that his journalists traded on intrusion and sensation. 'I've got nothing to be ashamed of, and this goes for everyone on the *News of the World*.' While he did not seek to suggest it was a 'grandiose ideal', the paper was proud to 'reveal big stories and titillate and entertain the public, while exposing crime and hypocrisy'. I knew from my own occasional visits to Wapping how highly Coulson was thought of. Framed copies of the front pages of his most memorable scoops had pride of place along the corridors, hung like trophies in a hall of fame.

Part of Coulson's appeal to a party eager for publicity was his flair and ingenuity as a campaigning newspaper editor. Tackling knife and gun crime were regular fare but the focus was firmly on strengthening law and order rather than engaging in politically motivated causes. By exposing grievances and using the *News of the World*'s influence to change government policy, he believed the tabloids could justify his claim that they did more for the people of the country than 'any other newspapers in the world'. He was the driving force in sustaining pressure for the introduction of 'Sarah's law', the right of parents to discover whether their children were at risk from paedophiles living in their neighbourhoods. When the *News of the World* began publishing pictures of child sex offenders in the summer of 2000 to highlight the background to the murder of six-year-old Sarah Payne there was a storm of protest about the danger of 'mob rule' but the then editor, Wade, and her deputy, Coulson, held their nerve, published more photographs the following Sunday and then launched a mass petition. Coulson continued the campaign when he succeeded Wade as editor in 2003 and the Home Secretary, John Reid, finally responded in June 2006 by promising to study 'Megan's law' in the United States, the first of a series of initiatives which culminated in March 2010 with the government's decision to give all parents the right to check whether people with access to their children were sex offenders. Generating a million signatures in support of 'Sarah's law' was said by Coulson to have been an experience which more than anything else strengthened his belief in the campaigning role of newspapers and their ability to represent the views of their readers. Another much-publicised scoop was the discovery of footage of British troops beating up unarmed Iraqi civilians in 2006, a revelation which prompted a government inquiry.

Coulson's upfront approach to the job of being editor of a tabloid newspaper had clearly made an impression on George Osborne, who had the misfortune to feature on the *News of the World*'s front page during the summer of 2005 when he was Cameron's campaign manager. 'Top Tory, coke and the hooker' was the headline over an allegation by a former 'vice girl' that the shadow Chancellor had a 'youthful fascination with cocaine', a claim he vehemently denied and dismissed as a 'desperate smear'. Osborne had made the editor's acquaintance before the story broke and according to a profile of Coulson by the *Guardian Weekend*'s columnist John Harris, the two men ended up developing an 'increasing mutual respect'. On meeting again not long after his resignation, Osborne suggested to Coulson that he might be interested in becoming the Conservatives' director of communications. He was told the party needed some 'really serious firepower' in dealing with the media.

Conscious no doubt of the way cynical journalists would interpret Osborne's role in recruiting a disgraced newspaper editor, Cameron issued the briefest of statements when the appointment was announced in May 2007. Coulson would make 'a formidable contribution' to building the 'most effective strategy and operation' for winning the next election. The new director of communications was equally short and sweet: he was looking forward to helping the Conservatives 'return to government' under Cameron's leadership. Having had the good fortune to secure such a high-powered position, Coulson had no intention of allowing himself to become the story and it was clear, as was already the case with the party's chief strategist, Steve Hilton, that he had no intention of answering journalists' questions or of being accused of gossiping with reporters and feeding media speculation. A pointer to what he could expect if he followed Alastair Campbell's example was provided by the *Daily Telegraph*'s headline 'Phone-tap editor is new Tory spin doctor'. When responding to a reader's question for the *Independent*, Cameron's answer was the one he subsequently gave whenever asked to justify the appointment: he was satisfied Coulson 'was not aware' a journalist had engaged in telephone tapping but as editor he 'did the right thing, took responsibility and resigned'.

Such was the disarray at campaign headquarters when he started work in early July that Coulson had no shortage of advice from political commentators. Gordon Brown, only recently installed in Downing Street, was continuing to savour the political honeymoon enjoyed by a new Prime Minister. Anger among Conservative MPs at the downgrading of the party's support for grammar schools, defeat in the Ealing Southall by-election, and the ridicule heaped on his head for visiting Rwanda while Britain battled with summer floods had called into question Cameron's ability. Labour's lead in the opinion polls ranged between 7 and 9 per cent, heightening speculation that Brown might be tempted to seek a fresh mandate in the autumn. Les Hinton, News International's executive chairman, was hedging his bets, anxious to reassure the Prime Minister that Rupert Murdoch's executives were impressed by the swift action he had taken to deal with a run of crises such as the foiled terrorist attack and widespread flooding. He told *Esquire* that Brown had been under-estimated; he had a 'formidable intellect' and seemed all set for a commanding first year as Prime Minister. 'Cameron has made some horrible misjudgements but is still a fresh, eager, clever man.'

Each initiative aimed at restoring Conservative morale and halting

Labour's advance in the opinion polls was analysed by the Westminster press corps for the Coulson effect. By early August, journalists started to detect a harder edge to Cameron's speeches. His promise to square up to a 'bare-knuckle fight' with the government to save district hospitals was an early example of the headline-grabbing phrases which began to pepper his comments. When interviewed on *Today* about a spate of violent gang attacks, he said that unless society was tougher on yobbish behaviour it would not be possible to deal with 'anarchy in the UK', the much-used phrase which had appeared the previous day in a front-page headline in the *Sun* on a report about the danger of letting 'yobs rule the streets'. The murder that week of eleven-year-old Rhys Jones in a shooting at Croxteth Park in Liverpool gave added weight both to his warning and to the speeches which he had been giving since the start of the year on the need to tackle Britain's 'broken society'. In February, in response to the shooting of three teenage boys in south London, he said the murders showed that British society was 'badly broken' and that it was time fathers were made to look after their children. To publicise his speeches readers of the *Daily Telegraph* were given free copies of *Breakdown Britain*, the Conservatives' guide to 'fixing our broken society'. When Cameron used a *Daily Mail* article to call for 'zero tolerance of knives, let alone guns', his initiative was hailed on the front page: 'Crime: Tories finally get tough'. In an exclusive interview for the *Sun*, he outlined plans for sixteen-year-olds to spend six weeks of their summer holidays putting 'something back into Britain' through a programme of 'patriotic national citizenship service'.

There was no let-up that summer: when the *News of the World* revealed that troops in Afghanistan were paying higher tax as a result of changes in the Budget, Cameron addressed their complaints on a visit to British bases in Helmand province and he renewed his promise to deal with their grievances in a forces' manifesto. Renewed hints that Brown might use Labour's annual conference as a springboard for an autumn election meant there was no escaping the fallout from the Conservatives' ill-fated campaign in the 2005 election and their controversial proposals for curbs on immigration. When challenged on *Newsnight*, Cameron was unexpectedly forthright: immigration was 'too high' and had placed 'too great a burden on public services', which was why it needed to be 'better controlled'.

Instead of the usual summer run of 'silly season' political stories, the Conservatives offered a populist agenda which succeeded in capturing journalists' attention. With Coulson's help, Cameron was starting to exploit the weaknesses in the government's handling of law and order and mount a far more effective challenge to Labour's record. Trevor Kavanagh, the *Sun*'s columnist, thought his former colleague had solved the Conservatives' desperate need for a publicity supremo who understood tabloid journalism. He told *Today* that Coulson would have advised Cameron that he would be missing a trick if he failed to take advantage of the phrase 'anarchy in the UK'. When the *Independent* canvassed political correspondents for their opinion, there was praise for the way Coulson orchestrated the party's summer fightback. Crime and immigration were picked out by Patrick O'Flynn, chief political commentator for the *Daily Express*, as two of the issues where Cameron had been weak and which were 'dear to our readers' hearts'. Fraser Nelson, political editor of the *Spectator*, had observed the way Coulson went through press statements 'line by line', and it was his ability to guide Cameron on exactly how a speech would be reported which was cited by Daniel Finkelstein, comment editor for *The Times*, as the reason why the party had been so anxious to hire a seasoned tabloid journalist.

Notwithstanding their summer fightback, the Conservatives were at Brown's mercy. A gathering momentum behind calls for a snap autumn election dominated the build-up to his first appearance as Prime Minister at Labour's annual conference in Bournemouth. In a speech which made repeated patriotic references to 'British' and 'Britishness', he delivered a string of pledges on education, health and cutting crime which seemed to suggest he saw himself as the true champion of Conservative values, ready to go to the country within weeks. Next day the *Sun* bucked the pre-election hype and launched a highly personal attack. 'Not his finest hour' said the headline over a five-page spread which denounced Brown for his failure to honour Labour's 2005 election pledge by renewing the promise of a referendum on the new European Union constitution. A petition form was printed the following day inviting readers to join a campaign to ensure the British people had their say on the EU treaty. If the *Sun* was ready so soon to use its ardent Euroscepticism as a weapon to attack Brown, his chances of securing the paper's endorsement, should he decide to call a snap election, had been knocked for six. Coulson would have been encouraged by the shift in sentiment at News International and would have known there was all to play for at the Conservatives' annual conference the following week. After Osborne's pledge to increase the threshold for inheritance tax, and the rousing reception for Cameron's off-the-cuff address, the *Sun* boosted Tory spirits by advising the Prime Minister to 'think twice' before taking the electorate for granted.

As Brown dithered over whether to go to the country, journalists on rival newspapers sensed that media proprietors were taking a fresh look at the Conservatives. According to the *Independent on Sunday*, Murdoch rang Cameron to congratulate him in person on his conference speech. By eventually deciding it was too risky to seek a fresh mandate and put his premiership at risk, Brown extended an all-important lifeline to Cameron, giving him every opportunity to continue reviving and reorganising his party. In the three months since joining the staff at party headquarters, Coulson had transformed the Conservatives' ability to respond to the dictates of the popular press and, with the threat of an immediate election having been lifted, his bridge-building skills were about to be deployed in helping Cameron steer Tory policy towards News International's commercial interests as well as helping to reflect its political agenda.

On seeing for myself the engaging nature of the Cameron–Coulson partnership in action, mixing it with editors and media executives as guests of the Journalists' Charity, I realised how well attuned the Tory leader was to the ongoing concerns of the industry. During my time as the charity's immediate past chairman, I had made the acquaintance of senior members of News International's management and I recognised the significant financial contribution which the company made as a leading benefactor. Coulson's presence at the annual lunch in March 2008, sitting at a table with his former colleagues and so evidently enjoying their company, seemed to suggest there were no hard feelings about his abrupt resignation the previous year. Cameron and his publicity chief were welcomed by the charity's chairman, Bob Warren, the *News of the World*'s long-standing executive editor. Once the speeches began there was no mistaking a friendly meeting of minds. Without prompting, but no doubt as a result of Coulson's advice, Cameron knew precisely which buttons to press. He praised Britain's great tradition of campaigning journalism and singled out the *Sun*, the *Observer*, the *Mail on Sunday* and the *Sunday Times* for their investigations into the plight of forces families, the scandal of fraudulent television phone-in programmes and the financial irregularities of MPs at Westminster. Of even greater significance to the audience was Cameron's pledge that a future Conservative government would continue to support the self-regulation of newspapers through the Press Complaints Commission. He thought the voluntary regulatory system was 'working better' than it had done in the past, although he had an open mind about how it might be strengthened in the future. When owning up to how he felt on the occasion when Carlton Television got into trouble with the broadcasting regulators and was fined £1 million for a programme which 'went wrong', he was reminded from the floor that it was in fact £2 million, a correction which he took his stride, complimenting by name Laurie Upshon, a fellow former employee at Carlton, for having a better memory. Cameron could not be faulted on his repartee or the jokes which he made at his own expense. He even suggested Coulson had been hired on the strength of the phrase 'hug a hoodie'. If three words which he had never uttered could do him so much damage, he said, just think what 'the person who wrote them' could do to the Labour Party.

Cameron's endorsement of self-regulation was particularly well received because of an increasing investment in newspaper websites and the hope that online revenue might stem the loss of income from falling sales and a decline in press advertising. To the industry's great relief the PCC, rather than the government-appointed broadcasting regulator, Ofcom, had taken on responsibility the previous year for regulating the content of video and audio material on newspaper websites. Self-regulation gave newspapers far greater editorial freedom in their audio-visual output than that enjoyed by public service broadcasters, whose bulletins and programmes were rigorously monitored. The long-term aim of the proprietors was to expand the audio-visual content which readers were being offered online to a point where newspapers might be able to generate digital programmes in competition with established radio and television stations.

In order to encourage investment in preparation for the digital switchover, the industry was seeking a curb on the BBC's commanding online presence, an argument which George Osborne had advanced in a recent speech. Murdoch's legendary hostility to the BBC, fuelled by his constant battles with the corporation over the development of Sky Television, had increasingly been directed against the continued expansion of the BBC's online output. Newspapers said they found it almost impossible to charge for access to their websites because of the free online news and information services available from the BBC. Media companies were urging the government to intervene on their behalf. Like the other major publishers, News International was struggling to achieve a return on its investment in newspaper websites, an aspect of the business in which Coulson had personal experience. Before being appointed deputy editor of the *News of the World* in 2000, he spent a year with the group's dot-com division and helped to set up the *Sun*'s website www.page3.com, the first of the company's online enterprises to make a profit. Cameron made no mention in his speech of the industry's ongoing dispute with the BBC, nor did he reveal that the party's research department had in fact been examining the future development of public service broadcasting.

One of the central conclusions in a discussion document which was released three weeks later was that the BBC's 'dominant online presence' created a 'real danger' of crowding out innovation. It also proposed that broadcasting regulations should be eased to allow newspaper proprietors and independent broadcasters the opportunity to open new super-local television stations. Commercial operators who started fledgling local stations providing news and weather would need to be nurtured and protected in order to prevent 'any potential stifling' by the BBC. In a preface to the document, the shadow Culture Secretary, Jeremy Hunt, said the aim of the Conservatives was to encourage the 'creative diversity' of Britain's broadcasting sector. As a blueprint for the future development of the industry, it offered newspapers a chance to reinvent themselves as significant players in a digital world, an enticing prospect for hard-pressed national and local press proprietors whose income base was threatened by a loss of property and classified advertising to the internet.

Of particular significance for Murdoch's executives was the recommendation that new television stations established by newspaper companies should be free to follow their own editorial line without fear of breaching the rules on political impartiality which applied to public service broadcasters like the BBC and ITV. Britain enjoyed what was probably 'the most lively and varied' national press in the world and the argument of the Conservatives' research department was that if the country was quite relaxed for newspaper editors to be partisan, why should broadcasting not evolve along the same lines? Public service broadcasters would be required to maintain political impartiality but the digital switchover would allow for the development of a broadcasting sector as diverse as in the USA, where Fox News catered for 'right of centre viewers' and CNN addressed a 'more liberal audience'. 'Why should "Telegraph TV" – or for that matter "Guardian TV" – be prevented from following the editorial lines pursued by their newspapers if they were to become digital channels and not simply broadcast on the internet?'

Here was an open invitation to media companies to plan for a future free from the constraints which they had complained about in the past.

Ofcom, the broadcasting regulator, had already acknowledged in its report *New News, Future News* that there was an argument for suggesting that 'small niche channels' should have the freedom to be politically partisan in their output because the rules were becoming 'less enforceable'. But the party's discussion paper went much further: a future Conservative government was indicating it would have no objection if Murdoch decided to launch a British equivalent of Fox News, his highly politicised American television station. With the growing sophistication of their websites, the *Sun* and the *News of the World* were starting to demonstrate they could compete head on with both the BBC and ITV by offering online videos featuring investigations and exclusive interviews. Often the material was so sensational or politically charged that it commanded the news agenda and clips from the footage, with the logo of each newspaper burned into the corner, began to feature regularly in mainstream news bulletins and programmes.

By giving an explicit warning that a Conservative administration would prevent the BBC from attempting to 'crowd out innovation' in a 'multi-channel, multi-platform' era, the corporation was under immediate pressure to justify its existing plans to expand the growing reach of BBC news online by offering local as well regional coverage. Hunt advised the BBC Trust to reject any move by the BBC to offer local video news on demand because of the threat it would pose to local newspapers, which were struggling to 'reinvent their business model'. Before the management had time to reply, they were engulfed in the damaging furore which ensued after the BBC Radio 2 presenters Jonathan Ross and Russell Brand left obscene messages on the telephone answering machine of Andrew Sachs, the *Fawlty Towers* actor. Ross was suspended and Brand resigned but the lack of editorial control and the failure to honour guidelines on taste and decency left the BBC's hierarchy at the mercy of the Murdoch press. 'BBC £14 million fat cat scandal' was the *News of the World*'s front-page banner headline in November 2008 over a report revealing 'a staggering £14.3 million paid in salaries to management fat cats'. Using the Freedom of Information Act, the paper forced the BBC to reveal that more than fifty of its executives earned more than the Prime Minister's salary of £189,994. Cameron leaped into the controversy next day with a signed article in the *Sun* carrying a headline which pulled no punches: 'Bloated BBC out of touch with the viewers'. His experience at Carlton Television taught him the value of a broadcasting industry which had three streams of income – advertising, subscription and the licence fee – to finance programme making and he wanted to 'stick with that structure'. But he said the BBC had over-reached itself, had 'become bloated with many of its executives over-paid' and had 'lost touch with the values' of the people who supported it through the licence fee. The BBC had a privileged position which 'must not be abused' and the 'squeezing and crushing of commercial competitors online or in publishing needs to be stopped'. Because of inadequate procedures for controlling programme standards and inept commercial decisions, the management had called into question their own competence, a ready-made opportunity for Cameron to put in writing the Conservatives' pledge to encourage innovation in the broadcasting industry by reining in the BBC. Tony Blair used a discreet telephone call to say he was 'instinctively sympathetic' to Murdoch's plans to expand his satellite television services; the Tory leader was honoured with a two-page spread in the *Sun* to offer the reassurance that Murdoch's television stations and newspapers would have every chance to take advantage of the digital switchover.

While there are often relatively innocuous diary items about the socialising which takes place between media magnates and leading politicians, there tends to be something akin to a gentlemen's agreement between the largest newspaper groups to draw a veil over their respective commercial and political links. News International, Associated Newspapers (publishers of the *Daily Mail*) and Telegraph Media Group (*Daily Telegraph*) rarely engage in a dog-eat-dog style of journalism when reporting each other's business affairs because they know they have a mutual interest in trying to safeguard the light-touch regulation of their industry and to minimise government intervention. However, newspapers outside the loop of self-interest have no such inhibitions and the Conservatives' charm offensive had not gone unnoticed. The *Guardian* suggested in July 2006 that if Blair had turned down a chance during his trip to the USA that summer to address a gathering of Murdoch and his executives at the Pebble Beach golf resort, then Cameron would have been invited instead. Two years later the *Independent*'s front-page splash had the headline 'Cameron, Murdoch and a Greek island freebie'. Political editor Andrew Grice revealed that the Conservative leader delayed the start of his August summer holiday in 2008 to hold private talks on Murdoch's luxury yacht *Rosehearty* when it was moored off a Greek island. After drinks on board Cameron attended a dinner party and flew on to Turkey the following day for his family holiday. When asked the following October why the talks had been kept secret, a Conservative press officer said there was 'nothing unusual' about a politician attending a 'social event' hosted by Murdoch; details of the trip had been 'fully and properly declared'.

Although the major groups were reluctant to wash each other's dirty linen via the pages of their newspapers, they were united in their belief that the BBC needed scaling back and they were only too happy to see the Murdoch press taking the lead. 'Cameron: We'll freeze the licence fee' was the bold headline in March 2009 over the *Sun*'s report that the Tory leader was determined to curb the 'BBC's bloated bureaucracy and waste of cash'. It welcomed his promise to cap the annual licence fee so as to 'choke off the taxpayer funding that gives the BBC an advantage over rivals such as Sky'. When Conservative MPs moved a motion in the House of Commons to revoke a £3 increase due as part of a six-year settlement, they were heavily defeated, despite a warning from Jeremy Hunt that an inflation-busting rise in the licence fee was unnecessary and would disadvantage struggling rival broadcasters.

Cameron's unstinting support was about to be rewarded with the kind of patronage which the Murdoch press has no shame in exercising. There was no contest when News International came to choose the politician to be the first guest on SunTalk, an internet radio station which was launched in April 2009. Listeners to the opening programme were welcomed to the 'home of free speech' by the presenter Jon Gaunt and he invited callers to his morning phone-in to put their questions to 'the next Prime Minister, David Cameron'. Alternatively listeners could text the answer 'yes' or 'no' to the question 'Is Cameron ready and fit to be the next Prime Minister?' Gaunt's opening sally was to enquire whether Cameron would deliver the 'full-blooded Conservatism' of Margaret Thatcher or a 'watered-down version'. Cameron said his generation faced different challenges, not just 'a broken economy, but a broken society', and the big difference between himself and Gordon Brown was that the Conservatives would halt the 'spend, spend and borrow, borrow' of Labour and bring public expenditure under control. After half an hour Gaunt announced that the text vote was showing that 78 per cent thought Cameron was fit to govern the country. 'Good morning, Prime Minister' was the cheery hello of the sports reporter, 'Motormouth' Ian McGarry.

Five weeks later, on the morning of polling day for the 2009 elections to the European Parliament, SunTalk lived up to its promise to herald 'a radio revolution' by broadcasting its daily three-hour phone-in while voting was taking place. Unlike, for example, the USA where there are no restrictions, broadcasting on election days in Britain is politics free as long as the polling stations are open. As a result of a combination of regulation and convention, news bulletins and programmes on radio and television confine their coverage to factual reports about the weather and level of turnout and limit themselves to showing footage of the general public and party leaders turning up at polling stations to cast their votes. Partisan interviews or commentary are prohibited in line with the requirement that public service broadcasting must remain impartial and free of political bias. No such constraints apply to the online audiovisual output of newspapers, however, and Gaunt was able to celebrate the fact that the *Sun* was presenting a programme which he claimed was making broadcasting history. 'We are a newspaper of the air and we are making democracy come alive. No one else is talking politics across the airwaves this morning. The only place you can do that here in Britain is on SunTalk.' Gaunt had no inhibitions about promoting the station's politics and he interspersed his phone-in with repeated reminders to listeners to read that morning's editorial in the *Sun*, which recommended readers to vote Conservative as 'the only way' to get Britain to hold a referendum on the Lisbon Treaty.

News coverage during the preceding four weeks of campaigning in the elections for both the European Parliament and English county councils had been all but obliterated by the emerging scandal over abuses in the expenses and allowances paid to MPs at Westminster. Voters seemed determined to give a good kicking not just to Gordon Brown's government but also to the entire political establishment. *The Times* declared it was the European election that 'never happened' but, like its stablemate the *Sun*, it recommended readers to vote Conservative because it was the only party which was promising the British people a referendum and would seek to withdraw from the 'pointless internal deliberation designed to cement power centrally' within the EU.

Conservative candidates polled well in both elections. The party lost one seat in the European Parliament but on 27.7 per cent the Tories had by far the largest share of the vote, higher than in 2004. In the council elections, the Conservatives gained 233 seats while Labour lost 273. Brown, facing the biggest electoral test of his premiership, was humiliated. Labour lost five seats in the European Parliament and with the party's share of the vote falling to a mere 15.7 per cent, it finished in third place behind the United Kingdom Independence Party. Public anger at MPs' greed and their attempt to keep their expenses a secret triggered a sizeable protest vote which benefited UKIP and also the British National Party, which won its first two European seats. But Cameron was able to argue that the Conservatives were at last winning votes 'in every part of the country'. Looking ahead to the general election, party strategists could for the first time since Blair's landslide in 1997 see tangible evidence that the Murdoch press was prepared to recommend voting Conservative. Another encouraging pointer was that in the absence of any serious debate about European issues during the build-up to polling day, the *Sun* urged readers to sign a petition supporting Cameron's demand that Brown should face the electorate.

In the two years since his appointment Andy Coulson had played a pivotal role behind the scenes in rebuilding the traditional links between the Conservatives and News International and the rapprochement had reached a point where Cameron was almost certain of having the *Sun* on his side once an election was called. At a personal level Coulson seemed well on the way to detoxifying his own share of the blame for the phone-tapping scandal which had ousted him from the *News of the World*. His sure touch in guiding the party's media offensive was acknowledged in October 2008 when he was named public relations professional of the year by *PR Week*. Danny Rogers, the editor, believed Coulson's main strength was his capacity for damage limitation. Time and again he 'gained control of a story by responding quickly and decisively'. When the shadow Home Secretary, David Davis, resigned unexpectedly from Parliament in June 2008 in protest at the government's decision to press ahead with proposals for the 42-day pre-charge detention of terrorist suspects, Coulson 'quickly leaked the story to television news, forcing Davis to rush out his announcement'. Another victim was the Prime Minister, for it was Coulson who was 'instrumental in getting senior Tories to describe Brown as a "ditherer" at every opportunity'. His irritation was confirmed when the *Independent on Sunday* revealed that in the previous two months Downing Street had counted fifty-three mentions in newspapers of the Prime Minister being called a 'ditherer', a taunt which he personally blamed on the orchestration of the Conservatives' spin machine. Black Dog, the *Mail on Sunday*'s diarist, described the laughter in Cameron's office whenever there was a call to Coulson's mobile phone. His ringtone was a recording of the 'foot-in-the-mouth gaffe' which Brown made in his House of Commons statement on the recapitalisation of the banks when he slipped up by suggesting 'We not only saved the world. . . er, saved the banks. . .'

Given his pride in the success of the *News of the World*'s ten-year campaign to allow parents access to information about local paedophiles, Coulson would have immediately seen the potential of the *Sun*'s decision in November 2008 to launch a petition to prevent a repetition of the brutal death of Baby P. After his mother and stepfather were convicted at the Old Bailey for their part in the baby's death, the paper asked readers for their support in demanding that the social workers in the case should be sacked together with Sharon Shoesmith, head of children's services for the London Borough of Haringey. Cameron was the first party leader to give his backing. In a signed article on the day the petition was launched he said his wife Samantha could not bear to watch news reports of the trial. 'Baby P was cruelly let down in life, but we won't let him down in death.' The *Sun*'s petition attracted over 1.4 million signatures, nearly half a million more than the one for 'Sarah's law', and it took six of the paper's journalists to carry the sacks of completed forms up Downing Street to the No. 10 front door.

Political correspondents were forced to rely on second-hand insights into Coulson's influence and handiwork because he continued doing his utmost to keep the lowest possible profile and work behind the scenes. Through his network of friends and contacts at News International he would almost certainly have picked up on the management's fear that ongoing inquiries by the *Guardian* might uncover fresh evidence of illegal hacking into messages left on mobile phones. On 9 July 2009, the second anniversary of the day he started work at Conservative headquarters, his photograph stared out from the *Guardian*'s front page under the headline 'Revealed: Murdoch's £1 million bill for hiding dirty tricks'. After months of work the paper's investigative reporter Nick Davies was able to disclose that News International had paid out more than £1 million in out-of-court settlements in three cases involving the 'use of criminal methods to get stories'. Davies claimed that 'suppressed evidence' showed that the royal editor, Clive Goodman, was not the only journalist on the paper using private investigators to hack into mobile phones and there could be 'hundreds more legal actions by victims' of the *News of the World*.

Coulson knew the previous afternoon that he was back in the headlines once the *Guardian* released a summary of the story on its website. In an attempt to stay one step ahead of their competitors, while ensuring at the same time that they can demonstrate ownership of an exclusive story, newspapers have resorted to releasing key facts in time for evening news bulletins, in the hope this will help alert the public and generate extra sales the following morning. But the tactic of pre-empting publication of a sensational exclusive does sometimes influence the dynamics of a story and although the *Guardian* certainly succeeded in mobilising critics of the Murdoch press, it also gave the Conservative Party and the Metropolitan Police time to plan their response. Reports in the BBC's early evening news bulletins were based on the details given on the *Guardian*'s website but Jon Snow, presenter of *Channel 4 News*, followed up the story by interviewing John Prescott, Labour's former deputy Prime Minister, another of the public figures whose mobile phone messages were alleged to have been intercepted. Prescott said he always thought his phone was tapped; he demanded a police investigation because these latest revelations 'reflected badly' on the officers who conducted the original inquiries; and he called on Cameron to sack Coulson. Snow then asked for a response from the Conservative MP John Whittingdale, chairman of the House of Commons Culture, Media and Sport Select Committee. Whittingdale promised that his committee would meet the following morning and would consider whether to reopen the inquiry it conducted in 2007. In evidence which he gave at the time, News International's executive chairman, Les Hinton, told MPs that he was 'absolutely convinced' that the royal editor was the 'only person' involved in illegal phone hacking.

Events moved rapidly next morning once politicians and journalists had had a chance to read the details of the *Guardian*'s investigation, which was spread across two inside pages under the headline 'Trail of hacking and deceit under nose of Tory PR chief'. When asked to comment on leaving home for Westminster, Cameron dismissed calls for Coulson's dismissal. It was 'wrong for newspapers to breach privacy without any justification' but the editor resigned and was offered a job with the Conservatives because as party leader he, Cameron, believed in 'giving people a second chance'. The phrase 'second chance' was seen as a recognition of the fact that Coulson was somehow implicated but Cameron insisted his communications director was now doing an 'excellent job in a proper and upright way at all times'. Cameron's determination to stand by Coulson was strengthened immeasurably a few hours later when the Metropolitan Police assistant commissioner John Yates announced that the *Guardian*'s report did not require further investigation because 'no additional evidence' had come to light since the original prosecutions. The police had uncovered nothing to suggest Prescott's phone was tapped and in the 'vast majority of cases' which were investigated there was 'insufficient evidence' to show that interception had actually been achieved. Yates had not previously been involved in the *News of the World* case but he was no stranger to controversial corruption inquiries, having conducted the inconclusive investigation into the 'cash for peerages' scandal in 2006. He was well versed in the deadlines of the news media and his statement ruling out another phone-tapping inquiry was in time to make the lead headline on *Channel 4 News*.

In the opinion of rival newspapers the swiftness and sheer certainty of Yates's response appeared to stop the story in its tracks. However, the *Guardian* was undeterred and reported triumphantly next morning that its investigation had triggered three new inquiries. Keir Starmer, the director of public prosecutions, had agreed to review the evidence in the original prosecutions; the Press Complaints Commission announced a fresh inquiry; and in an attempt to discover whether Hinton had misled MPs, the Labour-dominated parliamentary select committee agreed to reopen its 2007 inquiry and for the first time put questions directly to Coulson. Nonetheless within the space of twenty-four hours the Metropolitan Police had effectively vindicated Cameron's judgement in backing his communications chief. Party officials rallied to his support insisting there had been 'extensive due diligence' before his appointment and that there was 'nothing new' in the *Guardian*'s story.

In the course of his investigation Nick Davies tried to establish whether the former editor was aware of a £700,000 out-of-court payment to Gordon Taylor, chief executive of the Professional Footballers' Association, whose mobile phone was one of those alleged to have been hacked. An e-mail reply from his office said the story did not 'ring any bells with Andy' and later, in a brief statement, he said he had no knowledge of 'any settlement' with Taylor. Yet again journalists had failed to penetrate the protective shield which staff at party headquarters threw around their director of communications. That Sunday, welcoming the decision of Assistant Commissioner Yates – 'one of Scotland Yard's most experienced detectives' – to rule out another police investigation, the *News of the World* published a full-page editorial defending its journalistic standards, complete with the banner headline, 'No inquiry, No charge, No evidence'.

With so little fresh information having been volunteered either by the management or by Coulson himself, News International had little difficulty in holding a consistent line when the select committee reconvened. For well over three hours, he and three executives kept the MPs at bay. They insisted the jailed royal editor was a 'rogue reporter' and they had not known what he was up to. Coulson made no secret of the fact that the *News of the World* spent 'more money than most newspapers' in pursuit of stories. Although 'mistakes were made' and 'things went badly wrong', his instructions to staff were clear:

> *We did not use subterfuge of any kind unless there was a clear public interest in doing so . . . They were to work within the PCC code at all times . . . If a rogue reporter decides to behave in that fashion, I am not sure there is an awful lot more I could have done.*

Coulson, who before the phone-hacking scandal was tipped by colleagues to be the next editor of the *Sun*, said he was not looking for sympathy but on resigning he had given up a twenty-year career with News International and everything which he had worked towards since the age of eighteen.

While he was deemed by MPs to have been culpable for the phone hacking which took place, Coulson escaped relatively lightly when the select committee's report was published in February 2010. He was criticised for a 'serious management failure' but the committee acknowledged it had 'seen no evidence' that the former editor knew what was happening. By contrast the report was excoriating in its assessment of News International and the 'collective amnesia' which afflicted its executives when they appeared as witnesses. They were taken to task for their 'claims of ignorance . . . and deliberate obfuscation'; it was 'inconceivable' that no one else knew that phone messages were being intercepted illegally. Both the Press Complaints Commission and the Metropolitan Police were rebuked for their inadequate follow-up investigations. A second inquiry by the PCC had not 'fully or forensically' considered all the evidence. Yates was reprimanded for not giving MPs more detailed evidence about the extent of the phone hacking, a failure considered 'regrettable and improper', but one which he explained on the grounds that it was hard to get prosecutions for the illegal accessing of voicemails.

News International responded to the report with its own counter-attack and accused the Labour-controlled committee of producing biased and distorted findings in pursuit of a 'party political agenda'. On a majority vote, the committee included reference in its report to an unrelated industrial tribunal hearing at which a former *News of the World* sports reporter was awarded £800,000 after he complained of 'a consistent pattern of bullying behaviour' while Coulson was editor. Although the seemingly interminable saga over the suitability of Cameron's communications chief continued to command extensive coverage in the *Guardian* and the *Independent*, other newspapers made only passing reference to Coulson's culpability. Defending press freedom was judged to be a far more productive wicket for the *Daily Mail*, which concentrated instead on the select committee's recommendations regarding the threat posed by libel and privacy laws.

Across the media, among editors, producers and correspondents, there was a widespread feeling that Coulson had shown himself worthy of the 'second chance' which Cameron had afforded him and there was a reluctance to take advantage of what was beginning to look like a political vendetta. Having a former journalist in a key role at the heart of the Conservatives' media machine found favour with most reporters because they preferred dealing with a communications director who understood the news business and who was well versed in the rules of the game when it came to offering preferential access or exclusive interviews. With only two or three months to go to the general election, traditional political loyalties were also beginning to kick in and stories which were particularly damaging to the Tory leadership were often being downplayed by the papers of News International, Telegraph Media Group and Associated Newspapers. One editorial line which remained common to all three groups was their belief that only a change of government could deliver decisive action to slim down the BBC and encourage the kind of light-touch regulation which the industry said was urgently needed to improve the financial viability of online and digital services.

After winning plaudits from Rupert Murdoch's newspapers for the Conservatives' sustained attack on the 'bloated' BBC, Cameron was presented unexpectedly with another opportunity to nail his colours firmly to the proprietors' mast. Complaints about heavy-handed interference in commercial broadcasting had already been taken on board at party headquarters but when Ofcom provoked a dispute in the market for pay television, the regulator's executives failed to think through the likely political consequences. Cameron and his shadow ministers were working up a new initiative aimed at demonstrating the Conservatives' determination to cut back on Whitehall bureaucracy. High on their list of potential targets were the growing number of quangos – quasi-autonomous non-governmental organisations – which Labour had created and which were said to be costing the country £34 billion a year. Ofcom, established in 2003, was facing mounting criticism for the extravagant salaries of its staff and for engaging in what the industry considered was often pointless research and consultation. When it decided in June 2009 to challenge the price charged to competitors for rebroadcasting Sky Television's premium sports and movie channels, BSkyB accused the regulator of making an 'unwarranted intervention' which would require programmes to be sold for less than their true value. Rival operators such as British Telecom and Virgin Media welcomed Ofcom's proposal to challenge both BSkyB's dominance in pay television and its near monopoly in televising FA Premier League matches. Subscription television was the cornerstone of BSkyB's success and the *Sun* immediately rallied to the defence of its sister company. 'This is the world gone mad,' said the paper's columnist Fergus Shanahan, who railed against the 'Ofcom busybodies' for trying to reward losers while punishing Sky Television for showing 'top-flight footie and the latest films'. Shanahan urged the Business Secretary, Lord Mandelson, to intervene. Needing no encouragement, Cameron seized the opportunity and gave a pledge ten days later to cut the number of quangos and reduce the 'scope of their influence'. Ofcom was singled out as a prime example of an 'unaccountable bureaucracy' which was taking decisions which should be the responsibility of ministers 'accountable to Parliament'. Under a Conservative government, Ofcom's remit would be 'restricted to narrow technical and enforcement roles' and its policy-making functions would be returned to the Department for Culture, Media and Sport. 'Ofcom as we know it will cease to exist.' Cameron's announcement, in a hurriedly arranged speech to the think tank Reform, conjured up the prospect of a fundamental shake-up in the way the industry would be regulated. The message to Rupert and James Murdoch could not have been any more reassuring: once installed in Downing Street, Cameron would have an open door for media magnates and be as welcoming as both Tony Blair and Gordon Brown had been in the past. His own experience at Carlton Television, accompanying Michael Green to meetings with ministers in both Conservative and Labour administrations, had taught him the value of face-to-face bargaining. Sensitive government decisions which might affect the political allegiances of influential media companies could not be sub-contracted out to faceless bureaucrats. Not surprisingly Cameron's promise of a 'bonfire of the quangos' was greeted with a chorus of approval: the *Sun* hailed the news that among the 'official busybodies' to be axed were the 'hugely expensive brigade of bossy boots who run meddling quangos like Ofcom'; the *Daily Mail* said Cameron deserved credit for taking on Britain's 'monster' quango state.

When it emerged the following week that James Murdoch had agreed to give the James MacTaggart Memorial Lecture at the August Edinburgh Television Festival, the Tory front bench saw another chance to climb aboard the continuing press campaign to rein in the BBC. In an interview for the *Sunday Times*, Ed Vaizey, spokesman on media and arts, promised that his party would consider whether the corporation should be forced to sell off Radio 1. Angered by the refusal of the BBC Trust to publish the salaries of executives and presenters earning more than £100,000, Vaizey said a future Conservative government reserved the right to freeze the licence fee, as Cameron had already proposed. 'The BBC should get its tanks off our lawn' was the headline over an editorial praising both Vaizey's intervention and an earlier request by the shadow Culture Secretary, Jeremy Hunt, that the BBC should abandon its plans to extend local online news services in order to avoid damaging the regional press. 'The BBC should stick to broadcasting and leave the written word to newspapers and their online commercial rivals.'

James Murdoch could hardly have orchestrated a timelier curtain raiser to his MacTaggart Lecture than if he had written the editorial himself and his presence at the festival was a reminder of the influence which his family wielded. In the 1989 MacTaggart Lecture, Murdoch senior predicted that once consumers were able to take advantage of the multi-channel digital world of the future, the BBC would be hard pressed to justify the 'compulsory poll tax' which financed its services. At the time Sky Television was losing £2 million a week and he challenged the 'sneering' attitude of the old BBC–ITV duopoly which was 'protected by public subsidy and state privilege' and which was 'innately unsympathetic to markets and competition'. Twenty years later, not to be outdone, Murdoch junior ratcheted up the anti-BBC rhetoric by arguing that in an expanding digital and online market place the corporation was spearheading 'a land-grab, pure and simple' which in the 'scale and scope of its current activities and future ambitions is chilling'. Independent digital journalism needed to be able to charge a fair price otherwise the BBC would 'throttle' the news market. 'Dumping free, state-sponsored news on the market makes it incredibly difficult for journalism to flourish on the internet.' Unless the 'expansion of state-sponsored' journalism was curbed, Murdoch suggested, it risked creating the type of news media which George Orwell described in his novel *Nineteen Eighty-Four*. 'As Orwell foretold, to let the state enjoy a near-monopoly of information is to guarantee manipulation and distortion.'

His withering attack on the BBC and the 'authoritarianism' of an 'unaccountable' Ofcom was launched with the edict 'We can't go on like this', a line which would reappear in a Conservative election poster. Murdoch's lecture reinforced and developed the argument which Cameron had advanced the previous month that Ofcom's regulatory approach had to be reorientated away from intervention if there was to be any chance of preserving the diversity, dynamism and innovation of the UK's media industry. A regulator armed with a set of prejudices also harmed the consumer. When the European Commission required Sky's broadcasting rights to Premier League football to be divided up so that no one company could buy all the rights, customers ended up paying more because they needed two subscriptions. Murdoch's *cri de coeur* for 'genuine independence' in the news media was brought to a conclusion with a pay-off which seemed to encapsulate the motivation of the Murdoch dynasty: 'The only reliable, durable and perpetual guarantor of independence is profit.'

When the festival was opened up for debate the following day Murdoch renewed his assault on the BBC and the 'immense problems' which were created for the independent sector by the expansion of its online news and information services. Jeremy Hunt agreed with Murdoch that the level of investment in the BBC's websites was provoking legitimate objections. News online was an 'important part of the value' which many licence fee payers obtained for their money but the increasing number of sites made it difficult for other organisations to run viable operations. Most newspaper editorials sympathised with Murdoch and welcomed Hunt's promise to restrain the BBC's growth. 'Murdoch was right' said a headline in the *Guardian*; an editorial in the *Independent* expressed similar sympathy under the headline 'The BBC's unhealthy dominance'.

The timing of Murdoch's lecture, within months of a general election, was no coincidence, according to David Elstein, a former head of programming at Sky and chief executive at Channel 5. He told *Newsnight* that the BBC Trust had no alternative but to prepare for a possible change of government, which explained why it backed down when the Conservatives wrote a 'very fierce' letter calling on the corporation to abandon the development of ultra-local television services. 'I think James Murdoch has chosen his moment . . . I think David Cameron will listen much more sympathetically to News Corporation.' Elstein's insight was further confirmation that the Murdoch family were finally convinced their business interests would be best served by a change of government. Hunt had been unstinting in his efforts to back up Cameron's speeches by repeatedly reassuring newspaper proprietors that an incoming Conservative administration would follow a twin-track strategy of giving them greater freedom to develop online services while at the same time being resolute in forcing the BBC to downsize services where new commercial operations were threatened. By constantly seeking to publicise weaknesses and flaws in the corporation's responses, Hunt and his frontbench colleague Ed Vaizey were able to exploit deep-rooted press hostility towards the BBC and, by injecting a sharp political edge into the regular reportage, they did even more to unsettle the management and encourage headlines claiming the BBC was in 'retreat'. Mark Thompson, the director-general, was the target of the next offensive. His annual salary of £834,000 was 'too high' and his successor should be paid no more than the Prime Minister's annual salary of £192,250. Hunt outlined the Conservatives' proposal for a cap on the pay of all BBC executives in an interview for *The Times*. Even if salary levels were 'much more realistic', he was confident there would be no shortage of applicants because of the 'privilege' of being director-general and of working for the BBC. Ten days later, in another exclusive interview, he told the *Daily Mail* that a Cameron-led administration would scrap the BBC Trust, replacing it with a 'truly independent body', and would consider whether parts of the BBC's commercial arm, BBC Worldwide, should be sold off.

Hunt's flurry of initiatives through September 2009 had to compete with other new policies in a wider agenda for change which the Conservatives were promoting in the weeks leading up to the all-important annual party conferences, the last before the general election. The BBC's misfortune was that it lacked the collective strength to fight back. A sense of defeatism which the Conservatives were helping to engender within the management was then being used by the party leadership to reinforce their assertion that a new Tory administration would be far more radical than a re-elected Labour government in opening up the digital and online market to the benefit of the commercial sector.

Messrs Cameron, Hunt, Vaizey and Coulson had only a matter of days to wait for the realignment which they had striven so hard to achieve. 'Labour's lost it' said the banner headline on the *Sun*'s front page on the morning after Gordon Brown's speech to the Labour conference in Brighton. After 'twelve long years' in power the government had 'lost its way . . . and now it's lost the *Sun*'s support too'. There had never been much doubt that the *Sun* would switch sides but the pre-planned brutality of its attack on the Prime Minister in the middle of his final pre-election conference stunned even Labour's hard-bitten media handlers. An inside page was illustrated with a large wilting red rose and each copy of the paper included a full-size poster with pictures and graphs depicting the grim policy failures of the 'hard labour' which the country had endured under Blair and Brown. An editorial demanded a clear response in the months leading up the election: 'Cameron's Conservatives must earn voters' trust by setting out their promising policies in detail' but the *Sun* 'believes – and prays – that the Conservative leadership can put the "great" back into Great Britain'. Next day's edition was devoted to the personal stories of the 'fed-up man in the street, wounded war heroes, families of dead soldiers, victims of crime and NHS superbugs' who were 'let down' by Labour. Just as Tony Blair was photographed looking at the 1997 front page declaring 'The *Sun* backs Blair', so David Cameron was pictured holding the 'Labour's lost it' edition. Printed alongside was his promise not to take '*Sun* readers for granted' and to 'earn their votes'.

When news of the paper's switch to the Conservatives reached Brighton on the evening of Brown's speech there was raw anger at the top of the party. Delegates and trade union leaders shared the leadership's annoyance at what they considered was a blatant attempt to sabotage positive reporting of the Prime Minister's pre-election rallying cry. However, among activists on the left there was almost a sense of relief that the party had at last broken free. They welcomed the fact that ministers would no longer feel they were under pressure to appease the Murdoch press. Labour's fifteen-year courtship of the *Sun* had required both Blair and Brown to look the other way when confronted by the aggressive and often anti-competitive business practices of News Corporation, which liked to style itself as the 'globe's leading publisher of English-language newspapers'. Margaret Thatcher's government raised no objection in 1981 when Rupert Murdoch purchased *The Times* and the *Sunday Times*, to add to the *Sun* and the *News of the World*; it approved the launch in 1989 of Sky Television, Britain's first satellite channel, and then allowed a merger with British Satellite Broadcasting in 1990 to form BSkyB. Murdoch's acquisitions and investments effectively drove a coach and horses through the spirit if not the letter of the regulations aimed at restricting cross-media ownership and many stalwarts of Old Labour were disappointed when, within a year of becoming party leader, Blair flew to Australia to trail his coat in front of Murdoch's executives. Nonetheless, the *Sun*'s backing of Labour in the 1997 general election campaign symbolised the strength of press support for Blair. To lose that backing after more than a decade was a significant setback for Brown and

Michael Crick was correct in predicting in his report for *Newsnight* that delegates would not enjoy reading their newspapers over breakfast.

For the Prime Minister, smarting from having been ditched in such a sudden, savage way, there was no escape next morning during a round of radio and television interviews. When Jim Naughtie asked on *Today* what he thought about being dumped, Brown said he believed the *Sun*'s readers would have welcomed his announcement of action against anti-social behaviour and new guarantees for treating cancer patients. 'When I get up in the morning I don't automatically read the newspapers, I get on with my work, the job in hand.' But he lost his composure during a bad-tempered exchange on Sky News when Adam Boulton persisted in asking questions about his style of leadership. 'You are sounding a bit like a political propagandist yourself' was Brown's retort. Instead of staying for the usual post-interview pleasantries he immediately stood up, cutting the conversation short, only to find on getting to his feet that his microphone was still attached to his lapel. Inside the conference hall there was an equally tetchy atmosphere. In a speech on equality, the party's deputy leader, Harriet Harman, claimed the nearest the *Sun*'s political analysis got to addressing 'women's rights is Page 3 news in briefs'. Insisting the conference would not be bullied by a newspaper, she tried to rally delegates by urging them not to be bitter about the defection: 'Don't get mad, get mobilised.' Her plea was reinforced by Tony Woodley, joint general secretary of the Unite trade union, who won a standing ovation as he tore in half a copy of that morning's edition. Murdoch, a hate figure for trade unionists for having sacked so many print workers, was once again being demonised by the left. Having been more than happy to support 'Blairite free market policies', the *Sun* was switching back to the Conservatives and big business, 'the leopard getting its spots back', said Woodley. Labour had no need of an 'Australian-American and his son' who never backed the minimum wage and who were yet again interfering in British politics.

Invitations to conference receptions held by newspapers and other media organisations are highly prized among delegates and are also a draw for ministers anxious to talk to editors and journalists. To add insult to injury the evening of the leader's speech was the night of News International's party, being hosted by the former *Sun* editor Rebekah Brooks (née Wade), newly promoted to the post of chief executive. She had taken her husband's name following her marriage to the racehorse trainer Charlie Brooks and relished her role on the conference circuit as an ambassador for Murdoch's newspapers. Brown made no secret of his refusal to attend the reception, as did Lord Mandelson, who cancelled a planned dinner with James Murdoch. Brooks spoke to Mandelson on the phone and he told her in no uncertain terms that News International would regret its decision. After news leaked out of the ear bashing he gave her, he was challenged on the seafront by Cathy Newman of *Channel 4 News*. He denied delivering a four-letter tirade: 'I said they will be regarded as a bunch of chumps.' But there were no second thoughts at News International and after years of friendly relations with the Murdochs and their executives, Mandelson finally gave vent to his anger, accusing them of 'crude politicking' and doing a deal with David Cameron. 'What the *Sun* can do for the Conservatives during the election is one part of the contract and, presumably, what the Conservatives can do for News International if they are elected is the other side of the bargain.'

Ever since the infamous front-page headline 'It's the *Sun* wot won it' claimed credit for having helped to swing the 1992 general election in the Conservatives' favour, there has been an ongoing disagreement among political strategists and psephologists about the extent to which any one newspaper can influence voters. By deserting Labour for the Conservatives in a way which caused maximum discomfort for the Prime Minister, the *Sun* reopened the argument because its treatment of Brown drew immediate parallels with its contemptuous portrayal of Neil Kinnock before he lost unexpectedly to John Major. Academics dispute the impact of the press on polling day. Anthony King, professor of government at Essex University, believes the theory that endorsements affect elections is 'unsupported by the evidence' and John Curtice, professor of politics at the University of Strathclyde, is even more dismissive, having argued that the aggregate effect of newspapers' influence 'approximates to zero'. But politicians and journalists tend to disagree and as the debate progressed on air and in print the consensus was that Labour would suffer.

The *Sun*'s columnist Trevor Kavanagh was much in demand. He told Radio 4's *The Media Show* the switch in allegiance would not have happened without the 'agreement' of Rupert and James Murdoch. 'The *Sun* has a readership of ten million and our readers are swing voters . . . they do move in elections.' Kavanagh's claim that his paper's readers were open to persuasion was supported by the Labour MP Martin Linton, author of *Was It the* Sun *Wot Won It?*: 'Readers of the *Sun* and the *Daily Mirror* are from the same social group but the *Sun*'s readers are less committed to a party, less interested in politics, so more easily influenced by attacks on character and distortion.' Linton estimated that the *Sun*'s 'character assassination of Kinnock and distortion of Labour's policies' probably saved twenty-five to thirty seats for the Conservatives in the 1992 election. Kinnock shared Linton's analysis and thought it had been obvious for some time that the paper was 'edging' back towards the Conservatives. He told *The World at One* he was convinced that being subjected to the *Sun*'s 'perpetual attack' did make a difference to some people's perception of himself and the party. Harold Evans, the celebrated former editor of the *Sunday Times*, agreed with Linton and Kinnock that voters were far more likely to be influenced by negative, one-sided reporting than a recommendation to vote one way or another. 'What matters much more is the slow prejudicing effect of misreporting over a period, prejudicing people's minds by the steady drip of hostile and negative reporting.'

Labour delegates left Brighton encouraged by a YouGov poll conducted after Brown's speech which suggested a six-point improvement in Labour's rating, halving the Conservatives' lead. But the *Sun* had moved on, turning the spotlight onto Cameron as he prepared for his party conference in Manchester. 'My blueprint for Britain' was the headline over a double-page spread that listed his ten key pledges. Next day the *Sun* printed an interview by its columnist Jane Moore entitled 'Cameron the family man', which described how he proposed to Samantha 'as we watched *Mean Streets*'. Listeners to SunTalk were urged by Jon Gaunt to get 'behind a landslide victory' for Cameron. Unencumbered by the need for political impartiality, Gaunt gave his online audience a vivid account of his day at the Labour conference, watching the Prime Minister's speech: 'I wanted someone to pass the sick bucket when Sarah Brown said her hero was Gordon Brown . . . He is a busted flush . . . He ruined this country . . . We say David Cameron should be the next Prime Minister . . . Brown is dead.'

6
EXPENSES

As MPs struggled during the spring and summer of 2009 to come to terms with the enormity of the unfolding scandal about their parliamentary allowances and expenses, David Cameron was presented with an unprecedented opportunity to change the face of the Conservative Party in ways which had eluded previous leaders. After spending three and a half years doing all he could to promote a modernising agenda, he had become as frustrated as his predecessors by the painfully slow progress in speeding up the selection of women, gays and non-white candidates. Cameron's problem was not just the resistance of local associations but also the low rate of turnover within the parliamentary party and a consequent dire shortage of vacancies in winnable seats. When morale was at rock bottom during the years the Labour Party was busily entrenching its hold on power after Tony Blair's comprehensive 1997 victory, I often heard young activists speak of their fear that it could take a generation to rejuvenate the Tory Party. Just as hospital admissions are curtailed when wards fill up with patients who do not have homes to go to, so the modernisers complained that they faced the political equivalent of 'bed blockers', Tory grandees who were comfortably ensconced in some of the safest seats and who had no intention of standing down simply to make way for new blood. Tory 'knights of the shires', honoured for their past loyalty to the governments of Margaret Thatcher and John Major, were a formidable force, secure in their personal fiefdoms and, as the *Daily Telegraph* was about to reveal with such damning clarity, they had been only too happy for the taxpayer to go on subsidising their highly desirable country houses and lavish amenities. Leaked details of extravagant and outlandish claims for maintaining these second homes became the catalyst for the old guard's final denouement; at last Cameron had the chance to install candidates who he believed were far more representative of the country his party was seeking to govern.

In their day Neil Kinnock and Tony Blair both gained political kudos from confronting far-left Labour MPs and the so-called barons of the trade union movement. Cameron, desperate to avoid a renewed outbreak of civil war with his party's die-hard Eurosceptics, was wary of picking a fight with the troublesome top Tories who had been such a drag on his modernising ambitions. There had been neither an opportunity nor a suitable excuse to slap them down and political commentators took delight in reminding him that he remained untested when it came to the challenge of handling an ideological split within his party. In the 1980s Kinnock enforced his authority over a rebellious parliamentary party by securing the expulsion of Labour MPs who supported the Militant Tendency; a decade later Blair provoked a clash with the left in order to demonstrate his determination to abandon the historic commitment to public ownership which was enshrined in Clause IV of the party's constitution. Both confrontations were purposely played out in the full glare of publicity for the benefit of the news media because the two party leaders needed to show the public visible evidence of their success in taming outdated and divisive forces which undermined their chances of electoral success. Cameron, indelibly tarred by his opponents as a Tory toff, would have to get tough with some of the grandest of the grandees but, like Kinnock and Blair before him, he was only too pleased to encourage the media to take full advantage of the comeuppance which awaited those members of the Tory hierarchy who, with the help of hidden subsidies, had been able to enjoy a lifestyle reminiscent of the landed gentry.

Another unexpected dividend from the drama which transfixed

Westminster was the Conservatives' ability to present themselves as the champions of full disclosure and restitution for the taxpayer. Cameron managed to keep one step ahead of the government as it slowly dawned on MPs that their excessive claims would have to be repaid and that control over their allowances as well as their pay would have to be taken away from the House of Commons and administered independently. In the all-important battle to influence the news agenda Gordon Brown lost the initiative and in responding to what was an unpredictable but fast-moving story, the Tory leader demonstrated a far surer touch, thanks to the guidance of his director of communications, Andy Coulson.

Day after day, as it published yet another batch of highly incriminating expenses claims, the *Daily Telegraph* was able to command the undivided attention of politicians and journalists, all desperate to discover what fresh horrors were in store for the Westminster village. Not only had the paper secured a scoop which would shatter the public's trust in their elected representatives but it succeeded in reordering the daily agenda, giving a fresh twist to the 24/7 news cycle. By trailing next morning's disclosures on its website the previous evening, the *Daily Telegraph* secured a much-enlarged online readership while managing at the same time to virtually dictate the running order of the main radio and television news bulletins, gaining free publicity which generated additional sales next morning. In the thirty-five consecutive days of its investigation the paper sold more than a million extra copies and attracted thirty million hits to its website.

Coulson's expertise in exploiting an unpredictable but agenda-setting scandal was honed during his career on the *Sun* and the *News of the World*. His skill in predicting how a story was likely to be covered by competing news outlets enabled him to identify where the Conservatives were at greatest risk and then advise on the timing and impact of the party's reaction. Cameron was trapped in a political minefield. Tory MPs were responsible for having made some of the most outrageous claims and their calculated exploitation of parliamentary allowances shocked the country just as much as did all the other abuses which the *Daily Telegraph* was exposing. Cameron's rapid responses, backed up by the announcement of some headline-grabbing initiatives, kept the Prime Minister on the defensive while reinforcing the message that the Conservative leadership acknowledged the true extent of the public's disgust at the unforgivable greed of so many MPs.

The *Daily Telegraph* nearly missed its coup in obtaining details of the allowances and expenses claimed during a four-year period. At least five other newspapers had been offered access to a disk containing a copy of claim forms, receipts and correspondence which the Stationery Office had scanned electronically at the request of the parliamentary authorities as the House of Commons prepared for the eventual but partial publication of data relating to the payments made to MPs. But only the *Daily Telegraph* agreed to publish information relating to the claims of all 646 MPs, irrespective of party affiliations, and for the relatively modest outlay of £110,000 it bought the exclusive rights to a story which dominated the news agenda for weeks, all but destroyed the public's faith in the probity of serving politicians, and set in train the biggest upheaval at Westminster for a generation.

Staff scanning the documents were being guarded by soldiers on leave from Iraq. It was their plight in being forced to moonlight in order to earn extra money to help pay for additional kit for front-line duty that was one of the inspirations for a clandestine operation to find a newspaper which was prepared to meet their mutually agreed objective of holding all MPs to account. Tortuous cloak-and-dagger negotiations were eventually conducted on behalf of the whistleblowers by John Wick, a former SAS officer, who hawked the disk around a number of editorial offices. Initially newspapers were offered a sample of the kind of information which had been copied from the hard drive of the Stationery Office computer.

Rumours had been circulating for some weeks about the existence of a illicit disk when in February 2009 the *Mail on Sunday* revealed that the Home Secretary, Jacqui Smith, had designated a spare bedroom in her sister's house in London as her 'main' home and had claimed more than £116,000 in 'second' home allowances on her family house in her

Redditch constituency. Later that month the *Mail on Sunday* revealed that the employment minister, Tony McNulty, who lived three miles from the House of Commons, had nominated as his 'second' home a house in his Harrow constituency which was in fact his parents' main home. The source of these two leaks was not identified but initially some newspapers were being offered access to an individual MP's file at £5,000 a shot. A sample of the data on the disk was shown to the *Sunday Express*, which caused fresh embarrassment for Smith by revealing that her expenses claim included 88p for the cost of a sink plug and a bill for two pay-per-view adult films which her husband later admitted to having watched.

The closer the expenses scandal got to the heart of the government the greater the pressure on Brown to intervene in what Downing Street had previously said was a matter for the House of Commons. In the hope of defusing the mounting furore over Smith's and McNulty's claims, the chairman of the Committee on Standards in Public Life, Sir Christopher Kelly, was asked by the Prime Minister to conduct a wide-ranging review of parliamentary allowances. A week later, after it was revealed cabinet ministers were claiming for 'second' homes while living rent free in London in grace-and-favour apartments, Brown realised that mounting public anger meant there would have to be an immediate shake-up of the entire system. According to the latest estimate, the annual cost of MPs' expenses was likely to reach a new record of £93 million and he could not risk holding off until the committee reported in the autumn. Downing Street briefings suggested he was thinking of taking the moral high ground by linking expenses to daily attendance, a move which would favour Labour MPs while disadvantaging those Conservatives who held directorships or owned expensive country homes. An interim scheme was approved at a cabinet meeting in late April but instead of making a parliamentary statement or holding a news conference, Brown announced his initiative by way of video messages on the Downing Street website and YouTube.

Less than a month after advising the House of Commons to wait for the Kelly review, MPs were astonished to be informed via a social networking site that they would be asked within days to approve a new flat-rate daily allowance to be paid on their actual attendance at Westminster. Allowances for 'second' homes would be abolished and so would claims for food, furniture and fittings. 'A U-turn on YouTube' was how Nick Robinson described Brown's sudden change of mind in his report for the *Ten o'Clock News*. A report for *Newsnight* highlighted sections of the YouTube video, which showed the Prime Minister adopting odd facial expressions and smiling awkwardly. Sketch writers could hardly believe their good fortune and his inept performance, rather than the substance of his proposals, commanded most attention in next morning's newspapers. Quentin Letts filled almost two pages of the *Daily Mail* describing the 'weird video announcement' from the Downing Street bunker. Letts was struck by the way the Prime Minister's 'head jerked and his lips stretched wide into an inexplicable smile'. Brown's suggested solution of MPs being paid a daily attendance allowance of £150 proved to be as ill fated as his YouTube debut and it was abandoned within days. Some limited changes were approved, including a requirement that MPs should produce receipts and declare all earnings from second jobs, but they voted to keep their all-important 'additional costs' allowance pending the outcome of Kelly's review. Brown's piecemeal approach and his wounded retreat to business as usual when MPs opposed the abolition of payments for 'second' homes left him in an exposed and vulnerable position when a fortnight later the *Daily Telegraph* began publishing leaked data from its illicit Stationery Office disk.

In a concerted attempt to prevent further one-off disclosures such as those involving Smith and McNulty, there had been a redoubling of John Wick's efforts to find a newspaper which would do justice to the story. *The Times* was approached; there were also discussions with the *Sun* and the *News of the World*. Wick's associate Henry Gewanter, a public relations consultant, approached the *Daily Telegraph*. After lengthy negotiations and a ten-day period during which the paper had exclusive right of access to the disk, the editor, Will Lewis, promised full disclosure of every MP's expenses. The paper agreed to pay £100,000 for the disk and £10,000 to Wick and Gewanter for their time and expenses. Lewis was under pressure to do a deal because midway through the negotiations *The Times* revealed that it had been 'approached by a businessman' who was asking £300,000 for details of all MPs' expenses claims.

A team of journalists assigned to work on the story faced the daunting challenge of having to get to grips with a mountain of paperwork. The disk contained copies of one and a half million receipts, four years' worth of correspondence between the individual MPs and the House of Commons fees office and other assorted documents relating to their claims and allowances. Wick estimated that all told there were four million separate pieces of information, which had been scanned electronically at the Stationery Office and which had then been transferred to an 'unregistered' copy of the hard drive. In order to protect the identity of those involved in the leak, Wick, Gewanter and the *Daily Telegraph* have purposely remained as vague as possible about precisely what happened. Sometimes there is reference to a single 'ultimate source' or 'the mole' but in *No Expenses Spared* – 'the inside story of the scoop which changed the face of British politics' – the authors, Robert Winnett and Gordon Rayner, indicated there was a wider conspiracy. The book described how the Stationery Office workers and their guards were so scandalised by what they had seen in the files that 'they had decided to orchestrate a leak'. One of the civilian staff who was involved in 'passing the disk to Wick' told of the anger he and his colleagues felt when they discovered that MPs were 'claiming a fortune on their expenses' while they were being paid a pittance. Ending up being guarded by serving soldiers who were trying to earn enough money to buy essential equipment was 'a large factor' in their decision to leak the information. The mole told the authors he had no regrets: 'I'm bloody glad I did it.' Wick later confirmed that it had been a joint effort. He told an Oxford Union debate in October 2009 that the £100,000 was shared out between the 'people who gave the information . . . and who have now lost their employment'.

On seeking legal advice Wick was assured from the start that the data could not be considered to have been 'stolen' because the disk was an 'unregistered' copy and therefore it could be argued that its existence was the result of lax security precautions at the Stationery Office rather than theft. To the surprise of both the staff and their guards they had noticed that unlike most sensitive official documents which were scanned, the data relating to the MPs' claims and allowances had not been given a security classification, such as 'confidential' or 'restricted', and in their view the files were not protected by the Official Secrets Act. The *Daily Telegraph*'s chief in-house lawyer, Arthur Wynn Davies, agreed with Wick that the disk itself 'did not constitute stolen property'. He feared the parliamentary authorities might still seek a High Court injunction on the grounds that the disk was stolen or that publication breached the data protection laws. If legal action was taken he was convinced the paper would have 'an overwhelming public interest defence', its position having been strengthened by a ruling from the information commissioner that the expenses claims should be published. In order to demonstrate good faith, the paper was determined to give each MP an undertaking that their personal security would not be compromised; addresses, bank account numbers and other personal details would not be published.

Faced with such a mass of data, Lewis and his team agreed they would have to prioritise their investigation and they began by examining the files relating to the allowances paid to cabinet ministers. Thirteen, including the Prime Minister and the Chancellor of the Exchequer, were identified as having made questionable claims and they would be among the first to be exposed because Lewis feared that the *Sun*, which had been allowed access to the files of twenty MPs, might try to pre-empt the *Daily Telegraph*'s exclusive. Without even being allowed to tell their own colleagues what was afoot, the team had to work under great secrecy as they feverishly sifted through the documents, first to discover if public money had been misappropriated, and then to see if they could establish the evidence. Lewis was anxious to start publication of their stories with a 'shock and awe' edition detailing the payments made to the cabinet. On subsequent days the paper intended to examine the claims of junior ministers, the shadow cabinet and then the eye-catching receipts submitted by Conservative grandees. Downing Street had less than twenty-four hours' notice of the *Daily Telegraph*'s exclusive. The Prime Minister's office was informed at one o'clock that e-mails would be sent out within the hour giving Gordon Brown and his cabinet colleagues every opportunity to respond to the allegations to be published next day.

Instead of trying to outsmart rival newspapers by delaying publication until later in the print run, Lewis opted to go with the story from the first edition, so as to be in time for the late evening news bulletins and thus create the maximum impact. Under his editorship the paper was investing heavily in its website – www.telegraph.co.uk – but he had faced an uphill struggle convincing some of his senior correspondents that the days were long gone when they could ignore the impact of the internet by attempting to hold back stories until publication next morning. If the *Daily Telegraph* was to succeed in establishing a commanding online presence it had to claim 'ownership' of its exclusives immediately, thus increasing traffic to the website and helping promote sales. If any of its journalists were still uncertain about the editor's strategy for keeping pace with the competitive pressures of the 24/7 news agenda or his resolve to secure a future for the *Daily Telegraph* in a multi-media environment, their doubts were dispelled by the way in which the paper's momentous revelations would go on commanding wall-to-wall coverage, day after day.

Two hours ahead of their main news bulletins the political editors of the BBC, ITV and Sky News were invited by Fiona Macdonald, the Telegraph Media Group's public relations executive, to attend a briefing on the scope of the investigation and to hear an outline of next morning's exclusive. All three channels led with the claims about the misuse of cabinet ministers' allowances in their ten o'clock programmes. Macdonald had started what would become a regular procedure for giving broadcasters advance warning of next day's revelations. She told me that at around eight o'clock each evening she would ring the three editors – Nick Robinson (BBC), Tom Bradby (ITV) and Adam Boulton (Sky) – to alert them to the contents of next morning's front-page story.

At about the same time 'taster' stories would be posted on the paper's website trailing the story but without naming the MPs. Between forty-five and sixty minutes later the first details would be released online. Such was the level of interest in the *Daily Telegraph*'s disclosures that broadcasters on the news channels would relay the information as soon as it was released. Some evenings Jon Craig, a political correspondent for Sky News, would appear with a computer screen beside him in order to point to the latest developments and read out what was being said. Rarely had there been a political story of such magnitude which was tailor made for the rolling news channels and where the source was so eager to do everything possible to sustain non-stop reporting by offering broadcasters a continuous supply of startling disclosures. The resulting saturation coverage subjected MPs and the House of Commons authorities to collective trial by media. For the politicians there would be no escape from the all-embracing nature of the scrutiny they would have to endure; all the public could do was look on in anger and amazement and hope that either the government or opposition parties might give a lead in reforming the system.

'The truth about the cabinet's expenses' was the bold double-deck headline which streamed across the *Daily Telegraph*'s front page on Friday 8 May 2009. Startled readers might have thought at first glance that a world war had just been declared, so stark was the presentation. Staring out from the 'shock and awe' edition were Gordon and Andrew Brown and between their two photographs was a copy of a receipt showing that the Prime Minister had paid his brother more than £6,000 over a 26-month period for 'cleaning services' at his London flat. Included in the story was a quote from Downing Street which explained that the Prime Minister shared a cleaner with his brother Andrew, head of media relations at EDF, a French-owned energy company. Another story on an inside page suggested the Prime Minister had used his parliamentary allowances to 'boost his expenses claims' by switching his designated 'second' home shortly before moving into No. 10. The Chancellor, Alistair Darling, was said to have changed his 'second' home designation four times in as many years and received almost £10,000 towards repaying expenses incurred in buying a new London flat. Even though it had yet to complete a detailed examination of the claims of all 646 MPs, the paper said it was convinced the 'systematic misappropriation' of allowances was one of the 'great scandals of modern public life'. A large proportion had used their additional costs allowance – worth up to £24,222 a year – to pay the mortgage interest on 'second' homes which could then be 'refurbished, decorated and sold at taxpayers' expense'. A step-by-step guide to working the system explained the concept of 'flipping', how an MP could nominate a London property as a 'second' home for refurbishment and then flip the designation to a constituency home, so that it could be improved too.

Unidentified insiders quoted in *No Expenses Spared* gave a graphic account of the consternation in Downing Street when at two o'clock in the afternoon the Prime Minister was presented with the e-mail which asked for his response to the allegations to be published next day. His media advisers had been 'at pains to cultivate a good working relationship' with the *Daily Telegraph* and were upset to have been hit by the story like 'a bolt from the blue'. Brown cleared his diary to prepare his response and 'looked really shocked' once officials began to assemble copies of the e-mails listing the questions which were being asked about claims made by other members of the cabinet. He was said to have been particularly 'concerned' by suggestions that the Communities Secretary, Hazel Blears, had avoided paying £13,000 in capital gains tax when she 'flipped' her 'second' home. She had infuriated him the previous week by criticising the government for its 'lamentable failure' to get its message across to the electorate. In a calculated swipe at his disastrous attempt to use new media, she concluded a comment column for the *Observer* with the line 'YouTube if you want to but it's no substitute for knocking on doors'.

Brown was said to have spent most of the afternoon and early evening sitting at his 'extra-large' computer screen drafting his response and when it finally arrived the journalists noticed that it was typed in the 'large, bold letters' which the Prime Minister tended to use, having lost the sight of an eye in a rugby accident in his youth. Jack Straw, the Justice Secretary, was the first to reply. He acknowledged errors in his claim for council tax and mortgage payments and said he had 'repaid the difference'. Brown, like Straw, did not dispute the figures but insisted there had been no wrongdoing on his part as he had simply paid his brother for the shared cost of a cleaner. For Will Lewis and his editorial team the replies from the Prime Minister and the Justice Secretary were a source of relief because there seemed to be no suggestion that the government might be attempting to block publication either through an injunction or by calling in the police.

When Brown saw the *Daily Telegraph*'s front page and found his cleaning bills had become the splash he 'erupted in fury', a mood which was said to have got 'even worse' when he heard *Today* leading on reports questioning the validity of his expenses. Senior aides arrived to find that the Prime Minister had stayed up much of the night agonising over the story and was 'positively incandescent' at what he considered was an unjustified attack on his personal integrity. Officials noted that he was displaying a 'strong instinct for self-preservation' and that his focus was on 'clearing his own name and that of his brother' rather than on discussing how to speed up reform of the system for reimbursing MPs' expenses. Unnamed ministers were 'troubled' by Brown's 'narrow-minded reaction' and felt he was failing to show leadership and get a grip on the situation.

Throughout the day, as radio and television programmes demanded answers from ministers, the common refrain was that all their allowances and expenses had been 'approved' by the House of Commons fees office. When Blears was challenged she argued that all her claims were 'within the rules', which became another much-repeated mantra. In interviews giving their first reaction Gordon Brown and David Cameron both said it was the 'system' which was wrong and which needed to be changed. By early evening these initial responses were being rapidly overtaken by events. Newsrooms were on a state of high alert, having been primed to expect 'further astonishing revelations'.

Official confirmation that the leak was genuine and from the computer which stored the files of all 646 MPs came from Sir Stuart Bell, chairman of the House of Commons Finance and Services Committee and a member of the commission which administered the expenses system. When *The Times* ran its story earlier in the year claiming newspapers were being offered a purloined disk for £300,000, Bell promised an investigation to see if any data had been stolen. As soon as the first details appeared in the *Daily Telegraph* he acknowledged that parliamentary security had been breached. He told *Channel 4 News* he considered the thirteen ministers were the victims of the kind of 'selective leaking' which was 'not good for democracy'. When pressed by the presenter, Jon Snow, he was confident that 90 per cent of MPs would have 'nothing to apologise for' if their claims were published. Snow's principal interviewee was Heather Brooke, a freelance journalist and freedom of information campaigner, for whom publication of the *Daily Telegraph*'s scoop was a bittersweet moment. She had spent the previous five years trying to force the parliamentary authorities to answer questions about MPs' expenses and it was largely as a result of her repeated applications under the Freedom of Information Act, and her refusal to take 'no' for an answer, that the files were scanned and prepared for publication. Having been 'constantly obstructed', she considered the House of Commons had only itself to blame for 'creating a black market' in data which should have been published the previous October.

Brooke's frustration was shared by other journalists who had tried to investigate the closely guarded procedures for reimbursing claims under the terms of the 'additional costs' allowance. A number of MPs had already been exposed for abusing the system and the parliamentary authorities had also been forced to try to defend the existence of the infamous 'John Lewis list', which gave guide prices on claims for furniture and other household items. On two occasions MPs nearly succeeded in gaining parliamentary approval for legislation to exempt themselves from the requirements of the Freedom of Information Act. But the combined might of Speaker Michael Martin, senior MPs and several distinguished parliamentary officials was no match for Brooke's dogged determination and her relentless campaign to obtain a breakdown of the expenses paid under the 'additional costs' allowance. A ruling in her favour from the Freedom of Information Tribunal, upheld by the High Court, declared that disclosure was in the public interest and the data was due to be released by July 2009.

When the story broke, MPs had already spent some weeks checking through their own files in readiness for publication. The importance of the illicit disk was that it contained unedited copies of receipts and correspondence complete with addresses, bank numbers and other personal details, information which had been blacked out at the Stationery Office. In pre-empting publication of the redacted version which the House of Commons had reluctantly agreed to release, the *Daily Telegraph* not only outwitted the MPs but was also in a position to exploit data which the parliamentary authorities had gone to such lengths to censor. Unless the paper's journalists were able to identify which addresses had been nominated as either a 'main' home or a 'second' home, and unless they could then establish whether or not these designations had been changed, they would not have been in a position to determine which MPs had 'flipped' between different properties in order to claim extra allowances. In her book *The Silent State*, Brooke said the *Daily Telegraph*'s journalists did 'a phenomenal job' in going through the unexpurgated expenses files and in helping the public understand what they contained. 'I don't begrudge them anything, even if they did take away my scoop.'

'The ministers and the money' was the banner headline for the second tranche of revelations which concentrated on the middle and junior ranks of government. One of the first backbenchers to have her allowances scrutinised was Margaret Moran, Labour MP for Luton South, who had claimed £22,500 for treating dry rot at a semi-detached house in Southampton which she designated as her 'second' home, although it was a two-hour drive from both her constituency and the House of Commons. The splash in the *Sunday Telegraph* revealed that five Sinn Fein MPs, none of whom had taken up their seats at Westminster, had nevertheless claimed nearly £500,000 between them on renting three London properties which they designated as their 'second' homes.

Having been spared the embarrassment of finding their own expenses under scrutiny during the initial three days of the investigation, the Tory leadership were able to spend the weekend preparing for the worst, seeking the advice of Andy Coulson and then thinking through what to say. His strategic guidance to Cameron on how best to respond to a media firestorm was about to be tested to the limit. Thanks to the timing of the *Daily Telegraph*'s daily disclosures, the Conservatives had an opportunity to prepare a strategy for damage limitation, an option which was not afforded to either the Prime Minister or his ministerial colleagues, to their great personal annoyance.

On the fourth day of disclosures photographs of six members of the shadow cabinet filled half the front page under the headline 'The Tories and taxpayers' money'. Inside the paper, half way down page five, was the headline: 'Cameron is Mr Clean with only twenty pages of claims'. His 'second' home expenses were described as being 'some of the most straightforward' of any member of the shadow cabinet. While the files of some of the shadow cabinet were ninety pages long, his ran to a mere twenty pages and his only claim in addition to mortgage interest and utility bills was for £680 in 2006 to pay for repairs to his Oxfordshire 'constituency cottage', which included clearing wistaria and vines from a chimney.

Included in the paper's list of excessive payments was £7,000 to Michael Gove for furnishings, £7,000 to Alan Duncan for gardening, and £2,000 to Oliver Letwin for fixing a pipe under a tennis court. But near the top of the front-page story was mention of the first apology by a party leader. Shadow ministers were notified at noon the previous day that their expenses were about to published, giving Coulson ample time to give his advice on how the party might respond. Cameron took the lead. He issued a press statement at eight o'clock and then gave a series of television interviews in which he expressed his regret, ready for the moment when the details started to appear that evening on the *Daily*

Telegraph's website. Fiona Macdonald had already given political editors advance warning of what to expect, which enabled broadcasters to plan their coverage and get television crews in position.

'Cameron said sorry' was the headline on the BBC's *Ten o'Clock News*, which then named the six shadow ministers whose questionable claims were to be revealed next morning. If the government and the House of Commons were unable or unwilling to offer a collective apology, there was no such hesitation on the part of the leader of the opposition, who was only too keen to express contrition on behalf of MPs.

> *Clearly tomorrow is going to be another bad day for Parliament and frankly a bad day for the Conservative Party. The public are really angry. We have to start by saying: 'Look, the system that we used, that we operated, that we took part in – it was wrong and we are sorry about that.' In my view claims should be published online immediately they're made.*

Cameron gave a pledge to take firm but unspecified action against Conservative MPs found to have exploited the system. His apology was prominent next morning in most of the national newspapers and it topped the front pages of the *Daily Mail* and the *Guardian*.

Clearly having been caught off guard, Gordon Brown was anxious to follow suit and according to the London *Evening Standard* he 'scribbled his version' that morning while on the train to Harrogate, where he was to address a conference of the Royal College of Nursing. He stopped short of a personal apology, preferring a more general expression of regret. 'I want to apologise on behalf of politicians, on behalf of all parties . . . Just as you have the highest standards in your profession, we must show that we have the highest standards.' But by waiting three days and then failing to use the word 'sorry', the Prime Minister attracted fresh criticism and was accused by some journalists of simply trying to play 'catch up' after Cameron's swift apology the previous day, which his aides hoped had gone some way towards neutralising the embarrassing disclosures about shadow ministers.

Next morning's *Daily Mail* claimed Labour MPs were bemused by the way the Prime Minister had allowed Cameron to 'beat him to the punch' and failed to recognise that it was simply no good blaming the system. But Brown and his colleagues were still seething about the way they had been treated and were convinced the *Daily Telegraph* had purposely waited three days before exposing the Conservatives. In an editorial that morning the paper insisted it had kept its promise to extend its investigation to the opposition. 'We have been as good as our word. Leading Conservatives are today revealed to have mounted highly questionable raids on the public purse, "flipping" their properties to claim more than one second home allowance.' Cameron's pre-emptive apology was to be welcomed and showed a 'pleasing contrast' with Brown's refusal to 'accept any blame'; the Tory leader had taken the first steps towards restoring 'a more honourable ethos' to Parliament.

The editorial made no mention of the highly effective two-way contact which the paper's journalists were establishing with the hands-on operation which Coulson was co-ordinating at Conservative headquarters. In *No Expenses Spared*, Robert Winnett and Gordon Rayner justified their conclusion that Cameron's expenses claims were 'pretty straightforward . . . boring, even' on the grounds that the total amounts of his yearly 'second' home claims – £20,902 in 2004/5 – were already in the public domain. Ahead of publication, Winnett contacted the party's head of media, Henry Macrory, and told him he thought there was 'nothing much we didn't know' in Cameron's claim. Macrory replied: 'It's just that one repair bill, isn't it?' Winnett took that as confirmation that the Conservatives had already gone through the claims of the shadow cabinet. He discovered subsequently that once the *Daily Telegraph* started trailing its story about the Prime Minister's expenses, Coulson spoke to Cameron, warned him that the Conservatives would be next, and they agreed to start preparing a response. Coulson would have known instantly the potential magnitude of the story, no doubt having been given a steer by former workmates at the *Sun* and the *News of the World*, two of the newspapers which had briefly had access to some of the names on the disk. Next day a team of specialist researchers under the party's director of political operations, Oliver Dowden, were installed in rooms alongside Cameron's office and told to comb through the expenses files of every Conservative MP.

Unlike Labour, where Brown's colleagues were being left to their own devices, there were 'co-ordinated responses' from members of the shadow cabinet and Winnett found that the control which Cameron was exercising in marshalling the party's reaction to the *Daily Telegraph*'s disclosures put Coulson and Macrory in a 'far stronger position to answer questions than their Labour counterparts'. The contrasting responses of Brown and Cameron made quite an impact on the editor the more he became aware of the unbelievable abuses which his journalists were unearthing. *No Expenses Spared* suggested that Will Lewis had no intention of ever disclosing the content of a 'heated' conversation he had with the Prime Minister on the day the cabinet's expenses were published. But the following year he told the annual lunch of the Journalists' Charity that in the course of his telephone call Brown left little unsaid. 'Suffice it to say I haven't been called such names since I played Sunday league football . . . I resisted the temptation to call a hotline for anti-bullying.' Whereas Brown 'wasted several days' having convinced himself he was the victim of a personal attack, Cameron 'tapped into the public's anger' and responded far more effectively.

Listening to Lewis answering questions about what went through his mind before he sanctioned the riskiest investigation of his career, I was struck by the friendly manner with which he complimented Coulson for his role in co-ordinating the Conservatives' response. The clear implication was that an editor whose constant fear initially was that the disk might have been a hoax had ended up establishing a good rapport with a former editor whose media contacts were proving invaluable in helping Cameron stay one step ahead of Brown. Coulson crossed the line when he left the *News of the World* and entered the world of political public relations but he made no secret of the fact that he remained a great defender of campaigning journalism, a tradition which he had encouraged Cameron to support. Once competing news outlets realised the extent of the leaked information which was in *Daily Telegraph*'s possession there was a chorus of approval among rival editors and journalists for the devastating impact of its investigation. Editorial executives on newspapers which rejected the disk were kicking themselves for having missed out on a sensational story over which the politicians had lost control. Lewis recalled with satisfaction how Coulson reacted with 'pure astonishment' the moment he was informed of the ludicrous expenses which some of the Conservatives' longest-serving and most respected MPs were requiring the taxpayer to meet in order to finance hidden subsidies for their country retreats.

Another double-deck headline – 'Paying bills for Tory grandees' – barely did justice to the breathtaking nature of the fifth day of disclosures. Flipping designations between 'main' and 'second' homes seemed somewhat mundane when compared with the ingenuity shown by eight of the party's landed gentry in justifying their parliamentary allowances. Upstanding 'knights of the shires' were about to discover that the rest of the country did not share their opinion that the taxpayer had an obligation to help meet the cost of maintaining their manor houses and stately homes. Reputations would be shredded in the political tsunami which was engulfing Westminster and their pained reaction that anyone should have dared to question what they considered was their entitlement only served to heighten the public outcry.

Topping the list of the most extravagant receipts unearthed so far was a £2,115 bill for clearing the moat around the Lincolnshire manor house of Douglas Hogg, 3rd Viscount Hailsham and a former Conservative Agriculture Secretary. Parts of Kettlethorpe Hall dated from the thirteenth century and Hogg's files showed that in 2004/5 he was reimbursed a total of £23,083 for the upkeep of his property and garden. Each year he submitted a schedule of his maintenance and cleaning expenses and he asked the fees office to pay a proportion equal to the maximum available under his annual 'additional costs' allowance. The schedule included £18,000 for a gardener, £14,000 for a housekeeper, £671 for a mole-catcher and a £31 call-out to have bees removed. Contributing towards the cost of clearing Hogg's moat secured an immediate place in the lexicon of British political folklore for outrageous parliamentary expenditure. On emerging from his London flat next morning he was challenged by *Channel 4 News* and spent four minutes denouncing the *Daily Telegraph* as he continued to walk briskly along the pavement. He had not claimed directly for his moat or housekeeper; these were simply items listed in his schedule of expenses.

Hogg's inclusion of 'moat clearing' might have been considered nothing more than a joke but for the fact that it transpired to be just the first of many preposterous but equally excessive demands which the House of Commons fees office deigned to sanction. Included in Sir Michael Spicer's £20,902 claim for his 'second' home – a manor house in Worcestershire – was the cost of hedge cutting around his helipad and £620 for the installation of a chandelier. Spicer, effectively the party's most senior MP in his role as chairman of the influential 1922 Committee for Conservative backbenchers, was held in high regard but when he tried to dismiss reference to his 'helipad' as nothing more than a family joke, the paper pointed to its inclusion in the bill submitted by his gardener. By examining an MP's claim receipt by receipt, the paper's journalists were finding a never-ending list of bizarre examples. Their scrutiny of the allowances paid to another distinguished former minister, David Heathcoat-Amory, led to the discovery that over a three-year period the fees office had paid out £389 for 550 bags of horse manure used by the gardener at his stone-built country home near Glastonbury. Mention of the 'manure parliament' was instantly suggested as another entry in an A–Z of the escalating scandal of MPs' expenses. One of three grandees who had been singled out for charging for the maintenance and refurbishment of a swimming pool was Michael Ancram, the Marquess of Lothian and a former deputy leader of the party.

The build-up to the sensational revelations about the 'Lords of the Manor' became all the more entertaining after ITN's political editor, Tom Bradby, broke the story in its 6.30 p.m. bulletin. He suggested one grandee might 'even have claimed for a butler'. Andy Coulson was so alarmed he rang the *Daily Telegraph* for clarification. Housekeepers but not butlers had been claimed for and, on condition only David Cameron was alerted, he was told that one claim was for a moat to be cleared. Coulson was said to have replied: 'Fuck me. A moat?' Advance guidance of the horrendous headlines to come again proved invaluable to Cameron and once he had been briefed by Coulson he took the precaution of immediately repeating his apology of the previous evening. He coupled it with a warning that any MP found guilty of an infringement could expect to face disciplinary action. 'Cameron to sack his MPs who defy the rules' was the *Daily Telegraph*'s page 2 headline, indicating that for the second day running the Tory leader was out in front and prepared to admit that trotting out the excuse that the claims were 'within the rules' only added to the public's disgust.

As he left home and was asked by journalists if he could justify payments for swimming pools and moats, he said the claims revealed that morning represented an 'abuse of taxpayers' money'; they were 'out of order'; and he was going to 'deal with it'. Cameron headed straight for his office for what became a day of reckoning with his shadow ministers. After seeing them one by one they went to another room where their claims were examined by an accountant who advised on the appropriate amount to be repaid. Backbenchers were summoned to a meeting of the 1922 Committee, where they were informed that a panel was to be established which would scrutinise each MP's file and enforce restitution of excessive claims. Hitherto unimpeachable grandees who thanks to their impregnable majorities held such sway over the upper reaches of the parliamentary party were told in no uncertain terms that refusal to co-operate meant immediate expulsion. By mid-afternoon Cameron was ready to meet the news media and at a hastily arranged news conference he signalled his readiness for a public showdown with the Tory hierarchy which would prove to be as symbolic as Tony Blair's confrontation with the Labour left over Clause IV.

First came another apology: 'I want to start by saying sorry. Sorry that it's come to this and sorry for the actions of some Conservative MPs.'

Rapid repetition of the S-word was intended to contrast the sincerity of his regret with that of Gordon Brown. A fresh apology was a prelude to a display of collective contrition which again turned the headlines to Cameron's advantage and highlighted the woefully inadequate response of the government. He had been 'completely appalled' to find that some of his MPs had taken money from the taxpayer for swimming pools and moats when so few of their constituents could afford a comparable lifestyle. 'People want something done. The fact is today I can actually announce people are writing out cheques and handing them back to the House of Commons.' Cameron then proceeded to give a roll call of repayments: 'So Michael Gove will pay back the £7,000 for furniture. Oliver Letwin will pay back the £2,000 for the pipe under his tennis court. Alan Duncan will repay £5,000 for gardening bills. . .' Cameron gave a personal undertaking to repay the £680 claimed for repairs to his own 'second' home; three MPs who submitted bills for maintaining swimming pools agreed to reimburse the fees office; and the shadow Welsh Secretary, Cheryl Gillan, rounded off the restitution by writing out a cheque for £4.47 for dog food which had been 'mistakenly' included in a food bill. If shadow ministers had not agreed to return the money, they would have been sacked. The parliamentary party would have to abide by new rules in future: no Conservative MP would be able to charge for furniture, household items or food; there would be a ban on 'flipping' between designated homes; and capital gains tax would have to be paid on homes against which claims had been made.

'Cameron leads payback' was the teatime headline on the BBC News Channel; *Channel 4 News* described him as a 'man of action, the man of the moment'. But by mid-evening he was competing for attention with Hazel Blears. She appeared on Sky News at nine o'clock brandishing a cheque for £13,332 to repay capital gains tax on the sale of her 'second' home. Her dramatic display of contrition was upstaged in the BBC's *Ten o'Clock News* with a report on what the political editor Nick Robison said had been a race by the Prime Minister to catch up with Cameron. Harriet Harman, the leader of the House, prepared the ground by announcing that new rules were being considered. Political correspondents were then summoned to Downing Street to hear Gordon Brown announce an 'independent and radical review' of all claims and receipts submitted during the preceding four years. He said there would be new limits on the amount of mortgage interest which could be claimed. 'I hope and believe all political parties will approve this.' *Newsnight*'s political editor, Michael Crick, said the Prime Minister struggled to 'seem in charge' whereas Cameron had been 'decisive' in telling Conservative MPs they either made restitution or faced expulsion from the party.

The sight of MPs falling over each other in their haste to write out cheques on what after all was only the fifth day of the story was vindication, if any was needed, that publication of the illicitly acquired data was in the public interest. Cameron's swift crackdown on dubious claims, and his ruthlessness in being prepared to name and shame even members of his own shadow cabinet, was hailed by the *Daily Telegraph* as the first sign that the 'penny is beginning to drop' and that voters would not accept the failure of the political establishment to stop some MPs 'crudely and shamelessly' exploiting their parliamentary allowances. Its editorial was topped with the headline 'Courageous Cameron shows how to lead', a sentiment shared by *The Times*, which praised him for taking the 'first, confident step' towards tackling public anger and for taking command on a 'rudderless' House of Commons. In a signed article in the *Sun*, Cameron apologised to its readers for a 'shocking week' for British politics. If elected a Conservative government would tackle the country's problems with the same 'responsibility and thrift'.

For the Tory leader to be attracting plaudits from the press was all the more galling for the Prime Minister given that he was still smarting from the attack on his own integrity and the news media's refusal to give him any credit for his previous efforts to reform the system. But his lack of an overall strategy and his inability to co-ordinate a fightback to match the urgency and conviction of Cameron's response was compounded by even greater ineptitude on the part of the Speaker, Michael Martin. In his first response to the scandal he opted to go on the offensive rather than seize the chance to build on the Prime Minister's initial apology 'on behalf of politicians, on behalf of all parties'. Because the unauthorised disclosure included details of 'bank accounts, style of signature and verbal passwords', suggesting a 'criminal offence or offences may have been committed', the police had been informed. Martin feared that the person who sold the data was capable of 'selling this information further'; therefore that individual could not be left 'in situ', able to offer the data to the 'highest bidder'. But Martin compounded his failure to join the chorus of apologies by unexpectedly rounding on MPs who dared to suggest the House of Commons should be reforming itself rather than calling in the police. The Labour MP Kate Hoey argued that it was 'an awful waste of resources' to ask the Metropolitan Police to investigate the leak when the newspapers were handling personal details 'very responsibly by blanking them out'. Martin, red faced and jabbing his finger, said that while it was easy for Hoey to deliver her 'public utterances and her pearls of wisdom' on Sky News and give quotes to the *Daily Express*, he could not stand by and allow an employee of the House to sell private data. When the Liberal Democrat Norman Baker asked for all the expenses claims to be published as soon as possible, he was admonished for being 'keen to say to the press whatever the press wants to hear'. By defending the Westminster club rather than taking the first opportunity to show contrition, Martin sealed his own fate. Campaigners for greater openness believed the Speaker had become the principal road block to reform because of the way he had encouraged the House of Commons commission to thwart the Freedom of Information Act. A parliamentary motion was tabled that evening by the Conservative MP Douglas Carswell calling on Martin to stand down so that he could be replaced with a Speaker with a mandate to 'clean up the Commons'.

Martin's misjudgement of the mood of the House became all the more embarrassing as the day wore on and details started to emerge about the subsidies being paid to Tory grandees for the upkeep of their country estates. Public disbelief at the ease with which wealthy Conservatives had managed to fleece the taxpayer turned to raw anger once the *Daily*

Telegraph discovered that some Labour MPs might have committed the criminal offence of false accounting. 'Phantom' mortgages were about to join moats, swimming pools and adult films in the A–Z of the scandal. Elliott Morley, a former Labour agriculture minister, commanded the whole of the front page on the seventh day of the investigation. A report alleging the 'most serious' disclosure so far was topped with a triple-deck headline which left little unsaid: 'MP who claimed £16,000 for mortgage that did not exist'. Morley took 'full responsibility' for a mistake in his accounts and said he had repaid the money but his swift apology was not enough to prevent suspension from the party. David Chaytor, Labour MP for Bury North, suffered the same fate after his expenses made the front-page splash on the ninth day of the story: 'The MP and phantom £13,000 mortgage'. He apologised unreservedly for an 'unforgivable error' in his accounting procedures.

To have gone on paying not one but two non-existent mortgages was a reminder if any was needed of the shortcomings of the fees office and the ineffectiveness of the Speaker's supervision of staff under his control. Martin's abject response to the public outcry over expenses followed persistent criticism of his stewardship of the House of Commons since his failure in December 2008 to stop an anti-terror squad from the Metropolitan Police searching the office of Damian Green, the shadow immigration minister. Jill Pay, the Serjeant at Arms, had advised the Speaker that Green was about to be arrested as part of an investigation into the leaking of Home Office statistics. She believed the police had authority to search Green's room but when Martin was forced to admit to the Commons that the police did not have a warrant he was accused of not having done enough to protect the rights of MPs. His mishandling of the police raid and his evident mismanagement of the expenses saga were issues which rival newspapers could investigate. Having seen their daily counterparts beaten hands down during the previous nine days by exclusives derived from the expenses disk, the Sundays had identified the likeliest scapegoat. Their headlines signalled the opening scene of another political drama: 'Speaker "waged a reign of terror" over expenses'

(*Sunday Times*); 'Pack your bags, Speaker Martin' (*Sunday Express*); 'Mr Speaker, you have brought this House into disrepute. You must go' (*Mail on Sunday*).

Speculation about the Speaker's fate dominated the Sunday morning political programmes and the Liberal Democrat leader, Nick Clegg, had no hesitation in leading the attack. He told *The Andrew Marr Show* he was prepared to break the convention that party leaders refrained from criticising the Speaker because Martin had shown himself to be a 'dogged defender' of a 'rotten parliament' and needed to be replaced with a radical reformer. William Hague, the shadow Foreign Secretary, agreed on *Sky News* that the call for Martin's resignation was 'reaching crisis point' and would have to be resolved. 'Mr Speaker's last stand' was the *Daily Mail*'s front-page headline next morning, heralding the start of another critical day for the House of Commons as MPs awaited a fresh statement on his intentions. For the eleventh day of its investigation the *Daily Telegraph* had specifically targeted Martin and claimed that some of the leaked correspondence revealed how officials under his control had colluded with MPs in allowing them to make inflated claims on their mortgages. Later that morning, after it was confirmed that Douglas Carswell had tabled his motion calling on Martin to step down, lobby correspondents were told that the Prime Minister would accept the 'will of the House'; it was not for the government to 'pass judgment' on the Speaker. Martin bowed to the clamour for an apology but remained as combative as the week before. In his opening remarks he acknowledged that the 'men and women of the United Kingdom' felt they had been let down 'very badly' by himself and the House. 'We must all accept blame and to that extent that I have contributed to the situation, I am profoundly sorry.' He called for an urgent meeting with party leaders to discuss reform of the expenses system but the Speaker was no longer in control of events. After Martin rebuffed the Labour MP David Winnick for having asked for at least an indication of when he might retire, Carswell demanded to know when MPs would be allowed a chance to elect a new Speaker to lift the House 'out of the mire'. Martin was having none of it. He refused to allow discussion of a vote of confidence, saying it was in the form of early day motion and only a substantive government motion could be debated. MPs were aghast at his attempt to brazen it out and while his critics piled on the pressure in radio and television interviews, his fate was sealed at a discreet meeting with the Prime Minister in Speaker's House. Early next morning the Press Association news agency confirmed that Martin intended to resign. At the start of business, straight after prayers, he made a brief 33-second statement announcing that he would relinquish the office of Speaker the following month. Martin was the first occupant of the Speaker's chair to be ejected by MPs since Sir John Trevor in 1695. 'A very British revolution' was the succinct headline next morning over the *Daily Telegraph*'s front-page report of a 'momentous day' at Westminster. Martin's fate was 'symbolic of the rottenness of a political system which was once the envy of the world'. He had precipitated his own removal by his 'fumbling and inadequate' response to the paper's disclosures.

A rude awakening was in store for the many MPs who had so far escaped scrutiny and who perhaps harboured the thought that journalists investigating their expenses might call it a day now that they had succeeded in forcing the first Speaker out of office for 300 years. David Cameron too was in for a surprise: Douglas Hogg's moat clearing was about to be surpassed by a country house extravagance which would amaze the nation. Sir Peter Viggers, Conservative MP for Gosport, followed Hogg's practice of asking the fees office for the maximum yearly allowance on the annual running costs of his country home. The breakdown for 2006/7 included 'pond feature, £1,645', which on inspection of the receipts was invoiced as a 'floating duck island . . . Stockholm model . . . price includes anchor blocks, duck house and island'. The *Daily Telegraph*'s sleuths had identified the iconic symbol of the entire expenses saga but for once Will Lewis and his team failed to clear the front page for the revelation which grabbed the attention of the world's news media.

The '£1,600 duck house' was mentioned in the third line of the headline and there was a picture of one of the Tory grandee's 'feathered friends' but the main focus of the splash was on the allegation that a

Conservative whip, Bill Wiggin, a contemporary of Cameron at Eton, had been reimbursed for a 'phantom' mortgage; he had been claiming interest on a unmortgaged property. *No Expenses Spared* provided an explanation for the muddled story line on the fourteenth day of the investigation: Andy Coulson had made numerous calls on Cameron's behalf in an attempt to put pressure on the paper not to give Wiggin the same prominence as the two Labour MPs whose 'phantom' mortgages had already been exposed. Coulson's argument was that Cameron had been assured that Wiggin had made an 'innocent – albeit stupid – mistake' by accidentally claiming for his constituency address when he meant to claim for his 'second' home in London. Lewis considered it would be 'wrong to treat Wiggin differently' from other MPs with questionable claims so he insisted the allegation went on the front page; it would be up to the public to decide whether Wiggin's 'defence of ignorance stood up to scrutiny'. In revealing what went on behind the scenes that day *No Expenses Spared* identified but did not elaborate on two significant pointers to the conduct of the Conservatives' media strategy: if necessary Coulson could be as persistent as Peter Mandelson and Alastair Campbell when it came to trying to browbeat journalists, and for his part Cameron was inclined to be too protective of his inner circle and could lose the objectivity required of a party leader.

A close-up of a brightly coloured mallard was prominently displayed on the front page alongside photographs of Wiggin and the former cabinet minister Ruth Kelly – who claimed for flood damage to her 'second' home on her expenses – but the layout lacked clarity. A confusing array of information and images suited Cameron and Coulson because it diluted the impact of the story about Wiggin's 'phantom' mortgage. As a consequence the front page did not do justice to Viggers's ridiculous claim, the details of which were relegated to a page 3 story. An aerial photograph reproduced from Google Earth showed his large country house, grounds and pond complete with its 'Stockholm duck house' based on the design of an eighteenth-century building in Sweden. An official in the fees office marked the item 'not allowable' but Viggers had included 'pond feature' in his handwritten list of expenditure. He subsequently acknowledged he made a 'ridiculous and grave error of judgement' in asking the taxpayer to contribute towards its cost.

Unlike Hogg, who hung on for a week before indicating that he would stand down at the next election, Viggers was 'forced' to announce his retirement immediately after a brief discussion with an 'incandescent' Cameron, who told *GMTV* next morning that if the MP had refused to stand down he would have faced expulsion. A third grandee to confirm that day that he too would not be seeking re-election was Anthony Steen, Conservative MP for Totnes, who told the party leadership of his decision after it was disclosed he claimed £459 for a woodland consultant to inspect the 500 trees in the grounds of his country home. The three casualties were MPs of long standing – Viggers (1974), Steen (1974) and Hogg (1979) – and they formed the advance guard of what would become a dramatic cull of Tory old-timers who lorded it over some of the party's safest seats.

In the fourteen days since the *Daily Telegraph* began publishing the results of its trawl through the data on the Stationery Office disk, its reporters had examined less than a third of the MPs' files but they had already managed to identify the two most memorable claims; the last of the hapless trio was about to earn the accolade for the most petulant response. Steen's interview for *The World at One* encapsulated the breathtaking arrogance of those MPs who believed the public had no right or justification to know how they spent their taxpayer-funded allowances. Steen insisted that he had behaved impeccably and the fuss was all the fault of the 'wretched' Labour government which had 'completely mucked up the system' by introducing the Freedom of Information Act.

I have done nothing criminal. And you know what it's about? Jealousy. I have got a very, very large house. Some people say it looks like Balmoral, but it's a merchant's house from the nineteenth century. What right does the public have to interfere in my private life? None. Do you know what this reminds me of? An episode of Coronation Street. *This is a kangaroo court.*

Cameron, shocked by what he heard, told interviewers he had given Steen a clear instruction: 'One more squeak like that and he will have the whip taken away from him so fast his feet won't touch the ground.'

For a young party leader keen to assert his authority, desperate to clear out dead wood to make way for fresh talent, the expenses scandal was a blessing in disguise. Moats and duck houses reinforced the image of a party ruled by wealthy toffs but the merciless treatment meted out from the start was a vivid illustration of Cameron's determination to try to decontaminate the Tory brand. Summary justice sent a powerful signal to his party and the news media: if any other Conservative MPs were found to have made equally absurd or inflated claims they too would get short shrift. In the two weeks which had elapsed since the scandal broke, Cameron had taken command of the internal disciplinary process and was exercising tight control over the presentation of the party's reaction in what had become a highly unpredictable media frenzy. He had no way of knowing in May 2009 that the House of Commons was in the opening phase of what would become, as the Prime Minister later remarked, the 'biggest parliamentary scandal for two centuries'. Right up until the 2010 general election and beyond there would be no escape in the Westminster village from the repercussions of the indefensible abuse of parliamentary allowances. Whereas Cameron managed from the start to get a grip on the unfolding story, Gordon Brown was slow to appreciate the dynamics of what was happening or to understand the potential damage to Labour's prospects in the imminent European Parliament and local authority elections. During the week Cameron started to read the riot act, Brown was still in the process of defending Geoff Hoon and James Purnell, two cabinet ministers who had not paid capital gains tax on the sale of second homes but who the Prime Minister believed had stuck to the 'letter of the law'.

Labour's lumbering disciplinary procedures were sometimes no match for what Anthony Steen claimed was Cameron's 'kangaroo court', which usually managed to pre-empt the *Daily Telegraph* by forcing the hand of recalcitrant MPs well before details of their expenses had been released. When a single, massive story takes command of the 24/7 agenda instant responses are required from politicians if they are to have any hope of influencing the direction of the coverage. Unlike Labour, where it took time to co-ordinate the reaction of Downing Street, government departments and the party machine, the Conservatives' media team had firm control over the story line and a much better chance of responding in time to meet news deadlines. Elliott Morley and David Chaytor were both suspended from the parliamentary party on the day their 'phantom' mortgages were disclosed but by the time their suspensions were announced that afternoon the story had been running on television, radio and newspaper websites since the previous evening and journalists were already moving on to the next group of MPs to be targeted. Ben Chapman was the third Labour MP to be accused of claiming for a 'phantom' mortgage and the first to announce that he would voluntarily stand down. He denied doing anything wrong but took the initiative because he was anxious not to embarrass his local party in the marginal constituency of Wirral South. Similarly Dr Ian Gibson, Labour MP for Norwich North, indicated he was prepared to stand down as soon as he was notified that the paper intended to reveal the fact that he sold his 'second' home to his daughter for half its market value. But instead of accepting his decision party officials banned him from seeking re-election, at which point Gibson resigned as an MP and triggered a by-election.

On some occasions the instant justice meted out in the leader's office failed to satisfy Tory party activists. Andrew Mackay, one of Cameron's senior parliamentary aides, tendered his resignation after realising that he and his wife Julie Kirkbride were about to be exposed for 'double dipping' – where a husband and wife each claimed a parliamentary allowance on houses designated as 'second' homes. Cameron told Mackay joint claims were 'unacceptable' and his resignation was relayed to the *Daily Telegraph* well before it managed to release its findings, a pre-emptive strike which took some of the heat out of the story. Mackay hoped to remain an MP but party members in his Bracknell constituency had other ideas and after being barracked at a Friday evening meeting, he declared he would stand down at the election. He had no wish to become a 'distraction', which suggested to journalists that he had lost Cameron's support and was perhaps hoping his wife might have a better chance of surviving if he stepped down.

When challenged by activists in her Bromsgrove constituency, where 5,000 signatures were collected in support of a 'Julie must go!' campaign, she declined to attend a public meeting and instead offered to talk it over with local voters on the doorstep. Her proposed door-to-door visit was overtaken by fresh disclosures concerning a £50,000 extension to her 'second' home and a £1,040 claim for two sets of posed photographs of herself. Cameron said Kirkbride was doing the 'right thing' by proposing to meet her constituents but she realised her position was becoming untenable and was quoted that morning saying she would stand down if the leadership considered her conduct was unacceptable. *No Expenses Spared* described the moment she rang to confirm she would not be seeking re-election. Cameron, who was with Andy Coulson, was in the process of being interviewed by the *Daily Telegraph* and was explaining why he believed MPs who claimed for 'phantom' mortgages should face fraud charges. He left to take Kirkbride's call and on his return the 'strained expression on his face' underlined his concern at the loss of prominent MPs. A Labour casualty that day was Margaret Moran in Luton South, who decided to stand down rather than face deselection at a disciplinary panel.

Aggrieved politicians can become dangerous loose cannons during a prolonged bout of political instability and the ease with which even experienced Conservatives were managing to shoot themselves in the foot must have reminded Cameron of his time as a young political adviser in the final years of John Major's premiership. Rebel MPs were able to trash Major's government with impunity because he lost control at

Westminster, a nightmare scenario for any party leader. Cameron faced a comparable threat to his own authority because MPs were throwing caution to the wind in their desperation to defend themselves. Sir John Butterfill, Conservative MP for Bournemouth West, agreed to be interviewed by *Newsnight* on discovering that the *Daily Telegraph* intended to reveal next day that he had paid no capital gains tax on a £600,000 profit from the sale of his country house. His claim for a 'second' home allowance on the property included costs for a 'servants' quarter' occupied by his housekeeper and gardener. When questioned by Kirsty Wark, Butterfill admitted his one mistake in claiming mortgage interest was his failure to separate out the value of 'the servants'— er, the *staff* wing'. His slip of the tongue reinforced his status as a Tory grandee, a salutary reminder if one was needed that he made the right decision in offering to repay £20,000 and in opting not to seek re-election.

Rent-a-quote MPs who can be relied upon by journalists to offer an opinion are another potential source of irritation at a time when the leadership is doing all it can to manage reaction to a difficult story. In her four years as Conservative MP for Mid Bedfordshire, Nadine Dorries had established a high profile as an independent-minded backbencher prepared to offer an opinion on controversial issues and sometimes say the unsayable. Cameron was swift to disassociate the party from her unexpected attempt to justify the 'second' home allowance. She accused the *Daily Telegraph* of engaging in a 'McCarthyite witch hunt' which was pushing some MPs to the point of suicide. Dorries, who claimed for rent and furnishings for two second homes, told *Today* that MPs considered a 'lump sum of money' in their 'additional costs' allowance to be part of their salary as it made up for pay rises which they had been denied. 'MPs are walking around with terror in their eyes waiting to see if they're next to get an e-mail from the *Daily Telegraph* at 1 p.m. The atmosphere is unbearable and some MPs are seriously beginning to crack.' Instead of pausing for thought she went straight to Radio 5 Live as a guest on Victoria Derbyshire's morning phone-in. Undaunted by the hostility of the callers and the alarm she was causing at party headquarters, she castigated the paper's journalists for giving MPs only five hours in which to respond. 'They say they'll put it in the paper whatever an MP says. Conversations are recorded and there's no right of reply.' Dorries had her own conspiracy theory: exposing MPs' expenses was part of an attempt by the *Daily Telegraph*, a Eurosceptic newspaper, to encourage voters to cast a protest vote for the United Kingdom Independence Party so as destabilise Britain's relationship with Europe.

When the shadow leader of the House, Alan Duncan, caused a sensation by suggesting MPs were being forced to 'live on rations' because of public anger over their expenses, Dorries sprang to his defence. She told the Jeremy Vine show that while assisting at a road accident she was too frightened to admit she was an MP because of a backlash caused by 'horrific stories spun in the media' which were totally untrue. Duncan, MP for Rutland & Melton, had only himself to blame for getting caught on film complaining about the plight of MPs. His repayment of £4,000 for gardening was one of the first made by a shadow minister and made him a target for pranksters. Secretly filmed footage of a pound-shaped flowerbed being dug in the lawn of his constituency home became a hit on YouTube. In a surprising show of hospitality Duncan invited the culprit for a drink and chat on the terrace of the House of Commons. Heydon Prowse, editor of the magazine *Don't Panic*, had a penchant for undercover filming and the unsuspecting Duncan did not realise a buttonhole camera was recording his musings on the future of the House of Commons. 'Basically, it's being nationalised. You have to live on rations and are treated like shits . . . I spend my money on my garden and claim a tiny fraction. And I could claim the whole bloody lot, but I don't.' Initially Duncan insisted his remark about having to 'live on rations' was meant as a joke but later he apologised unreservedly, saying he understood that the last thing people wanted to hear was an 'MP whingeing about his pay and conditions'. Nonetheless his fear that high achievers from the outside world would be put off entering Parliament was endorsed by Sir Patrick Cormack, Conservative MP for South Staffordshire. He told *The World at One* that meeting the costs of being an MP was 'an extremely expensive business' and in lieu of expenses the annual salary should be doubled. 'One is expected to give liberally to all manner of charities, one is expected to attend all manner of events, and one is expected constantly to be putting one's hand into one's pocket.' On his return next day from holiday Cameron urged his parliamentary party to demonstrate that it shared the 'public's real fury' and was prepared to 'clear up the mess of expenses'. Duncan's apology for making a 'bad mistake' was accepted but a month later Cameron demoted him to shadow prisons minister and he was replaced as shadow leader of the House by Sir George Young; Cormack, an MP since 1970, added his name to the roll call of Tory grandees announcing their retirement.

Horror stories apart, the Conservatives continued to benefit from the close working relationship which Coulson maintained with the *Daily Telegraph*. Invoking instant disciplinary procedures, perhaps an instruction to make immediate repayment or leaving an MP with no alternative but to stand down, gave the party the edge over Labour and the 'punishment' usually became one of the top lines in each new story, reinforcing Cameron's image as a no-nonsense party leader. Gordon Brown, still so resentful of what he considered was Labour's unfair treatment, suggested that ministers facing questions from the *Daily Telegraph* about their expenses should issue their replies first to local newspapers and the Press Association. *No Expenses Spared* quoted Downing Street aides saying they hoped their 'low level harassment' might embarrass the paper into ending its investigation. Brown made another miscalculation in breaking off relations: when the House of Commons finally published the redacted version of each MP's file, the *Daily Telegraph* made sure the Prime Minister remained the prime focus of its story. 'Blackout: the great expenses cover-up' was the bold, two-deck headline and reproduced below was a heavily blacked out entry from the Prime Minister's claim. Except for the date – 23 November 2005 – only two lines were still visible: 'Mr G. Brown' and 'Total now due £83.70'. When the censored document was compared with the original on the disk it turned out to be his telephone bill but it had been so heavily redacted that even the British Telecom logo was blacked out. Other redacted entries from Brown's file were reproduced on inside pages and the paper said the continuing cover-up made a mockery of the Prime Minister's declaration that 'transparency to the public is the foundation of properly policing this system'.

For the first time since the leaks began appearing there was a level playing field for the news media. All journalists, as well as the public, had equal access to the files when they were released online at 6 a.m. on Thursday 18 June. Reporters could hardly believe what they saw on the House of Commons website. Instead of being able to check through an MP's claim in the hope of finding incriminating details which might have been missed, they were confronted by an almost impenetrable wall of black ink. So much of the detail had been censored that most of the entries were indecipherable and the media's unanimous verdict was that the parliamentary authorities were guilty of a cover-up which would prove to be even more humiliating than their attempt to thwart the Freedom of Information Act. Before being released on the parliamentary website each MP had been able to check his or her file and at their behest the process of redaction had gone much further than the Stationery Office originally proposed. Instead of simply removing sensitive data such as signatures, addresses and other personal details, the MPs had blacked out page after page of receipts, rendering the text that remained almost meaningless. There was widespread support across the media for the *Daily Telegraph*'s contention that if it had not been able to publish the leaked version of MPs' expenses, the public would never have known about 'flipping' between 'second' homes, 'phantom' mortgages and the avoidance of capital gains tax. Data which did not make the redacted versions included the correspondence regarding Douglas Hogg's moat and Sir Peter Viggers's floating duck island and any reference to the Prime Minister's brother.

Next morning most newspaper front pages reflected renewed public fury over what the *Independent* dubbed 'The Blackout'. Brown's 'censored invoice for cleaning' made the *Sun*'s front page and was widely reproduced. Any hope on the Prime Minister's part that publication of the files might put a stop to stories about his own claims was misplaced and he again became an obvious target for the *Daily Telegraph* once Will Lewis felt able to go public about the role played by John Wick. Wick's account of the anger of the soldiers guarding staff at the Stationery Office linked the expenses scandal directly to Brown and his alleged failure as Chancellor of the Exchequer to provide sufficient resources for the troops on duty in Iraq and Afghanistan. The story of the soldiers' fury and the motivation of the mole who handed over the disk filled the front page on two consecutive days; the reportage could hardly have been any more explicit in pointing a finger of blame. Brown's expenses included £36 a month for a sports package on Sky TV and it was this one item which was said to have 'particularly enraged the staff' and encouraged them to leak the MPs' files in order to 'shame the government into finally supplying the right equipment for the thousands of soldiers risking their lives in Afghanistan'. Identifying Brown as the original focus of the whistleblowers' anger was seized on by the *Sun* in support of its long-running campaign to force ministers to admit they had failed to give 'our boys and girls' the equipment they needed to take on the Taliban. Bereaved families and relatives began quoting the story line that the expenses leak had been prompted by soldiers moonlighting to buy the right body armour, commentary which reinforced the connection between the Prime Minister's expenses and their desperation and anger.

Just as John Major suffered terrible collateral damage from the 'cash for questions' scandal in the mid-1990s, so Brown was finding it almost impossible to extricate himself from the charge of inaction over the abuse of parliamentary allowances. Prime Ministers engrossed in the affairs of government have nothing like the freedom of manoeuvre enjoyed by leaders of the opposition and the incumbent tends to get the blame for wider failings in public life, but Cameron's ruthlessness in toppling Tory grandees did suggest he exercised firmer control than Brown and it also served as a regular reminder of the changing face of his party.

A gratifying political dividend for the modernisers was the growing realisation that a wide array of safe seats would require new candidates, an unparalleled opportunity to inject fresh blood into the Tory heartlands. In the week that Julie Kirkbride was fighting to remain an MP, Cameron found a neat, newsy way to take advantage of the speculation that up to half of all MPs would either stand down or be defeated in the forthcoming election. The prospect of the biggest clear-out at Westminster since 1945 gave him the chance to respond to the clamour for 'honest politicians' by offering to recruit candidates who had no political experience or previous connection with his party. 'If you believe in public service, if you share our values, if you want to clean up politics, come and be a Conservative candidate.' More than a hundred constituencies, dozens of them considered winnable seats, had vacancies and the party began to assemble an eclectic mix of political outsiders for a new A-list of possible candidates.

Cameron's bid to attract fresh talent from all walks of life smacked of opportunism but any potential critics among the Tory hierarchy were silenced the moment the party realised Dr Ian Gibson's resignation had triggered a by-election which any leader would die for. Norwich North was considered a safe Labour seat but by sheer good fortune the Conservative candidate was a spin doctor's dream, a 27-year-old political novice who if elected would become the country's youngest MP. Instead of finding she was fighting a long-shot Labour-held seat, 163rd on the Conservatives' target list, Chloe Smith was suddenly in with a sporting chance of beating a local party which was hurt by the expenses scandal and divided by Labour's decision to ban Gibson from standing again. Cameron visited the constituency six times to give his support and surprised the media by turning up to deliver leaflets for her at 6 a.m. on polling day, a first for a leader of the opposition, as far as *Newsnight*'s veteran political reporter Michael Crick could remember. Smith, a management consultant with Deloitte, took the seat with a majority of more than 7,000, a margin which exceeded the vote of the Labour candidate, Chris Ostrowski. The swing to the Conservatives was 16.5 per cent, not far short of the 17.6 per cent they had secured the previous summer in the Crewe & Nantwich by-election in the wake of Labour's misjudged campaign accusing the Conservative candidate Edward Timpson of being the 'Tarporley toff'. The runaway success of a 'Cameron babe' in what the *Daily Telegraph* dubbed the 'expenses by-election' added fresh momentum to Cameron's push to increase the party's female representation. Smith had become not only the youngest Conservative MP for thirty years but also the party's youngest-ever woman at Westminster, the very personification of what the London *Evening Standard* said was an 'impeccable Cameroonian'.

Another first was also taking shape in Anthony Steen's constituency of Totnes, where, at a cost of £40,000, the party had invited the 69,000 voters to take part in a postal ballot to select a Conservative candidate from a shortlist of three. Dr Sarah Wollaston, a general practitioner in a nearby practice who had no political experience, won the nomination by a comfortable margin and Eric Pickles, the party chairman, hailed the open primary selection process as a 'great success for democracy'. In a second postal primary, held in the Gosport constituency of Sir Peter Viggers, local voters chose Caroline Dinenage, daughter of the veteran television host Fred Dinenage. At 17.8 per cent, the turnout in Gosport's postal vote was slightly down on the 24.6 per cent participation in Totnes but the Conservatives had made a radical break with the traditional selection process and Pickles believed that giving 'power to the people' was one way of rebuilding trust in the political process.

A run of positive stories about Cameron's success in feminising the list of prospective MPs could not last and Smith's role as a standard bearer for the future face of the party made little impact in the neighbouring constituency of South West Norfolk, where local activists tried to overturn their original choice. Within days of selecting Elizabeth Truss as candidate a group of grassroots supporters reacted angrily when told of her affair five years earlier with Mark Field, a married Conservative MP. Truss, a mother of two, faced deselection and as Cameron rallied to her support, insisting that her affair had been 'publicly known', the headline writers had a field day. Simon Walters, the *Mail on Sunday*'s political editor, was out in front with his report claiming that the moral conduct of a 'Cameron cutie' had enraged Norfolk's 'turnip Taliban', the local Tory 'turnip heads who made the Taliban look progressive'. Ahead of a recalled meeting, Cameron appeared to relish the prospect of a Clause IV-style confrontation and he warned the constituency that if she was rejected he would impose an all-women shortlist. In the event Truss, deputy director of the think tank Reform, was reaffirmed as candidate by a four-to-one majority.

Sir Jeremy Bagge, a former high sheriff of Norfolk, who tabled the motion to deselect Truss, claimed the local membership had been 'deceived and betrayed' by party headquarters. His spirited stand against the influence of the modernisers encouraged resistance in a number of other constituencies where A-list outsiders were being promoted. Cameron acknowledged that his drive to offer voters a diverse range of candidates had necessitated 'some leaning' on local parties but his cajoling had succeeded in scaling back the predominance of white, middle-class men and in making the party more representative of the country at large. If the Conservatives won the 2010 general election with a majority simply of one, the tally of women MPs was expected to increase from eighteen to sixty and the number of black and Asian MPs to go from two to twelve. Cameron had spent four years trying to rebrand his party and although the expenses scandal damaged the public's trust in politicians it did nonetheless help usher in a generation of Conservative candidates who believed they constituted a better cross-section of society.

7

DEALING WITH THE NON-DOMS

One of the recurring hazards of becoming party leader is being dogged by embarrassing news stories about the business interests and tax affairs of prominent figures who have a role in what is sometimes referred to as the 'kitchen cabinet'. A politician on the fast track to the top tends to attract rich and powerful supporters. In return for their desperately needed financial backing and tactical advice, these friends and advisers acquire an insight into the powerful interplay between the key figures in what they hope might one day become a future government. Political journalists, suspicious and often envious of the access enjoyed by a privileged few, subject a party leader's confidants to an unrelenting scrutiny.

Given the continuing hostile focus on David Cameron's privileged background, members of his inner circle had no excuse for not resolving potential conflicts in their own affairs so as to limit the likelihood of their close association being exploited by the media and harming the leader's electoral prospects. But he too was at fault for not demanding greater clarity about the tax status of two wealthy individuals whose support he greatly valued. Lord Ashcroft, the party's deputy chairman and leading benefactor, and Zac Goldsmith, an adviser on quality of life issues, prized their position as insiders and their familiarity with a potential Prime Minister. But despite repeated opportunities they both failed to declare publicly that they were non-domiciled for the purposes of taxation. When their true status was finally confirmed only a matter of months before the 2010 general election, Cameron's embarrassment was all the greater because he had presented Labour and the Liberal Democrats with an open goal and had only himself to blame for having missed an ideal occasion to insist on full disclosure.

Non-domiciled residents (non-doms) have long been a bête noire for Middle England, able to enjoy an untaxed offshore income and avoid paying a fair share towards the upkeep of the country; they are only taxed on what they earn in the United Kingdom. Gordon Brown promised on becoming Chancellor in 1997 that he would find a way to tax their foreign assets but he backed off when faced with the prospect that many of them might move abroad. To Brown's annoyance, George Osborne seized the initiative at the Conservatives' 2007 party conference by proposing a £25,000 annual levy on non-doms as a way of meeting the cost of raising the threshold for inheritance tax to £1 million. Such was the popular acclaim for the shadow Chancellor's ingenious solution to two pressing grievances that he was credited with forcing Labour to think again about a snap general election, a high point for the party after a difficult summer coming to terms with the early months of Brown's premiership. Having taken the high ground by declaring that a future Conservative government would require all non-doms to register, Cameron could so easily have stolen a march on Labour and called for immediate transparency within his own party, at least for all office holders and candidates.

Turning the adversity of the MPs' expenses scandal to the Conservatives' advantage required the adroit use by Cameron of the news media and an unerring sense of certainty about how best to present himself and his party, attributes which unexpectedly deserted him when faced by a crisis within his coterie of friends and advisers. For once he seemed paralysed by indecision, unable to come to terms with the danger he faced if he allowed opposition parties and the media to make all the running when seeking to expose the tax arrangements of Ashcroft and Goldsmith. His hesitation was all the more inexplicable given the rapid and resolute action he took against Tory grandees and members of his shadow cabinet. In the turmoil of the first few weeks of the *Daily Telegraph*'s disclosures about the abuse of parliamentary expenses, the politicians were at the mercy of an unprecedented frenzy. Cameron's success in limiting the damage was due in large part to the clarity of his message. The aim was to keep one step ahead of Labour and the Liberal Democrats by ensuring that those Conservative MPs who had abused their parliamentary allowances were the first to apologise and then became the first to start paying back their excessive claims. The absence of a comparable game plan to tackle the fallout from the unmasking of two celebrated Tory non-doms was again all the more surprising given Cameron's record as a streetwise politician. His early years as a bit-part player in some of the dramas which precipitated the collapse of John Major's government should have been a constant reminder that journalists will go to extraordinary lengths to rework long-running political scandals if they sense they have not been told the truth. Where he had the edge over Gordon Brown in securing advance warning of what might be afoot was that he could call on the expertise of a former newspaper editor whose career had been built on the campaigning journalism of the *Sun* and the *News of the World* and their success in probing the private finances of the rich and powerful. Alastair Campbell had interpreted the media mindset for Tony Blair; Andy Coulson could not only match Campbell's ability to predict where a story might go next but he could also offer Cameron far greater insight into the way newspapers manage risky investigations which might be based on leaks or other equally dubious sources.

Coulson's guidance on how the *Daily Telegraph* would continue to exploit its illicit data would have been far superior to anything on offer to the Prime Minister from his advisers in Downing Street. In the two years he had spent as director of communications at Conservative headquarters, Coulson had maintained and strengthened his range of contacts within the newspaper industry and the occasional references in *No Expenses Spared* to his role behind the scenes in managing relations with editors and their executives explained why Cameron found his advice so indispensable. Given the back-up that was available to him, the absence of any co-ordinated damage limitation on non-doms suggested Cameron's loyalties got the better of him. The questions he left unanswered would eventually leave him open to accusations of weak leadership.

Once journalists detect evidence that they might have been misled, an otherwise manageable issue can hog the headlines. Reporters working for rival news organisations are usually keen to follow up a competitor's story only if it seeks to expose attempts by powerful organisations and individuals to withhold information which should be in the public domain. Whenever Blair was caught in a scandal Campbell always said that a cover-up invariably made matters worse. If all the incriminating data was released as soon as possible there might be greater discomfort initially but experience had shown that openness paid dividends; negative coverage tended to subside more quickly and there was often far less damage long term.

Through a combination of scandalous self-interest and an appalling lack of collective judgement, the House of Commons went to inordinate lengths to justify withholding information from the public. Evidence of a sustained cover-up by MPs was if anything more shameful than their greed and when he reflected on the repercussions of the scandal in a speech in the summer of 2009, Cameron admitted that the 'simple act of providing information' had brought about the biggest shake-up in the political system for a generation. 'It is information – not a new law, not some regulation – just the provision of information that has enabled people to take on the political class, question them, demand answers, and get those answers. That's exactly as it should be.'

Requiring all Conservative MPs to submit their expenses to forensic examination did secure favourable headlines but it was nonetheless a humiliating experience, especially for those senior parliamentarians who always considered their own conduct above reproach. A lingering sense of resentment rebounded with a vengeance after the party discovered that Cameron's insistence on the 'simple act of providing information' had not been applied with anything like the same rigour to his inner circle of aides, friends and benefactors.

Tony Blair's reliance on a variety of financial backers whose precise status was in some instances as questionable as that of leading Tory donors had left Labour as exposed as the Conservatives to the accusation that they were benefiting from the proceeds of untaxed foreign assets. The two parties had spent the previous three decades trading insults with each other about the degree to which they were in hock to shady donors, a problem which had got steadily worse because of the increasing cost of posters and press advertisements. To deflect attention from Blair's entanglement in the 'cash for peerages' scandal, Labour MPs stepped up their attacks on Lord Ashcroft, who had not only become the Conservatives' largest donor but had also been given a key role in preparations for the 2010 general election.

Unresolved questions about Ashcroft's extensive business interests in Belize had dogged him since his first appointment as party treasurer, a post he held from 1998 until William Hague's defeat in the 2001 general election. Hague lobbied for Ashcroft to be granted a peerage, which was finally approved in 2000 after initially being refused by the Political Honours Scrutiny Committee. Ashcroft's donations assumed even greater importance after the 2001 defeat and his financial support for campaigning in marginal constituencies was said to have helped the Conservatives secure twenty or more of the seats they gained in the 2005 general election. Michael Howard's failure to deliver victory against Tony Blair was analysed by Ashcroft in his booklet *Smell the Coffee: A Wake-up Call for the Conservative Party*, which suggested the party's image was so tarnished that voters were repelled by the Tories even when they backed their policies. Howard and Ashcroft had disagreed over whether his money should go direct to specified candidates or to central party funds and Ashcroft had also been critical of Howard's right-wing election strategy. His analysis of what the party should do to widen its appeal was shared by Cameron and one of his first decisions within two weeks of becoming leader in December 2005 was to set aside the differences of the past and appoint Ashcroft to the post of deputy chairman with responsibility for the target seat campaign. Ashcroft's wife Susan contributed £20,000 to Cameron's leadership campaign, the biggest single donation, and her husband's subsequent support for the party included a loan of £3.6 million. If Cameron harboured doubts about his deputy chairman's tax status he must have kept them to himself and the assumption was that he relied on Hague's much-repeated assurances that Ashcroft had given 'unequivocal undertakings' that he had 'fulfilled the obligations' imposed on him to become 'a permanent resident' in the UK – an arrangement which Hague told Blair 'will cost him (and benefit the Treasury) tens of millions a year in tax'.

Opposition complaints about Ashcroft's role at the heart of the Conservatives' campaign resurfaced after Brown decided against a snap election in the autumn of 2007 and the parties began to dig in for the long haul to 2010. Anxious Labour and Liberal Democrat MPs in marginal constituencies joined the clamour for Cameron to come clean about the way the Tories were funding their target seats. Ashcroft defended his role in a letter to the *Guardian*. He denied 'hand-picking' Tory candidates for marginal constituencies; his donations and gifts from other donors were being made to a central fund worth about £2 million a year which directed help to target seats. 'I do this because I am a passionate Conservative.' Blair's ill-fated pursuit of donations from business leaders was an attempt to match Ashcroft's support while at the same time reducing Labour reliance on trade union contributions.

Doubts about Ashcroft's true tax status were fuelled by the revelation that the House of Lords expenses register showed that his main residence remained in Belize and that he continued to declare on his personal website that 'if home is where the heart is, then Belize is my home'. After the Liberal Democrat peer Lord Oakeshott proposed a bill to require all peers to declare whether they were domiciled for UK tax, the Conservative leader in the Lords, Lord Strathclyde, gave an assurance that Ashcroft would either 'have to comply' or lose his seat in the Upper House. Another line of attack was opened up by Gordon Prentice, Labour MP for the marginal constituency of Pendle, who lodged a freedom of information request for access to the precise wording of Ashcroft's assurances to the Honours Scrutiny Committee. Cameron should have needed no reminding after experiencing the 'sleaze' allegations of the Major years and seeing the devastating impact of Blair's mauling during 'donorgate' that unasked or unresolved questions about political funding have a nasty habit of getting answered at the most awkward moment.

While there might have been extenuating circumstances for not demanding clarity from Ashcroft on his appointment as deputy chairman, a failure to insist on total transparency was all the more surprising in the case of Zac Goldsmith, heir to the billionaire financier Sir James Goldsmith. He joined the party during the Conservatives' 2005 annual conference, at the height of the surge in support for Cameron's challenge for the leadership. As a founder and editor of the *Ecologist*, he had made a name for himself as an environmental campaigner and was almost immediately appointed deputy chairman of the Conservatives' quality of life policy group; the following year his name was added to the A-list of prospective candidates and he became a leading advocate of the leader's slogan 'Vote blue, go green'. After an open caucus in March 2007, Goldsmith was selected to fight the Liberal Democrat-held seat of Richmond Park. Again Cameron had no excuse for not ensuring that the relevant questions were asked before giving him priority in the selection process, an omission which was even harder to explain given Goldsmith's personal fortune and his father's role in funding the Referendum Party, which took votes from the Conservatives in the 1997 general election. In that election, Cameron lost well over 1,000 votes to a Goldsmith-backed candidate when he was defeated by Labour in Stafford. Nursing his own disappointment, he would almost certainly have had some sympathy at the time with the former Conservative minister David Mellor, who lost his seat in Putney and urged Sir James Goldsmith, who had stood against him, to stop trying to 'buy up the British political system' and 'get off back to his hacienda in Mexico'.

Having experienced at first hand the reach of the Goldsmith family fortune and the impact of the seemingly limitless amount which was spent promoting Referendum Party candidates, Cameron could hardly plead ignorance when Sir James's son was forced to acknowledge that he was a non-dom. Zac Goldsmith made no mention of his tax status when selected to stand in Richmond Park and as soon as it was revealed by the *Sunday Times* in November 2009, his opponents had no hesitation in implicating Cameron and in accusing the Tory candidate of having 'dodged' paying taxes in the UK, an omission which it was said made him unfit to stand for Parliament. Goldsmith was in fact tax resident in the UK, he had always paid tax on his locally generated income, and he asserted he was non-domiciled only in relation to his inheritance in a family trust in the Cayman Islands. But his promise to relinquish his non-dom status well before the election was of little comfort to Cameron, whose unyielding efforts to rebrand the Tory Party seemed to be on the point of unravelling. In his weekly column in the *Sun*, Kelvin MacKenzie said the revelation that another old Etonian had 'looked in his wallet' and decided to be a non-dom explained why the 'rich boys' club' which dominated the Tory leadership was languishing in the opinion polls.

Initially the party said it could not comment on Goldsmith's 'private affairs' but the non-dom story was beginning to spiral out of control and Cameron was forced to intervene. He urged Goldsmith to become 'a full UK taxpayer as rapidly as can be done', a belated response given Cameron's ongoing blind spot about the status of Lord Ashcroft. Goldsmith's disclosure looked like becoming the start of a chain reaction of negative pre-election publicity and the story line was slipping out of Cameron's control. Conservative targeting of winnable seats had so alarmed Labour and the Liberal Democrats that there had been repeated complaints to the Electoral Commission, which agreed in February 2009 to investigate the legality of donations totalling £4.7 million made in the name of Ashcroft's company, Bearwood Corporate Services. Another looming hazard was the fear that the Cabinet Office would be forced to reveal the exact form of the undertaking given when his peerage was granted.

By mid-December, desperate to head off further damaging revelations, Cameron realised there was probably no alternative but to subject Conservative non-doms to the same rigorous scrutiny as Tory grandees. One possible quick fix was to float the idea of an immediate change in the law by strengthening the government's Constitutional Renewal Bill. Cameron called for cross-party agreement on a last-minute amendment to require all MPs and peers to be full UK taxpayers, a move which would block the chance of any non-doms standing for Parliament in 2010. Labour and the Liberal Democrats claimed Cameron was simply trying to distract attention and their cynicism was well founded. Next day the Electoral Commission revealed that in the space of eighteen months Goldsmith had donated £264,000 towards the office costs of the Richmond Park Conservative Association, a contribution which the Liberal Democrats claimed was probably partly financed by the £500,000 a year which they estimated he must have saved through non-dom status on his share of the family's £300 million inheritance.

By donating the equivalent of £3.50 for every voter in Richmond Park, Goldsmith was said to be 'buying' the constituency, precisely the charge which political opponents were making against Ashcroft for his funding of target seats. His pivotal role as Tory benefactor and strategist was a source of pride and in an updated version of his autobiography *Dirty Politics, Dirty Times*, Ashcroft revealed that over the years he had given 'well in excess of £10 million' to the party. If the Tory high command had thought of following Alastair Campbell's guidebook on crisis management, the initial furore over Goldsmith would have been the justification for clearing the decks and ensuring full disclosure of the deputy's chairman's tax status. Mid-December was obviously a pivotal moment and if Cameron had been as ruthless then as he had been earlier in the year over MPs' expenses he might have stood a chance of averting a prolonged run of dire headlines which derailed the Conservatives' pre-election campaign and fuelled fresh doubts about his leadership and the party's reliance on a few big donors.

Ashcroft set the ball rolling in March 2010 when he published a statement on his website which finally confirmed his status as a non-dom. His hand had been forced by the freedom of information commissioner and the imminent release of the relevant wording. He wanted to get in first and give a fuller explanation. In his dialogue with the Cabinet Office in March 2000 it had been agreed that the interpretation of taking up 'permanent residence' meant that he would be 'a long-term resident' and would declare his UK income. 'My precise tax status therefore is that of non-dom.' He claimed his position was comparable to that of two of Labour's biggest donors, Lord Paul and Sir Ronald Cohen, who were both 'long-term residents' and also non-doms. As to the future, he agreed with Cameron that anyone sitting in either the Lords or the Commons should be treated as resident and domiciled for tax purposes, a condition he accepted.

Ashcroft's statement raised more questions than it answered, as did publication of the undertaking he originally gave. In authorising its release, the freedom of information commissioner issued a terse rebuke to the Conservative leadership for having persisted in giving 'evasive and obfuscatory' explanations. To be presented two months before polling day with the confirmation that there had been a ten-year cover-up at the top of the Tory Party was enough to whet the appetite of most political journalists. Who-knew-what-when stories have endless permutations and the obfuscation over Ashcroft's status was all the more embarrassing because Cameron and his colleagues had prevaricated time and again whenever they were challenged by television and radio presenters. William Hague's formulation that Ashcroft had 'fulfilled the obligations imposed on him' was the key line in carefully rehearsed answers which they all tried valiantly to stick to. In one interview in December 2007, Cameron insisted Ashcroft was 'resident in the UK and pays taxes in the UK' but his subsequent answers were less precise and he suggested interviewers should put their questions on tax direct to the deputy chairman.

After Zac Goldsmith confirmed his non-dom status, Cameron must have realised the party could no longer defend the ambiguity but rather than insist on full transparency, as he had over MPs' expenses, he stood by as the party chairman, Eric Pickles, and other leading figures were required to go on squirming on camera. Shortly before Ashcroft's statement there was a noticeable change of tack: William Hague said he was confident the deputy chairman understood there could be 'no ifs and buts' once non-doms were banned from sitting in the Commons and the Lords. Sir George Young, shadow leader of the House, was equally convinced that Cameron's initiative in seeking a change in the law would 'resolve the issue'. Their answers were taken as a tacit admission of what had always been suspected.

Ashcroft's statement was the opportunity which Cameron had been waiting for. He told the BBC he was delighted his deputy chairman had 'come out' and shown that like Lord Paul he had honoured his original undertakings and would meet any future obligations. But Ashcroft's long-overdue explanation provided no escape because the story line had moved on. Hague and Cameron were under fire for not having levelled with the public much earlier, as soon as they were aware that Ashcroft had used the loophole of being 'a long-term resident' to keep his non-dom status. When challenged next day by reporters to give chapter and verse on precisely when he was advised that Ashcroft was not paying UK taxes on his foreign earnings, Cameron's irritation got the better of him and he made the mistake of rubbishing the validity of the question. 'I admire people who try to flog a dead horse. But the horse is dead and should no longer be flogged.' His put-down was uncharacteristic but another reminder of his original miscalculation in thinking the story would play itself out. Whenever politicians accuse the news media of flogging a dead horse their opponents can usually be relied upon to give the story fresh legs. Labour were only too keen to oblige. Lord Mandelson, the Business Secretary, tried unsuccessfully to persuade the House of Lords to launch an inquiry into whether the Upper House had been misled and in the Commons, the leader of the House, Harriet Harman, called for an investigation into whether, as a consequence of pocketing 'tens of millions' a year in unpaid tax, Ashcroft had been allowed to use the 'Belize dollar' to buy up marginal constituencies in Britain. To Cameron's relief, four days after Ashcroft's initial statement the Electoral Commission ruled in his favour and declared that 173 donations totalling £5.1 million made via Bearwood Corporate Services between February 2003 and December 2009 were 'legal, permissible and correctly reported'. But Ashcroft and the Conservatives did not escape criticism. The commission said it had been unable to obtain 'meaningful information' about Bearwood's Belize-based parent company and party officials were rebuked for being 'unwilling to agree' to be interviewed about the donations. What mattered to Cameron was that at last there was a positive outcome which the party could trumpet. Liam Fox, the shadow Defence Secretary, told *PM* that the investigation proved that Ashcroft's status and donations were 'perfectly legal' and no different to the financial help given by Labour's non-doms; if their opponents and the media failed to accept that conclusion it would begin to look 'like a witch hunt'. But yet again deliverance from the trials and tribulations of what journalists had dubbed the saga of 'Lord Cashcroft' was proving elusive.

In a final round of pre-election politicking the Labour-dominated Select Committee on Public Administration launched an investigation to discover how Ashcroft managed to maintain non-dom tax status without the knowledge or approval of the Honours Scrutiny Committee. Conservative MPs boycotted the inquiry on the grounds Labour were playing politics and they felt vindicated when the correspondence over Ashcroft's peerage was leaked to the BBC on the morning of the hearing. When the *Today* presenter Evan Davis suggested the documents proved that the party had been misled, Hague insisted that his original concern was to secure a guarantee of Ashcroft's permanent residence rather than to question his personal tax status. He only discovered the true position after a conversation with Ashcroft 'at the turn of the year' and he asked for Cameron to be informed. Hague conceded that he was personally at fault for having suggested to Tony Blair that in terms of taxation there would be a considerable benefit to the Treasury once Ashcroft took up residency. 'In retrospect it was a mistake to say tens of millions, because it may have cost him millions, it may cost him millions – we don't know.'

Hague remained the focus of much of the coverage in next day's newspapers. The *Guardian* suggested he must have been aware of the deal to protect Ashcroft's tax privileges but after a three-week run the crisis was abating. Even Sir Hayden Phillips, the senior civil servant who had been in charge of processing Ashcroft's peerage, was forced to admit on *The World at One* that he had not appreciated the different tax implications of being a 'permanent resident' as opposed to a 'long-term resident'.

Cameron could not escape blame for having allowed the story to derail the Conservatives' campaign strategy. Much of the pre-election coverage in early March was dominated by the fallout from Ashcroft's initial statement and allegations of a cover-up lingered on in the headlines until the middle of the month, blunting the impact of the party's policy initiatives. The loss of a full week's campaigning against Labour caused consternation among party strategists and commentators. 'One more wobble and the game's over' was the *Sunday Telegraph*'s headline over Michael Dobbs's assessment of the leadership's failure to prepare for an all-too-predictable media onslaught into their private lives. Doubts about Ashcroft's tax status were 'bound to be messy, just as they were blindingly obvious' and Cameron and Hague should have dealt with it 'ages ago'. In his column in the *Sunday Times*, Martin Ivens said the stream of negative headlines showed a lack of grip on Cameron's part; his mistake was to have calculated that the story would not run. An editorial in *The Times* reached the same conclusion: Cameron and Hague 'hunkered down', hoping the story would go away, but in doing so they put 'political convenience ahead of principle'.

Labour MPs, already heartened by a narrowing in the opinion polls, could hardly believe their good fortune that Cameron had been so inept. An imminent strike at British Airways provided ammunition for Conservative MPs to retaliate and they made much of their counter-charge that Gordon Brown's administration was a wholly owned subsidiary of Unite, the trade union for cabin staff, which was Labour's largest contributor, having donated £11 million since 2007. A chance to trade insults about the largesse of rival political paymasters was a useful diversionary tactic but it did nothing to quell unease among the party faithful about the extent to which their campaign had been destabilised. Unlike Labour, still struggling to patch up the wounds of the perpetual feuding between Brownites and Blairites, the Tory rank and file had by comparison been a model of self-discipline, determined whatever their differences to present a united front. Nonetheless Ashcroft's assertion that he broke his silence in order to ensure his tax affairs did not 'distract' attention from the campaign tested the patience of some leading Conservatives. Peter Bingle, chairman of Bell Pottinger Public Affairs, was the first to break ranks. He told *Channel 4 News* that unless Cameron took control of 'a shambolic campaign' the Conservatives would throw away victory at the election. Lord Tebbit thought Ashcroft should have revealed his non-dom status 'years ago' because he should have known better than to have kept quiet about something he would be unhappy to 'read about in tomorrow's *Daily Mail* . . . and that *Daily Mail* test is the one that matters above all in politics'. Another concerned voice was that of Barry Legg, a former chief executive of the party, who told *The World at One* he thought Cameron should have sacked Ashcroft the moment he discovered that the deputy chairman had failed for so long to correct the impression that he was paying 'tens of millions' in tax. 'Ashcroft is the second most powerful man in the party, he runs the marginal seats campaign, he has a big say in which MPs get elected . . . He should have stood up straight away and corrected this misapprehension.'

Securing a clean bill of health from the Electoral Commission for the legality of Ashcroft's donations gave Cameron a chance to draw a line under an appalling own goal but he bided his time and waited for several days before answering questions. In an interview for the *Ten o'Clock News* with the BBC's political editor, Nick Robinson, he defended his stewardship of the party's finances and denied he had been too weak to confront Ashcroft. 'What people have seen from me is the answer to the questions which needed answering . . . about where he pays his tax. It was done before the election and it was done by me.' Cameron revealed that when he became leader the party was in debt to the tune of

£20 million but he had 'sorted out the funding' and the debt had been more than halved. 'I have made it less reliant on a few wealthy people. I have paid off loans including a very large loan to Michael Ashcroft so the party is not in his debt one piece.' Later the party confirmed rumours that Ashcroft intended to stand down as deputy chairman after the election to concentrate on his media and business interests. An announcement that he would quit front-line politics also killed off speculation that Cameron might offer him a post in a future Conservative administration; a prospect which the Prime Minister of Belize, Dean Barrow, said would damage Anglo-Belizean relations.

Cameron's spirited performance in seeking to redefine the party's relationship with Ashcroft seemed to reassure his critics. Tory MPs were further comforted by the verdict of opinion pollsters that Labour and the Conservatives had probably limited the damage to each other by pulling off a score draw. In the opinion of Andrew Hawkins, the chief executive of ComRes, playing it as Ashcroft v. Unite amounted to a policy of mutually assured self-destruction, which meant that ultimately neither party gained an advantage. Peter Kellner, president of YouGov, agreed that the Conservatives' best defence was to tar Brown with the same brush by reminding voters of Labour's reliance on union money. He thought the danger for the Tories was that a story about their rich donors had metamorphosed into a question mark over the competence of Cameron and Hague and whether they had been tough enough in standing up to Ashcroft.

There could hardly have been a sharper contrast between the non-dom train crash and Cameron's success in turning the disaster of MPs' expenses to the Conservatives' advantage. Andy Coulson's fingerprints were all over Cameron's hands-on media strategy when it came to tackling the excesses of Tory MPs but the hidden world of the wheeler-dealing that goes on behind the scenes in the financing of political parties is usually a no-go area even for a media chief. As the Ashcroft–Goldsmith saga spiralled out of control I am sure Coulson would have felt as exasperated as Alastair Campbell did when he had to pick up the pieces after it was revealed Tony Blair had accepted a £1 million donation from the Formula 1 boss Bernie Ecclestone at the height of the row about whether to ban tobacco advertising, on which motor racing depended. Cameron, like Blair, probably felt he could not shirk personal responsibility for his role in trying to attract party funding and there was probably no way he could have prevented the collateral damage that Ashcroft's eventual disclosure inflicted on the party. But leaving unexploded ordnance lying around an election battlefield is not the best tactic and he should have called in a bomb disposal team much earlier rather than attempt to defuse the problem two months before polling day.

8
LEADERS' WIVES

Long before the three main parties reached their historic agreement to give the go-ahead for three live televised leaders' debates, the foundations were being laid for another epic step in the inexorable shift towards a US-style 'presidential' election. From the moment her husband finally took control of 10 Downing Street, Sarah Brown decided she would be like no previous Prime Minister's wife: she would unashamedly present herself as the first First Lady of British politics. Single-handedly she began refashioning the public's expectation of the role to be performed by the premier's spouse. Instead of continuing to pursue her earlier career as a public relations consultant, or opting to become a demure and often silent companion, she transformed herself into an informal ambassador for the Labour government and, through her use of Twitter and other social media sites, she managed to by-pass official channels and started to develop an engaging dialogue with the public. Her ability to converse directly with potential voters, and her skill in softening the image of her husband by showing he was a caring family man and not simply a rather unpleasant political obsessive, began to have a profound impact on Labour's tactics and could not be ignored by their opponents.

Campaign strategists for the Conservatives and Liberal Democrats realised they would need to respond and that they too would have to prepare for their own leaders' wives to have a much higher profile than in previous general elections. David Cameron and Nick Clegg had been enthusiastic in their support of televised debates so they could hardly complain when the Prime Minister began to rely on his wife's attempts to import another American initiative to help bolster his dismal opinion poll ratings. But the more women journalists complimented Sarah Brown on becoming 'the kind of First Lady we could all be proud of', the greater the dilemma for Cameron and Clegg. Samantha Cameron and Miriam González Durántez were working mothers managing to continue their own highly successful careers; they had always appeared content to be photographed supporting their husbands but had never sought to portray themselves as political activists. Neither had shown any desire or inclination to join the pressurised world at Westminster inhabited by politicians, journalists, lobbyists and public relations consultants, a milieu in which the Prime Minister's wife had always thrived and which through her own network of contacts she was eager to exploit.

Sarah Brown's great strength over previous Prime Ministers' spouses was that as the wife of the Chancellor of the Exchequer she had served a lengthy apprenticeship next door at 11 Downing Street. She had seen from the inside the pressures on Tony Blair's family and how his wife tried to cope with constant media exposure and the incessant demands of the 24/7 news cycle. Cherie Blair took a fresh and distinctive approach to the duties expected of a Prime Minister's wife. She continued her legal career as a QC and crown and county court recorder while caring for her young family and also finding the time to attend numerous official events. Firm convictions were an indelible part of her persona and she was determined to go on supporting the sometimes controversial causes in which she had an interest. The depth of her political commitment gave a sharper edge to the traditional interpretation of the daily duties of a premier's spouse and if need be she did not hold back from advancing her own beliefs. Cherie Blair's determination to be true to herself made her a target for tabloid newspapers, a useful lightning rod for Tony Blair's critics, which meant extra care had to be taken managing her appearances at political events.

Successive Prime Ministers have always been generous hosts, staging a non-stop round of receptions for an infinite variety of worthy purposes; being photographed entering No. 10 is a special moment for countless individuals. But instead of holding largely informal gatherings where journalists were not welcome, Tony and Cherie Blair broke new ground by staging many more events which offered access to the news media, prompting complaints from the Conservatives that Labour was using Downing Street far more frequently as a platform for political advantage than Margaret Thatcher or John Major ever had.

In recent years leaders' spouses have been much in demand during general election campaigns because their presence attracts media interest, enhances television coverage and provides a constant supply of fresh pictures for newspapers and magazines. Much time and effort goes into finding suitable locations and the imperative for party managers is to make sure such occasions are properly controlled; an ill-judged photo-opportunity can blight a politician's career. Margaret Thatcher was frequently accompanied by her husband Denis but he made it a general rule to be rarely seen and certainly not heard. His determination to steer clear of the cut and thrust of daily politics was shared by Norma Major. Glenys Kinnock was at her husband's side for the main events of the 1992 general election and, in conceding Labour's defeat, he paid tribute to the dignified way she had withstood what he considered was the spiteful press comment which they both had to endure. In 1997, during the highly disciplined general election campaign, Labour did all they could to promote the Blairs as a young, dynamic family. The party was on constant gaffe-watch and photo-opportunities involving Cherie Blair were carefully choreographed to ensure that there were no slip-ups which journalists could exploit.

With the imminent approach of the 2010 general election political strategists knew that the tried and tested routines which helped secure Blair's three election victories could no longer be relied upon. When rules were finally agreed in early March for the broadcasting of three ninety-minute televised debates, campaign managers were in uncharted waters. A guarantee that the Liberal Democrats' leader would get equal time with Labour and the Conservatives held out the prospect of a genuine three-horse race and one which each party knew would have to be sustained by three highly personalised campaigns. Domestically Messrs Brown, Cameron and Clegg were evenly matched. To the delight of their respective spin doctors they each had attractive wives and young children and were devoted fathers. In presentational terms their status as happily married men was ideal but to gain maximum impact there would need to be regular photo-opportunities involving their partners, a requirement which was considered all the more pressing by the two challengers because of the ease with which the Prime Minister's wife was managing to exploit the news media.

For three years Sarah Brown had in effect been a full-time publicist on her husband's behalf and her emergence as an unacknowledged First Lady added a new chapter to the British handbook on campaign tactics. Politicians' conversations on social networking sites were helping the parties reach sections of the public for whom politics were usually a turn-off but Mrs Brown's engagement with would-be electors had reached an unprecedented level and turned her into an online phenomenon. Her unexpected success in the fast-changing world of new media put the Conservatives and the Liberal Democrats at a disadvantage; and it increased the pressure on their campaign managers to package and to promote David Cameron and Nick Clegg in ways which did more to capitalise on the active support of their wives. Sarah Brown's boost for a presidential style of electioneering had another unexpected spin-off once the contest was underway because it began to have a marked influence on the focus of campaign reporting. As polling day approached, the media's concentration on personalities rather than policies was a source of increasing annoyance among the women MPs and candidates who were contesting the election. Much to their combined chagrin they found that the coverage they were managing to secure was being far exceeded by the level of media exposure for the leaders' wives.

By giving up her career as a public relations consultant Sarah Brown acquired the time and opportunity to begin developing her innovative and very personal media offensive on behalf of her beleaguered husband. Just as Cameron was consumed by his desire to rebrand the so-called 'nasty party', so was she on a mission to detoxify the image of Gordon Brown. A rapidly changing media landscape worked to her advantage and provided a friendly platform for the kind of comment and conversation which her immediate predecessor never had the opportunity to exploit. Whenever Cherie Blair had dared to express an opinion she was roundly and regularly condemned by newspaper columnists; there was an even greater hue and cry if anything she said could somehow be interpreted as having been political or an attempt to interfere in the affairs of government. Her misfortune was to miss out on the explosion in the use of social networking sites such as YouTube, Facebook and Twitter and the brevity of the new-found freedom of expression which was taking hold across the age ranges and at all levels of society whenever people communicated instantly through internet message boards or via texts on their mobile phones. Personal privacy was happily being relinquished in a new online world of self-revelation. If the public were prepared to volunteer their innermost thoughts and feelings there seemed to be no reason why politicians should not attempt to join the conversation.

From her courtship by Gordon Brown through to their marriage in 2000 and the loss the following year of their baby daughter Jennifer, Sarah Brown had never wavered in her dedication to the cause of humanising her husband's dour image. Journalists were fascinated by the challenge she faced in trying to force the Chancellor to undergo a makeover and when she stood with him in his moment of triumph on the steps of 10 Downing Street in June 2007 they knew this was the day she had been waiting for. Columnists complimented her on the new Prime Minister's appearance: she was 'the key player behind the throne', concluded Cassandra Jardine (*Daily Telegraph*), and Anne McElvoy (*Evening Standard*) congratulated her on 'masterminding the proceedings'. Feature articles giving insights into the success of the 'new First Lady' made unflattering comparisons with the demeanour of Cherie Blair. When Sarah Brown curtseyed on meeting the Duchess of Cornwall at the First Ladies' Commonwealth lunch in Kampala, the *Daily Express* praised her for 'ending a decade of Labour snubs to royalty'.

A natural empathy with the press pack was evident once her husband began representing Britain at summits with world leaders and she started taking her place alongside the other wives at social gatherings. She struck a pose which seemed to attract universal praise and the *Daily Telegraph*'s columnist Liz Hunt thought her high approval rating reflected the fact that she was 'a very different character from the pugilistic and openly political Cherie'. On her family's departure from Downing Street Mrs Blair told the waiting media scrum, 'I don't think we'll miss you,' a remark which reflected a long-standing mutual hostility. By contrast Sarah Brown's image was regarded as endearing and she was able to 'draw on a well-spring of deserved public sympathy' in the wake of Jennifer's death after her premature birth, followed by the 'joy of her son John's arrival' but then yet 'more heartache' when her second son, James Fraser, was diagnosed with cystic fibrosis.

Achieving an instant affectionate response from women journalists was just the encouragement she needed as she prepared to open up a second front in her bid to expand the political role of a British First Lady. In her earlier career as a partner in the public relations agency Hobsbawm Macaulay she worked on behalf of numerous charities and good causes and built up a wide network of media contacts. She seemed to know instinctively what she needed to do to start promoting 'Sarah Brown' as a personality in her own right. Within a matter of months she was writing regularly under her own by-line as a celebrity commentator and columnist. She contributed to a new cookbook, *Mums' Recipes*; wrote for the *Sun* on the need for children to read books rather than play computer games; provided a column in support of the *Daily Telegraph*'s Christmas charity appeal; and secured a two-page spread in the *Daily Mail* with 'a moving tribute to her mother' to launch the paper's Inspirational Women of the Year awards, an exercise she repeated the following year, writing about the 'extraordinary women she meets every day'.

In becoming a regular press contributor she managed to walk a political tightrope with apparent ease. Newspapers and magazines would not have accepted her copy if she had simply tried to push a Labour line but equally she knew that Downing Street needed to be reassured that any views she might express would not conflict with official policy. Editorial executives and government press officers admired her news judgement and her ability to censor herself. She steered clear of blatant political propaganda and by aligning herself so clearly with charities and other worthy causes she avoided embarrassing the government or the party. She was careful not to be caught off guard, rarely gave interviews, and refused to volunteer off-the-cuff answers to reporters' questions.

With the benefit of six months' experience and a high approval rating from commentators Sarah Brown began 2008 more determined than ever to project her new-found image as a confident First Lady. During the Prime Minister's official visit to India at the start of the New Year, she wore embroidered silk gowns specially created for her by the leading Indian designers Abu Jani and Sandeep Khosla. 'Didn't Sarah look lovely' was Allison Pearson's verdict in the *Daily Mail*. A charity lunch she organised at Lancaster House attracted widespread publicity and the fashion writers were well and truly hooked: 'Sarah Brown in Jaeger and Carla Bruni-Sarkozy in Dior'. She topped the celebrity pages greeting George Clooney, who was in Downing Street to highlight the Darfur crisis in his role as a UN peace messenger. A feature in *Glamour* giving women advice on how to be more confident was followed in July by a three-page fashion shoot in *The Times*, and she topped that in early September by posing for countless photographs with the supermodels Naomi Campbell and Erin O'Connor at a fundraiser for Fashion for Relief. Mrs Brown's ability to command the attention of diary columns and fashion pages in support of good causes was applauded by the wider commentariat: 'The woman is a charity powerhouse' (Viv Groskop, *Evening Standard*); 'She is an asset to the Prime Minister and a credit to the nation' (Yasmin Alibhai-Brown, *Independent*).

Sarah Brown did not have to wait long before she was presented with an ideal opportunity to deploy her new-found celebrity status on behalf of her embattled husband. Gordon Brown had taken a battering during the build-up to Labour's 2008 annual conference. Turmoil in the financial markets and the rescue of Northern Rock had been followed by a challenge to his leadership by rebel MPs and dismal opinion poll ratings. He arrived in Manchester determined to launch a fightback and his wife was about to deliver a stunning *coup de grâce*. Breaking conference tradition, she stepped on to the stage to introduce 'my husband, the leader of the Labour Party, your Prime Minister'. She was greeted with a lengthy ovation after thanking delegates for the chance to praise her husband: 'I'm so proud that every day I see him motivated to work for the best interests of people all around the country.' He reciprocated on behalf of 'Team GB': 'I am very proud to be her husband.'

Her unexpected platform debut injected the bravura of an American political convention into the rather less theatrical world of a Labour Party conference. She could not be faulted on her timing as her emotional gesture seemed to chime seamlessly with the mesmerising campaign being waged by Barack and Michelle Obama in the lead-up to the US presidential election that November. Activists across the British political spectrum were transfixed by the contest between Obama and John McCain and were desperate to learn lessons which might be relevant in the forthcoming general election. Sarah Brown raised the stakes when she started to assume the political mantle of a First Lady, and her touching conference endorsement of the Prime Minister was another defining moment in the shift towards American-style campaigning. Television news bulletins captured the drama of the occasion and next day's newspapers were filled with photographs of their platform embrace. But once opinionated women columnists had time to reflect on what they saw, they were divided over the merits of her unprecedented intervention.

The so-called 'queens of mean' split into two camps: some praised her for helping Gordon Brown to 'look human' but others thought she had taken a step backwards for women politicians and especially the wives of other party leaders. Fiona McIntosh, columnist for the pro-

Labour *Sunday Mirror*, praised her 'gutsy and totally unexpected move' and the electrifying effect it had on the conference: 'The real show-stopping moment came when she turned to her awkward beleaguered husband and gave him a proper "I fancy you" kiss on the lips.' Zoe Williams (*Guardian*) said she was a 'phenomenal asset' because she made his 'smile seem real . . . she makes you trust him'. But Janet Street-Porter (*Independent on Sunday*) deplored the Prime Minister's willingness to be influenced by the US presidential election and for encouraging his wife to ape Michelle Obama and Cindy McCain. Sarah Brown would have been more impressive if she had taken the microphone and announced she was running for Parliament 'instead of acting as her fella's warm-up'. Jenny McCartney (*Sunday Telegraph*) agreed: the wives of the two presidential candidates were 'effectively political figures in their own right', dazzling voters to buy a stake in their family. By forcing herself on to the stage to buoy up Gordon Brown's 'flagging political fortunes' she would leave Tory aides with no alternative but to start 'plotting furiously how best to deploy the glories' of Samantha Cameron.

Brown used his wife's build-up to good effect and wasted no time rounding on David Cameron for the Conservatives' criticism of the government's handling of the banking crisis. He delivered a pointed put-down to the effect that he favoured apprenticeships but saying it was 'no time for a novice'. Unexpectedly Cameron was also in the firing line at a personal level for having presented his family in a way which the Prime Minister could not match despite his wife's undoubted public relations expertise. Earlier in the year a report by the BBC's political correspondent Carole Walker included shots of the Camerons having breakfast with their five-year-old disabled son Ivan; she made a point of explaining in her commentary that the Browns refused to allow their sons to be filmed. Cameron defended on camera why he favoured giving the media access: 'The public have a right to know quite a bit about you, your life and your family, what makes you tick and informs your thinking . . . Nothing influences me more than my family . . . so this is a natural thing to do.' Photographs and footage of him caring for Ivan appeared regularly in press and television reportage and was said by friendly interviewees to have been the most important factor in softening his approach to politics.

Brown had clearly become exercised by the images of the Camerons *en famille* and the repeated media references to the disparity in the way the two sets of parents behaved. The Camerons' Christmas card was a family photograph with Ivan in his father's arm; Brown insisted, unlike the Blairs, that his family would never be used in his seasonal greetings. In a pre-conference interview for Kay Burley of Sky News, he went out of his way to express his determination to ensure his sons continued to have 'an ordinary childhood' without the 'glare of publicity'. When he and Sarah visited the Olympic Games in Beijing he purposely avoided sitting next to John and Fraser to make sure they could not be photographed with him. They both 'enjoyed it very much' but they were 'behind the scenes', a reminder to the media that the two boys were off limits. His irritation with Cameron for not insisting on the same level of protection for his three children was not a minor difference of opinion; Brown intended to make a political point. It took the Prime Minister several minutes to calm down the delegates applauding his wife and he seized the opportunity to insist that he was a politician and not a celebrity. 'Some people have been asking why I haven't served my children up for spreads in the papers. And my answer is simple. My children aren't props; they're people.'

In launching his below-the-belt assault on Cameron, Brown seemed oblivious to the fact that moments earlier he had happily used his wife as a prop, a contradiction not lost on Labour's opponents. Her vivid demonstration of the political power of a First Lady was a fitting curtain raiser for her next assignment. Within twenty-four hours of his conference address, Brown flew to New York to deliver a speech to the United Nations. His wife had a separate engagement helping to host a charity dinner in Manhattan for a hundred of the 'world's most influential women'. She joined Queen Rania of Jordan and Rupert Murdoch's wife Wendi in welcoming a line-up of guests that included the Alaska governor Sarah Palin, who interrupted her campaign as Republican candidate for vice-president. Yet again the Prime Minister was upstaged by his wife and, like the rest of the British press, the *Daily Mail* made much of the moment 'when Sarah B. met Sarah P.', when the woman who surprised the Labour conference discussed tactics with the woman who had 'electrified US politics'.

Immediately on her return Sarah Brown was deployed to campaign on Labour's behalf in the critical Glenrothes by-election, which the government eventually won with a comfortable majority in the week that Barack Obama was elected President. She paid seven visits to the constituency and was described by journalists as the Prime Minister's 'secret weapon', having 'hit the phones and doorsteps and cajoled and hassled the locals into backing her man'. The *Sun* said it was the 'tale of two Sarahs': the 'moose-shooting hockey-mom' whom Republican insiders blamed for Obama's victory and the Prime Minister's wife who helped increase Labour's vote against the Scottish Nationalists and had 'come to his rescue again'. Like any other committed activist she knew that the one overriding lesson of the presidential election was that political parties – and especially Labour – had to follow Obama's example and find new ways to exploit the internet.

The Democrats used social networking sites with devastating effect to build a campaign that reached way beyond the confines of the party faithful. More than twenty million people signed up to the My Vote website as Obama mobilised grassroots workers and attracted a record-breaking number of small donations. Sarah Brown was inspired to develop her own online presence. Writing in a direct, accessible style, she began posting online news and comments about her life in Downing Street and the events she was attending. Her insights regarding the famous people she met, and titbits of information about the interesting places she visited, were positive and non-partisan and her followers responded with a warmth which added to the appeal of her simple, easy-going reportage. Once she played to her strengths as the Prime Minister's wife and began posting items of celebrity news she began to attract wider attention.

An entry on her Facebook page about the American heiress and socialite Paris Hilton propelled her to the top of the diary columns in May 2009. They met at the African First Ladies Health Summit in Los Angeles and Mrs Brown was obviously star struck by the American heiress: 'Nothing about her public image prepares you for the first meeting. She's a smart, caring, considerate person. Who knew?' Her chatty dispatches on Twitter took the rest of the media by surprise when *The Times* discovered that the Prime Minister's wife was busily tweeting on subjects ranging from ironing, cake baking, trips to the cinema and the plight of Aung San Suu Kyi, the imprisoned Burmese politician. Anyone who responded to her tweets seemed to be getting a reply, except in the case of the paper's correspondent Suzy Jagger, who noted with disappointment that journalists were clearly not considered bona fide members of the Twitterati. Within two months of joining Twitter in March 2009, Mrs Brown had attracted 150,000 followers, well short of the 500,000 for the site's runaway star Stephen Fry, but her story of everyday life in Downing Street was clearly captivating an ever-expanding network of admirers. After six months her network of followers had expanded to 770,000, far outstripping Fry, and within a year she was boasting a following of 1.1 million, which the *People*'s political editor, Nigel Nelson, said made her 'the most popular woman in Britain'.

Her breakthrough into the world of new media was all the more encouraging for the party because of Labour's sluggish and much-troubled fightback against the right's dominance of the political blogosphere. Once she succeeded in establishing a commanding position on Twitter, other Labour big hitters joined her in trying to take advantage of what was considered to be the liberal-left bias of the site. Some political commentators ridiculed the banality of Sarah Brown's observations about the social whirl of her daily comings and goings but her critics overlooked the importance to the party of her ability to appeal to a non-political audience which might be attracted by Labour's values and aspirations. Her tweets achieved a far wider circulation than her Twitter network because they were often picked up by journalists and reproduced in the mainstream news media. The shrewdness of her strategy as far as the party was concerned was that she had managed to depoliticise her conversations with the public and by avoiding the pitfalls which proved so troublesome for Cherie Blair she escaped a political backlash from Labour's opponents.

A non-stop round of charity events in the first half of 2009 owed much to her flair as a natural networker and consummate PR. She organised photo-opportunities with A-list celebrities, which had a compelling 'wow' factor for the tabloid press. Fashion writers were full of praise for her evolving dress sense during a flurry of gatherings involving the G8 and G20 countries. Gordon Brown's role in helping to co-ordinate the financial community's response to the banking crisis ensured star billing for his wife in the obligatory photo-shoots for the First Ladies. She was assembling an album to die for: exchanging gifts for the children with Michelle Obama at the White House; shedding a tear at the Auschwitz concentration camp as her husband signed the visitors' book; holding an umbrella for Naomi Campbell during a rainy visit to Glastonbury; showing guests the vegetable patch which Michelle Obama had suggested for the Downing Street back garden. Her unique selling point for the newspapers was that her up-to-the-minute postings on Twitter were adding fresh information for journalists and caption writers. At a ceremony for D-Day veterans in Normandy she stood beside Carla Bruni-Sarkozy and Michelle Obama but, as the *Daily Mail* pointed out, she was the only member of the 'First Wives Club' to provide a running commentary: 'Just attended very moving service for D-Day at Bayeux Cathedral – so many British veterans here to pay tribute.'

By midsummer the audience for her Twitter feed was approaching 400,000 and her constant updates supplying titbits unavailable elsewhere in the mainstream media strengthened her position as a much-sought-after contributor to newspapers and magazines. The Prime Minister's relationship with the Murdoch press was becoming increasingly fractious as a result of the media's relentless hostility towards his government and Andy Coulson's ceaseless efforts on behalf of David Cameron to persuade newspapers such as the *Sun* to switch to the Conservatives. But

Sarah Brown's by-line retained considerable appeal among the editorial executives of News International and she was invited to be the guest editor of *Fabulous*, Britain's 'biggest weekly glossy magazine', given away each Sunday with the *News of the World*. Her cover star was Jools Oliver, wife of the chef Jamie Oliver, whom she interviewed about fertility treatment in support of Wellbeing of Women, a charity of which she was patron. Colin Myler, the paper's editor, praised the way she worked with staff in the office and he asked her again the following year to co-ordinate another special edition tackling women's health problems. A campaign by the *Sun* against domestic violence featured a by-lined two-page spread in which she explained how she wept when reading how a 'young mum of two — also called Sarah Brown — was killed by her violent partner'.

Her ability to work to the agenda of the tabloids, combined with her prolific output, served as a reminder to the public that she and the Prime Minister were able to relate to the concerns of ordinary people. Glenys Kinnock admired the way she doubled up with her husband in drumming up support for the government's initiatives: 'Sarah is brilliant on women's rights; she's a real global leader, she has galvanised first ladies around the world to pay attention.' When the *Guardian* ran a feature in September 2009 which posed the question 'Can Sarah save Labour?' she was a week away from another star billing at the party's annual conference in Brighton and the *Sun*'s brutally executed decision to ditch Gordon Brown in favour of David Cameron. Party activists were in awe of her tireless drive to promote the Prime Minister and they set great store by the influential role which they were convinced she could play during the forthcoming general election. Michelle Obama's introductions had made compelling viewing during the presidential election and Sarah Brown was not to be outdone. 'My husband. My hero!' was all it took to repeat the frisson which she created in 2008 but she realised she would have to strengthen her heartfelt tribute of the previous year; her bruised and battered partner was in need of life support, not just emotion.

Because we've been together for so long, I know he's not a saint — he's messy, he's noisy, he gets up at a terrible hour – but I know that he wakes up every morning and goes to bed every evening thinking about the things that matter. I know he loves our country and I know he will always, always put you first.

She enhanced her plea by emphasising how touched she was that someone as intense as her husband still made time for family, friends and everyone who knew him. 'That's why I love him as much as I do.'

Rapturous applause reflected a sense of gratitude for her unstinting loyalty and admiration for a public display of affection for a party leader who delegates felt was being needled unfairly by his tormentors in the media. Not surprisingly a show of unity on the conference floor did not impress the 'queens of mean', who again thought British politics had been debased. Amanda Platell (*Daily Mail*) doubted whether the 'Michelle-isation of our Sarah' would impress voters and Janet Street-Porter (*Independent on Sunday*) was convinced party managers were mistaken if they thought the way to sell politics was to 'bring on the wives'. But their critique had not kept pace with the importance within the Brown household of Sarah's emotional support, the motivation perhaps for the undoubted sincerity of her plea for compassion in understanding her husband's failings.

For some months there had been a noticeable and rather unpleasant undercurrent in press commentary questioning his grip on the premiership and persistent speculation that he might step down voluntarily. In the run-up to the conference, the Downing Street press office had categorically denied reports in the blogosphere suggesting that Brown was on the point of resigning because of his 'worsening health'. Severe depression and failing eyesight were mentioned as possible reasons and there was consternation among party officials when Brown was asked in a pre-conference interview on *The Andrew Marr Show* if he used 'prescription painkillers and pills'. Marr justified his question on the grounds that voters knew the medical history of an American President; he wondered if his eyesight might be 'a reason for standing down at some point'. Brown's firm 'no' was followed up with a rather plaintive rebuke: Marr's line of questioning was the sort which was 'all too often entering the lexicon of British politics'. He lost the sight in his left eye after a rugby accident but a retinal detachment operation saved his right eye and his sight was 'good . . . and people understand that you can do a job'. The complaints which rained down on Marr's head were a testament to the anger of conference delegates: Neil Kinnock was aghast that a BBC presenter had stooped to such 'abominable poking and prying'; Peter Mandelson was appalled that Marr gave credibility to politically motivated bloggers who were circulating groundless 'smears and rumours' on the internet suggesting the Prime Minister was taking anti-depressants.

Nonetheless questions about the strength of his eyesight had become part of a wider media narrative about the Prime Minister's competence and could not be ignored. A fortnight later Downing Street confirmed that during a recent examination two 'minor tears' had been discovered in the retina of his right eye but there had been 'no deterioration'. Given the continuing story line it was hardly surprising that speculation about the degree to which his sight might be impaired became an issue once again after the *Sun* reproduced an 'error-filled' handwritten letter which Brown had sent to Jacqui Janes, the mother of a twenty-year-old soldier killed in Afghanistan. 'Bloody shameful' was the front-page headline over the story of a 'soldier mum's disgust at condolence letter' that misspelled her name and contained other spelling mistakes. Alongside a reproduction of the letter was a second story criticising Brown for failing to bow his head when laying a wreath at the Cenotaph on Remembrance Sunday. His embarrassment was compounded next day when the *Sun* published a transcript of his telephone call to Mrs Janes apologising for having mistakenly spelled her name 'James' and for also having had to correct the spelling of her son Jamie. When Brown acknowledged that she might have felt his 'writing was not right', she begged to differ and said it was an 'insult to my child' to send her a letter with twenty-five spelling mistakes. He denied making mistakes: 'Listen to me, please . . . maybe my writing looks bad . . . I don't think what I said in it was disrespectful at all.' Mrs Janes stood her ground: 'The spelling mistakes are disrespectful . . . I can't believe I've been brought down to the level of having an argument with the Prime Minister of my own country.'

Without advance warning, or a chance to explain himself, Brown was suddenly on the ropes, being brutally punished by a once-loyal newspaper, not knowing what might happen next. When the *Sun* abandoned Labour for the Conservatives the day after his conference speech the previous month, it wrote Brown off as a political failure but the story about his 'hastily scrawled insult' was far more wounding. His 'amazing late-night phone bust-up with a grieving Forces mum', and her complaint that he was failing to show sufficient respect for a soldier who was 'fifth-generation infantry', reinforced the paper's campaign for better equipment for 'our boys' and more support for the relatives of those who had lost their lives in Afghanistan and Iraq. Several service families sprang to Brown's defence and said they were touched by his handwritten letters even though they were in black felt pen and the writing was somewhat disjointed; the *Guardian* attributed Brown's 'notoriously bad handwriting' to his 'poor' eyesight and suggested he followed the example of Margaret Thatcher and Tony Blair in enclosing a printed copy of handwritten letters. At his monthly news conference that morning Brown was mortified to have learned from a tape recording made without his knowledge that he might have caused further offence when he phoned Mrs Janes on the evening of Remembrance Sunday. 'The words I was using, even if she had found them difficult to read which I understand from my writing, were sincerely meant . . . You know, I am a shy person . . . but I also do feel the pain of people who are grieving.' Ministers who rallied to Brown's support were encouraged by e-mails and texts to BBC programmes, Sky News and other broadcasters which accused the *Sun* of bad taste for having exploited Mrs Janes's grief. Peter Mandelson, the Business Secretary, claimed the paper's 'crude politicking' was part of a 'contract' formed between the Murdoch press and the Conservative Party which bound them to one another:

What the Sun *can do for the Conservatives during the election is one part of the contract and, presumably, what the Conservatives can do for News International if they are elected is the other side of the bargain . . . When the* Sun *creates news in this way, this is then followed up by Sky News, which puts pressure on the BBC to follow suit.*

But the die was cast: negative stories about the Prime Minister were now the order of the day and he would have to get used until polling day to the kind of hostility from the Murdoch press which Neil Kinnock had been forced to endure during the lead-up to the 1992 general election.

When parting company with Labour, the *Sun* accepted that Brown was 'a good man but flawed' and its editorial paid tribute to the 'love and loyalty' of Sarah Brown but she too had been discarded, replaced in the paper's affection by David Cameron's wife. Both women had accompanied their husbands the previous June to the wedding of News International's chief executive Rebekah Brooks but the Prime Minister's wife would no longer be feted with regular double-page spreads in the group's top-selling tabloids. Samantha Cameron's pin-up status was assured the moment she arrived at the Conservative conference in Manchester and was photographed by the *Sun* showing off 'her dolphin ankle tattoo' in a pair of Zara shoes. Jane Moore, the paper's top columnist, complimented Cameron on his 'wise choice' in marrying Samantha, 'a successful businesswoman in her own right'. Next day she was photographed wearing a £65 'off-the-peg 1940s-style polka-dot dress' from Marks & Spencer, only for newspapers to discover the following week that it had been run up specially on the orders of the executive chairman, Sir Stuart Rose, after the company discovered that the 2,000 supplied to its stores had sold out within days.

Party conferences have become mini-fashion parades for the leaders' wives and the women's pages were able to compare and contrast Samantha Cameron's effortless, casual chic with the designer elegance of Sarah Brown's outfits. Julie Burchill provided the *Sun*'s assessment of the new potential First Lady: 'Sam Cam struts her stuff, shakes her shiny hair and allows Dave to bask in the glow of her high-end gorgeousness.' But Burchill did not forget Sarah Brown and she praised the two women for being in a class of their own: 'Having both experienced the death of a child, they are both tough and tender . . . They are there to stand by their man – and how very charmingly they do it.'

On 25 February 2009 the Westminster village was stopped in its tracks by the sudden death of Ivan Cameron at the age of six. On Gordon Brown's initiative Prime Minister's Questions were cancelled as a mark of respect. David Cameron had spent the previous evening at home with his three children celebrating Shrove Tuesday and enjoying what *The Times* said was one of his designated 'family nights'. Ivan, who suffered from cerebral palsy and a rare degenerative form of epilepsy, had a seizure after what was described as a 'very, very bad night'. His parents went with him to St Mary's Hospital, Paddington, arriving at 5.45 a.m.; he died at 6.30. MPs heard the news on reaching the House of Commons and there was immediate cross-party agreement on a temporary suspension of parliamentary hostilities. In his brief life Ivan had acquired a political persona of his own because friend and foe alike acknowledged that caring for a disabled son had influenced Cameron's political views and explained why he had become such a passionate defender of the National Health Service. There was the same sense of shock as after the fatal early-morning heart attack suffered by the Labour leader John Smith, when, like Brown, John Major ordered the cancellation of Prime Minister's Questions.

Ivan's death was front-page news next morning and most papers carried a photograph of the distraught couple taken as they returned home from hospital. Much of the coverage focused on their dedicated care of Ivan and the struggle that parents face looking after a disabled child. Whenever television crews had been given access to their home, or they were all photographed together, the pictures invariably showed that Ivan's place was centre stage, being cherished within the family, an image which columnists said was an example of how best to care for a disabled child. In her column in the *Sunday Times*, India Knight praised

Cameron for not having been deflected by those who criticised him for parading Ivan: he 'wasn't tucked out of sight . . . instead there was palpable love but no whitewash'. Rather than concentrate her attention on David Cameron and the 'emotional making of this great statesman', the *Daily Mail*'s Jan Moir said it would be wrong to under-estimate the role of Samantha in the family dynamic: 'The pale agony of her face, as she returned home on a cold February morning without her first born, was awful to behold.' On his return from a fortnight's compassionate leave Cameron's first task at Question Time was to thank well-wishers for their condolences; he knew that the Prime Minister's message of support 'came right from the heart'. Although Gordon Brown made no mention of his and Sarah's own loss of their daughter Jennifer, they understood the Camerons' grief. 'The death of a child is a loss no parent should have to bear,' he said.

Samantha Cameron returned to the public eye by attending a launch party for the French fashion house Lanvin and once again photographs of her began adorning diary pages and society magazines. In June she won *Glamour*'s award for accessories designer of the year, a reminder that whatever the political fortunes of her husband she had no intention of surrendering her four-day-a-week job as creative director at Smythson of Bond Street. Cameron applauded her no-nonsense approach in a BBC interview. Whatever happened she would continue her 'incredibly successful' career because 'that is part of our relationship, that we are different'. In October Fraser Nelson, the *News of the World* columnist, congratulated her for saying she had no intention of staying for the whole of the Conservative conference. 'She only gets twenty-five days' holiday a year, and can think of better use of it. What a girl.'

Samantha Cameron's fleeting visit to the conference, being photographed on her arrival and then sitting in her M&S polka-dot dress listening to her husband's speech, lacked the high octane of Sarah Brown's rallying cry to the party faithful but it was still an equally important public relations coup. She was faultless in her role as a First Lady in waiting, totally supportive of her husband while gracefully eschewing politics. She also was also able to play to her strengths as a trendsetter in fashion and accessories and, to the delight of the party's media strategists, her brief appearance generated umpteen features assessing her choice of outfits, shoes, bags and belts. According to a count in the *Guardian* there were 386 separate photographs of her in the national press during 2009, a non-stop fashion parade which the *Daily Mail*'s Alison Tyler said owed much to her trendy look of 'High Street mixed with upmarket designer' which made her appear 'so natural, so normal'. She was named best-dressed woman in politics by *Tatler*, just in front of Carla Bruni-Sarkozy, an award which only confirmed Janet Street-Porter's conclusion that 'Sam Cam's wardrobe has been subject of more scrutiny than any Tory policies'.

From the start of 2010 the quickening political tempo gave fresh impetus to the competing fashion statements of the two leaders' wives. Their rival power-dressing was on display at London Fashion Week in February. Sarah Brown, patron of the British Fashion Council, opened the event wearing a printed dress by Erdem Moralioglu, a designer who supplied a floral-print skirt worn by Michelle Obama. Elsewhere she stuck to the high street brands of Wallis and Marks & Spencer and wore around her neck a gold pendant which *The Times* understood was a Valentine's Day gift from the Prime Minister. Samantha Cameron was in the front row at another show next to Alexandra Shulman, editor of *Vogue*, and sporting an Erdem printed blouse with a jacket by Malene Birger. The two wives did not meet at rival catwalks but the *Daily Mail* was ready to declare that one all-important election battle was finally under way: 'Sam v. Sarah. Who gets your vote?' *Guardian Weekend* indicated its left-leaning bias with a reverse billing: 'Sarah v. Sam'. In addition to being evenly matched in their ability to command the attention of the fashion writers, the two wives had another compelling attraction. They had both lost their first-born child, a link that could not be overlooked in the mindset of journalists and one which satisfied the news media's craving for human interest angles. The two mothers were spared the indignity of having to respond to mawkish questions themselves but their husbands were considered fair game and neither could complain. Brown was desperate to demonstrate that he could grieve, that he was as normal as the next man; and having flagged up that caring for his disabled son was probably the most important game-changer in his political life, Cameron also had to engage when asked.

'Brown weeps on television' was the inevitable headline on the *Mail on Sunday*'s exclusive preview of an interview in which the Prime Minister opened his heart about the death of Jennifer and Fraser's three-year battle with cystic fibrosis. His eyes welled up with tears and his wife 'also sobbed in an extraordinary display of emotion' in front of a studio audience. Sarah Brown played a leading role in preparing her husband for his pre-recorded appearance, on the ITV programme *Piers Morgan's Life Stories*. Ahead of the broadcast, which was aired on 14 February, she did a web chat for the social networking site Mumsnet and described how 'DH' – her darling husband – was taking charge of plans for Valentine's Day and was 'surprisingly romantic (for a Scot and a man)'. Alastair Campbell's advice was that to avoid any perception of spin when projecting his human face, Brown should try to be 'genuinely authentic'. David Cameron was urged by the *Daily Telegraph* to resist the temptation to follow suit. Politicians who invited questions about their emotional lives were 'nearly always facing political crisis and reaching out for a sympathy vote'. *The Times* reminded the Prime Minister that he was open to a charge of cynical electioneering given his strictures in 2008 to the effect that his children 'aren't props, they're people'.

Conservative Party strategists told journalists that Cameron had no intention of being interviewed by Piers Morgan; the former editor of the *Daily Mirror* was a declared Labour voter and a close friend of Brown, and the Tory leader was wary of embarking on a risky confrontation. In the event his own voice cracked with grief when asked a similar question about Ivan's death in an interview that same week with the Scottish channel STV. In acknowledging the 'amazing' public response to his family's tragedy and the great support which this had been, he began to falter over his words: 'Erm, so I'm sure that, that helped. It's diffic—' At that point his voice trailed off and as he struggled to recover his composure, he apologised for stumbling and admitted that two weeks' leave was probably not enough to get over the shock. 'I probably should have taken a bit longer. . . It is something that just hits you in an incredible way and it takes quite a long time before you can even start to put things back on track.' The timing of the interview had not been ideal and ten days later, on the first anniversary of Ivan's death, he spent the evening at home with his wife rather than attend an awards dinner to receive the prize of politician of the year from *Asian Voice*.

Another reason for Samantha Cameron's distress that evening was said by the *Sun* to have been a press briefing from an unidentified Labour source noting that she did not seem to spend much time supporting good causes. The tactic being mooted was that Labour would target her during the campaign: 'Much will be made of Sarah's charity work and journalists will be encouraged to compare the amount of work Mrs Cameron does for charity.' Labour denied being responsible and insisted there was 'no basis in fact' for a suggestion which the Conservatives attacked for being 'insensitive and unpleasant'. Mrs Cameron had always accepted that her job with an upmarket brand like Smythson could be exploited by her husband's political opponents and a *Sunday Times* profile said her anxiety about the potential for negative reaction explained why she refused to give interviews. When Smythson opened its first store in Los Angeles in 2007 she invited *Harper's Bazaar* into her home for a four-page profile and photo-shoot and was promptly accused by Labour MPs of profiting from her husband's position. 'Come back Cherie, all is forgiven' was the taunt which was said to have hurt her most.

An instant denial of any possibility that Labour was thinking of targeting Samantha Cameron was in line with Gordon Brown's categorical assurance that there would be no negative briefings by anyone in his party about the personal lives of politicians and their families during the course of the election campaign. Media strategists for all three main parties had been issued with strict instructions following the resignation the previous year of Brown's personal press officer Damian McBride after he was exposed for having invented obscene slurs designed to smear David Cameron and George Osborne. McBride's downfall was a seismic event for Labour's discredited spin doctors, the ultimate point of no return for the attack dogs unleashed by Blair and Brown. E-mails sent from McBride's Downing Street address in January 2009 suggested fictitious story lines for use by the pro-Labour blogger Derek Draper, who was seeking material for his new website, Red Rag. McBride's ideas were rated 'absolutely totally brilliant' by Draper and although there had been a bit of 'poetic licence', they were 'mainly gossipy, and intended to destabilise the Tories'. The line of attack against Cameron would imply there were unanswered questions about his family wealth and university life and the aim was to force him to publish his full financial and medical records: 'He could clear up exactly how much the Camerons are worth ... and he could make clear that he's not hiding any embarrassing illnesses.' Lurid scenarios intended to 'put the fear of God into Osborne' included one aimed at his wife: 'Why are friends of George Osborne letting it be known that his wife Frances has been feeling emotionally fragile since his Yachtgate troubles in the summer?' Brown wrote handwritten letters expressing his 'great regret' to all those subjected to the unsubstantiated claims made by his Downing Street head of media strategy; all concerned had been told that such actions have 'no part to play in the public life of our country'.

In the year that had elapsed since McBride's resignation there had invariably been swift and resolute action across the political divide whenever there was any hint that party activists might be on the point of resorting to underhand briefings about the private lives of politicians. Sarah Brown's extensive charity work and her unstinting support for her much-harassed husband had so impressed the Westminster village that it reinforced the notion that politicians' wives and partners were untouchable and were most certainly off limits when it came to the machinations of spin doctors and their media clientele. Occasional 'Tory toff' jibes about the Camerons' wealthy friends and relatives attracted some publicity but gained little traction except in the *Guardian* and the Labour-supporting *Daily Mirror* and Labour's attack dogs made no attempt to rekindle the ill-fated class war which was waged during the Crewe & Nantwich by-election.

By early March 2010 all that needed to be resolved on the Tory side was an agreement on the role which Samantha Cameron might play once campaigning stepped up a gear in the approach to polling day. In her *Sunday Times* profile she was credited with having said that she had no intention of becoming 'an all-singing, all-dancing political wife' but her ability to generate compelling photo-opportunities and attract favourable coverage was an asset which the Conservatives' media team were anxious to exploit. There was consternation at party headquarters when the shadow arts minister, Ed Vaizey, told a Channel 4 documentary, *Cameron Uncovered*, that Mrs Cameron might have voted for Blair during the Labour landslide in 1997. He claimed she would be going into this election thinking: 'Is Cameron the real deal or should I stick with Brown?' Vaizey beat a hasty retreat after being rounded on by Central Office. All he meant to do was portray her as a woman with her 'own political views'; he knew that she had worked 'night and day' on her husband's campaign in Stafford in 1997 and that, as she said, she had 'never voted Labour'. David Cameron had no alternative but to resolve the uncertainty and he told ITV's *Alan Titchmarsh Show* that his wife had worked out for herself the kind of role that she wanted to play. She would join him on the campaign trail and would also make public appearances in her own right in support of the kinds of social action project which a future Conservative government intended to encourage.

'Britain get ready' was Cameron's cheery salvo as he warned viewers that they were going to see 'a lot more' of an 'amazing woman, working mum and successful career woman' who had helped transform a great British business. 'She said to me the other day when we were having breakfast, "I know I work hard and I have my own business but I want you to do this, I want you to win. I'm right behind you."' Cameron's answers to a volley of lifestyle questions from Titchmarsh were mocked by the sketch writers. Quentin Letts (*Daily Mail*) said Cameron's list of 'little personality details' was depressing but probably unavoidable. 'He was soon gushing about "the family I adore". The whole thing was like a script for an old Oxo advert.' But Cameron's tormentors missed the other potential news line which he freely volunteered when Titchmarsh asked if he intended to expand his family: 'If the stork drops one off.'

Cameron's intriguing answer was a clue to what was in store: his wife's promotion to the front line of the Tory campaign would be like the launch of a new product; she was about to be marketed in a way which would more than match Sarah Brown's skilful presentation of herself as the unacknowledged First Lady and cheerleader for Team Brown. Whether they liked it or not, voters would be getting a chance to savour another first for a British general election, not an import from American presidential elections, but a wholly home-grown phenomenon. The three leaders' wives were about to be treated by the tabloid press as WAGs – short for wives and girlfriends, a term usually applied to the larger-than-life and expensively attired partners of Premier League footballers. Newspapers and magazines have invested heavily in celebrity reporting and believe one of their great strengths is an ability to offer readers a spread of photographs, insights and gossip which television and radio cannot match. Cameron's interview with Alan Titchmarsh was the signal to the media that Samantha Cameron was happy to come out and play, that she was ready and willing to leap from the safety of the fashion pages to the brash and far less respectful world of the WAGs. Their likes and dislikes get endlessly compared and contrasted and as journalists compete to feed the addiction of their readers, the privacy of family life has to take second place; even innermost thoughts become public property. Celebrity reporting was Andy Coulson's forte and his hotline to the *Sun* and the *News of the World* would ensure top billing for 'Sam Cam', the 'secret weapon' which party headquarters had been longing to deploy at the election battle front.

Kathy Lette, the Australian novelist and a long-standing friend of Sarah Brown, identified the Prime Minister's wife as his 'secret weapon' once she began attracting publicity by inviting Naomi Campbell and other A-list celebrities to attend events in support of her charitable causes. 'Sam Cam's our "secret weapon" says David' – the headline in the *Daily Express* over a report that his wife had already launched a counter-attack by giving her first television interview to another ITV programme, *Trevor McDonald Meets David Cameron*. If the Prime Minister thought he could win votes by inviting Piers Morgan to present him as a romantic heart-throb, the Tory leader was more than capable of offering an alternative love story. Just as Sarah Brown was proud to lay on a public display of affection for her husband, so Cameron's wife was happy to play the romantic. There seemed no limit to the lengths to which the two couples were prepared to go in airing their most intimate moments. Gordon Brown told Morgan that sitting next to Sarah on a plane ended up becoming a 'modern love story'; he said he 'knew she existed' but did not know much about her. 'No', they did not join the 'Mile High Club', but she was 'very beautiful, very elegant' and he found he just kept asking Sarah questions about herself. 'You might say love at first flight. I don't know. I don't know. I thought she was very nice.'

Samantha Cameron told Trevor McDonald that she was hooked by her husband on a holiday romance. There had been some 'tough times' in their eighteen years together but 'I can honestly say that in all that time he's never let me down . . . He loves politics and I think so much of the Dave that I first met and fell in love with is Dave the politician.' She was filmed in the family home and she readily enlarged on her husband's 'very irritating' habits. 'One of the brilliant things about him is he loves cooking. But he makes a terrible mess.'

Her well-scripted answers suggested the handiwork of Andy Coulson and immediately caught the eye of the *Daily Mail*, which noted similarities in political 'wifespeak'. Michelle Obama admitted her husband had trouble 'putting his socks actually in the dirty clothes'; at the Labour conference Sarah Brown said the Prime Minister was 'not a saint – he's messy, he's noisy'; and in reprimanding her husband for making a 'terrible mess', Samantha Cameron added the line that 'he's not very good at picking up his clothes'. Coulson's role behind the scenes in helping the Camerons prepare for their interview with Trevor McDonald was confirmed by the *Guardian*, which subsequently discovered that he was allowed to preview the programme before transmission. ITV denied the move was highly unusual: there was 'no harm' in allowing Coulson and his staff an opportunity to see the film given that the producer's editorial control was 'absolute and there were no opportunities to make any changes other than factual points'.

Nonetheless Samantha Cameron's television debut was a coup for ITV and at last the 'queens of mean' were in business. Jan Moir (*Daily Mail*) was captivated by the opening salvo of the 'Sam v. Sarah WAG election'. All of that 'yummy mummy, handbag-making nonsense' would have to be set aside and, 'like an oiled gun being rolled towards the Tory ramparts', she would have to counter the exponentially increased public profile of Sarah Brown and try to ramp up the Conservatives' diminishing lead in the opinion polls. Another of the *Daily Mail*'s columnists, Amanda Platell, was shocked to hear Samantha's words come tumbling out in Estuary English. During the interview she uttered twelve *you know*s, four *sort of*s and six *really*s – four of them in a single sentence. 'How on earth, I wondered, does a baronet's daughter end up talking like the Clinique girl in the Bluewater shopping centre?' But the party's spinmeisters were reassured by the subsequent headlines, such as 'Tories benefit from a Sam Cam bounce'. After a month in which the Conservatives' opinion poll lead had been halved to around 5 points, the *Trevor McDonald Meets David Cameron* programme was credited in an Opinium survey with helping to restore it to double digits.

With the three party leaders already in training in preparation for the first of their televised debates, Nick Clegg was immediately put on the spot: was his wife prepared to make it a three-horse race with Sarah and Samantha? From the outset Miriam González Durántez, who retained her Spanish citizenship, had shown no interest in turning out for the WAGs. But whatever she might have wished, she had already been signed up by the media and was being marked down in the fashion stakes. Jane Moore (*Sun*) was surprised to see her pitch up at the Liberal

Democrats' spring conference in mid-March 'wearing a grey bin liner and a handbag seemingly made by the Wombles'. Instead of purchasing a bag from Smythson of Bond Street, hers was the height of 'eco-chic' and made from 'discarded ring pulls by under-privileged women in the shanty towns of Brazil'.

Clegg reassured the press pack that González, mother of his three sons – Antonio, Alberto and Miguel – would be joining him at least one day a week on the campaign trail. When the couple were interviewed together for ITV by Mary Nightingale, she recoiled on being described as a political wife. 'I dislike that name . . . I don't have a role, I'm just married to him.' She was an international trade lawyer and had no intention of going round the country presenting a 'sugar-coated image' of herself simply to win votes for her husband. 'I don't have the luxury of having a job that I can simply abandon for five weeks and I imagine that is the situation for most people in the country . . . I am willing, of course, to help Nick because he is my husband. I want the best for him and of course I love him.'

Clegg and González met when studying at the College of Europe in Bruges and were both subsequently employed by the European Commission; he was elected a member of the European Parliament in 1999 and became MP for Sheffield Hallam in 2005. No pre-election interview with Clegg was considered complete without reference to his infamous gaffe about having slept with 'no more than thirty' women before he met his wife, a claim which prompted the unforgettable *Sun* headline: 'Lib Dem Nick's Cleggovers'. He assured Nightingale that this was not correct and his wife thought 'the whole thing was absurd'. But, true or false, his supposed sexual prowess was the best-known 'fact' about the Liberal Democrat leader and one for which Piers Morgan shamelessly took the credit. When interviewing Clegg for *GQ* in April 2008, Morgan asked him if he was good in bed. After replying that his wife was the 'only judge of that', Clegg foolishly got drawn into admitting that other women might have an opinion. Morgan pounced: 'Well, how many are we talking – ten, twenty, thirty?' Clegg replied: 'No more than thirty.'

Morgan said that if Clegg had bothered to check he would have seen he asked the same cheeky question of every other *GQ* interviewee and he could easily have chosen the option of 'mind your own business'. Clegg told *Grazia* that he panicked; he feared Morgan might get to a hundred. 'He was just reeling off numbers, ten, twenty, thirty, so I just interrupted, and before you know it, it became a claim that's turned into a myth.'

His wife's assertion that an MP's partner could be 'supportive without being submissive' impressed Elizabeth Day, a feature writer for the *Observer Magazine*, who caught up with her in the boardroom of international lawyers DLA Piper. González embodied the 'new breed of Sam Cams, the independent career women and mothers who happen to be married to politicians'. She seeped unapologetic glamour: 'Today she is wearing a grey silk shift dress, a chunky gold necklace and fashionable high-heeled ankle boots.' Her refusal to take time out to go campaigning attracted the support of women writers who agreed with her that the media's obsession with the leaders' wives was 'patronising'. Nonetheless she was prepared to answer questions on the occasions she accompanied her husband to campaign events. Even if she was absent when her husband was being interviewed, journalists admired from afar her elegance and aloofness: 'Spanish, glamorous and defiantly laissez-faire about her husband's choice of career' (Carole Cadwalladr, *Grazia*); 'achingly fashionable' (Tim Walker, *Daily Telegraph*).

If the political correspondents thought they might be in with a chance of regaining the initiative from the fashion writers, they were mistaken. 'Glam Sam' was the *Mail on Sunday*'s headline over a collection of photographs of 'Samantha the supermodel' from a 'twelve-year-old fashion shoot discovered in an Isle of Wight attic'. The pictures were taken a year or two after the Camerons' wedding in 1996 and showed that she 'once cut an altogether more vampish dash' sprawled on the floor in a mini-dress and high-heeled boots. Fashion writer Alison Jane Reid, who organised the shoot, said the camera loved Mrs Cameron. She had all the features a model needed: 'clear, radiant skin, a symmetrical face, wonderful long hair, a model's body and those legs, a mile long'.

Even before the women's pages had time to give their opinion on Sam Cam's 'more seductive streak', she was back on the front pages with an announcement which put the politicos in a spin. 'Wham bam! Sam Cam to be mam (she'll need a new pram)' was the *Sun*'s inimitable take on a story which delighted the tabloids and put a spring into David Cameron's step. Bounding into his morning news conference, he complimented the headline writers, saying he never realised so many words rhymed with 'Sam Cam'. The couple had decided to try for another child after Ivan's death the previous year but it 'sometimes took a while before the stork drops one down the chimney'. A September baby was not ideal because it clashed with the party conference but they were 'completely thrilled' that one was on the way to join Nancy and Arthur Elwen.

No spin doctor would have thought it possible to time Cameron's confirmation of his wife's pregnancy to within six weeks of polling day but it was precisely the lucky break he needed as he tried to calm Tory jitters while Westminster waited for the Prime Minister to call the election. Gordon Brown's drive to Buckingham Palace on the Tuesday of Easter week had been so heavily trailed in advance that his opponents responded immediately with their pitch to the electors. Alternative pictures being offered by the Conservatives included footage of a pregnant Samantha Cameron filmed for WebCameron, the online video site which the party launched in 2006 to offer glimpses of the Camerons' family life. She was shown boiling a kettle at their London home and then sipping her drink as her husband sat at a computer. When asked if she needed any tips on campaigning, he replied: 'She's a natural . . . she's eclipsing me completely.' Mrs Cameron chipped in: 'I think the bump is.'

Conservative-supporting newspapers were captivated by images of the pregnant Samantha but the more she was paraded as David Cameron's 'secret weapon' the greater the admiration for Nick Clegg's wife. Feisty correspondents began to applaud her decision to carry on as normal in the face of a general election. 'Miriam, we salute you. We love you for acting like an independent, modern mother and wife.' (Alison Tyler, *Daily Mail*.) 'Regardless of our politics we warmed to her no-nonsense approach.' (Vanessa Feltz, *Daily Express*.) The *Sun*'s double-page spread – 'The race to Number 10 . . . and now the wives are out' – identified her as the 'most exotic-sounding of the three leading Westminster WAGs' but also complimented her on being 'a great role model for young girls'. *The Times* commissioned a Mumsnet panel to give their opinion and she was admired for being 'silent but strong'. Some respondents said they were offended by the way Brown and Cameron were exploiting their wives and they would not be swayed by Mrs Cameron's pregnancy. A similar verdict was offered by a *Sunday Times* YouGov poll, which suggested that 89 per cent of those surveyed thought the wives would have no impact on their vote. Nonetheless the tabloid fashionistas were assembling photographs of their ever-changing outfits ready for a contest to determine the most stylish wife. Encouraging the political WAGs to raise their game had provided plenty of light relief for the media during the pre-election skirmishing but the dissolution of Parliament, the launch of the manifestos and the looming televised debates were about to impose new strains and stresses on the leaders' wives. Their husbands were about to participate in what would become the game changer of the general election and the strength of their wives' moral support would be more important than their sartorial prowess.

9

THE TV DEBATES

The Labour and Conservative campaign strategists always gave the impression that they rather enjoyed their traditional pre-election joust with the broadcasters over the possibility that one day they might deign to approve a televised leaders' debate. Eager producers were encouraged to make their pitch; they would emphasise the impact of presidential debates on the outcome of successive US elections and would then explain why they believed there was no justification to go on denying British voters an opportunity to see and hear how their party leaders might respond if they too were required to appear together in a television studio and were forced to address the issues of the day. Often there would be lengthy and purposeful negotiations on the structure and supervision of such programmes but invariably, usually at the last moment, one of the political parties would pull out, blame the other side – and perhaps the BBC as well – and the whole charade would collapse with recriminations all round. Prime Ministers and leaders of the opposition tended to remain above the fray, preferring instead to make lofty pronouncements when it suited them about how they believed Question Time in the House of Commons was a far more effective substitute.

In 2010, though, against the odds, an agreement was reached with surprising good grace to stage three separate ninety-minute debates during the final three weeks of the general election campaign. After waiting for nearly fifty years British television was finally given the go-ahead to transform its contribution to the conduct of a general election campaign. Little did the broadcasters know that their breakthrough would have such a profound effect on the electoral process that it would set in train the biggest shake-up in the politics of the United Kingdom since the coalition government of the Second World War.

The Americans had been the pioneers in using television to engage the electorate, and the Republican-v.-Democrat format adopted for presidential debates was long regarded as being an ideal fit for the traditional two-party politics of the United Kingdom. However, a complicating factor in later years was the slow but steady increase in the number of Liberal Democrat MPs, which started to exert increasing pressure on the two main parties to allow the opportunity for a third leader to participate. To the surprise of many within the broadcasting industry, Labour and the Conservatives agreed unexpectedly not only to go ahead with a televised confrontation but also to accept a three-way split. A guarantee of an equal share of the time for the Liberal Democrats changed the dynamics both of the debates themselves and of the course of the election. Instead of the leaders of the two main parties going head to head as they might have expected, a relative outsider had been given an unprecedented opportunity to challenge the established order. Gordon Brown and David Cameron entered the first debate having overlooked the fact that their greatest vulnerability was that they could be portrayed as the leaders of the 'two old parties', the embodiment of a failed political system. Equal billing gave Nick Clegg an unparalleled chance to introduce himself to the public at large and present the case for 'fairer' politics.

In the year which had elapsed since the *Daily Telegraph* began publishing details of the systematic abuse of parliamentary allowances, there had been no lessening in the public's distrust of MPs. Initially a widening sense of disenchantment with the established political process looked like encouraging a new wave of high-profile independent parliamentary candidates. But the few who put themselves forward seemed unable to turn an anti-politics mood to their advantage. In the early months of 2010 pollsters and political pundits were confused by contradictory messages from opinion surveys. On the one hand it appeared that disillusion might lead to a low turnout but conversely there seemed to be the potential for a sizeable protest vote if only it could be mobilised. A narrowing in the opinion polls added to the uncertainty, which in turn fuelled the expectation that for a vast swathe of the public the three televised debates might determine how they would vote.

Clegg's tactics could not be faulted. He seemed to know intuitively how the electorate's deep-seated scepticism could be harnessed to the Liberal Democrats' advantage. He was the undisputed winner of the first debate and the Liberal Democrats' opinion poll rating advanced by 10 to 12 points within the space of a week, the largest leap ever recorded during the course of an election campaign. While Clegg was able to communicate with viewers in a natural and engaging manner which eluded Cameron and Brown, his opponents managed to retaliate by drawing attention to controversial policies in the Liberal Democrats' manifesto. But waning support for his party's policy agenda did not dampen enthusiasm for Clegg's vision of a fairer electoral system and as polling day approached there were calls for tactical voting to try to ensure greater co-operation between any newly elected government and opposition parties.

Achieving a balanced parliament, where parties would be forced to share power, was an option which began to attract growing support in the final stages of the campaign. The sight of the three leaders each continuing to argue his corner appeared to have reinforced the determination of those among the electorate who felt a new approach was needed. Uncommitted or uncertain voters had been fired up by the televised debates. After the election many said their hope of securing change and a hung parliament did influence the way they voted.

The first televised confrontation of this kind had taken place in 1960. British electors had been forced to wait half a century to see their own version of a format which had become commonplace during election campaigns in democracies around the world. Such was the debates' impact on the 2010 campaign that there was an immediate realisation within the political establishment that there could be no turning back; that in future no party might earn a mandate to govern the country unless its leader had been prepared to engage with the electorate via the forum of televised debates. Broadcasters accepted that they too faced a fresh challenge: the format of the three programmes did not ensure rigorous interrogation of the party leaders, they were not held to account through supplementary questions, nor were they required to give a proper explanation as to how their parties intended to deal with the key issue of the day: the record deficit and the wider economic crisis. But despite their limitations, the debates succeeded in dominating the campaign and they appeared to have secured their place as an essential component in the direction of any future general election.

Unlike American Presidents, bound by fixed four-year terms of office, British Prime Ministers have enjoyed the right to go to the country on a date of their choosing, within a five-year period. Their freedom of manoeuvre held the key to the years of prevarication over televised debates. Once an election was in the offing there was usually a distinct tactical advantage in favour of either the government of the day or the main opposition party. Until the surprise agreement of 2010 the leader with the strongest hand had always been reluctant to put that at risk by entering into an unpredictable confrontation. The often devious ways in which Labour and the Conservatives were able to twist the arguments for and against televised debates to their own political advantage became a long-standing abuse of the two-party system. Suddenly unlocking the door to a new world of three-way political engagement precipitated an unprecedented shake-up at Westminster. Fear of making a leap into the unknown explained the tortuous delay and it was only by being prepared to abandon the ritualistic postures of their predecessors that Cameron and then Brown rose to the challenge and helped to revive flagging participation in the political process.

British politicians had watched with fascination the first of America's televised debates, in the lead-up to the 1960 presidential election.

Richard Nixon was a skilled and powerful debater who thought he could easily take advantage of his inexperienced rival, John Kennedy, but in fact the reverse was the case. Kennedy was the more handsome of the two, he was tanned and at ease, and appeared to be in command of their exchanges. By contrast Nixon, who had refused make-up and had a noticeable five o'clock shadow, looked shifty and left a negative impression with viewers. Kennedy took part in a further three debates with Nixon and he explained subsequently in a BBC interview why they played a vital part in the Democrats' campaign and his election as President. 'A good deal of the press supports Nixon and this way we could discuss these issues face to face with Nixon without going through the press.'

Sir Alec Douglas-Home became the first Prime Minister to be challenged to a televised debate when the leader of the opposition, Harold Wilson, threw down the gauntlet during the run-up to the 1964 election. Wilson had been highly impressed both by Kennedy's performance and by the impact of the Democrats' use of television to counter a Republican bias in the American press. Labour faced similar hostility from Conservative-supporting newspapers and Wilson was just as keen to appeal directly to voters but his challenge to a debate was in vain. Sir Robin Day, the legendary BBC inquisitor, extracted an explanation from Douglas-Home which stood the test of time for successive incumbents:

> *I am not very attracted by the idea of confrontations of personality. If you are not careful you will get a* Top of the Pops *contest. I dare say I would win it, I am not sure. You will get the best actor as leader of the country and an actor will be prompted by a script writer. I would rather have our old ways. I debate with Wilson in Parliament and I shall decide if I want to confront Wilson, not if Wilson wants to confront me.*

Douglas-Home, an Old Etonian, who had renounced his hereditary earldom to stand for Parliament, was defeated by Labour and once Wilson was safely installed in Downing Street he adopted the same stance as his predecessor. He rejected Edward Heath's challenge to a debate in the 1966 election, a mutual stand-off which Wilson and Heath maintained in the elections of 1970 and 1974. Wilson's political secretary Marcia Williams was convinced that no Prime Minister wanted to appear on equal terms with a leader of the opposition: 'Harold's office would have rubbed off on Heath, to Heath's advantage . . . and would have given him a lot of exposure in a setting which Heath wanted.'

James Callaghan, who succeeded Wilson as Prime Minister, was the first incumbent to rise to the challenge. After his already weakened government had been battered by the industrial strife of the 'Winter of Discontent', he seemed on the point of being defeated by the Conservatives and readily accepted London Weekend Television's invitation to take part in a debate in advance of the 1979 election. Margaret Thatcher was advised by her celebrated media strategist Sir Gordon Reece to reject the offer. She was ahead in the opinion polls and he feared that the first woman to lead the Tories into a general election might come off worse when up against a confident television performer like Callaghan. 'Take him on, Maggie' was the *Sun*'s advice but her reply to LWT set out the reasoning which she later repeated from a position of strength as Prime Minister in both the 1983 and 1987 elections: 'Personally, I believe that issues and policies, not personalities, decide an election. We are not electing a President.' Likewise her successor, John Major, had no hesitation in rejecting Neil Kinnock's request that he should join a televised debate which the Hansard Society was offering to organise in advance of the 1992 election. Major's refusal dominated the final session of Prime Minister's Questions. He had clearly come armed with a carefully prepared answer for Kinnock: 'If I accurately recall my Shakespeare: "He draweth out the thread of his verbosity finer than the staple of his argument". Appropriately, that comes from *Love's Labour's Lost* and Labour will lose.' Kinnock needed little prompting with his supplementary: 'The Prime Minister reads quotations from Shakespeare. Let me give him one from the Right Honourable member for Finchley

[Thatcher]: "He is frit."' But the Prime Minister was having none of it: 'Every party politician that expects to lose tries that trick and every politician who expects to win says "No".'

Five years later the tables were turned. Leading a Conservative government that faced almost certain defeat after eighteen years in power, a beleaguered Major followed Callaghan's example and did all he could to initiate a debate with Tony Blair, leader of the rebranded New Labour. Michael Dobbs, a former deputy chairman of the Tory Party, opened negotiations with BBC and ITV. Major had been warming to the idea for some time, which encouraged senior broadcasters to devise a range of possible formats. Once again there was an impasse but the failed negotiations of 1997 laid bare the wily politicking which takes place when a failing government faces a resurgent opposition; the discussions were also significant because for the first time a structure had been devised which would give the Liberal Democrats a voice. Thirteen years later a bruised and battered Gordon Brown would face the same plight as Major; the one difference would be that despite having the upper hand, David Cameron – unlike Blair – kept his word and did not pull the plug at the last moment on the debates of 2010.

The fiasco of 1997 was the last serious attempt to strike a deal until Brown, Cameron and Clegg authorised their aides to start bargaining with the broadcasters. One lesson which the three parties took on board more than a decade later was the importance of keeping their discussions private, for Major's abortive negotiations had been played out in the full glare of publicity and rapidly descended into political point scoring.

Major's campaign strategists advised him that he had nothing to lose by subjecting himself to a televised debate with Blair. At his final meeting with Conservative backbenchers before the dissolution of Parliament there was much banging of desks when he declared that he was 'relishing the chance to pin Blair down' on the detail of Labour's policies. The BBC proposed a ninety-minute programme to allow an hour's debate between Major and Blair under the chairmanship of David Dimbleby; there would be a separate stand-alone interview with Paddy Ashdown for the Liberal Democrats, and closing statements from all three. A similar format was proposed by ITV: Jonathan Dimbleby would chair the debate and there would be time for additional questions from Sue Lawley and Michael Brunson. Initially Major felt the structure was too rigid and would allow Blair 'too many opportunities to trot out his soundbites'. He was reassured there would be opportunities to challenge the Labour leader.

Both programmes would have audiences, though it was not intended that they would participate, and this became a stumbling block for Labour's negotiator, the shadow Lord Chancellor, Lord Irvine. He wanted the audience to take part and ask questions, an option which the deputy Prime Minister, Michael Heseltine, considered was a wrecking tactic: 'What Labour want to do is send in people to cheer for Blair and to boo for Major.' The Conservatives accused Labour of having cold feet and my own conversations at the time with Blair's press secretary, Alastair Campbell, confirmed as much. 'We don't care a stuff if Major does or does not want a debate . . . What we don't welcome is the idea of a television debate becoming a dominant issue in the campaign.' Campbell rounded off a pretty clear steer that a debate was unlikely by reminding me that Ashdown's role had become a problem for the broadcasters. Suggesting that he should be interviewed separately had enraged the Liberal Democrats' campaign manager, Lord Holme of Cheltenham. The prospect of 'only the two great men' being allowed to have a debate and then the interviewer going across to Ashdown who was 'stuck in a room on his own' was quite unacceptable.

With the negotiations rapidly descending into farce Labour called the Conservatives' bluff by setting a midnight deadline, which Michael Dobbs took as confirmation that Blair had been planning to 'pull the plug' all along. Campbell confirmed to me that Labour would waste no more time 'playing politics' with the Conservatives: 'The idea we don't want Blair to be cross-questioned is balls. What we didn't want was a format like Prime Minister's Questions. We wanted an audience to ask the questions.' Brian Mawhinney, the Tory chairman, retaliated next morning on *Today* by pointing an accusing finger at Blair himself: the BBC, ITV and the Conservatives all wanted to go ahead with televised debates but 'Blair is terrified, he's chicken'. In an attempt to remind voters that it was Labour who had reneged, the Conservatives dressed up a volunteer as a chicken who prowled around outside Labour's campaign events armed with a placard which said 'Chicken Blair won't debate'.

Blair's landslide victory in 1997 led to a resumption of the pattern of previous years: an incumbent, backed by a massive majority, had no intention of jeopardising the premiership and for another two general elections the door remained firmly closed to the possibility of a televised debate. In advance of the 2001 campaign, in the vain hope that Blair might be enticed to take part, programme planners at the BBC and ITV made a joint proposal for two one-hour debates. William Hague and Charles Kennedy, respectively leaders of the Conservatives and the Liberal Democrats, both accepted but Labour declined on the grounds that the two broadcasts would not 'significantly add to the public interest in or understanding of the issues'. My notes of Campbell's briefing revealed the real reason: the Prime Minister was so far ahead in the opinion polls the risk was not worth taking, especially as Hague had demonstrated superior debating skills at the dispatch box. I thought one telling argument which Campbell advanced went some way towards explaining his own concern as the Prime Minister's director of communications. He feared the media's concentration on the 'process of the debates' might make it more difficult for Labour to present their policies to the electorate:

All we would get is endless discussion about the personalities of the leaders and flashbacks to the key moments of the past like Richard Nixon sweating . . . There would be nothing but blah-blah about the ballyhoo of it all for days on end . . . We think you will have more discussion and more focus on policy without televised debates.

Campbell could hardly have been more explicit: if a party was in a commanding position in the opinion polls and was managing successfully to dictate the news agenda, it made no sense to participate in a confrontation which would allow two rival candidates to gang up on a leader who might then end up being diverted from focusing on the campaign by the kind of uncontrollable media frenzy which a television spectacular would provoke. Blair's media strategists were regarded by their opponents as the ultimate control freaks and, whatever the short-term embarrassment they might have to endure, they were resolute in their determination to eliminate all potential upsets.

In the 2005 election Blair finally secured the format he had always wanted and in which he felt most comfortable: a half-hour grilling from a live audience. *The Leaders' Debate* was the BBC's innovative solution to the never-ending stalemate. The three leaders agreed to be questioned consecutively, for thirty minutes each, in the same studio by a *Question Time* audience, moderated by David Dimbleby. A theatre in east London was chosen as the venue but its location was not revealed and reporters were kept away. Questions were invited on key issues including the Labour government's support for the American-led invasion of Iraq, the economy and the National Health Service.

Charles Kennedy opened for the Liberal Democrats, followed by the Conservative leader, Michael Howard, and then the Prime Minister. Kennedy appeared relaxed and at ease, eager to rehearse the reasons why the Liberal Democrats had opposed the Iraq War; he was applauded after declaring he was 'ashamed of what the government did in the name of our country'. Howard looked uncomfortable, even nervous, but insisted he would have supported the war even if he had known that Saddam Hussein had no weapons of mass destruction; it was 'the right thing to do'. Facing a barrage of hostile questions, which were often greeted with applause, Blair stood his ground while accepting there were people in the audience who disagreed 'very, very strongly' with his decision to take the country to war. He was booed on several occasions and, as the questioning moved on from Iraq and the economy to hospital waiting lists, beads of perspiration began to trickle down his brow. At one point several members of the audience shouted in agreement when two women complained that government targets were making it difficult to get doctors' appointments for their children. But even under sustained fire Blair remained clear and forthright and the format allowed him every opportunity to subject himself to a level of verbal assault which some party leaders would have found either too intimidating or too difficult to handle.

While the three leaders had no opportunity to challenge each other they were subjected to rigorous probing and the audience leapt at the chance to participate and put the politicians on the spot. Occasionally Dimbleby interjected with supplementary questions if he felt the point at issue had not been properly addressed. *The Leaders' Debate* was no substitute for the confrontation which broadcasters and the opposing parties would have preferred but the programme did at least succeed in getting the three leaders into the same studio and gave the audience a chance to hold them to account.

For an avid student of British politics there was only one lesson to draw from the absurdities of the previous fifty years. In an age of reality television party leaders had no alternative but to get used to live studio audiences and to being judged on their performance in front of the camera. Televised debates were already a regular feature of leadership contests; there might even be considerable kudos in becoming the first party leader to signal a break with the past. David Cameron's experience as political insider and television executive pointed to only one conclusion: he would be ready come what may to take on any opponent in a televised pre-election confrontation. He gave the pledge during the first of three full-scale televised debates which he held with David Davis in the final round of the 2005 Conservative leadership election. Immediately after Cameron made it his personal commitment, Davis followed suit in his own opening remarks. Their debates and joint appearances in television studios became a notable feature of the contest and their readiness to confront each other live on air was welcomed by Adam Boulton, political editor of Sky News, who chaired the last of the three programmes. He explained in an article in the *Sunday Telegraph* why he was convinced the boldness of the two Davids demonstrated television's ability to empower viewers to make political choices and constituted an overwhelming case for leaders' debates at the next election. 'Blair's exaggerated fears don't matter now . . . All that is needed is agreement to participate from the next Labour leader. We should not let him or her wriggle out of it.'

Cameron's debates with Davis did not go as well as he might have hoped; occasionally he lacked the flair and fluency which he had demonstrated so clearly when speaking without notes at the party conference and some commentators considered his opponent was the more effective debater of the two. Any doubts were set aside after Cameron's two-to-one victory in the leadership election. As Boulton had pointed out, the priority for the Conservatives was to make sure that a new Labour leader was not allowed to repeat Tony Blair's outright refusal at three general elections to debate with his opponents. In May 2007, a month before the Blair–Brown handover, Cameron used his WebCameron blog to issue a direct challenge to the Prime Minister in waiting. Rather than leave it until the general election, Brown should agree immediately to head-to-head discussions on the big issues facing the country, a demand which had the backing of the Liberal Democrat leader, Menzies Campbell. They both argued that in the absence of a contest for the Labour leadership, the electorate deserved a meaningful debate on Brown's future plans. Brown dismissed the idea out of hand.

Boulton was also as good as his word and at Brown's first Downing Street news conference he asked for an assurance that the new Prime Minister would agree to a televised debate. Brown promised on taking office that he intended to deliver 'a new style of politics' and the question was particularly relevant given the speculation that Labour might go for an autumn election. Without hesitation Brown resorted to the answer given by previous incumbents: Britain did not need US-style presidential debates because there was a thirty-minute televised debate between himself and Cameron in the House of Commons every week. 'To draw parallels with America is not right . . . There is a time and a place for deciding elections . . . I am getting on with the job of government'. In his report that evening for the *Ten o'Clock News*, the BBC's political editor, Nick Robinson, included an archive clip of a young Brown berating Margaret Thatcher for not agreeing to a televised debate. Robinson said that what had changed was that Brown was Prime Minister, and like Thatcher, he could refuse.

Tactically Brown might have thought he had made the right call; no Prime Minister wanted to pre-empt decisions that were better taken nearer an election. But his stance was at odds with the pace of modern politics and the importance which political activists attached to televised debates. The six contenders for deputy Labour leader faced viewers' questions and interrogation both on *Question Time* and in a special edition of *Newsnight*; Nick Clegg and Chris Huhne, the two contenders to succeed Campbell as Liberal Democrat leader, clashed on *The Politics Show*; and there were angry exchanges between Boris Johnson and Ken Livingstone when three main candidates for mayor of London appeared in their first televised debate on ITV's *London Talking*. Barack Obama's success in televised debates with Hillary Clinton when campaigning for the Democratic nomination provided Cameron with another chance to goad the Prime Minister. But Brown stuck to his line that the United States did not have an equivalent of Prime Minister's Questions; instead he rounded on Cameron for making a mockery of his call for 'an end to Punch and Judy politics'.

When Brown walked away from a snap election in the autumn of 2007 he must have hoped that the long march to polling day in May 2010 would allow him plenty of time to restore Labour's fortunes. Soldiering on until the end of their mandates did not save either Callaghan or Major, and Labour's campaign team knew that risks would have to be taken if there was to be any chance of defeating Cameron. Lord Mandelson, the Business Secretary, gave the first hint that Brown might follow the example of Callaghan and Major and agree to a debate. Downing Street immediately denied that Brown had changed his mind, but Mandelson, deputy Prime Minister in all but name, was quite explicit. His own mind was 'open' to giving voters a chance to choose between Brown and the 'words and nice smile' of Cameron. 'I think people would see through the smile . . . Cameron exudes effortless superiority in public but loses his rag in private . . . The more the public sees of them [Cameron and Osborne], the more they'd realise that Gordon is the man of substance.'

Mandelson was expected to take a commanding role in Labour's election campaign and by going public with his thoughts he gave the impression that Brown was perhaps being bounced into taking part. A subsequent off-the-record briefing confirmed that the Prime Minister had discussed the possibility and was planning to make a surprise announcement in his speech to Labour's annual conference in September. Nonetheless Downing Street's official denial opened up a new line of attack for the Conservatives. 'It looks like another case of Brown the bottler,' said a party spokesman. Cameron was 18 points ahead in the opinion polls and a leading article in *The Times* wondered what strategy Tory headquarters would adopt to counter Mandelson's election battle plan of presenting Brown as the underdog. Given that Cameron seemed to be heading for an overall parliamentary majority, was it perhaps the time for him to change his mind? 'With every successive opinion poll, a live debate is beginning to look like an unwarranted risk.' Simon Heffer reached the same conclusion in his column in the *Daily Telegraph*: 'Dave becomes the one with more to lose'. Another cautionary note was struck by the *Independent*, which carried a signed article from the Liberal Democrat leader, Nick Clegg, outlining his demand for equal time. He said British politics were marred by profound unfairness and there needed to be 'fair competition' between the parties. 'Labour's time is up, and the Conservatives think it's automatically their turn, but I think in these difficult times we need to do something altogether different.'

Eight months out from the 2010 general election Cameron was facing a point of no return. If he was having second thoughts about a televised confrontation with Brown, this was the moment to start backpedalling. But there appeared to be no doubt in his mind: Prime Minister's Questions were 'no substitute for a proper prime-time studio debate'. He was standing by the line he used at the height of the speculation surrounding a 2007 election when he declared he was ready for a showdown with Brown. 'Any time, any place, anywhere. I will even pay for the taxi to take him to the studio. In fact, I'll even drive the cab.' And, whatever Brown might want, he was quite prepared for a three-way debate which gave Clegg the chance to participate.

Mandelson's unexpected support caused a flurry of excitement among rival television executives. Sky News stole a march on the BBC and ITV by announcing in September 2009 that it would host a live debate and 'empty chair' any leader who refused to take part. Some informal discussions had already taken place and the BBC and ITV promised to continue working together to reach an agreement with the parties. But John Ryley, head of Sky News, would not be dissuaded if extended negotiations ended in failure. His channel would not accept the status quo: 'Public confidence in politics is at the lowest ebb. Something must be done to help restore faith in our political system.' Ryley said broadcasters knew precisely why politicians went through such contortions to stop televised debates: 'They understand that studio debates really can transform an election campaign. One unguarded answer can give the lie to a policy fudge or expose a lack of experience otherwise hidden from electors.'

Brown's confusing on off stance over whether he would agree to a leaders' debate seemed to mirror his indecision of 2007 over the possibility of calling a snap autumn election. On the eve of the party conference Nick Robinson told the *Ten o'Clock News* that the Prime Minister intended to confirm that he was willing to confront Cameron on television. A draft of his speech indicated that he was prepared to take part in debates both during and before the election. In the event his address concentrated on policy rather than election tactics; he made no reference to confronting Cameron and afterwards he declined to give journalists a straight answer. But broadcasters were convinced they had been given the green light and they decided to seize the initiative. A formal proposal for three live election debates was made jointly by the BBC, ITV and Sky News. Brown responded next day with a statement on Labour's website confirming that he was willing 'in principle' to take part and would like the debates to focus on subjects including public services, the economy and foreign affairs. 'It is right that the parties debate the issues not just in Parliament but in every arena where the public will join the discussion . . . I relish the opportunity of making our case directly to the people of this country.' Instead of commanding the agenda Brown's equivocation got the better of him and he failed to ensure that he got the credit for a radical transformation in the conduct of a British general election campaign. Kevin Maguire, the *Daily Mirror*'s political editor, hailed the decision as a 'glorious opportunity' for Brown to appeal directly to voters. A showdown with Cameron and Clegg would be a 'lifeline' when Labour was 'behind in the polls and the BBC and much of the press sucks up to Cameron'.

As television executives and party strategists prepared to work out a structure for the three debates there was evidently tension behind the scenes. Brown hoped the debates could start in the autumn but Cameron was insisting they should be as close to polling day as possible. Clegg's role was also a point of contention: Brown wanted to go head to head with Cameron and then have a separate debate with Clegg. In the event the parties set aside their differences and broke a fifty-year stalemate by agreeing to hold three ninety-minute debates in the final weeks of the campaign. A running order was fixed by the broadcasters: ITV's debate would be first, followed by Sky News and the BBC; the three programmes would be hosted by their respective presenters, Alastair Stewart, Adam Boulton and David Dimbleby. The next task, delayed until the start of the New Year, was the tricky problem of agreeing the rules but the die was cast and the parties braced themselves for an election that would be like no other.

However he eventually performed, Nick Clegg had the satisfaction of knowing that he had secured an unimaginable prize for the Liberal Democrats: an equal share with Labour and the Conservatives in three prime-time programmes. Clegg had been gifted an opportunity which Charles Kennedy and Paddy Ashdown had battled for unsuccessfully in previous elections. To the irritation of the two main parties the Liberal Democrats often tended to punch above their weight as a result of the rules requiring television and radio to provide balanced coverage during election campaigns. National news bulletins and current affairs programmes broadcast by the BBC usually worked on a rough basis that Labour and the Conservatives were each allowed around 30 to 40 per cent of air time and the Liberal Democrats the remainder. Given their number of parliamentary seats an allocation of 3:3:2 was regarded by their opponents as being over-generous but the Liberal Democrats argued that it was their share of the vote which counted. Once an election was called the party always went to inordinate lengths to ensure that no programme was ever without a Liberal Democrat voice. Experience had shown the effectiveness of their tactics; guaranteed exposure raised their profile and activists were constantly being reassured by the leadership that once the campaign was underway the party's opinion poll ratings would improve. By agreeing that Clegg could have equal time in the three leaders' debates, Labour and the Conservatives had inadvertently moved the goalposts even further in the Liberal Democrats' favour: broadcasters would be under pressure to work to a new ratio of 1:1:1 once the campaign started and the rules on balance took effect. With their opinion poll rating hovering at just under 20 per cent Ming Campbell remained optimistic; he told *The World This Weekend* that television and radio exposure for the Liberal Democrats would not be squeezed once the campaign started and they were guaranteed more air time.

Tim Montgomerie, editor of ConservativeHome, the party's website for activists, was one of the first to express rank-and-file concern at the willingness of the Tory leadership to allow Clegg equal time. Cameron had in effect given the Liberal Democrats 'a status that the third party in British politics has never had before'. Political commentators were equally nonplussed by the Conservatives' generosity: Matthew Norman suggested in his column in the *Independent* that the Liberal Democrats were enjoying a 'Christmas miracle'; Cameron had better realise he would be up against an 'impressive television act' who scored brilliantly in the focus groups which the American pollster Frank Luntz was conducting for *Newsnight*. Norman's colleague Andrew Grice, the *Independent*'s political editor, said that having watched Clegg at one of his hundred town hall meetings he understood why people liked him and why he would probably appeal to the ten million people expected to tune in to the debates.

Getting an agreement on a format for the programmes was taking longer than expected. A well-sourced exclusive in the *News of the World* suggested that Brown and Cameron wanted the studio audience to sit in silence and be banned from applauding. Andy Coulson, Cameron's head of communications, led the negotiations for the Conservatives and *The Times* said it could confirm that there had been 'sharp differences' between the three parties. Much of the press coverage focused on the American consultants who were being hired to advise the three leaders and help with rehearsals. Their briefings on potential pitfalls were also having an influence on shaping the structure of the programmes because the negotiators wrongly assumed that experience of the US presidential debates was most relevant to the British situation.

Early in March, two months from polling day, the three parties and the broadcasters finally struck a deal. Their 76-point agreement confirmed that the leaks were correct: the rules were so strict that much of the spontaneity looked like being drained from the debates. Members of the audience would be able to ask questions but they could not raise supplementary points and applaud only at the beginning and end of the programme; opening statements and replies would be subject to tight time limits. Nick Robinson was nonplussed by the restrictions: 'The debates will involve an audience that can't clap or cheer or boo or heckle . . . questioners who can't react to the answers they're given . . . and television interviewers who cannot demand answers to questions from evasive politicians.' Any potential for one or other of the leaders to gain an unfair advantage – or for the broadcasters to have any leeway – seemed to have been well and truly blocked. Handshakes between the leaders would be restricted to the end of each programme; close-up cut-away shots of individual members of the audience would be permitted only if they were being directly addressed; and there were rules on the type of podiums to be used and the eye line of the moderators.

Three locations were chosen – Manchester (ITV), Bristol (Sky News) and Birmingham (BBC) – and the pollster ICM was commissioned to recruit audiences of 200 people from within a 30-mile radius of the host cities according to gender, age, ethnicity and social class to reflect the population at large. Separate leaders' debates were proposed for Scotland, Wales and Northern Ireland but this failed to satisfy either the Scottish National Party or Plaid Cymru. Both threatened legal action against the BBC unless their leaders were included but their objections were ignored by the three main parties. Cameron hailed the debates as the antidote to stage-managed politics. In an article for the *Sun* he predicted they would transform the campaign: 'It's not exactly the *X Factor*. We're not classic prime-time entertainment. But I believe they will energise politics.'

Channel 4 managed to cock a snook at its three more powerful competitors by pre-empting their much-trailed debates. *Ask the Chancellors*, a live televised confrontation between Alistair Darling and his two shadows, George Osborne and Vince Cable, provided an engaging dress rehearsal. 'Mr Dry, Mr Angry and Mr Smooth' – as they were dubbed by *The Times* – decided in advance to disregard the oppressive safeguards insisted on by their leaders and they opted instead for a no-holds-barred argument. In the event they each agreed that in order to restore Britain's economic credibility the cuts in public spending would have to be tougher than those imposed in the 1980s by Margaret Thatcher's government. Darling and Cable ganged up against Osborne over the Conservatives' election pledge to abandon Labour's increase in national insurance contributions and they were equally critical of Osborne's intention to make an immediate start on reducing the deficit by finding £6 billion of efficiency savings. 'Poor, poor judgement' was Darling's verdict; 'utterly incredible' said Cable.

Sketch writers had been gagging for an opportunity to sharpen their debate pencils and their consensus was that Cable outshone his rivals. Benedict Brogan suggested his *Daily Telegraph* readers should go to the bookies and put money on the Liberal Democrats doing better than the pollsters were predicting. 'Cable played the plague-on-both-your-houses middle which got him the applause . . . There is clearly an appetite out there for a message that taps voter cynicism.' Cable's ability to milk the applause led to three complaints from the Conservatives that Channel 4 had allowed the programme to be skewed in the Liberal Democrats' favour. Cable was able to present himself as 'a referee between two opponents' rather than face tough questions over his own policy positions. Andy Coulson was quoted in *The Times* as having warned the broadcasters that the Liberal Democrats must not be allowed to score 'open goals' in the three leaders' debates.

Ask the Chancellors was perhaps of greater relevance and a better guide to what might influence British audiences than some of the costly advice of the assorted American pollsters and consultants who had been hired to give tips to Brown and Cameron. All three leaders were being coached well away from prying eyes, and journalists had great fun identifying the politicians and spin doctors recruited as stand-ins to help with role playing. Not having the resources of Labour and the Conservatives to call on top-flight American election gurus, the Liberal Democrats were concentrating their tactics on working out how Clegg could build on Cable's performance and inflict even more damage on the 'two tired old parties'. Their best hope in the election was that by increasing their share of the vote and winning more seats they might hold the balance of power if there was a hung parliament. Charles Kennedy told *The Andrew Marr Show* that he would have given an 'arm and a leg' for a chance to take part in a televised debate. Under Kennedy's leadership the Liberal Democrats won a record sixty-two seats in the 2005 general election and his advice was to adopt a different stance from Brown and Cameron. They would both want to play it safe so Clegg should not get overloaded with policy details and be ready for some 'general spontaneity and taking risks'. Clegg showed every intention of taking his predecessor's advice. He told *Today* that he would not be 'over-prepared or over-rehearsed' because he wanted to keep his contributions to the debates as 'fresh as possible'.

In pre-match posturing ahead of the opening debate in Manchester, Cameron acknowledged that as front runner he was under the greatest pressure. Preparation had been stressful and he was still feeling 'nervous about getting it right'. Instead of limiting himself to self-deprecatory remarks he launched into a critique of the format for the programmes. There was a danger they might disappoint the public if there was only enough time for the three leaders to take about eight questions during a ninety-minute debate. 'I do worry that we may have ended up with a format that's going to be a bit slow and sluggish . . . I do hope the public won't feel short changed.' He had learned from his own experience of speaking around the country at seventy-two Cameron Direct meetings that it was possible to get through twenty-five questions in an hour; he thought it was important viewers felt the leaders were answering the public's concerns. Cameron could hardly have made a worse move by appearing to doubt the competence of the referee and the quality of the pitch before the first ball had been played. Andy Coulson helped to negotiate a tightly controlled running order to ensure that Cameron was safe in his comfort zone and the suggestion the debates might be 'slow and sluggish' provoked a tart response from Jonny Oates, the Liberal Democrats' director of election communications. He revealed on *The World at One* that it was the Conservatives who were behind the ban on applause during questions and answers: 'From where I was sitting it was clear the Conservatives were not seeking an open debate . . . Cameron should get on with debating rather than arguing about rules he was instrumental in securing.' John Ryley, head of Sky News, was also surprised that the Tory leader was 'pre-emptively distancing himself from the restrictions his advisers so carefully negotiated'. In fact the rules governing the three programmes were 'far less restrictive' than those which applied to presidential debates and Cameron should remember he was playing for the 'highest stakes imaginable' in a game-changing event.

Cameron had succeeded in adding to the impression that he was over-confident, over-prepared and perhaps a touch over-mighty in his bearing towards the Liberal Democrats' leader. He was advised by the *Daily Telegraph*'s columnist Bruce Anderson, an early supporter of Cameron's bid for the Tory leadership, to regard Clegg as 'an amiable lightweight'. Anderson's fellow columnist Benedict Brogan was not so sure. He thought Clegg could easily emerge the winner by playing to Britain's undecided, angry middle ground: 'He plans to surf to influence on a wave of indifference.' A favourable advance billing for the Liberal Democrats irritated Alastair Campbell, who had taken the role of Cameron in rehearsals with Brown and who feared that Clegg posed an equal threat. Campbell complained that the Liberal Democrats should not have been given equal billing; that was never even contemplated during the abortive negotiations on Blair's behalf in 1997.

If Cameron thought privately there was a risk he was heading for a fall his unease was not helped by Clegg's luck in winning the right to be the first of the three to be asked by ITV's moderator, Alastair Stewart, to make an opening statement. His pitch from the start was that he was the reasonable man between two squabbling opponents, able for the first time to introduce himself to the nation. 'Now, they are going to tell you tonight that the only choice you have is between the two old parties who've been taking it in turns to run things for years.' Presenting himself throughout as a fresh and open-minded politician, his prime objective was to keep reminding viewers that the Liberal Democrats offered the only alternative to voting Labour or Conservative. 'Don't let them tell you that the only choice is between two old parties that have been playing pass the parcel with your government for sixty-five years now, making the same old promises, breaking the same old promises.'

Brown's tactics were never in doubt and, as expected, he launched an aggressive and sustained attack on the Conservatives' pledge to make an immediate start on reducing the £167 billion fiscal deficit by imposing cuts of £6 billion. The country had to make a decision on whether to put funds into the economy, as the government proposed, or take them out, as Cameron was demanding. 'We mustn't make the mistakes of the

1930s or 1980s when unemployment rose for five years after the official end of the recession.' Unless Labour could make sure that the money in the economy was protected the recovery was at risk. 'Get the decisions right now and we can have secure jobs, standards of living rising and everybody better off. Get the decisions wrong now and we could have a double-dip recession.'

Because of his poor eyesight Brown was allowed to stand to the right of camera and for the first debate Cameron stood at the central podium, a position that he must have hoped might give the impression he was Prime Minister in waiting. He opened with an unprompted apology for the scandal of MPs' expenses: 'Your politicians – frankly, all of us – let you down . . . I'm extremely sorry for everything that happened.' His main thrust was that the country faced a choice: either to 'go on as we are' or to deal with the deficit, get the economy growing and avoid the 'jobs tax' of an increase in national insurance contributions. He defended the £6 billion cut; it represented £1 out of every £100 which the government was spending. Effectively what the Prime Minister was saying was that he wanted to 'go on wasting now' so that he could put up taxes later. 'The idea that you have to go on wasting money to secure the recovery is wrong.'

Opening up the debate to questions gave the Prime Minister repeated opportunities to challenge Cameron and they sparred over a range of issues. Brown secured one of the few laughs of the evening by mocking the Conservatives' constantly updated poster campaign. Billboard advertising was concentrated on target constituencies and the first much-vandalised poster appeared in January. It featured an obviously air-brushed photograph of Cameron wearing an open-necked shirt; alongside was the slogan 'We can't go on like this. I'll cut the deficit, not the NHS'. A later series of posters featured a large picture of Brown with a wide grin on his face; listed beside the photograph were his alleged failures as Prime Minister. Brown thanked Cameron for having done more for his image than any newspaper editor by plastering his smiling face on billboards around the country – 'and I'm very grateful to you and

Lord Ashcroft for funding that'. Another rehearsed dig took advantage of the widely spoofed poster of Cameron: 'Be honest with the public. You can't airbrush your policies even though you can airbrush your posters.' Later he jabbed: 'This is not question time; it's answer time, David.'

Clegg took advantage of the spats between Brown and Cameron to remind viewers of his criticism of the 'two old parties'. At one point he remarked: 'The more they attack each other, the more they sound the same.' Although his advances were rebuffed, Brown seemed at times to be falling over himself to line up with Clegg against Cameron; his aim clearly being to undermine the Conservatives. 'I agree with Nick' — repeated seven times by the Prime Minister — became the catchphrase of the debate and the most memorable one-liner. While lacking the punch of Ronald Reagan's famous off-the-cuff put-down — 'There you go again' — to Jimmy Carter in the 1980 presidential debate, it developed a life of its own. Clegg was presented with an 'I agree with Nick' rosette next day and party workers regarded Brown's attempt to woo their leader as an indication of the pivotal role which the Liberal Democrats might play in the event of a hung parliament.

Cameron stood back from his lectern and although occasionally looking ill at ease, pursing his lips, he maintained his cool and authority and refused to be goaded in the face of Brown's frequent interruptions. He mocked the Prime Minister's attempt to gang up with Clegg: 'Gordon says Nick agrees with Gordon but Nick says he doesn't agree with Gordon. So I'm confused.' Immigration was one issue on which Cameron was convinced the Conservatives were accurately articulating the public's concern. He resolutely defended the party's manifesto pledge to place a cap on immigration from outside the European Union: 'I want us to bring immigration down so it's in the tens of thousands, not the hundreds of thousands.' Brown, seizing every opportunity to build an alliance with the Liberal Democrats, defended the government's proposal for a points system: 'I agree with Nick: an arbitrary cap won't work.' A graph on an ITV website monitoring real-time audience reaction showed that Cameron's determination to bring immigration down to pre-1997 levels was popular with viewers. His criticism of the early release of prisoners registered his highest score on the BBC's equivalent measure: a worm-like graphic being produced for the corporation by a group of thirty-six undecided voters who were registering their opinions on an electronic keypad.

At its peak the audience for the first debate hit 9.9 million and the broadcasters' initial attempts to offer viewers and listeners instant reaction as the debate progressed were about to be dwarfed by the impact of a clutch of opinion polls. As the data from the surveys began to be released it showed that Clegg's approval rating was reaching staggering proportions. A Sky News poll taken after the first sixty minutes put Clegg and Cameron level on 36 per cent and Brown on 28 per cent. ITV's programme poll put the Liberal Democrat leader well in front: Clegg 45 per cent, Brown 36 per cent, Cameron 19 per cent. A larger survey of 4,000 viewers by ComRes for *ITV News* indicated that his lead was overwhelming: Clegg 43 per cent, Cameron 26 per cent, Brown 20 per cent. The *Sun*'s YouGov poll of 1,000 viewers, issued within four minutes of the programme finishing, suggested that an even larger majority agreed the Liberal Democrat leader 'performed best overall': Clegg 51 per cent, Cameron 29 per cent, Brown 19 per cent. The margin of victory in a Populus poll for *The Times* was immense: Clegg 61 per cent, Cameron 22 per cent, Brown 17 per cent.

Television's historic achievement in securing the live debates had already generated massive press coverage but now it was being eclipsed by a sensational story which would be front-page news next morning. Political journalists who had gone to Manchester to monitor the exchanges were waiting in a nearby hotel ballroom to be briefed by party propagandists the moment the debate finished. The newspapers hoped to claim ownership of the story, at least overnight, because the opinion polls gave them a chance to drive the agenda forward. Aides for the three party leaders were desperate to put their gloss on the debate and there was a cacophony of claim and counter-claim in what became known as 'spin alley'. George Osborne, the shadow Chancellor, thought Cameron did well and 'spoke from the heart'; William Hague, the shadow Foreign Secretary, described him as the 'leader of change'. Lord Mandelson begged to differ: 'Cameron tanked . . . behind Cameron's veneer was just more veneer.' Brown had 'nothing to worry about', in the opinion of the Home Secretary, Alan Johnson. He gave his assessment of all three: 'Brown won on substance, Clegg on style and Cameron lost on both.' But it was Lord Ashdown, the former Liberal Democrat leader, who was in most demand as the polling data emerged and he indicated the programme had been a game changer. 'This debate has shown the Nick Clegg the House of Commons refuses to allow people to see. He walked away with it. For the first time we have the public able to see the real Nick Clegg and they loved it.'

Clegg's relaxed, confident performance and his supreme ability to capitalise on a platform which had never before been given to a third party leader electrified the campaign. Two-thirds of those who had been questioned by the pollsters said the debate would make a difference to how they viewed the election. Next morning the burning issue on *Today* was the magnitude of Clegg's approval rating and speculation as to whether it would cross over into voting intentions. On the morning after the debate the *Sun*'s daily tracker poll by YouGov indicated the highest lead for Cameron since the start of the campaign. It put the Conservatives on 41 per cent, Labour on 32 per cent and the Liberal Democrats 18 per cent. Ashdown, on a whirlwind round of interviews, was confident there would be an instant boost in the Liberal Democrats' predicted share of the vote: 'Clegg has made this election a three-way race and if the Liberal Democrats now get 25 per cent and Labour are cut back to between 27 and 28 per cent it changes the whole dynamic of the election.' He agreed with *Today*'s presenter Evan Davis that Clegg had stolen Cameron's charisma: 'Yes, Clegg leached charisma away from Cameron . . . Clegg won hands down and the Conservatives will certainly go for us now.'

Ashdown chuckled as he delivered his prediction that Clegg was about to become a target for the Tories. But his banter hardly did justice to the foreboding at party headquarters and the realisation among Cameron's aides that the first televised debate had been a disaster; their strategy of fighting the election as a two-horse race against Labour looked like being torpedoed by the Liberal Democrats. Cameron's demeanour generated a sense of alarm among his minders as soon as they started watching his opening exchanges against Brown and Clegg. They noticed immediately that something was wrong. Among the reporters in spin alley monitoring the debate was Joey Jones, political correspondent for Sky News, who observed the Conservatives' reaction. 'They seemed taken aback by Cameron's far-away, into-the-distance look. By contrast it was obvious Clegg had precisely the right eye line to camera. A televised debate is an artificial arena and Clegg was making the uncomfortable look comfortable and the artificial look natural.' Jones's assessment pinpointed two failings in the Conservatives' preparation for the debate: Cameron's rehearsals with American consultants had clearly paid little attention to basic television techniques and he seemed to have approached the debate on the basis that it was a town hall meeting rather than a conversation with viewers at home.

Clegg had wisely avoided over-burdening himself with the kind of ploys which might work in the more formalised setting of a US presidential debate but were in danger of falling flat in a country which, after all, had come up with formats for television reality shows that had been copied around the world. Cameron's homely anecdotes based on people he had met on his travels sounded as staged as the contrived and badly delivered jokes which Brown tried to make at Cameron's expense. Clegg handsomely outscored them both where it mattered most to the viewer: he name-checked members of the audience on ten separate occasions while managing at the same time to maintain eye contact with the right camera. Clegg's rehearsals were, in the words of Joey Jones, 'lights, cameras, action' and he spent real time looking down the lens.

A seasoned television professional and former Sky News anchor, Scott Chisholm, was named by the *Daily Mail* as one of the advisers credited with helping groom Clegg for his appearances. Chisholm's guidance when coaching clients was to pitch their answers as if they were speaking to a ten-year-old because if they 'use words that viewers have to process in order to understand, then they will miss the next three to six words you say'. Electric Airwaves, the company which employed Chisholm, said he assisted in 'a personal capacity, as a mate' without payment. Another insight into the care taken with Clegg's preparation was revealed in a set of instructions written by John Sharkey, the party's strategic communications adviser and chairman of its campaign team. The notes were left in the back of a taxi and the driver handed them to the *Sun*. 'Clegg's secret election dossier found in cab' was the headline next morning. It showed that Clegg was warned not to 'act weird' like Brown; instead to be 'normal'; and also to act more like Cameron because he talked a lot in the 'language of values and we need to do this'. The upshot of all the preparation was that the Liberal Democrat leader walked away with the accolade of being a natural television performer. Gary Gibbon, political editor of *Channel 4 News*, marvelled at Clegg's appealing manner and his 'I've lost my puppy' look.

Clegg claimed the credit himself in an interview for the *Daily Telegraph* for having realised that he would be more effective if he largely ignored the studio audience and concentrated on talking to viewers at home. 'I wasn't told to do it. I thought there are millions out there and 200 in there. It seemed obvious.' Clegg also kept his word by making sure he did not over-load himself with information immediately before arriving in Manchester for the debate. An hour-long walk in countryside on the edge of the Peak District had, in the words of the *Independent on Sunday*, been a 'non-negotiable fixture' in his campaign diary for the day. When party officials tried to book him into a hotel near the Granada studios, he protested: 'No way. I need fresh air and greenery, not air conditioning.' Close aides interviewed by Paul Lewis of the *Guardian* said that rather than try to win a 'logical argument with numbers or statistics' the aim had been to leave viewers thinking that Clegg's 'alright . . . a decent bloke'. Initially he thought he had fluffed the first half of the debate and it was not until he spoke to his wife and calls started coming through on BlackBerrys with the results of the instant polls that he realised how well he had done. Miriam stayed at home and missed big chunks of the programme because she was talking on the telephone to her parents in Spain, who were looking after their three children. The boys' return home had been delayed due to the grounding of flights after a cloud of ash from an erupting volcano in Iceland persisted for several days in UK airspace.

Cameron's mistake was to assume that his mastery of party conferences and the ease with which he could deliver an off-the-cuff speech would somehow give him the edge in the artificial setting of a studio where the audience had been instructed not to respond. When in conversation with journalists on the Conservatives' campaign coach, he was frank about his own shortcomings and the way he under-performed; he realised he should not have treated a televised confrontation as if it was a Cameron Direct public meeting. 'A television debate puts you directly into someone's front room. There is a certain amount of artifice in them you have to understand. It is not town hall debates, which I sort of thought they were.'

Cameron was facing an uncomfortable inquest into his election tactics as well his television techniques. Among the ranks of the party's former campaign strategists there had already been signs of a fair degree of unease about his willingness to go ahead with the leaders' debates when the Conservatives were comfortably ahead in the opinion polls. One of the first to advise against participating was Lynton Crosby, the celebrated Australian political strategist, who was hired to sharpen up Michael Howard's campaign in 2005 and who helped mastermind Boris Johnson's victory in 2008 in the election for mayor of London. Another member of the old guard who had made no secret of his fear that Cameron was taking an unnecessary risk was Margaret Thatcher's trusted media adviser, Lord Bell. When James Callaghan challenged Thatcher to a debate ahead of the 1979 general election, her team felt there was a danger of the confrontation turning into a nightmare for the Conservatives. 'We knew there would be this strident schoolmarm beating up nice cuddly old avuncular Jim Callaghan. It would have been very bad for her, so we turned down the invitation without telling her.' When asked by the *Daily Telegraph* for his verdict on Cameron's performance Bell reiterated his opinion that the Conservatives had made a 'stupid' mistake. The debate was bound to favour Clegg: 'He was the new boy, the invisible boy, the person who people didn't have a prejudice or a view about. That is what you expect if you are foolish enough to go through with the debate.' Agreeing to take part in an exercise which was 'so artificial' as a mechanism for choosing a government was a grave tactical error. 'We don't have a presidential system and we shouldn't be using a technique that relies on you having one.'

Andrew Sullivan provided an American perspective on the first debate in his column for the *Sunday Times*. He agreed with Bell that Cameron had been ill advised to take heed of the US strategists Anita Dunn and Bill Knapp, partners in the Washington-based political consultancy Squier, Knapp, Dunn Communications, which advised Barack Obama. The classic American ploy when ahead in the polls and up against an unpopular incumbent was for the challenger to show he was up to the task.

> *The golden rule is: you do not attack. Stay presidential. Risk little. Appear calm. But Cameron's adviser, Anita Dunn, must not have realised that this classic risk-minimising debate strategy only really works in a two-person debate. With a third candidate, you run the risk of seeming listless if that pleasant young man to your right suddenly gets his testosterone flowing. As Nick Clegg did. Suddenly, the calm prime-ministerial-material tactic risked making Cameron seem like the less powerful challenger.*

However, when Cameron was interviewed by the *Daily Telegraph* the day after his appearance in the leaders' historic confrontation he argued that it was worth handing an easy victory to the Liberal Democrats in the first debate just to get them established as a fixture in British politics.

Look, I have been calling for these debates for five years. I challenged
Blair, I challenged Brown, I challenged when I was ahead in the polls,
and when I was behind in the polls. I just think they are a good thing.
You give the third party a big advantage in doing that but it's a price
worth paying for the benefit of having a political debate and being able to
get your point across.

The first debate had been 'great, a brilliant opportunity' to communicate
directly with millions of people on the issues he cared about.

Nevertheless, Bell's prescient prediction of a nightmare scenario
for the Conservatives required some rapid positioning by the party's
campaign team. As they set to work, Cameron did his best not to appear
rattled in public. After he readily acknowledged to reporters that Clegg
did have a 'very good debate', he tried to cheer up the troops by joining
the Take That superstar Gary Barlow for the launch of an *X Factor*-style
talent contest for schoolchildren. Backed by Barlow's endorsement,
and with the songwriter sitting at the piano, Cameron took to the
stage, determined to make light of the most ominous setback of his
campaign. 'On the television debates I felt like I was part of Britain's
worst boy band, so it's a pleasure to share the stage with a member of
Britain's best boy band ever.' Back at headquarters there were grim
faces as the party absorbed the implications of Clegg's success and the
unexpected difficulty which Tory candidates might face in winning
back seats from the Liberal Democrats in southern England and the
south-west. Nick Robinson told the *Ten o'Clock News* that Clegg was
not used to sporting a winning smile: 'Clegg the outsider, the public
schoolboy, former MEP and Eurocrat, is now taking on the political
establishment.' Michael Crick's report for *Newsnight* confirmed the
Conservatives' worst fear: the *Sun*'s latest opinion survey had slashed
Cameron's lead. YouGov's daily tracking poll put the Conservatives on
33 per cent, the Liberal Democrats up eight points at 30 per cent and
Labour on 28 per cent.

After a full day to regroup a fresh battle plan was ready. Two new targets were about to be attacked in equal measure: Clegg the 'unknown politician' and the 'dire prospect' of a hung parliament. I was reminded of similarities with the Conservatives' erratic performance in the 1992 general election, when a 25-year-old David Cameron was one of the headquarters staff sent scurrying around trying to pick up the pieces after yet another setback to John Major's campaign. Almost twenty years on the former party apparatchik was himself the leader and, as with his predecessor, it was his task to inspire a new generation of young activists. Instead of being asked to launch a hatchet job on John Smith's ill-fated shadow Budget or Neil Kinnock's surprise last-minute flirtation with electoral reform, the Tory researchers of 2010 were being instructed to update their briefings on the Liberal Democrats' leader and prepare position papers in the event of an inconclusive election result.

Saturday lunchtime's news bulletins confirmed that the Conservatives were fighting on a new front: Cameron was warning of the dangers of a hung parliament. At a rally in Gloucester, he declared that only a Conservative government could cut the cost of politics.

A bunch of politicians haggling and not deciding in a hung Parliament would not be making long-term decisions for the country but short-term decisions for their own future. Do you think they would agree to cut the size of the House of Commons, to cut MPs' pay, to cut the perks? The hell they would.

George Osborne sent out a campaign e-mail claiming that weak policies in the Liberal Democrats' manifesto were backed up by figures which fell apart under scrutiny. By contrast Clegg and his wife Miriam were enjoying heightened media attention and laid on a lively double act when they visited a hospital maternity ward in Kingston-upon-Thames where one of their sons was born. After her husband rounded on the 'old parties' and insisted that 'something exciting is about to happen', she played to the cameras and declared, 'I agree with Nick' – before reminding him that he had better not get used to it.

Late-night news bulletins began setting the scene for another traumatic day for Brown and Cameron. Opinion polls commissioned by the Sunday newspapers were indicating that the dramatic surge in support for Nick Clegg might be about to blow the contest wide open. By far the most sensational were two surveys which the *Mail on Sunday* claimed were pointing to one of the 'most astonishing election turnarounds' for a century. One poll put the Liberal Democrats a point ahead of the Conservatives and another suggested their lead could be as high as six points – the first time for 104 years that Liberals had been in the lead at a general election; Labour were trailing in third place. A YouGov poll for the *Sunday Times* indicated that Clegg was the most popular leader of any party since Winston Churchill with a personal approval rating higher than Tony Blair's at the height of New Labour's popularity. Although the polls were divided as to whether the Liberal Democrats had pulled ahead, or whether the Conservatives were still in front, their overall conclusion was that the election had become a genuine three-way contest.

A BPIX poll published by the *Mail on Sunday* and the *News of the World* put the Liberal Democrats on 32 per cent, up a staggering 12 points within a week, the Conservatives on 31 per cent and Labour on 28 per cent. A OnePoll survey for the *People* put the Liberal Democrats on 33 per cent, the Conservatives on 27 per cent and Labour on 23 per cent. Three other polls suggested the Liberal Democrats' advance had not been so great. YouGov (*Sunday Times*) had the Conservatives on 33 per cent, Labour on 30 per cent and the Liberal Democrats on 29 per cent; ComRes (*Independent on Sunday*, *Sunday Mirror*) gave the Conservatives 31 per cent, the Liberal Democrats 29 per cent and Labour 27 per cent; ICM (*Sunday Telegraph*) put the Conservatives on 34 per cent, Labour on 29 per cent and the Liberal Democrats on 27 per cent.

Dramatic headlines proclaiming a surge in support for the Liberal Democrats provided a telling illustration of the continuing power of Sunday newspapers to dictate the news agenda. Their success in generating a flurry of stories which provoked panic at the top of the two main parties seemed to fly in the face of regular predictions by media analysts during the long build-up to the 2010 campaign that the national press would probably be far less influential than in previous general elections. Despite a long-term decline in circulation, newspapers have managed to retain their ability to influence and often command the daily news agenda. Once polling companies found it was possible to produce a constant supply of up-to-the minute surveys, editors found a new way to maintain their political clout in a highly crowded media market place. Instead of questioning people in the street, as in previous elections, polling companies began to conduct most of their surveys on the telephone and then increasingly online. With the help of computer programs to take account of different statistical weightings, the results could be compiled on a daily basis in time for newspaper deadlines. In the 2005 general election more than fifty opinion polls were commissioned, a figure that was about to be exceeded many times over following the switch from weekly to daily polling. For the relatively modest outlay of around £5,000 per survey a national newspaper had the wherewithal to create its own headlines. The *Sun* began publishing its daily tracker poll in February 2010 and YouGov's president, Peter Kellner, promised it would 'follow the fortunes of the parties in real time'. Day-by-day polling had never been attempted before in a British general election and Kellner was confident YouGov's polls would reflect 'not only the drama but the trends that will shape the final outcome'.

His prediction that the innovation of daily polling would have an impact on the political process was proved correct within a matter of days. A YouGov survey for the *Sun*'s sister paper the *Sunday Times* – published at the end of February – sparked a run on the pound because it gave the first indication that the drop in support for the Conservatives pointed to the likelihood of a hung parliament. 'Brown on course to win election' was the front-page headline over an opinion poll that put Labour two points behind the Conservatives, the closest gap between the two parties for more than two years. Labour's predicted share of the vote was 35 per cent, as against 37 per cent for the Conservatives, and it suggested that although Brown would fall short of an overall parliamentary majority, he would still win enough parliamentary seats to form a minority government.

A clutch of polls in Sunday newspapers charting an unprecedented post-leaders' debate surge for the Liberal Democrats served to highlight one of the great imponderables of the campaign. Predictions for a share of the vote could not be translated easily into a party's likely haul of parliamentary seats. An uneven distribution of votes across the country, plus the redrawing of constituency boundaries, injected great uncertainty into the electoral mathematics and the task of trying to forecast the likely overall result that would be delivered by Britain's first-past-the-post electoral system. Intense rivalry in a hundred or so marginal constituencies was another complicating factor but one which the Conservatives were convinced would work in their favour. Even though two polls suggested the Liberal Democrats were in front nationally, their vote was spread so evenly around the entire country that at best the party might only double its representation at Westminster. The *Mail on Sunday*'s poll was predicting Clegg would secure 121 seats; this fell to seventy-four in the *Sunday Telegraph*'s survey. All five polls indicated a hung Parliament, where no party would have an overall majority. Labour would remain the largest party with 260–280 seats; the Conservatives would secure 230–250.

Cameron, for so long the front runner, was having to face up to the kind of mid-election crisis which nearly derailed the otherwise well-ordered and heavily resourced campaigns of Margaret Thatcher and John Major. In their hour of need party strategists always knew that Conservative-supporting newspapers could be relied upon to mount hard-hitting offensives. A weekend of shock opinion poll findings was tantamount to a declaration of war by the Tory press against the Liberal Democrats; it was about to become open season for targeting Nick Clegg. The *Mail on Sunday* was the first to open fire: 'His wife is Spanish, his mother Dutch, his father half-Russian and his spin doctor German. Is there ANYTHING British about the Lib Dem leader?'

British newspapers have a well-deserved reputation for investigative journalism and an ability to trawl through the antecedents of up-and-coming politicians to unearth potentially embarrassing information, however trivial it might seem. During the long years of post-war Conservative government the party's research department established an equally legendary reputation for its thoroughness and skill in compiling dossiers on all manner of issues and policy options. Rival politicians were subjected to the most detailed scrutiny and one of Cameron's first tasks after joining the research department at the age of twenty-two was to read the text of speeches and interviews given by Labour MPs to discover inept quotes or slip-ups which John Major could use as ammunition when answering Prime Minister's Questions. During the 1992 general election Cameron's role as head of the political section involved the constant monitoring of media coverage of Neil Kinnock's campaign so as to prepare briefing papers for Major and the party chairman, Chris Patten.

When I recalled how effectively the Conservatives worked to destabilise Kinnock I was sure Cameron must have been hoping the researchers who succeeded him were being just as diligent as he once was and were busily delving into Clegg's political career and all his early speeches and statements. Long-forgotten remarks or conflicts of interest have a nasty habit of reappearing during election campaigns and more often than not the source of the information is a researcher employed by one or other of the political parties. After Major's dire start in 1992 he pulled out his fabled soapbox at Luton and revived his party's spirits with some old-fashioned street corner campaigning. Back at party headquarters, Patten had arranged for the political editors and correspondents of the six most trusted national newspapers to attend a private off-the-record briefing with the Prime Minister. One of the journalists suggested he might like to try a variant on the title of the cult horror movie *A Nightmare on Elm Street*. Major repeated it to himself once, then twice, savouring the words. In his next big speech he warned of 'A Nightmare on Kinnock Street', a line which was reworked for a *Sun* headline. Almost twenty years later I am still not at liberty to identify the journalist whose idea it was and I do not know which staffers from party headquarters attended the meeting in addition to Major and Patten. Nonetheless I have no doubt that the ploys which were used to harry Kinnock would have been meat and drink to an impressionable young researcher like Cameron.

Nick Clegg was in the firing line as never before and reporters assigned to dig into his background were soon producing results. Indeed he did not have long to wait to feel the full force of the blitzkrieg which was being fired up as part of the traditional two-way terms of trade between the Tory press and the party's research department. The day of the second televised debate was judged to be Clegg's moment of greatest vulnerability and the strength of the fusillade directed against him suggested the kind of covert co-ordination which I had witnessed before during crises in Conservative election campaigns. 'Clegg in Nazi slur on Britain' was the *Daily Mail*'s front splash and the most jaw-dropping of the headlines on offer. The story advanced a lurid interpretation of an article which he wrote for the *Guardian* in 2002: the 'passionately pro-Europe' Clegg argued that Britain's 'misplaced sense of superiority' and 'delusions of grandeur' were a greater cross to bear than Germany's 'memories of Nazism' during the Second World War. The *Daily Telegraph*'s treasure chest of illicit information in the purloined disk which contained copies of MPs' bank statements provided the basis for another dramatic headline: 'Nick Clegg, the Lib Dem donors and payments into his private account'. The *Sun*'s front page reworked the 'sleaze row' over the alleged misuse of party donations: 'Clegg on his face'. A proposal by the Liberal Democrats to introduce an amnesty for illegal immigrants provided the basis for the front page of the *Daily Express*: 'Clegg's crazy immigration policy'.

Lord Ashdown was the first to man the barricades in defence of his leader. On the Liberal Democrats' behalf he demanded an explanation from Cameron as to whether the Conservatives had encouraged their 'Tory attack-dog' newspapers to 'smear and unbalance' Clegg on the eve of the second debate. Lord Mandelson gave added potency to a chorus of complaints by claiming on *The World at One* that the stories were 'straight out of the Tory Party's dirty-tricks manual' and had not happened by accident. 'The Tories have pushed the smear button. This is pure Andy Coulson-style *News of the World* territory turned into political form. These are classic smears of the form we have seen directed against Labour in many general elections and which are now being directed at the Liberal Democrats.' Coulson had been Labour's *bête noire* since the *Sun* ditched Gordon Brown. Mandelson relished the opportunity to retaliate. But Nick Robinson leapt to Coulson's defence in his blog on BBC News Online. He wondered whether Mandelson was smearing Cameron's director of communications simply to lay the blame for the smears against Clegg firmly at the door of the Tories. Robinson argued there were plenty of reasons to suggest Coulson was not involved: the *Daily Telegraph*'s story originated from its file of bank statements obtained during its investigation of MPs' expenses; the *Daily Mail*'s story was sourced to a *Guardian* article which anyone could have found with a Google search; and the *Sun* might have had the 'odd chat' with Coulson but the editor was after all a good friend of his. Two hours after posting his entry Robinson updated his blog with the news that he had subsequently learned that 'political reporters from the Tory-backing papers were called in one by one to discuss how Team Cameron would deal with Cleggmania and to be offered the Tory HQ's favourite titbits about the Lib Dems – much of which appears in today's papers'.

Robinson's confirmation that there was a co-ordinated operation to brief journalists chimed with my long experience of being steered by Conservative researchers towards speeches and statements which their opponents must have hoped would remain overlooked. Politicians dread being reminded of inconsistencies and indiscretions from the past and the job of any political research department is to collate the relevant references, sources, dates and so on, and keep the data to hand for possible future use.

All week there had been a succession of stories which suggested Clegg had been the target of negative briefings. When challenged by reporters over claiming £84,000 in second-home allowances during a four-year period, he insisted he would repay any profit made on the sale of the property. The *Daily Mail* revealed that between leaving the European Parliament and being elected to Westminster he joined one of the European Union's largest lobbying groups, GPlus; his employment with the lobbying firm GJW had been 'airbrushed' from his official Liberal Democrat CV. Far from being the 'man to clean up politics and rid the corridors of power of the influence of lobbying firms', he was himself a former lobbyist. After the *Mail* topped its previous disclosures with its 'Nazi slur' headline, Clegg's frontbench colleagues could hardly contain their anger. Chris Huhne, the Liberal Democrats' shadow Home Secretary, accused the BBC of repeating the smears of the Tory press when the *Today* presenter John Humphrys asked him about Clegg's work for lobbyists. Clegg was incensed that the *Daily Telegraph* had used his bank statements to suggest he had misappropriated party donations: 'It is totally out of order. I received money from three friends, properly given, properly received, properly declared and properly used to pay a member of my staff.' Clegg was quite prepared to stand up to those who were trying to stop political change and, more to the point, he was ready to make light of it. 'I am the first politician who has gone from being Churchill to being a Nazi in under a week . . . I hope people won't be bullied into, be frightened into, not choosing something different.'

Clegg's chief of staff, Danny Alexander, was determined to follow up Nick Robinson's confirmation that there had been special briefings for the Tory press. When interviewed on *Today* he demanded a fuller explanation of the BBC's implication that the Conservatives had mounted an 'orchestrated smear campaign'. William Hague dismissed the accusation as 'total nonsense': 'It's up to Tory papers to decide how to deal with Cleggmania. Yes, we talk to political reporters . . . we tell journalists about policies . . . personal things have not come from us.' Robinson paid off the sequence by denying he ever suggested the Conservatives 'orchestrated these personal attacks'; every political party briefed journalists. 'Get real – that's what I say to the Liberal Democrats . . . files of research from the parties pop into my inbox all the time.'

There was an upside to having become the target for what the *Guardian* diarist Hugh Muir judged was the 'rabid media onslaught' of Andy Coulson in his role as 'virtual editor of all the right-wing papers'. Loathsome headlines were doing wonders for Clegg's image on social networking sites such as Twitter. In a report for *Channel 4 News*, Cathy Newman said her favourite tweet was the one which suggested Clegg should even take the 'blame for killing Bambi'. Whereas the pre-debate pressure on Clegg was upfront and out in the open, Cameron was struggling to counter the demoralising impact of a continuous drip-drip of negative asides about his poor judgement in having gone ahead with televised debates and then allowed the Liberal Democrats equal time. Andrew Pierce, the *Daily Mail*'s diarist, reflected on what he inferred was the suppressed anger of the Tory rank and file for their leader's ineptitude in offering Clegg a chance to portray himself as a serious contender: 'It's a political miscalculation so monumental that it's even being compared to Neil Kinnock bellowing "we're all right" days before he lost the 1992 general election.'

Cameron arrived with his wife for the second debate, staged in Bristol by Sky News; he was armed with a clear set of instructions from assorted political pundits to work out where the cameras were located and then to think of the viewer at home. His aides briefed journalists to expect a change in body language and a more relaxed performance. Gordon Brown knew he had no alternative but to continue presenting himself as a man of substance and experience. At a news conference earlier in the week the Prime Minister bridled when reminded that Clegg's debate debut had pushed Labour into third place in the opinion polls. 'I know a little about what it is to have a short political honeymoon. I wish him well in it.' Brown was first to speak and his opening line was an admission that he could not compete with the campaign's matinee idol and a super-slick Cameron.

This may have the feel of a TV popularity contest but, in truth, this election is a fight for Britain's future, your future, and your jobs. If it's all

about style and PR, count me out. If it's about the big decisions, if it's
about judgement, if it's about delivering a better future for this country,
I'm your man. Like me or not, I have a plan for Britain's future.

Once he had the chance to respond to questions he was far more
aggressive than in the first debate and determined to challenge Liberal
Democrat policy at every opportunity.

Cameron's opening line was a repetition of his promise that only by
voting Conservative could the electorate be sure of getting 'a new team
running the country'. Like Brown, he was itching to put Clegg on the
spot and the first question gave him the opportunity to challenge both
Labour and the Liberal Democrats on their pro-European stance. If he
was Prime Minister he would pass a law to guarantee a referendum if
there was ever a proposal to pass powers from Britain to Europe; and
unlike the Liberal Democrats, a Conservative government would not
join the euro. 'If I'm your Prime Minister' was a turn of phrase which
he repeated in several answers when outlining what his administration
would do.

Brown retorted that there were three million reasons why Britain
should not be on the margins of Europe: 'three million jobs depend on
the EU and 750,000 businesses trade with Europe'. Clegg tried to pre-
empt the suggestion he was soft on Europe by drawing on his experience
as an official in the European Commission working on the trade brief.
The EU was not perfect but there were 'a whole load of things' Britain
could not do on its own and he ridiculed Cameron for leaving the main
centre-right grouping to join a new bloc with hard-right parties from
eastern Europe:

How on earth does it help anyone in Bristol or anyone else in the country,
David Cameron, to join together in the EU with a bunch of nutters,
anti-Semites, people who deny climate change exists, homophobes? Of
course we need to change the EU. But you change clubs of which you are
a member by getting stuck in, not standing on the sidelines.

Brown could not wait to jump in with a soundbite designed to mock his opponents: 'You know who these two guys remind me of? They remind me of my two young boys, squabbling at bath time – squabbling about referendums on the EU when what we need is jobs and growth and recovery.' A photograph taken over Brown's shoulder revealed that Brown was working to a crib sheet and the quip about his two boys was one of several pre-prepared lines ready to be deployed.

Another lively spat developed over Clegg's explanation for the Liberal Democrats' opposition to the renewal of Trident, an 'old cold-war nuclear missile system'. Brown rounded on him for putting the defence of the country at risk: 'I say to you, Nick, get real, get real. Iran, you're saying, might be able to have a nuclear weapon and you would not be able to take action against them. But you're saying we've got to give up our Trident submarines.' Cameron joined in: 'I thought I would never utter these words: I agree with Gordon. You cannot put off this decision.' Cameron's sharpest retort to the Prime Minister was when he accused him of authorising Labour's scare tactics and the distribution of election leaflets claiming the Conservatives would axe free bus passes, television licences and winter fuel payments for the elderly. 'I think it's disgraceful. You shouldn't be frightening people in an election campaign. You really should be ashamed of yourself . . . These lies you are getting from Labour are pure and simple lies. I have seen these lies and they make me very, very angry.'

One surprise intervention during a discussion on MPs' expenses was by the programme's host, Adam Boulton, who ignored the ban on moderators asking follow-up questions. He pointed out that Clegg was on the front page of the *Daily Telegraph*, an interjection which was tartly dismissed with the rejoinder that it was a 'nonsense story, complete rubbish'. After Clegg claimed that some MPs from the 'old parties' who flipped their homes had still not been held to account, Cameron seized the opportunity to remind him that the Liberal Democrats were in no position to suggest they had done nothing wrong. 'Frankly, Nick, we all have problems with this. Don't anyone try to put themselves on a pedestal over this.' Clegg reiterated his criticism of 'old party politics'; young people wanted the chance to vote for a different political system. 'This is one of the most exciting elections . . . Don't let anyone tell you this time it can't be different; it can.' His call for cross-party collaboration produced the highest approval rating from a BBC panel monitoring the debate.

After the hiatus in 'spin alley' following the first debate rival propagandists were better prepared and their soundbites well rehearsed. Lord Ashdown was delighted it was now a real three-way choice between 'Clegg and two ugly sisters'; George Osborne thought Cameron delivered a 'stronger performance'; and Alastair Campbell believed the second debate proved that the 'Cameron bubble' had burst and that Clegg was no Barack Obama because he lacked a forward agenda for the country. YouGov's instant poll, published within eight minutes of the programme finishing, suggested Cameron had won the debate on 36 per cent, as against 32 per cent for Clegg; Brown remained in third place on 29 per cent. An *ITV News* poll by ComRes judged Clegg the winner on 33 per cent and Cameron and Brown having tied on 30 per cent. Most of the commentators agreed that the second debate was much more evenly matched. Steve Richards, the *Independent*'s columnist, told Sky News there had been no knock-out blow from Cameron to Clegg and the Liberal Democrat bandwagon was still the wild card in the election; *Newsnight*'s Michael Crick agreed that Cameron had failed to damp down the Clegg effect.

On the evening of the final debate in Birmingham, with only a week left until polling day, opinion pollsters were continuing to predict that the Conservatives would fall well short of an overall majority; the pundits agreed that in all likelihood there would be a hung parliament. Great store had been set by the third confrontation because the economy had purposely been left until last and the three leaders knew that effectively it was their one and only chance to convince the country at large why their party was best equipped to take on the key task of cutting the record budget deficit. Brown was desperate to prove that his handling of the financial crisis meant he should be trusted with securing the recovery; Cameron faced growing unease within his party for failing to 'seal the deal' with the wider electorate; and Clegg was anxious to retain as much as possible of the Liberal Democrats' unprecedented surge in support. Their opening salvos were a restatement of well-entrenched positions and the BBC's moderator, David Dimbleby, was in the frustrating position of knowing there was nothing he could do on the audience's behalf to demand greater clarity as to where the public spending axe might fall. Nadim Afsal must have feared broad-brush answers from the three party leaders because his opening question about the extent of the cuts had a sting in the tail: 'Why can't you be honest and tell us?'

Clegg claimed that the Liberal Democrats' manifesto set out in much greater detail than the other parties' their proposal for £15 billion worth of savings, which would include a public sector pay freeze, the scrapping of a new generation of biometric passports and the abandoning of the Eurofighter Typhoon project. Labour's four-year deficit reduction plan would start in 2011 and was based on 'tax rises that are fair, spending cuts that are equitable'. Brown promised that the NHS, schools and the police would be protected and the government would 'find the cuts in other areas'. Cameron defended the Conservatives' plan to save £6 billion immediately through efficiency measures in order to prevent Labour's increase in national insurance contributions. A one-year public sector pay freeze would start in 2011; people would have to retire a year later from 2016. 'If I'm your Prime Minister, I will do everything I can to protect the front-line services.'

Except for the headline cuts which each party outlined at the start of the campaign, there were no new insights into future action. Dimbleby adopted a number of ploys in an attempt to persuade the leaders to give greater detail: 'Let me repeat the question'; 'If you were elected, what would you do about taxes?'; 'Can we explore some of these ideas?' But Brown and Cameron were determined to stick to their scripts and attack their opponents, which gave Clegg the opening he was waiting for: 'Can I try and move beyond the political point scoring?' Brown retaliated:

'David and Nick are not addressing the question we face now.' Cameron was having none of it: 'Gordon Brown has to stop misleading families in this country.' Clegg berated them with his familiar reprise: 'Here they go again.'

If the outcome of the economic debate had perhaps been all too predictable, questions on immigration allowed Cameron to give a forthright exposition as to why he believed only the cap being proposed by the Conservatives would get a grip on numbers. He opened up an attack on Clegg by saying that 'people need to know that the Liberal Democrats propose an amnesty for illegal immigrants'. Clegg accused Cameron of misleading the audience: 'I'm not advocating an amnesty.' In turn he opened fire on both Cameron and Brown for trying to deny there was a problem when there were 'lots of people living in the shadows of our economy'. Brown was convinced that an amnesty for people who had come to Britain illegally would send out the worst possible message. 'I agree with David on this . . . I don't think Nick has presented his policy in the way it's in his manifesto.' Clegg's only escape was to repeat his line that they were both making misleading claims 'very much in the style of old politics'.

Cameron, encouraged by opinion surveys showing strong support for the Conservatives' controls on immigration, was determined to wound his 'profoundly misguided' opponent. If 600,000 people were offered the Liberal Democrats' amnesty, they could each bring in a relative so that meant '1.2 million potentially' would have access to welfare and housing. 'If that's the number, they should come clean about that.' Clegg: 'We're not wriggling.' He in turn wanted to know whether the Conservatives' cap applied to the 80 per cent of immigrants who came from the European Union. Cameron insisted he had already answered the question; a government he led would impose transitional controls on immigration from any new members of the EU. Brown could not resist joining the fray: 'I hate to enter into private grief here, because both of them have got this wrong.'

Dimbleby drew the debate to a close by asking the Prime Minister to make the last of the three final statements. Brown struck a sombre note and acknowledged that 'if things stay where they are' in the campaign, then Cameron, perhaps supported by Clegg, would be in office in eight days' time. 'I don't like having to do this, but I have to tell you that things are too important to be left to risky policies under these two people. They are not ready for government.' Lord Mandelson was waiting in 'spin alley' to brief reporters: 'Gordon Brown pulled it off. He won the argument.' But the reaction of viewers told a different story. A BBC panel monitoring the debate gave the highest score to Cameron on immigration and the Conservative leader topped the two instant opinion polls. YouGov's survey was the most decisive: Cameron 41 per cent, Clegg 32 per cent, Brown 25 per cent. ComRes had: Cameron 35 per cent, Clegg 33 per cent, Brown 26 per cent.

Next morning Conservative-supporting newspapers were in their element: 'Scrambled Clegg on toast' was the *Sun*'s front-page headline alongside a photograph of Clegg and an image of Brown superimposed on a piece of brown bread, with the strap line 'but Cameron's full of beans'. The *Daily Telegraph*'s verdict was that Cameron 'saved his best for last' under the headline 'Cameron on the money'. A snap Populus poll for *The Times* put Cameron and Clegg neck and neck on 38 per cent but the *Financial Times* said Cameron emerged from the debate as the 'clear election front runner'. Dimbleby was praised by the *Daily Telegraph*'s reviewer Neil Midgley for having 'carried the proceedings with an effortless authority'. Most commentators thought the format was flawed and the moderator should have had the power to demand clarity about the parties' plans for drastic cuts in public spending. At one point Dimbleby's frustration nearly got the better of him when he pointedly asked Clegg 'not to repeat what you've already said'. In his column in the *Financial Times*, Philip Stephens was disappointed that viewers were presented with 'three, rather shifty politicians running away from the truth'. The *Independent*'s Tom Sutcliffe was exasperated watching the three leaders: 'An unleashed moderator might have been able to cut the pious boilerplate and drive them to specifics more quickly. And mere humanity would suggest that the audience should be unmuzzled.' I agreed with John Lloyd (*Financial Times*) that the debate of the 2005 election, when the three party leaders were questioned at length by a *Question Time* audience, elicited far more explanation about the alternative policies then on offer.

Across the press commentary there was a ready acknowledgement that television delivered the game changer of the campaign and that pre-election debates were here to stay. An average audience of 8.4 million watched the final programme, down on the 9.4 million who tuned in to ITV, but more than twice the average of four million for the debate hosted by Sky News. Matthew Parris (*The Times*) concluded that the debates were not the lightning of the campaign but the 'lightning rod for voters' rage with politics'. Angry public alienation from the whole political system was the static looking for a conduit and the anti-party party led by 'a fresh-faced politician with clean hands' was the beneficiary. 'The lightning flashed. Clegg lit up. His party's fortunes flared.'

Pre-election forecasts that the online world of interactive social networking would have a potentially decisive role in the campaign proved premature. Philip Gould, Tony Blair's celebrated pollster, predicted the internet would be 'a giant autonomous force' once the campaign started and the debates took place. Online political activists were 'an army of the night that moves on its own and no one will be able to control its influence'. While Twitter, Facebook, YouTube and the rest played their part, old media rather than new media remained in the driving seat. I was struck by the all-embracing nature of the coverage and the way in which press, television and the web fed off each other; the combined effect of their output was that the anticipation and excitement generated by the three debates went on reverberating throughout the campaign for longer than party strategists had expected. The journalism of the national press remained the dominant force; without the build-up in the newspapers there would have been nowhere near the great sense of expectation before each debate. Once the programmes were on air, television was firmly in command but the impact of social networking was also being felt as political activists started to tweet as they watched. Within minutes of the debates finishing, instant opinion polls gave the press the chance to seize the agenda and influence the course of the reaction. Online chatter on Twitter and other sites was a useful source of instant comment and opinion for journalists and became a powerful campaigning force among the young and politically active. When the Tory press launched its blitzkrieg against Clegg on the eve of the second debate, he became an online hero; similarly when the viral graffiti artists got to work on the airbrushed poster of Cameron, the Conservatives' advertising campaigns became an online laughing stock and the party paid a heavy price. But the digital election campaign remained the preserve of a relatively small percentage of the total electorate and the consistent verdict of the opinion polls was that for a high proportion of voters the television debates had by far the greatest impact. Mark Penn, strategic adviser to Bill Clinton in the 1996 presidential debate, thought the debates delivered a salutary 'wake-up call' to the two main parties; they were also a warning to the Democrats and Republicans of the danger of the growth in a third choice. US-style debates helped to 'shake up the kaleidoscope' for UK voters and if the Liberal Democrats could use televised confrontations to break through 'tradition-bound Britain' then it could happen anywhere.

Tony Blair's refusal to take part in a televised confrontation ahead of the 1997 general election was based partly on Alastair Campbell's belief that the news media's fascination with the 'process of the debates' would make it harder for the party to present its case to the electorate. Campbell's complaint that political correspondents could easily become obsessed by 'processology' rather than policy was a regular refrain during his years in Downing Street; he trotted it out as a diversionary tactic whenever journalists got stuck into an aspect of the democratic process which did not suit his agenda. I was hardly surprised when after the second debate Labour drafted a letter to be sent to BBC, ITV and Channel 4 expressing concern that the broadcasters were not analysing rival manifestos and ensuring that the alternative policies were being 'fully, fairly and properly' covered. The phraseology suggested Campbell's handiwork in trying to achieve cross-party support for a complaint: 'We share a common belief that the focus on the debates, both the process surrounding them, and the polling before and after which they have attracted, has dramatically reduced the amount of air time dedicated to the scrutiny of the policies of the parties.' Needless to say the claim that the public were being sidetracked by the focus 'on process not policy' got short shrift from Labour's opponents; the Conservatives said it was a 'desperate whinge' and the Liberal Democrats had no intention of trying to 'dictate political coverage'.

David Cameron's decision to press on with the debates when the Conservatives were ahead in the polls was bound to remain a troublesome source of dissension within his party. Perhaps the last word should go to Adam Boulton, moderator for Sky News. He was struck by the Prime Minister's thank-you to all those involved. Brown said the three debates were the answer to people who claimed politics did not matter; they showed that 'big differences' existed between the parties and there were 'big causes' they could fight for. Boulton knew there were always plenty of easy excuses which either of the main two parties could have deployed to 'duck' the debates. For the first time the pairing of an incumbent Prime Minister and leader of the opposition chose not to and 'neither camp baulked' at including Nick Clegg on equal terms. 'Instead, both manifested a statesman-like acceptance of the realities of multi-party Britain.'

10

CAMPAIGN ROUND-UP

Chancellors of the Exchequer and their shadows play a game of cat and mouse in the build-up to a general election always conscious of the fact that one false move could prove fatal by polling day. Bill Clinton's phrase 'It's the economy, stupid', which became a slogan in his 1992 presidential election campaign, was just as applicable to the politics of Britain. Whether it was Edward Heath winning for the Conservatives after he campaigned against rising inflation in the 'shopping basket' election of 1970, or John Smith's mistake in 1992 of introducing a shadow budget which was attacked as Labour's 'tax bombshell' and became a vote loser, there has never been much doubt that the prospects for employment, prices and taxation have exercised a decisive influence on the voting intentions of vast swathes of the electorate. The banking and financial crises which preceded the 2010 general election meant the question of economic competence was bound to be uppermost in the minds of most voters once the campaign began. Given the overwhelming pressure to reduce the budget deficit while not jeopardising economic recovery, the parties knew that come polling day they would be judged on how they intended to handle cuts in public expenditure and cope with the pressure for higher levels of taxation.

George Osborne never needed reminding of the difficulties which the opposition faced trying to present a coherent case against a Labour government which had proved highly adept at using a succession of financial statements, pre-Budget reports and the Budget itself to manage the economy and win over public opinion. Calculations and policies prepared by the Conservatives' Treasury team constantly needed to be revised or perhaps abandoned because the figures on which they were based were out of date. If Osborne announced what looked like becoming a vote-winning tax change, there was always the likelihood it would be appropriated by Labour and then shamelessly incorporated into government policy.

In a decade as Chancellor, Gordon Brown became a masterful exponent of Treasury politics and he was proud of his record in having seen off numerous Tory shadows. His successor, Alistair Darling, renowned for his dour unflappability, had established himself as a worthy successor across the despatch box. Osborne could not be faulted on his durability in handling the most demanding brief of any of his colleagues on the opposition front bench. He had been shadow Chancellor for a full parliament, longer than David Cameron had been leader of the opposition, and despite being considered by his opponents as too young and inexperienced to win the respect of the City of London, his track record as a political strategist spoke for itself. His audacious proposal to raise the threshold for inheritance tax to £1 million won such acclaim among potential Conservative voters that it was credited as one of the factors which persuaded Brown to ditch the idea of a snap election in the autumn of 2007. Osborne also had the satisfaction subsequently of seeing Darling forced to respond and announce his own increase in the threshold.

Osborne was Cameron's closest colleague in their shared goal of taking the Conservatives back into government and his role in shaping their tactics was pivotal. He had responsibility for devising policies to tackle rising public debt and he was also the leading strategist in planning the party's election campaign. His greatest challenge was the overarching task of finding ways to convince the public that the Conservatives could do a better job than Labour in managing the economy and in stimulating and sustaining a recovery. Brown and Darling had continually accused

Osborne of being a Tory lightweight, of having lacked judgement during the banking crisis and of having no credible ideas for ensuring financial stability. Eight months before the election, to the surprise of friend and foe alike, Osborne presented himself to his party's annual conference as the Chancellor for an 'age of austerity', ready to promise more financial pain than the incumbent government dared to contemplate in public. His honesty was applauded by many commentators but his openness so far in advance of polling day was considered to be high-wire politics, a tactic which left the Conservatives at risk of a counter-attack by Labour. Political pundits lost no time raising the spectre of 1992: had Osborne repeated Smith's mistake of opening the door to the kind of scare tactics which the Conservatives used so successfully against Labour and in which the young Cameron had played a part?

Spending cuts were at the heart of the pre-election posturing in the autumn of 2009, as they would be during the campaign itself, and Osborne was determined to answer the charge that the Conservatives were short on detail. Internal polling suggested the electorate was ready for honesty about the need for cuts in order to reduce the largest budget deficit in Europe. As Chancellor in waiting Osborne seemed to have worked on the assumption that the public were prepared to take their medicine and he told colleagues he expected to become 'the most unpopular man in Britain within six weeks of an election'. His party conference speech in Manchester was well trailed in advance as a strategy to stop the country 'sinking in a sea of debt'. He announced a series of measures to shave £7 billion a year from public spending. A public sector pay freeze in 2011 for all but the lowest-paid workers would save 100,000 frontline jobs, including those of nurses and teachers; the state pension age for men would be raised to sixty-six from 2016, ten years earlier than planned; and the administrative cost of Whitehall bureaucracy and quangos would be reduced by a third. 'These are the honest choices in the world in which we live and we have made them today. Anyone who tells you these choices can be avoided is not telling you the truth. We are all in this together. The Conservatives have been straight with you today.' He repeated that refrain – 'We are all in this together' – seven times in his speech, and political correspondents were unanimous in their conclusion that Osborne was heralding an 'age of austerity' and was prepared to impose the biggest cuts in public spending for thirty years.

His candour in promising to cut the deficit faster than the government proposed was applauded by leader writers, who had lambasted the Prime Minister and the Chancellor for their failure at the Labour conference the previous week to mention the scale of the debt crisis and where instead they 'spewed out uncosted new policies'. *The Times* said Osborne had 'grown in stature' for having spelled out the nation's 'parlous public finances in all their gory detail'; the *Daily Telegraph*'s conclusion was that the Conservatives sounded like 'a government-in-waiting' for having delivered 'an honest, unvarnished assessment of some of the acutely painful spending decisions' an incoming administration would have to take.

Cameron rounded off the conference by telling the BBC that it would have been 'dishonest and irresponsible' not to have been clear about the dangers facing the country. 'It was, I thought, quite a contrast with the government. It was an opposition behaving like a government when we've got a government behaving like an opposition.' Opinion polls seemed to confirm Cameron's confidence in the likely popularity of their blueprint to get the economy back on track. A pre-conference lead of 12 points rose to 14 points the following week, giving the Conservatives a 42 per cent predicted share of the vote as against 28 per cent for Labour, enough to secure a parliamentary majority of 100 seats.

Announcing their strategy in October before a May election exposed the Conservatives to the probability that Labour would take counter-measures in both the pre-Budget report due in December and the pre-election Budget in the spring. To the Conservatives' annoyance Darling partially pre-empted their proposed pay freeze for up to four million public sector workers by announcing the day before Osborne's conference speech that the government had recommended to salary review bodies there should be no pay increases for 40,000 senior public servants and no more than 1 per cent extra for groups such as doctors, dentists and prison officers.

At the next opportunity for tit-for-tat tactics, Labour ignored Osborne's warnings of calamity ahead; instead they upped the level of borrowing and announced a doubling of the expected increase in national insurance contributions. Darling told MPs in his pre–Budget report that to start cutting the £178 billion annual deficit immediately would threaten economic recovery; he proposed to reduce it in an 'orderly way' over a four-year period. The Conservative leadership faced the stark reality of having to come to terms with an electioneering Labour Budget which would seek to justify continued high levels of public spending. Darling's calculation appeared to be that up to ten million voters earning more than £20,000 a year would resign themselves to a 1p rise in national insurance in 2011 in order to maintain spending for schools, hospitals and the police. 'The buck passer's budget' was the *Daily Mail*'s front-page verdict on the Chancellor's refusal to 'tackle Britain's terrifying debt'. The election battle lines were drawn: Brown and Darling would be able to claim that Conservative cuts jeopardised the recovery and Cameron and Osborne could argue in return that an avalanche of debt should not be financed with higher taxes. 'Pain postponed', as the *Independent*'s headline put it, pointed to a political gamble but one that perhaps might have greater appeal to voters than the shadow Chancellor's 'age of austerity'. The Conservatives' commanding lead in the opinion polls following their party conference began to narrow, suggesting that they were vulnerable to Labour's warning that the recovery might be wrecked unless the government went ahead with its £31 billion boost to public spending. Several surveys put Labour back to 30–31 per cent and suggested the Conservatives' share of the vote had been reduced to 40 per cent. End-of-year headlines predicting that official figures would show that the recession was over added a fresh sense of urgency to the pre-election planning. Cameron signalled that the Conservatives would kick off their campaign early in the New Year; Brown indicated that the government was keeping its options open over the date of the Budget, Labour's last throw of the dice before polling day.

Claim and counter-claim filled the air in the first few days of January 2010 as the two main parties traded blows over tax and spending. Darling published a 148-page document which estimated there was 'a £34 billion credibility gap' in funding the Conservatives' programme. The Chancellor's strategy was a mirror image of the 1992 'tax bombshell' dossier which John Major launched against Neil Kinnock in an attempt to undermine the credibility of Labour's tax and spending plans. Cameron and his chief strategist, Steve Hilton, were well aware of the propaganda value of calculating the size of a 'black hole' in an opponent's plans: in the 1992 election, when Cameron was head of the party's political section and Hilton the campaign co-ordinator, the Conservatives followed up their attack with posters warning of 'five years hard labour' if Kinnock was elected, a tactic which annoyed the shadow Chancellor John Smith. When asked at a news conference for a response to Darling's dossier, Cameron dismissed it as 'complete junk' but afterwards, in an interview with the BBC's political editor Nick Robinson, he tripped up over his long-term pledge to offer tax breaks for married couples. No doubt wishing to appear fiscally responsible, he said his commitment to recognise marriage in the tax system was something he definitely hoped to do within a parliament but he was not 'able to make that promise because we face this vast budget deficit'. Two hours later he rushed out a statement insisting a tax break was something the Conservatives would 'definitely do in the next parliament'. 'Cameron error gives Labour first blood' was the *Guardian*'s front-page headline next morning. Three days later he gave an interview for BBC Radio in which he admitted he had 'misdescribed' Conservative policy. 'I messed up and there is no other way of putting it. I was thinking about all sorts of different things . . . There's only one thing worse than messing up, and that is messing up and not admitting to it.'

Cameron's contrition was not unexpected given the fun and games there had been since he spoke at his news conference in front of the party's first campaign poster, not realising that the large airbrushed photograph of himself wearing an open-necked shirt, which was appearing on hoardings in marginal constituencies, was about to become the most mocked image of the campaign. Graffiti artists with paintbrushes began defacing the poster on billboards up and down the country. Even more imaginative versions appeared online on sites such as www.mydavidcameron.com. Beside the photograph of Cameron's smooth, blemish-free face was a slogan which the copywriter did not realise was open to limitless variations. It said: 'We can't go on like this. I'll cut the deficit, not the NHS.' Cameron's favourite was said to be the poster in Hereford which was altered to give him an Elvis Presley-style hair cut and a slogan tweaked to reference a line from one of Presley's hits: 'We can't go on like this. With suspicious minds.' Another less flattering second line got straight to the point: 'Fuck off back to Eton.' Brown could not resist joining in the Cameron-baiting at Prime Minister's Questions. 'His airbrushed poster has better lines on it than he has delivered. If you can't get your photograph right it's pretty difficult to get your policies right as well.' Cameron had plainly feared the worst and retaliated by asking Labour MPs to put up their hands if they had included a picture of the Prime Minister on their election leaflets, a ploy which enabled him to deliver the taunt 'He's been airbrushed out of the whole campaign'.

Finding he had become a laughing stock over a misjudged photograph so soon after having to admit he had 'messed up' on policy was another irritation in what was fast becoming a deeply unsettling episode at party headquarters. Tough talk in mid-January had pointed to a hardening in the Conservatives' resolve to press ahead with spending cuts. One option being considered by George Osborne was to make sufficient savings to allow him to reverse at least part of Labour's planned increase in national insurance contributions. But rising optimism among business leaders was supporting the government's argument that spending by the state was helping to keep down unemployment and strengthen the recovery. Opinion polls indicated a continuing improvement in Labour's position. After three halved the Conservatives' share of the vote, including one survey by YouGov cutting the Tory lead to 7 points, pollsters said a hung Parliament was becoming a real possibility. Cameron did not wait long to change tack. He told *The Politics Show* the Conservatives were 'not talking about swingeing cuts'; his aim was to make 'a start' in reducing the deficit and to take decisions 'on a five-year horizon'. Osborne insisted in a speech later that week that there had been no U-turn but amid reports of a bunker mentality developing among staff at party headquarters, the move was seen as a tactical retreat in response to fears that big cuts could put the fragile economic recovery at risk.

Newspaper headlines about the first wobble of the campaign did little to ease the jittery state of Conservative MPs. Lord Heseltine, the former deputy Prime Minister, was the first Tory grandee to voice unease about the narrowing gap in the polls. He told a meeting of party members in west London that he doubted whether Cameron could win the election outright. When approached by the *Sunday Telegraph* he urged the party leadership to realise they faced 'a hell of a battle'; there was no room for complacency. 'If I was a betting man, my money would be on the election resulting in a hung Parliament with David Cameron as Prime Minister.' Heseltine's grim forecast coincided with an opinion survey suggesting the Conservatives' lead was less than 6 points; if the determination of those questioned to turn out was taken into account, Labour could end up winning most seats despite a lower share of the vote.

Conservative activists gathering in Brighton for the party's spring conference, the last before polling day, were desperate to hear Cameron mount a fightback. Their sense of anxiety was heightened by another shock headline that morning on the front page of the *Sunday Times*: 'Brown on course to win election, as Tory lead plunges to two points'. For the first time since July 2007, people trusted Labour more than the Conservatives to run the economy. On an inside page Cameron's poster had been reworked to show anguish on his face and the slogan 'You can't airbrush this, Dave. The incredible shrinking Tory lead'. A montage on the *News of the World*'s front page underlined the gravity of the party's plight. Cameron's photograph was superimposed on an illustration of a war-time recruitment poster with the slogan 'Your country needs ME'. Advance briefings of Cameron's speech suggested that he intended to declare it was his 'patriotic duty' to defeat the Prime Minister because the country was in 'a complete and utter mess, and we have to sort it out'. Speaking without notes, he did all he could to reinvigorate his party's push for power. 'Every day that goes by I feel I have what it takes to turn this country around.' His twin objectives were to reassure the public that better times were to come while claiming it would be a calamity if Brown was re-elected.

> *I can feel we're looking down some dark tunnel. But there is a bright light at the end of it . . . I want you to think of the incredible dark depression of five more years of Gordon Brown and say 'No, we are not going to do that' . . . another five years of a government so dysfunctional and divided, weak, a bunch of ministers who cannot work with him and cannot get rid of him.*

Cameron tried to turn to his advantage Labour's taunt that he was nothing more than a slick public relations executive: 'Gordon Brown says I'm a bit of a salesman. I plead guilty. We are going to need some salesmanship . . . Britain is under new economic management and we are open for business again.'

Conservative-supporting papers rallied to the cause: 'I'm fit to run Britain' was the *Daily Telegraph*'s front-page headline alongside a photograph of Cameron on his morning run along Brighton seafront. But the leader writers were rather more cautious. The *Financial Times* considered that the erosion in Conservative support reflected the feebleness of the Tory campaign. Instead of issuing a few sentences to explain their principles and a smattering of policy to illustrate them, the party had 'churned out an endless stream of plans, agendas and benchmarks, many of which cut across one another'.

Whenever Cameron launched a head-to-head offensive deriding Brown, Nick Clegg seized the opportunity to remind voters how increasingly alike these 'two old parties' were, the line of attack he would use with devastating effect in the first of the televised leaders' debates. Neither Conservatives nor Labour could be trusted because 'their sums don't add up'. But while the Liberal Democrats were buoyed by the likelihood of the closest election result since 1974 and the possibility of holding the balance of power, Clegg faced unease at his party's spring conference in Birmingham because of fears he intended to reach a post-election pact with Cameron. He told *Today* that the Conservatives' pledge to slash spending so early in the recovery was 'economic masochism'; his role in a hung Parliament would be to act as guarantor of the economy and to demand financial sanity as a condition of support. He was adamant he would not waver in his conviction that the party with the strongest mandate from voters would have the moral authority to be the first to seek to govern. 'I am not the kingmaker. The forty-five million voters of Britain are the kingmakers. This election is a time for voters to choose, not a time for politicians to play footsie with each other.'

Alistair Darling's Budget, six weeks from polling day, was the last set-piece confrontation in the House of Commons, an opportunity which the government was determined to take to create clear political dividing lines with the Conservatives. As there was no money for a pre-election giveaway, and the Chancellor was clearly intent on postponing the pain of spending cuts until after the election, the Chancellor chose instead to remind voters that Labour made the right calls when faced by the upheaval of a global recession:

> *Because of the steps we took, opposed by the opposition, the recovery has begun, unemployment is falling and borrowing is better than expected. The choice before the country now is whether to support those whose policies will suffocate our recovery or support a government which has been right about the recession.*

Higher than expected tax receipts vindicated his assessment and had cut the record budget deficit from £178 billion to £167 billion but he trimmed his growth forecast to 3.25 per cent in 2011. There were two election sweeteners which cheered Labour MPs: a two-year stamp duty holiday on homes worth less than £250,000 and the phasing in of an increase in petrol duty. Darling's nakedly political pitch contained no vision for the future other than managing the recovery, and the lack of radical thinking gave Cameron the opportunity to claim it was the Conservatives who would have to clear up the 'complete mess' of Labour's failed policies. 'They're just going to carry on spending, carry on borrowing and carry on failing . . . They say "Don't do anything before the election, let's just sit tight and keep our fingers crossed".' Clegg argued that both Darling and Cameron were in denial about the necessary scale of spending cuts; the Budget had been nothing more than a political dodge. 'This isn't the preface to a new government but a footnote to thirteen years of failure.'

Treasury documents released after Darling's speech revealed that a further £24 billion would have to be found in efficiency savings and cuts to public services by the following March to meet targets agreed three years previously. When the BBC's political editor, Nick Robinson, asked the Chancellor if he accepted that the Treasury's own figures suggested tougher cuts than implemented by the Thatcher government in the 1980s, he agreed. 'They will be deeper and tougher . . . There may be things that we don't do, that we cut in the future . . . What is non-negotiable is that borrowing is coming down by half over a four-year period.' But by putting off crucial decisions until after polling day, Darling left the election battlefield open to a counter-attack by George Osborne, who promised the party would set out how it intended to cut the deficit faster than Labour. Cameron used an interview on *The Politics Show* to trail the Conservatives' first tax-cutting pledge of the campaign: a government he led would reverse part of Labour's planned increase in national insurance contributions to help workers and recession-hit businesses. Osborne's intention was to scrap the 1 per cent increase for all but higher earners, which would leave seven out of ten employees up to £150 a year better off. The announcement had been timed to secure maximum political advantage because Osborne was able to promote his plan that evening when he appeared with Darling and Vince Cable on Channel 4's live debate, *Ask the Chancellors*. To finance the cancellation of the planned increase, Osborne said the Conservatives would save £6 billion in government efficiency measures. The significance of his pre-election coup was reinforced by twenty-three business leaders who signed a letter to the *Daily Telegraph* warning that if national insurance contributions were increased in April 2011 it could threaten jobs and put the recovery at risk. Signatories included Sir Stuart Rose, executive chairman of Marks & Spencer, Justin King, chief executive of Sainsbury's, Paul Walsh, chief executive of Diageo, and Sir Christopher Gent, chairman of GlaxoSmithKline.

Rounding up friendly figureheads in industry and commence and asking them to sign letters of support was a tactic which Tony Blair used in the 1997 election when promoting the business-friendly policies of New Labour. Darling was left with the unenviable task of urging the twenty-three executives to have 'a long hard look' at what the Conservatives were up to. Lord Mandelson, the Business Secretary, had no hesitation in retaliating in style. He accused Cameron and Osborne of peddling 'a cynical deception' and was not surprised the Tories managed to win the support of business leaders who thought there could be 'a pain-free tax cut'. This gave the story fresh impetus and allowed Cameron to argue that Mandelson's provocation would backfire on Labour and that it was 'patronising and wrong' to suggest that business leaders had been deceived. Two of the signatories, Simon Wolfson, chief executive of Next, and Ian Cheshire, chief executive of Kingfisher, insisted they had not been taken in by a deception but wanted to protect business from 'a tax on jobs'.

After failing for the first three months of the year to identify an issue to drive forward their campaign Osborne had managed to put Labour firmly on the defensive while at the same time giving the party's well-resourced media operation an opportunity to build up momentum behind an easily understood news story which related to millions of potential voters. To keep their initiative in the headlines the Conservatives needed to draw in a steady supply of new supporters. By the end of the first day, the Confederation of British Industry, the British Chambers of Commerce and five other organisations said the Conservatives 'deserved credit' for opposing the increase in contributions; next day another fourteen business leaders added their names to the list. Stefano Pessina, executive chairman of Alliance Boots, said an increase in national insurance was 'not helpful at this time'. A fresh quote from Cameron helped to sustain the story: Brown and Darling had managed to get Labour 'on the wrong side' of working people and big business. By the end of the week those giving their endorsement included Sir Richard Branson, who had lent his support to New Labour in 1997 by joining Tony Blair for a photo-opportunity on a Virgin West Coast train.

When the Conservatives first raised the possibility early in the New Year of reining in the national insurance increase through £6 billion in efficiency savings Cameron acknowledged their proposals would have to be properly costed. He mentioned at the time that an entire episode of *Yes, Minister* was devoted to finding efficiencies which never materialised. 'I've got to find the savings before I can make the promise . . . If I can't, I won't.' Osborne's subsequent success in engaging Mandelson in a week-long pitched battle over their plan to avoid 'Labour's jobs tax' boosted staff morale after the much-criticised start to their campaign. A renewed sense of optimism prompted rapid retaliation when Labour launched a poster depicting Cameron as the cult 1980s detective Gene Hunt from the television series *Ashes to Ashes*. Cameron's face had been mocked up on the body of DCI Hunt, who was perched on the bonnet of his red Audi Quattro and the poster raised the spectre of a return to the social unrest of the Thatcher era with the slogan 'Don't let him take Britain back to the 1980s'. Within hours the Conservatives had reworked the poster to take advantage of the huge popularity of the cool un-PC cop by adapting his catchphrase to declare 'Fire up the Quattro. It's time for change'. A strap line at the bottom said 'idea kindly donated by the Labour Party' – a reference to Jacob Quagliozzi, a 24-year-old Labour supporter from St Albans who won a poster design competition sponsored by Labour's advertising agency Saatchi & Saatchi. Two cabinet ministers, brothers David and Ed Miliband, launched the poster at Basildon in Essex, prompting the *Sun* to compare the 'dopey duo' to the tone-deaf *X Factor* act of Irish twins Jedward for not having realised how 'popular the old-school cop is with Brits'. Tory headquarters claimed a score-draw with Labour in the election poster war after their earlier howler over Cameron's airbrushed face.

Ending the week on a high note prepared Cameron for the dissolution of Parliament the following Tuesday and he managed to pip the Prime Minister to the post by launching the Conservatives' campaign in between Brown's visit to Buckingham Palace and his short speech on the steps of 10 Downing Street. Having served as leader of the opposition for longer than Margaret Thatcher and Tony Blair, Cameron must have been encouraged after four and a half years to see the finishing line in sight at last. Supported by a crowd of 200 Tory candidates and party workers he stood on the Thames embankment opposite the House of Commons and welcomed what he said was the start of the 'most important general election for a generation'. Echoing the words of John F. Kennedy, he declared: 'Don't just ask what government can do for us. But what can we all do together to make society stronger.' He gestured across the river and said politicians had to 'make people feel proud again of that building over there'. Brown opted for a family-photo launch in Downing Street, standing in front of the entire cabinet to emphasise the unity and comradeship of the Labour government. 'I am not a team of one, but one of a team. I say to the British people: our cause is your cause. The future is ours to win – now let's go to it.' Nick Clegg started his campaign in the marginal constituency of Watford, where the Liberal Democrats were competing in a close three-horse race, an ideal location for him to challenge the grip of the 'old politics' of Westminster. 'The choice in this election is between more of the same with Labour and the Conservatives or real change with the Liberal Democrats.' Clegg fuelled the suspicion that the Liberal Democrats would insist on the

Prime Minister standing down in the event of a hung Parliament and the possibility of working with Labour. 'This is the beginning of the end of Gordon Brown.'

Unlike his two rivals, whose wives were in attendance, Clegg appeared in Watford without Miriam. She was sticking resolutely to her own election pledge to put career and family first rather than spend her five weeks' holiday on the campaign trail. Samantha Cameron was among the crowd by the Thames listening to her husband; once the Prime Minister finished his photo-opportunity with the cabinet, Sarah Brown joined him and they headed off to visit constituencies in Kent. She was photographed on St Pancras station with her arm round her husband's back escorting him along the platform. The three leaders had a full week's campaigning ahead of them before the launch of their manifestos and the first of their televised debates; they probably had no inkling of what was in store for their other halves. A YouGov opinion survey indicated that 89 per cent of people thought the leaders' wives would have little or no influence on how they voted but the editors of the national newspapers had a different opinion and were about to deploy even more journalistic talent than before to the task of reporting the daily comings and goings of the WAGs.

A reputation for publishing po-faced critiques about the *Sun*'s page 3 girls did not inhibit the *Guardian*, which launched Imogen Fox's daily 'stylewatch'. Sarah Brown's first campaign cardigan – lime yellow with a round neck – was worthy of only two stars; next day Samantha Cameron merited only one star for having 'panicked big time' and chosen an army-style jacket and a floral blouse. But Jan Moir, writing her *Daily Mail* 'war of the wives' column, complimented Cameron on her outfit, which 'spoke of the high street and affordability'. She was on a solo visit to the marginal constituencies of Leeds North East and Brigg & Goole and the *Sun* published a spread of photographs to record the 'first time the Tory leader's shy wife has hit the election trail alone'. Brown, campaigning with her husband in east London, was asked by reporters whether she was going to win it for her husband. 'Can you take on Sam Cam, Sarah?'

Labour officials said Brown had no intention of campaigning solo. At his morning news conference the Prime Minister said his wife wanted to join him whenever possible. 'It's her idea, and she wants to help the campaign, and we want to work together on that. She's the love of my life and we work well together and we like going round the country together.'

Gordon Brown appeared more relaxed when Sarah was with him and her calm composure softened his overbearing image. Her presence often ensured he received a warmer reception than if he had been meeting people on his own. Her role as his companion had enhanced value for the Labour Party due to the ease with which she could communicate with a wider audience. Sarah Brown's million-plus followers on Twitter were able to read regular updates: for example, 'On high speed train whizzing across Kent – fabulous day'. On day four of the campaign she was signed up by the *Daily Mirror* and the *Sunday Mirror* to write an election diary. In her first report she said she loved every single minute of life on the road, meeting 'so many amazing people'. But she always had to remember that her handbag was not complete 'without a spare phone charger, a pair of flats and a pretty pad to write down the details'.

When 2,000 people were surveyed by BPIX for the *Mail on Sunday*'s weekly opinion poll they were asked which wife they thought was having the best campaign. Samantha Cameron was way out in front. She was on 22 per cent as against 13 per cent for Sarah Brown and a puny 4 per cent for Miriam González Durántez. Unfortunately for the Liberal Democrats the survey was conducted before her first campaign photo-opportunity. She was pictured helping her husband build a dry stone wall on a farm in his Sheffield Hallam constituency. The *Sunday Express* noted her 'low key look in blue jeans and grey cardigan'. At last Moir had a real contest to report in her 'war of the wives' column:

Hola, Sheffield! Miriam González Durántez came out of her self-imposed political purdah . . . the Cleggs seemed to be making a point of resolutely not holding hands in cheesy Gordon & Sarah plc way. A shame, because they look like the kind of couple who really would hold hands over their regular Saturday-afternoon dry-stone-walling excursion.

Next day, in an interview by Mark Austin for *ITV News*, González was able to give her opinion on the 'frivolous' attention being paid to the three wives. 'I think that the voters deserve better, deserve more focus on the policies and less on the clothes . . . Patronising is putting it very diplomatically.' After her interview was broadcast she was listed in the *Independent*'s election highlights as 'heroine of the day'. The *Economist* agreed that Clegg's 'admirably independent wife' was 'arguably the star of the campaign so far'.

If the three wives were being judged not by the fashionistas of the press but by hard-bitten political heavies there would have been no contest: Sarah Brown was one of the most sure-footed minders in the business, ready like no other to guard her husband's back, an invaluable extra pair of eyes and ears, able to spot from a distance the potential pitfalls in a dodgy photo-opportunity or to smooth away an awkward doorstep confrontation. Her great misfortune was to have been away from the Prime Minister's side during what instantly became known as Bigotgate, his encounter with Gillian Duffy, a redoubtable 65-year-old grandmother living in the marginal constituency of Rochdale. As the Prime Minister's wife hurried to rejoin him in Manchester, after the agony of taking a distraught telephone call in which he told her what had happened, she must have gone over it again and again in her mind, repeatedly saying to herself 'If only . . . if only I'd been there'.

Gordon Brown's election gaffe made headlines around the world because it confirmed a near-universal suspicion that most politicians have a low opinion of the general populace. Mrs Duffy left her home simply to buy a loaf of bread, saw a commotion in the street around the Prime Minister as he toured the constituency and shouted a question at him. On being asked to come forward, she engaged him in robust but polite question and answer. One issue which concerned her was that too many people who were not vulnerable were able to benefit from services while others who really were vulnerable could not claim help. 'You can't say anything about the immigrants because you're saying that you're . . . but all these eastern Europeans what are coming in, where are they flocking from?' After the Prime Minister patiently explained to her that a million people had come from Europe but the same number of British people had gone into Europe, Mrs Duffy went on talking happily about her grandchildren and their hopes of reaching university, until he finally rounded off the conversation saying, 'Good. And it's very nice to see you. Take care.'

Without realising that the radio microphone which he had been wearing during the visit was still attached to his lapel, he climbed into his official car ready to be taken to Manchester. He sat beside the Downing Street director of communications Justin Forsyth and as they were driven off, he launched into a tirade about what had happened, lashing out and blaming his staff. For the next few seconds, while the car remained in radio range, everything he said was being transmitted from his live lapel microphone and was being recorded nearby by a Sky News satellite truck. The Prime Minister was obviously in a foul mood from the word go, believing for some inexplicable reason that his conversation with Mrs Duffy had gone disastrously wrong and that it would be replayed endlessly by television and radio news bulletins. His intemperate, abusive description of a life-long Labour supporter, within minutes of meeting her in the street, was breathtaking in its insensitivity, a blunder of such horrendous proportions that it instantly entered the annals of campaign howlers.

BROWN: *That was a disaster . . . should never have put me with that woman. Whose idea was that?*
FORSYTH: *I don't know. I didn't see her.*
BROWN: *Sue's, I think [Sue Nye, director of government relations, Brown's gatekeeper]. Just ridiculous.*
FORSYTH: *Not sure that they'll go with that one.*
BROWN: *They will go with that one.*

FORSYTH: *What did she say?*
BROWN: *Everything, she was just a sort of bigoted woman who said she used to be Labour. I mean, it's just ridiculous.*

Sky News had provided a radio microphone at Brown's request as was often the case during constituency walkabouts because it helped to reduce the amount of pushing and shoving among camera crews and sound recordists as they tried to keep pace with the Prime Minister and continue to film and record his conversations with shoppers and passers-by. The recording at Rochdale was made on a pooled basis to be shared out between the broadcasters and by the time Brown reached BBC Manchester for a radio interview on the Jeremy Vine show his accusation that 'that woman . . . was just a sort of bigoted woman' was headline news. Midway through the interview Vine replayed the BBC's copy of the tape and as the Prime Minister began to listen to a recording of his own words which he had no idea had even been made, he slumped forward, shielding his face with his hand. Radio interviews with ministers and party leaders are regularly filmed so that extracts can be used in television news bulletins and the picture of the Prime Minister, a pair of radio headphones around his head, hunched forward over the studio microphones, his face shielded from view by his left hand, became the unforgettable, iconic image of the 2010 general election.

Sarah Brown's utter devotion to her husband and the emotional strength which he drew from her presence should have been a constant reminder to Labour's election managers that together they were a formidable team but that unless she was there at his side his fractured personality left him vulnerable to mishaps in the unpredictable circumstances of a campaign walkabout. In the opening sentences of her first campaign diary for the *Daily Mirror*, when she described how she loved 'life on the road' with her husband, she mentioned his reputation for being impatient, bad tempered and rude. 'I have said before that he's not a saint, and that's true.' On the fateful Wednesday morning of his Rochdale visit she was in Scotland and due to rejoin him in Manchester later in the day. Jan Moir took up the story in her 'war of the wives' column: 'And where was she while her husband was crashing and howling around Rochdale like an old bear being bated in a pit? Strangely enough she was at Asda in Edinburgh, shopping for vinegar with Alistair Darling's wife, Maggie.' Moir monitored Sarah Brown's tweets as the news media went into overdrive reporting her husband's dash to Rochdale to apologise to Mrs Duffy: 'How ironic that while the Twitter website went viral with tweets about Duffygate and Bigotgate, the site's most famous tweeter maintained a discreet if desperate silence. "On a train with an erratic signal!" she chirped, to explain her strange absence from the furious online commentary.'

Sarah Brown reached Manchester later that afternoon and was by her husband's side, clutching his arm, smiling and laughing, as they went on an early evening walkabout in Oldham, mingling with pedestrians. Lord Mandelson told journalists that her absence in Rochdale had contributed to the Prime Minister's 'bad mood'. In her own account in the *Daily Mirror* of how she did all she could that day to support her husband, she said he was left 'distraught' by his election gaffe and immediately apologised to Mrs Duffy. 'People may say many things about Gordon but they cannot say he doesn't care. He phoned me as soon as it happened and was absolutely mortified. He went to see her because he hated the fact that he had hurt someone. His apology was from the heart.' In her diary entry for the *Sunday Mirror* she said she hoped her readers would not feel that Gordon's 'little trouble' in Rochdale overshadowed the key fundamentals of Labour's appeal to the electorate.

He forgot his microphone was on and said something he will forever regret about a lady he had just met. I wasn't with Gordon at the time, but I could tell from the tone of his voice when he called me that he'd done something he felt mortified about. If there's one thing everyone who knows him agrees on about Gordon, it's that he simply hates upsetting people. The idea that somebody would have been caused pain or embarrassment

> *by something he had done is the sort of thing that goes right to the core of Gordon . . . I am glad that he has also had the chance to meet the lady again and speak to her personally and privately too.*

She remarked somewhat ruefully that 'these are the sort of incidents you get on the campaign trail' while not daring to point out that it would almost certainly not have happened if she had been there. To begin with Mrs Duffy would have been charmed to have met the Prime Minister's wife and her presence would have changed the nature and perhaps the content of the conversation. When walking to their official car she would have immediately noticed that the radio microphone was still attached to his lapel. Her long experience in public relations arranging celebrity photo-opportunities had instilled in her the importance of remaining in total control whenever television crews and photographers were present. In the years she had spent accompanying her husband as Chancellor and then Prime Minister on trips around the world she had never once been caught on microphone saying a word out of place. If by chance he had got into the car with the radio microphone still attached she would almost certainly have been sitting next to him and would have noticed it immediately.

Gordon Brown's humiliation that day was compounded by Mrs Duffy's refusal to join him for a photograph together at her front door after he went to apologise four hours later. He emerged to a battery of cameras to explain how he had tried to make amends: 'I am mortified by what has happened. I have given her my very sincere apologies. I misunderstood what she said. She has accepted that there was a misunderstanding and she has accepted my apology. If you like, I am a penitent sinner.' Next day, Sarah Brown was once again firmly at his side, holding his hand tightly as he made a campaign stop at Wolverhampton and toured a factory on his way to the final televised leaders' debate in Birmingham. In his opening statement the Prime Minister did his best to make a virtue out of his misfortune while emphasising his competent stewardship of the economy: 'There's a lot to this job and, as you saw yesterday, I don't get all of it right. But I do know how to run the economy in good times and in bad. So it's not my future that matters – it's your future that's on the ballot paper next Thursday.'

Rarely in the increasingly controlled circumstances of modern electioneering does the news media alight on a gaffe which so neatly fits a story line which journalists always knew was desperate to escape. The 'Prescott punch' was the unforgettable moment of the 2001 general election, when, with split-second timing, Labour's deputy Prime Minister, John Prescott, landed a straight left jab on to the chin of an egg-throwing protestor during a fracas at Rhyl. Prescott learned to box as a teenage steward on cruise ships and he had a well-earned reputation as a political bruiser. In 2010 Gordon Brown's self-inflicted disaster was an accident which journalists felt was waiting to happen; his moods and bad temper were legendary and his cussed refusal to engage in the pleasantries which eased the friction between politicians and reporters meant he had very few friends in his hour of need. Bigotgate was the incredible culmination to a well-entrenched narrative which had him written off as Prime Minister, a narrative which David Cameron had ruthlessly exploited when he warned repeatedly of the electorate waking up to the danger 'of another five years of Gordon Brown'. For Conservative-supporting newspapers Brown's humiliation was justly deserved, his rightful comeuppance after years of mismanaging the country's affairs.

British newspapers have long been renowned for the partisan nature of their political reporting during general elections but there had been nothing to match the intensity of Brown's denigration since the highly disrespectful mockery of a much-maligned John Major in 1997. Press proprietors and their editors have always made a virtue of their promiscuity, regularly switching their allegiance between the parties in the hope perhaps of political favours, for commercial advantage or more usually because they want to be in tune with the views of their readers. After three general elections when much of the press remained loyal to Tony Blair, Brown's sole supporter among the national dailies was the *Daily Mirror*, which was as slavish in support of Labour as the *Sun* was for the Conservatives. All four of Rupert Murdoch's newspapers endorsed Cameron after deserting Labour; the Conservatives were also confident of the backing of the *Daily Telegraph*, the *Daily Mail* and the *Daily Express*.

As polling day approached the two radical left-of-centre dailies, the *Guardian* and the *Independent*, which had both been doughty campaigners for electoral reform, could hardly contain their excitement at the prospect of a hung Parliament and the possible introduction of a fairer voting system. Having supported proportional representation for more than a century, the *Guardian* believed Nick Clegg deserved 'considerable personal credit' for having waged a campaign which had encouraged an overwhelming national mood for real change and presented the British people with a huge opportunity. Five days before the country voted, a leading article opened with a resounding message to readers: 'Citizens have votes. Newspapers do not. However, if the *Guardian* had a vote in the 2010 general election it would be cast enthusiastically for the Liberal Democrats.'

The *Independent*'s front page on polling day was an equally bold declaration urging its readers to have the final say. Under the headline 'The people's election' it listed fifteen reasons why voters should celebrate a campaign that could 'change the face of British politics for ever' and see off Britain's 'iniquitous and rotten voting system'. Simon Kelner, the paper's editor in chief, had run a spirited campaign to promote the *Independent*'s claim to freedom from proprietorial influence. A special wraparound front page was printed for 300,000 copies which were given away free and it carried a provocative pre-election slogan: 'Rupert Murdoch won't decide this election – you will'. By then both the *Sun* and the *News of the World* had declared their support for the Conservatives and the *Independent*'s promotion so angered James Murdoch, chief executive of News Corporation Europe and Asia, and Rebekah Brooks, chief executive of News International, that they went to the paper's newsroom after visiting the adjoining offices of the *Daily Mail*. Kelner was at the paper's editorial desk planning next day's edition when he saw them arrive together brandishing a copy of the *Independent*. At this point, according to an account in the *Financial Times*, 'bemused journalists' heard Murdoch ask Kelner: 'What are you fucking playing at?' Kelner invited them both to his office where there was a heated fifteen-minute conversation. Kelner told colleagues afterwards that Murdoch complained that the advertisement 'besmirched his father's reputation'.

Over the years Rupert Murdoch has always insisted that he does not interfere with the day-to-day news judgements made by his editors. Where he does exert influence is over the editorial direction of his newspapers and there has never been any doubt, as revealed in the transcripts of his conversations with Tony Blair, that he did direct the line they followed over the Iraq War. Murdoch also made no secret of the personal interest he was taking in Cameron's prospects of becoming Prime Minister; the *Sun*'s decision to abandon Brown, whom he had known personally for many years, would have needed his authority.

Only a few days before James Murdoch's confrontation at the *Independent* an insight into his father's political interference emerged in the *Guardian* in an article by the former *Sun* editor David Yelland. He was so taken aback by the groundswell in support for the Liberal Democrats after the first televised leader's debate that he thought it could have a profound effect on the 'entirely partisan' relationship between the 'media elite and the two main political parties'. Yelland said that if Rupert Murdoch had watched the leaders' debate, Clegg would have been totally unknown to him; he was a party leader 'utterly beyond the tentacles of any of his family, his editors or his advisers'. People outside the political and media elites felt disenfranchised but Yelland thought that could change if Clegg pulled off a miracle:

> *Make no mistake, if the Liberal Democrats actually won the election – or held the balance of power – it would be the first time in decades that Murdoch was locked out of British politics. In so many ways, a vote for the Lib Dems is a vote against Murdoch and the media elite.*

Yelland backed up his argument with an authoritative insider's account of how as the *Sun*'s editor for five years he never met a Liberal Democrat leader and was told that his paper did not send a single reporter to the Liberal Democrats' conferences for 'fear of encouraging them'. While successive News International chiefs and assorted senior staff held parties at Conservative and Labour conferences, he said they never even attended those held by the Liberal Democrats.

> *It gets even worse. While it would be wrong to say that Liberal Democrats were banned from Murdoch's newspapers (indeed,* The Times *has a good record in this area), I would say from personal experience that they are often banned — except where the news is critical. They are the invisible party, purposely edged off the paper's pages and ignored.*

A Lib–Lab pact appeared to be a possible outcome when Yelland wrote his article but the scenario he painted of the Murdoch press perhaps becoming isolated had even greater resonance given the inconclusive result of the general election and the historic agreement by the Conservatives and Liberal Democrats to establish Britain's first post-war coalition.

11
ONWARD TO MAY 2015

By breaking the traditional mould of two-party politics David Cameron and Nick Clegg swept away the certainties of the past and left the entire British establishment with no alternative but to embark on the steep learning curve of having to adjust to the new realities of collaborative government. The boldness of Cameron's 'big, open and comprehensive offer' to share power with the Liberal Democrats, and the firmness with which Clegg and his colleagues grabbed the chance to enter a coalition once they realised there was no prospect of a viable pact with Labour, tapped into an evident and seemingly widespread urge for a national consensus on tackling the budget deficit and the need to face up to cuts in public spending. Cameron and Clegg had been gifted a hitherto unimaginable opportunity; when it came to public opinion, the coalition was pushing at an open door and their promise of a partnership to govern the country chimed with many people's expectations. Post-election opinion polls suggested that up to four fifths of those questioned wanted the new spirit of co-operation to succeed.

Once campaigning began in earnest, there was no doubt that, while always difficult to pin down, there was a distinct appetite for political change on the part of numerous voters. They were looking for a positive response to their anger at the abuse of MPs' expenses and although they could not explain how they thought this might happen, they wanted the politicians to turn over a new leaf. Clegg's mastery of the first televised debate, his ability to turn his back on Cameron and Brown, to look straight to camera and then to decry the 'two old parties' with such manifest conviction, challenged the assumptions on which both Labour and the Conservatives had based their election campaigns. As polling day approached and the opinion polls continued to indicate that the Conservatives were likely to fall short of an overall majority, the possibility of a hung Parliament did not seem to be causing unease among the electorate on anything like the scale which might have been anticipated. 'Cleggmania' failed to deliver the advance which the Liberal Democrats hoped for; they secured nearly a million extra votes but ended up with five fewer seats. Nonetheless the prominence which Clegg gained through the debates strengthened his negotiating hand once Cameron and then Brown began to bargain for the Liberal Democrats' support. In his two and a half years as party leader Clegg had struggled to make an impression on the electorate but securing equal billing with Brown and Cameron in front of millions of television viewers propelled him to the forefront of the campaign and he gained the kind of national recognition which it took Paddy Ashdown and Charles Kennedy decades to achieve. The post-war revival in Liberal fortunes from no more than a handful of MPs, and the party's long march back to a place in government, dated from the start of the televising of election campaigns in the mid-1950s and the willingness of the broadcasters to offer a guarantee of air time to smaller political parties so that they could put their case against Labour and the Conservatives. But without the ultimate breakthrough of achieving level pegging with Brown and Cameron in the televised debates of 2010 the Liberal Democrats could well have been squeezed even further and Clegg might not have been able to command the stage at Westminster and play the role of kingmaker.

When shadow ministers from the two parties began the unexpected task of stripping down their manifestos to see if they could agree on a programme for a coalition government, the Liberal Democrats were surprised by the Conservatives' willingness to compromise on long-standing commitments which had played such a central part in the election. In subsequent days, as the two sides began to offer an insight into what took place during their ground-breaking negotiations, their enthusiasm for the deal was all too apparent. Cameron and Clegg, both in their early forties, were like-minded modernisers, backed by colleagues of a similar age and outlook; older hands in the two parties could only admire the younger generation as it pulled off a deal which would probably have been unattainable in their day. When I shared a platform in a debate at Westminster with two of the old guard who had looked on with amazement as the events unfolded, they readily acknowledged that Cameron and Clegg leapt at the chance to establish a secure coalition government backed by a stable parliamentary majority. Lord Dholakia, the Liberal Democrats' deputy leader in the House of Lords and former party president, was among those being briefed on a regular basis; he said he could hardly comprehend how accommodating Cameron's team proved to be. 'I couldn't believe it at first but the Conservatives were prepared to accept 60 to 70 per cent of the Liberal Democrats' manifesto'. Michael Dobbs, the Conservatives' deputy chairman during the Major government, was similarly bowled over by the shared sense of enthusiasm for coalition government. 'Cameron was very comfortable with the arrangement which was being reached; he didn't have to be dragged into a coalition, it was his decision, just as he kept saying "yes" to televised debates when he could have said "no".'

Regaining possession of 10 Downing Street for a Conservative Prime Minister was the prize which almost slipped from Cameron's grasp as soon as Brown made his counter-bid to Clegg. If there had not been two such willing partners for a hastily arranged political marriage we might have seen a fragile Lib–Lab pact or, more likely perhaps, a minority government led by the Tories. Even the best possible result from the election might have left Cameron trying to run the country with a parliamentary majority of no more than ten or twenty MPs, forcing him to adjust to the constant threat of being held hostage by the right wing of his party.

A key condition of the coalition deal was the agreement on a fixed five-year parliamentary term plus the additional safeguard of a higher threshold for the dissolution of Parliament. A vote of no confidence would require a 55 per cent majority before the government could be defeated and the Prime Minister was forced to go to the country to seek a fresh mandate. Other factors added to an initial sense of euphoria about the future prospects for the coalition and its breathtaking audacity in declaring that the next general election would be held on the 'first Thursday of May 2015'. In addition to five seats around the cabinet table and a role for Clegg on the main cabinet committees, a Liberal Democrat was appointed minister in each of the key departments. Having the chance to gain experience of national government was a prize which had eluded the Liberal Democrats for so long and the historic importance of being back at the centre of power for the first time in decades strengthened the leadership's determination to show they could be successful coalition partners. They realised their ability to withstand short-term unpopularity would have a significant impact on the fortunes of third-party politics and their own credibility in a hung Parliament of the future. Another important building block in assisting the two parties to cement their accord was the extensive forward planning which had been conducted by the civil service under the guidance of the cabinet secretary, Sir Gus O'Donnell.

Once the available cabinet posts had been shared out, the newly installed Prime Minister and Deputy Prime Minister had to co-operate in the all-important task of constructing a shared regime to manage the new government's relationship with the news media so as to exercise control over the flow of information from the state to the public. Not only were Cameron and Clegg having to convince disenchanted MPs on the margins of their two parties of the need to work together but they also had to square up to the challenge of amalgamating two different and hitherto hostile teams of political propagandists. Both leaders knew only too well that their success in being able to promote a united message in the uncharted waters of coalition would be regarded by the media as a critical test of the new administration's ability to survive.

Among the political apparatchiks of Westminster and Whitehall, party spin doctors tend to be the most tribal and, given the highly partisan nature of the briefings which had been the constant daily fare of both Conservative and Liberal Democrat media teams during the election, the task of welding them together into one harmonious group required a transformation in the traditional mindset of political public relations. The outgoing Labour government was riven by disputes between the rival media operations of Downing Street and the Treasury. A Blairite v. Brownite fight to the death was evidence if any was needed of the folly of giving competing ministerial aides free rein to offer journalists anonymous information and tip-offs. Ultimately their negative briefings against each other were so corrosive they became like a cancer eating away at the Labour government's authority.

Cameron, who spoke so often in opposition of his determination to turn his back on the spin of the Blair–Brown years if he became Prime Minister, took with him into Downing Street key members of his election team; Clegg did the same. They both decided to take the risk of relying on media advisers who were campaigning and briefing against each other throughout the general election but who they believed were professional communicators at heart. The two leaders seemed convinced that a new co-operative spirit between Conservative and Liberal Democrat ministers would help heal any previous differences and enable their combined media team to speak with one voice on the government's behalf. Political appointees have to work alongside the information officers of each department and the added challenge for the civil service was the need to adjust to the traditions and beliefs of two parties rather than one.

Steve Hilton, Cameron's long-time aide, became his No. 10 strategy adviser and the Conservatives' media chief, Andy Coulson, former editor of the *News of the World*, was appointed the Downing Street director of communications. Coulson was joined on the media side by Gabby Bertin, Cameron's press officer since the days of his leadership campaign, and by the party's well-established press spokesman Henry Macrory. All three worked at a party headquarters as a closely knit team during the campaign; in the latter stages of the election they had to devise strategies to counter the post-debate surge in support for the Liberal Democrats and to warn of the dangers of coalition government. They would have been well aware, for example, of the Conservatives' co-ordinated effort to brief journalists ahead of the barrage of critical stories about Clegg which appeared in the Tory tabloids on the morning of the second leaders' debate. Appointments by the deputy Prime Minister to his new media team at the Cabinet Office included Clegg's press officer Lena Pietsch and the Liberal Democrats' director of election communications, Jonny Oates. During the hard bargaining to settle the rules for the televised debates Oates broke ranks and suggested there had been conflict with Coulson over the format for the programmes. Another illustration of the on-going spin war during the campaign was a *Mail on Sunday* profile which questioned Clegg's 'Britishness'; Ms Pietsch was identified as his 'German press spokeswoman'.

When highly partisan teams have spent so long making it their daily business to oppose each other, their tribal loyalties do become deeply ingrained and invariably have an impact on their ability to influence the news media. Former Conservative press officers would obviously tend to have more extensive contacts within Tory newspapers whereas the Liberal Democrats' media staff would almost certainly be better acquainted with broadcasters and left-of-centre journalists. News organisations spend considerable time and effort establishing speedy and accurate lines of communication with political parties, not least in the hope that they might get favourable treatment. Coalition government notwithstanding, newspapers of a Conservative or Liberal Democrat persuasion would still hope to get exclusive stories and access, given the strength of the political affiliations of their proprietors and editors. But the practice of the Blair and Brown governments of giving preferential status to journalists from the Murdoch press – a tendency which Cameron adopted once the *Sun* ditched Labour – caused deep resentment among political correspondents. The danger for Downing Street if it tries to play off one section of the press against another is that it will sour relations between rival groups of journalists and annoy broadcasters and other news organisations. If favouritism is suspected, as it has been in the past, it could make life even more difficult at times of strained relations between the media and a new government.

One tactical advantage for Cameron and Clegg is that under a joint Conservative–Liberal Democrat administration, the political influence which newspapers try to exert can no longer be exercised with quite the same degree of certainty. Indeed the fallout from the closeness of the three-party fight in the general election and the formation of the first post-war coalition might well be a lessening of the opportunities for collusion between media proprietors and the government of the day. Given the intensity of day-to-day coverage no government has any wish to alienate important sections of the media. But if coalition ministers fail to be even-handed or are tempted to exploit the traditional affiliations of the press, any underlying conflict in their briefings will almost certainly be interpreted as an early pointer to potential splits and could pose a threat to their collaborative venture. If, for example, spin doctors of a Conservative persuasion were found to be favouring the Murdoch press at the expense of other news outlets, or if the Liberal Democrats appear to be holding separate briefings for left-of-centre newspapers, one side of the coalition will have every reason to fear that the other is reverting to type. Once a hostile briefing war began ministers would soon find they were being threatened from within. Anonymous briefings would feed the inevitable story line that the Conservative–Liberal Democrat partnership was always bound to collapse and end in an acrimonious separation. Political journalists have already programmed themselves for constant 'coalition watch', waiting to pounce on the first signs of dissension.

Cameron and Clegg needed no reminding of the hazards ahead and it was their good fortune to have entered office on a flood tide of goodwill and a determination within the leadership of both parties to make a success of the first peacetime coalition since the 1930s. Their new administration will have the ability to command the news agenda for months on end with a succession of announcements and policy initiatives; that energy and drive to achieve early results will only add to the momentum. But however bold their venture, it is not without risks. Off-the-record but well-sourced briefings from 'insiders' attacking individual ministers or their decisions tend to be the first sign of distress at the top of any new government. Cameron knows from his own experience as a special adviser at the heart of John Major's troubled government in the early 1990s how difficult it can be to police the freelance activities of anonymous Downing Street 'sources'. Nonetheless there could hardly be a Prime Minister who is better equipped to have a go at fusing two rival spin machines to see if it is possible for a coalition to speak with one voice when faced with the ever-demanding pressures of a 24/7 news environment.

Overriding all other challenges in terms of presentation will be the need for the new government to demonstrate to the country that it has begun to reduce the budget deficit and started to deliver spending cuts while managing at the same time to protect front-line services. A single, overarching objective is a common characteristic during a coalition or pact. At a time when there are often many other competing story lines to deal with, the pressure within Whitehall to communicate a simple coherent message can be unrelenting because even marginal shifts in public opinion may determine whether a shaky administration stands or falls. In many ways the inconclusive result of 2010 mirrored the hung Parliament of 1974; a national crisis and a loss of confidence in the political system were contributory factors in what was a comparable election stalemate. A state of emergency had been declared after the failure to resolve a miners' strike and Edward Heath called the election to determine who ruled the country – the government or the mineworkers. Although the Conservatives gained a larger share of the vote than Labour, Harold Wilson secured four more seats and he was able to form a minority government after Heath failed to get a promise of support from the Liberal leader Jeremy Thorpe. A strict rota of power cuts imposed because of a shortage of coal had forced the country onto a three-day working week; the priority for the Wilson government was to restore full production as soon as possible and then work out how to ensure continued industrial peace in the pits and the power stations. He was able to argue that only a Labour government could heal the divisions caused by the Conservatives' 1971 Industrial Relations Act, just as Cameron and Clegg have claimed in the wake of Labour's defeat that only a Conservative–Liberal Democrat coalition has the capability to steer the country through the continuing repercussions of the banking and financial crisis and the determination to bring down the crippling budget deficit built up under Blair and Brown.

Wilson's government was given a renewed lease of life when his successor, Jim Callaghan, agreed the Lib–Lab pact with David Steel in March 1977, just the kind of arrangement which Brown would like to have negotiated with Clegg. In return for Steel's promise of support from his thirteen MPs if the government was threatened by a no-confidence motion in the House of Commons, Labour agreed to accept a limited number of Liberal policies. Rising inflation and spiralling wage demands proved too much for Callaghan and his colleagues and their focus on strengthening the trade unions and protecting the nationalised industries was seen as being increasingly at odds with public opinion. The pact collapsed in July of the following year. After rejecting the advice of union leaders to hold an autumn election, Callaghan hung on through the 'Winter of Discontent' until his defeat by Margaret Thatcher in May 1979. I was struck at the time, when reporting a succession of industrial disputes for the BBC, by the way Callaghan's ministers were forced to live a hand-to-mouth existence, striving desperately to hold the line against a tidal wave of adverse publicity. Every day there seemed to be a new crisis over price rises, or perhaps yet another threat of strike action. Journalists judged the Labour government's effectiveness through the prism of whether or not its policies on prices and incomes were succeeding. A similar test in relation to the coalition's all-embracing goal of reducing the budget deficit became the immediate yardstick by which the media started to assess the performance of the Conservative–Liberal Democrat partnership.

The coalition's vulnerability when constrained by a single paramount objective was exposed not long after Cameron and Clegg presented the media with an engaging display of bonhomie. They celebrated their unique collaboration by standing side by side in the Downing Street garden to answer journalists and demonstrate their release from the 'broken politics' of the past. Next morning they were feted by effusive front-page headlines: 'The great No. 10 love-in' was the *Daily Mail*'s verdict on the first joint news conference of the coalition. Little did they know that their political honeymoon would be shattered within a matter of days by the unexpected resignation of one of the five senior Liberal Democrats given a seat in the cabinet. David Laws, Treasury chief secretary, stood down after the *Daily Telegraph* revealed that he had broken the rules on MPs' expenses by claiming more than £40,000 to rent rooms in properties owned by his partner. Losing the minister specifically charged with the task of identifying cuts in public spending so soon after the coalition took office raised an immediate question mark over the strength of the Liberal Democrats' hard-won acceptance of George Osborne's strategy for an immediate £6 billion reduction in the budget deficit. Downing Street and the Treasury went into overdrive trying to reassure the news media that the loss of Laws would not deflect the new government from its overriding objective to get public expenditure under control. If confidence was to be restored the two parties had to present a united front in what had became the first test of the new administration's cohesion and durability.

Laws agonised for two days about what to do. He offered to repay the £40,000 immediately; he insisted that for eight years he had continued to rent rooms from his partner not for financial benefit but because of his desire to keep his 'sexuality secret'. But his failure to end the arrangement when the rules were changed in 2006 weakened his argument and his equivocation was seized on as a further illustration of Clegg's failure to subject his parliamentary party to the same rigorous examination which Conservative MPs were forced to undergo when Cameron attempted to identify potential abuses of the expenses system before they could be exposed by journalists. There could hardly have been a trickier baptism of fire for the coalition's newly merged team of media handlers but collateral damage was kept to a minimum. Andy Coulson and Jonny Oates managed to hold the line and deliver a consistent message as Cameron was forced to execute a swift mini-reshuffle of his cabinet.

There was little sympathy for Laws on the part of some Conservative MPs who were angered that the new government had been tarnished so soon by allegations of parliamentary sleaze. But there was no sign of poisonous off-the-record quotes emanating from within the government itself, a pattern which had been all too common under Blair and Brown. By apparent good fortune, two days before Laws's expense claims were revealed by the *Daily Telegraph* Cameron gave a pep talk to the coalition's newly appointed cadre of ministerial aides. He told the sixty-six special advisers nominated by the Conservatives and Liberal Democrats that they would 'automatically be dismissed' by their appointing ministers if they were caught preparing or disseminating 'inappropriate material or personal attacks'. They were also reminded in no uncertain terms to refrain from briefing against each other or their partners in the coalition.

In his resignation statement Laws acknowledged that he could not escape the conclusion that what he had done was 'in some way wrong'; his failure to act with 'a sense of responsibility' had disqualified him from carrying on the 'crucial work' of implementing spending cuts. His sudden departure was a bitter blow to Clegg's authority. Laws was a leading member of the team which negotiated the coalition agreement and he was regarded as an ideal partner for George Osborne, eager to assist the new Chancellor of the Exchequer prepare the emergency Budget which the Conservatives had promised within fifty days of the election. His qualifications for the post of Treasury chief secretary could not have been bettered. After achieving a double first in economics at Cambridge University, he became vice-president of an investment bank at the age of twenty-two and then managing director of another before he was thirty. As he remarked somewhat ruefully when writing to Cameron to tender his resignation, he regretted having to leave behind vital work which he felt 'all my life has prepared me for'. Laws first hit the headlines by revealing that on arriving at the Treasury he had been left a cryptic note by the outgoing Labour chief secretary, Liam Byrne. It said: 'I'm afraid there is no money. Kind regards – and good luck!'

Laws was replaced by another Liberal Democrat cabinet minister, Danny Alexander, who was switched to the Treasury from the Scottish Office. Alexander was also a target of fresh claims by the *Daily Telegraph*; he was accused of avoiding capital gains tax, an allegation he swiftly denied. Clegg could not escape a degree of personal responsibility for having encouraged the *Daily Telegraph*'s journalists to go on re-examining their secret stash of data on MPs' expenses in the hope they might be able to expose fresh abuses. When challenged about his own claims during the second televised debate Clegg made the mistake of adopting a holier-than-thou attitude. He implied the Liberal Democrats were less tainted by the expenses scandal than their opponents because it was MPs from the 'old parties' who flipped their homes and had not been held to account. Cameron's sharp rejoinder that the Liberal Democrats were in no position to put 'themselves on a pedestal' had clearly not been heeded, as Clegg discovered to his own discomfort. There was never the slightest doubt that the Tory press intended to keep the Conservatives' coalition partners firmly in their sights and the higher their profile the more interest they attracted. In mid-June, barely six weeks into the life of the coalition, Chris Huhne, the Energy and Climate Secretary, became the third Liberal Democrat cabinet minister to be targeted. After being followed by the *News of the World* he was forced to confirm that he was in a 'serious relationship' with another woman and was separating from his wife.

The Queen's Speech opening the new parliamentary session was hailed by the Prime Minister as a defining moment for the coalition. Her words left no room for doubt as to his government's intentions: 'The first responsibility is to reduce the deficit and restore economic growth.' Cameron used the occasion to declare an end to the 'years of recklessness and big government and the beginning of the years of responsibility and good government'. Their joint programme would be radical: 'It takes the deficit head on, it shows that Britain is reopening for business.' George Osborne reinforced Cameron's message the previous day by announcing how the Treasury had shared out between government departments the cuts of £6 billion promised during the election.

In the five weeks which were to elapse before the Chancellor delivered his first Budget, Cameron gave a series of newspaper and television interviews in an attempt to construct a compelling narrative to explain the 'purpose behind the pain' and the predicted sharp rise in unemployment once the spending cuts took effect. His assertion that the economy was in a far worse state than Gordon Brown had admitted was backed up by a surprise announcement from Alexander that the government intended to save £11.5 billion by abandoning numerous public sector projects, many of which were blamed on Labour's pre-election spending spree and wildly over-optimistic growth forecasts. Osborne maintained the momentum in his first Mansion House speech by confirming that the Budget would include a levy on the banks and further restraints on pay and bonuses. An increase in non-business capital gains tax was another of the measures well trailed in advance. Osborne kept the pundits guessing about his decision on value added tax: in the end he opted for a 2.5 per cent increase, and the new rate of 20 per cent would take effect from January 2011.

Instead of following the traditional pre-Budget purdah, Downing Street and the Treasury mounted a concerted attempt to remind the country that a freeze on public sector pay, together with a squeeze on the cost of public sector pensions and a curb on welfare benefits, were Conservative commitments during the election; the Budget, said Cameron, was the moment 'the rubber really hits the road'. Coalition politics had necessitated another change in previous practice. Rather than allow the Chancellor to keep his secrets to himself until revealed at the despatch box, which had been Blair's frequent complaint about Brown, Cameron and Osborne went out of their way to ensure their Liberal Democrat partners were properly consulted in advance. They held a joint meeting with Clegg and Alexander and all four signed off the Budget four days before it was announced to the House of Commons. On leaving the meeting Cameron went straight to give an interview with *The Times* in which he said regular cross-party talks with Clegg and his colleagues were part of a 'proper collective process' and were a source of strength. When reminded of his prediction during the election that coalition government would result in a 'bunch of politicians haggling' over short-term decisions about their own future, Cameron said he had enjoyed proving himself wrong and he paid tribute to the Liberal Democrats. 'I didn't predict that we would come together and agree properly robust fiscal action but we have, and that's all for the good.'

On the eve of a special conference in Birmingham where Liberal Democrat activists gave their 'overwhelming' support to the coalition agreement Clegg acknowledged that the deal with the Conservatives had caused 'both surprise and with it some offence' among party members. Labour seized every possible opportunity to claim they were attracting Liberal Democrat defectors, which in turn strengthened Clegg's hand in pushing ahead with plans for a referendum in May 2011 on electoral reform and the possible introduction of the alternative vote. Tory groups anxious to defend first-past-the-post made no secret of their intention to raise money to mount an effective 'no' campaign, which prompted Cameron to reiterate his undertaking to do all he could to avoid getting drawn into a dispute about a key condition of the coalition.

The first fifty days of Cameron's premiership were noticeably free of political conflict, as if he had been determined from the outset to present himself as a unifying force. After twelve people were shot dead in Cumbria by the taxi driver Derrick Bird, he met survivors of the massacre and paid tribute to the emergency services but warned of the danger of leaping to conclusions on gun control when what was needed was an understanding of what had happened. In an attempt to lessen anti-British rhetoric over the BP oil spill in the Gulf of Mexico, he put in a thirty-minute call to the White House to urge President Barack Obama to refrain from calling the company by its old name of British Petroleum and to remind him that the multinational employed thousands of British and American workers. The timing of the intervention would not have been lost on the President as Cameron had only just returned from a two-day visit to support British troops in Afghanistan. The first British Prime Minister to spend the night at Camp Bastion in Helmand province, he took the opportunity to honour a long-standing Conservative promise. He announced a doubling in the rate of danger pay, up from £14 to £29 a day for frontline soldiers, at an annual cost of £58 million.

Perhaps the most challenging of Cameron's early assignments was delivering the government response to the report of Lord Saville's inquiry into Bloody Sunday, when British paratroopers opened fire on a civil rights demonstration in Londonderry in January 1972 and shot dead thirteen marchers. Cameron, who was five years old at the time, told the House of Commons that for someone of his generation this was a period learned about 'rather than lived through'. He had never wanted to call into the question the behaviour of soldiers who he believed were the finest in the world but one did not defend the British Army by defending the indefensible. Just before he started speaking a huge cheer erupted around Derry's Guildhall Square as relatives inside could be seen giving the thumbs-up sign to the large crowd waiting outside to see Cameron's statement, which was about to be relayed on a large screen. Within less than a minute his words were being greeted with rounds of spontaneous applause as he outlined the inquiry's conclusions and embarked on a sweeping apology.

There is no doubt. There is nothing equivocal. There are no ambiguities. What happened on Bloody Sunday was both unjustified and unjustifiable. It was wrong. . . The families of those who died should not have had to live with the pain and hurt of that day – and a lifetime of loss. Some members of our armed forces acted wrongly. The government is ultimately responsible for the conduct of the armed forces. And for that, on behalf of the government – and indeed our country – I am deeply sorry.

Across the political divides of Britain, Northern Ireland and the Republic there was near-unanimous agreement that the tone and content of his apology could not have been bettered. Such was the praise for the sincerity of his response to the longest and most expensive inquiry in British legal history that he seemed to dispel many of the lingering doubts about his ability to speak on behalf of the country. Almost effortlessly he had assumed the mantle of a one-nation Tory, hoping to take the country with him but still enough of a realist to accept that a Prime Minister charged with the task of reducing the largest budget deficit of any major economy was hardly likely to secure instant popularity.

INDEX